SUNDAY YEAR A
WEEKDAY YEAR I

A BOOK OF PRAYER FOR EACH DAY
OF THE LITURGICAL YEAR

SARA McGINNIS LEE

LITURGY
TRAINING
PUBLICATIONS

Acknowledgments continued on page 423.

Daily Prayer is based in part on the pattern established in *Children's Daily Prayer*, by Elizabeth McMahon Jeep.

LTP prints the text of *Daily Prayer 2011* with ink that contains renewable linseed oil on paper that is 100% recycled and contains a minimum of 40% postconsumer waste.✪ Although many de-inking processes use highly toxic bleach, this paper was processed using PCF (Processed Chlorine Free) technologies. The printing process used to manufacture this book is a non-heatset process that significantly reduces emission of volatile organic compounds (VOCs) into the atmosphere.

LTP continues to work toward responsible stewardship of the environment. For more information on our efforts, please go to www.LTP.org/environment.

Printed in the United States of America.

ISBN 978-1-56854-890-6

DP11

To all those with whom I have prayed.
To all those for whom I pray.
To all those who have prayed for me.
—Sara

TABLE OF CONTENTS

INTRODUCTION

Rejoice always.
Pray without ceasing.
In all circumstances give
thanks, for this is the
will of God for you
in Christ Jesus.

1 Thessalonians 5:16–18

Welcome to *Daily Prayer 2011,* Sunday Year A and Weekday Year I! This edition of the well-loved prayer book provides a familiar order of prayer for each day of the liturgical year, from the First Sunday of Advent, November 28, 2010, to December 31, 2011. Readings from the daily Mass are provided, and the prayer texts and reflections are connected to the seasons, solemnities, feasts of the Lord, and the memorials of the saints. The prayers on these pages will inspire and bring you to a deeper appreciation for the word that is proclaimed and for Eucharist that is shared in the liturgical life of the Church.

THE ORDER OF PRAYER

Daily Prayer 2011 follows a simple order of prayer: it begins with an opening verse with the Sign of the Cross, followed by a psalm, a reading from the daily Mass, a brief reflection, Prayer of the Faithful, the Lord's Prayer, a closing prayer, and a closing verse with the Sign of the Cross. This order remains consistent for each day of the liturgical year, allowing its repetition to become part of your daily rhythm and routine.

Daily Prayer 2011 is organized by season, and the Psalter is located in the back of the book (pages 400–422). Everything you need is conveniently contained in this resource. Refer to the table of contents for easy reference.

DAILY HEADING

Daily Prayer is easy to use. A heading is provided for each day of prayer so you will always know where you are and what you should pray. The heading includes the date and the name of the liturgical observance. You will find the optional memorials are footnoted on the bottom of the page. The liturgical observances are those according to the norms prescribed by the United States Conference of Catholic Bishops' Committee on Divine Worship.

OPENING AND CLOSING VERSICLE WITH SIGN OF THE CROSS

The order of prayer begins each day with the Sign of the Cross and a versicle, or opening verse. The versicles are taken from the refrains proper to the Responsorial Psalms from the Mass; antiphons from the Liturgy of the Hours and Roman Missal; verses from the Acclamation before the Gospel (*Lectionary for Mass*), and lines from scripture, especially the Psalms.

PSALMODY

The psalms are an important part of Catholic prayer. As poetic readings from Sacred Scripture, the psalms reflect upon God's saving work in various ways—praise, thanksgiving, and lamentation. The psalms in Daily Prayer 2011 have been selected by their liturgical significance. Psalms for Advent implore for God's return; psalms for Christmas shout for joy; psalms for Lent evoke the need for God's mercy and forgiveness; psalms for Easter give praise for his glory and salvation; and psalms for Ordinary Time give thanks for all that is good. In some cases the psalm has been replaced with the Canticle of Mary. This Canticle is included at the end of the Psalter on page 422.

READING

Each day of prayer includes a reading from the daily Mass. This enables further reflection upon the word of God proclaimed during the Eucharistic celebration (Mass)—the source and summit of our faith. On some days, excerpts, not the full text, from the scripture passage have been selected. The Gospel is used for each Sunday, solemnity, and feast of the Lord.

REFLECTION

The author for this year has provided beautiful insights for meditation and reflection. These reflections are witty yet challenging as they guide the reader to a deeper relationship with God, neighbor, and self.

PRAYER OF THE FAITHFUL

The Prayer of the Faithful, sometimes referred to as the General Intercessions, Bidding Prayer, or Universal Prayer, is a prayer of the baptized who, through Christ, voice their concerns to God regarding the Church, the world, the oppressed, local needs, and other concerns. Thus, the prayers in this book connect the individual and small faith groups to the universal Church and those in most need of God's love and mercy. Although specific prayers are provided in this resource, others may be added.

THE LORD'S PRAYER

Jesus taught us how to pray. It is fitting to follow the Prayer of the Faithful with the Lord's Prayer, for it encapsulates the humility and reverence we give to our God—and neighbor—while asking for his mercy and forgiveness.

CLOSING PRAYER

The closing prayer follows the form of the traditional Collect. The prayers are "addressed to God the father, through Christ, in the Holy Spirit" (*General Instruction of the Roman Missal*, 54). Essentially, this prayer "collects" our daily prayer, the prayers found in this book, and those of our hearts and minds, those as individuals or groups, into one Trinitarian prayer, concluding with our assent of faith in the response "Amen."

USING THE BOOK

This resource may be used by individuals, families, or prayer groups; on retreats; to begin meetings or catechetical sessions, formational and youth ministry events; or as prayer with the aged, sick, and homebound. The prayers may be used at any time during the day, and, given this book's convenient size, it is easily transported to meet various prayer needs and situations.

The order of prayer may be prayed silently, or, especially for group prayer, prayed out loud. If used for prayer gatherings, it might be helpful to designate someone to open the prayer, lead the Prayer of the Faithful, begin the Lord's Prayer, and to conclude the prayer. Select an additional volunteer to proclaim the reading. Allow the faithful to read the psalm together either as an entire group or divide the stanzas among the faithful with alternating recitation.

Feel free to adapt these prayers for specific needs—intercessions (or petitions) may be added, music may begin and conclude the service, and the psalm, response to the Prayer of the Faithful, and the Lord's Prayer may be chanted and sung.

OTHER USES FOR DAILY PRAYER

Daily Prayer 2011 may also be used in other situations or for various needs.

• Use the Prayer of the Faithful during the Mass. The prayers have been written in accordance with the *General Instruction of the Roman Missal*, 69 and 70. Since this book contains prayers for each day of the liturgical year, you may use the intercessions for every day of the year for Mass.

• Use the included reflections as homily sparkers and catechetical tools.

CUSTOMER FEEDBACK

Daily Prayer 2011 is the tenth edition of an annual publication; *Daily Prayer 2012* is already being prepared. Because it is an annual, it can be changed from year to year to become a better tool for your daily prayer. As you use this book and adapt it for yourself, you may have ideas about how it can be made more useful for your prayer. Feel free to e-mail us at DailyPrayer@LTP.org.

ABOUT THE AUTHOR

Sara McGinnis Lee received a BA in Theology from Marquette University, and an MA in Theology from Aquinas Institute of Theology. She has been a high school and college campus minister for the Diocese of Belleville, teaches religious studies courses at McKendree University, and is a presenter for parish and diocesan programs. She spends much of her time raising her two young sons, Patrick and Dominic, with her husband Kevin.

✚ *The day of the Lord is near: Behold, he comes to save us.*

PSALM 85   *page 412*

READING   *Matthew 24:37–44*

Jesus said to his disciples: "As it was in the days of Noah, so will it be at the coming of the Son of Man. In those days before the flood, they were eating and drinking, marrying and giving in marriage, up to the day that Noah entered the ark. They did not know until the flood came and carried them all away. So will it be also at the coming of the Son of Man. Two men will be out in the field; one will be taken, and one will be left. Two women will be grinding at the mill; one will be taken, and one will be left. Therefore, stay awake! For you do not know on which day the Lord will come. Be sure of this: if the master of the house had known the hour of night when the thief was coming, he would have stayed awake and not let his house be broken into. So too, you also must be prepared, for at an hour you do not expect, the Son of Man will come."

REFLECTION

We begin Advent with a jolt. Stay awake, be ready! We may be thoroughly distracted by shopping, baking, family, parades, and events, but Jesus calls to us. Presents are fine, but prayer and outreach are better. Baking is good, but filling the hearts and bodies of the less fortunate is better. Celebration with our loved ones should reflect the love of God and make the world a better place.

PRAYERS   *others may be added*

We turn to God with awakened hearts and pray:

◆ O God, we wait for you.

For the people of God, that we may remain awake in faith until the coming of the Son of Man, we pray: ◆ *For the nations of the world, that the swords of war may be transformed by the peace of Christ, we pray:* ◆ *For those preoccupied with worldly activities, that Advent may be a time to focus on life in God, we pray:* ◆ *For this community of faith, that it may be a place of welcome and preparation for all who seek Christ, we pray:* ◆ *For all who sleep in Christ, that their waiting may turn into rejoicing on the last day, we pray:* ◆

Our Father . . .

God of our ancestors in faith,
you call all nations and peoples to
    your house;
help us to prepare for the time
    of judgment.
May your Word and Sacrament
    fortify us
as we remain awake and ready,
anticipating the glorious return of
    your Son,
Jesus Christ, our Lord,
who lives and reigns with you in the
    unity of the Holy Spirit,
one God, forever and ever.
Amen.

✚ *The day of the Lord is near: Behold, he comes to save us.*

1

✚ *The day of the Lord is near: Behold, he comes to save us.*

PSALM 85 *page 412*

READING *Matthew 8:5–11*

When Jesus entered Capernaum, a centurion approached him and appealed to him, saying, "Lord, my servant is lying at home paralyzed, suffering dreadfully." He said to him, "I will come and cure him." The centurion said in reply, "Lord, I am not worthy to have you enter under my roof; only say the word and my servant will be healed. For I too am a man subject to authority, with soldiers subject to me. And I say to one, 'Go,' and he goes; and to another, 'Come here,' and he comes; and to my slave, 'Do this,' and he does it." When Jesus heard this, he was amazed and said to those following him, "Amen, I say to you, in no one in Israel have I found such faith. I say to you, many will come from the east and the west, and will recline with Abraham, Isaac, and Jacob at the banquet in the Kingdom of heaven."

REFLECTION

Try to picture this: a beautifully laid-out dinner table, and gathered around it are our ancestors in faith—all saints, all souls, and all people who taught us and have passed on our Christian faith. This is promised to us as we begin this time of waiting for the Savior who will make it all possible. Our mouths water and our hearts burn within us.

PRAYERS *others may be added*

We come before our God of mercy, we pray:

◆ Bring us to your banquet.

That the Church may guide us to the heavenly table, a place of faith and harmony, we pray: ◆ *That the world may recognize the power of Christ to bring together east and west, we pray:* ◆ *That those paralyzed physically or by fear may be cured by the healing touch of Christ, we pray:* ◆ *That this community may be saved through the mercy of our God, we pray:* ◆

Our Father . . .

Lord of light and salvation,
your goodness and mercy
have healed and uplifted us.
May we respond in faith.
Lead us to your kingdom,
where all suffering and injustice ends.
We ask this through Christ our Lord.
Amen.

✚ *The day of the Lord is near: Behold, he comes to save us.*

✦ *Blessed are all who wait for the Lord.*

PSALM 40 *page 407*

READING *Matthew 4:18–22*

As Jesus was walking by the Sea of Galilee, he saw two brothers, Simon who is called Peter, and his brother Andrew, casting a net into the sea; they were fishermen. He said to them, "Come after me, and I will make you fishers of men." At once they left their nets and followed him. He walked along from there and saw two other brothers, James, the son of Zebedee, and his brother John. They were in a boat, with their father Zebedee, mending their nets. He called them, and immediately they left their boat and their father and followed him.

REFLECTION

Let us have an "immediate" response to God's call this Advent. Make one or two choices that significantly alter your normal December-mode in favor of a peaceful Advent. Decorate your home in violet instead of red and green. Give as many gifts to strangers and those in need as you would give to your family. Shop secondhand or look for third-world and environmentally friendly items for those on your Christmas list. Say "yes" to God and receive the gift of joy.

PRAYERS *others may be added*

We call upon the Lord, the God of mercy and peace, and pray:

◆ May our hearts respond "yes," O Lord.

That the successors of the apostles, our Bishops, continue to faithfully follow God's call, we pray: ◆ *That leaders called by Jesus to cooperate in his mission devote their lives in service, we pray:* ◆ *That all who make sacrifices out of faith know the companionship of the Lord, we pray:* ◆ *That young people in this community accept the invitation to ordination, religious life, and lay ministry, we pray:* ◆ *That those who have died be received by the loving embrace of God, we pray:* ◆

Our Father . . .

O Lord,
your call goes out through all
    the earth,
bringing forth disciples
who pray, teach, and give generously.
Help us as we wait for you.
Show us how to respond by sharing
    our gifts
and leaving behind whatever draws us
    away from you.
We ask this through Christ our Lord.
Amen.

✦ *Blessed are all who wait for the Lord.*

3

✝ *The day of the Lord is near.*

PSALM 85 *page 412*

READING *Matthew 15:29–37*

At that time: Jesus walked by the Sea of Galilee, went up on the mountain, and sat down there. Great crowds came to him, having with them the lame, the blind, the deformed, the mute, and many others. They placed them at his feet, and he cured them. The crowds were amazed when they saw the mute speaking, the deformed made whole, the lame walking, and the blind able to see, and they glorified the God of Israel.

Jesus summoned his disciples and said, "My heart is moved with pity for the crowd, for they have been with me now for three days and have nothing to eat. I do not want to send them away hungry, for fear they may collapse on the way." The disciples said to him, "Where could we ever get enough bread in this deserted place to satisfy such a crowd?" Jesus said to them, "How many loaves do you have?" "Seven," they replied, "and a few fish." He ordered the crowd to sit down on the ground. Then he took the seven loaves and the fish, gave thanks, broke the loaves, and gave them to the disciples, who in turn gave them to the crowds. They all ate and were satisfied. They picked up the fragments left over—seven baskets full.

REFLECTION

A child with autism. A grandparent with mental illness. A neighbor in a wheelchair. Someone at work or school who seems "different." What do these members of the People of God have to teach us? How will we be inspired by those whom we often ignore or exclude? God is closest to those who need him. We are each longing for wholeness in a unique way.

PRAYERS *others may be added*

Coming before God, we pray:

◆ Save us, O Lord.

For the Church to invite and include our weak and impaired members, we pray: ◆ *For international aid organizations to continue to urge us to provide for those in need, we pray:* ◆ *For those who long for full physical ability, that medicine, therapy, and the grace of God may heal them, we pray:* ◆ *For the eyes of all to be opened to what can be learned from and shared with each other, we pray:* ◆

Our Father . . .

Merciful God,
you hear our cries for healing.
May we learn compassion from you.
Show us how to share our own
    suffering
and bring us together through your
    redemptive love.
We ask this through Christ our Lord.
Amen.

✝ *The day of the Lord is near.*

✦ *The day of the Lord is near: Behold, he comes to save us.*

PSALM 85   *page 412*

READING   *Matthew 7:21, 24–27*

Jesus said to his disciples: "Not everyone who says to me, 'Lord, Lord,' will enter the Kingdom of heaven, but only the one who does the will of my Father in heaven.

"Everyone who listens to these words of mine and acts on them will be like a wise man who built his house on rock. The rain fell, the floods came, and the winds blew and buffeted the house. But it did not collapse; it had been set solidly on rock. And everyone who listens to these words of mine but does not act on them will be like a fool who built his house on sand. The rain fell, the floods came, and the winds blew and buffeted the house. And it collapsed and was completely ruined."

REFLECTION

It has been reported that some Christian home builders bury a Bible in the foundation of every house. Regardless of our personal opinion of this practice, it gives us a starting point for today's reading. What evidence do we find in our own homes of the foundation of our lives—religious art, sculptures, and symbols? Do we make a habit of spiritual reading, ethical purchases, or limited watching of TV? Tangible objects can contribute to an atmosphere of Christian living.

PRAYERS   *others may be added*

God, as we long for a strong foundation in you, we pray:

◆ Ground us in the rock of faith.

For the Roman Catholic Church, that our foundation in Peter may remain strong and true, we pray: ◆ *For our unstable world, that the care of natural resources becomes primary, we pray:* ◆ *For those without homes, that security may be found, we pray:* ◆ *For our parish leaders, that they keep before us our foundational purposes, we pray:* ◆

Our Father . . .

O Lord,
you alone are worthy of our trust;
you alone can protect us from all evil.
May we find ways to center our lives
    in you,
that we may we be grounded in
    our relationship with our Lord
    Jesus Christ,
your Son, who lives and reigns with
    you in the unity of the Holy Spirit,
one God, forever and ever.
Amen.

✦ *The day of the Lord is near: Behold, he comes to save us.*

✦ *Blessed are all who wait for the Lord.*

PSALM 40 *page 407*

READING *1 Corinthians 9:16 – 19, 22–23*

Brothers and sisters: If I preach the Gospel, this is no reason for me to boast, for an obligation has been imposed on me, and woe to me if I do not preach it! If I do so willingly, I have a recompense, but if unwillingly, then I have been entrusted with a stewardship. What then is my recompense? That, when I preach, I offer the Gospel free of charge so as not to make full use of my right in the Gospel. Although I am free in regard to all, I have made myself a slave to all so as to win over as many as possible. To the weak I became weak, to win over the weak. I have become all things to all, to save at least some. All this I do for the sake of the Gospel, so that I too may have a share in it.

REFLECTION

A servant of the Gospel, a "missionary" to the world, does whatever it takes to spread the Good News to all people in all places. In living out your faith and loving God, what sacrifices are you willing to make? To what extremes will you go? How will you stretch and challenge yourself in order to be more effective?

PRAYERS *others may be added*

Pledging ourselves in service to God, we pray:

◆ May it all be for the sake of the Gospel.

For lifetimes of love, careers of service, weeks of sacrifice, and days of devotion among the people of God, we pray: ◆ *For missionaries of Christ who go into challenging territories in their workplaces, schools, and the public arena, we pray:* ◆ *For those struggling to see their identity in Christ due to lack of self-esteem, trauma, or not having yet heard the Good News, we pray:* ◆ *For each of us to be willing to lay aside pride, indifference, or prejudice in our path to unity in Christ, we pray:* ◆

Our Father . . .

God, our Father,
your Son became human, enduring
    suffering and death,
in order to bring the Good News of
    your love to all people.
Your servant St. Francis Xavier
    was zealous in his devotion to
    the Gospel.
May we, too, be missionaries in our
    own way,
making brave choices and
    great sacrifices.
We ask this through Christ our Lord.
Amen.

✦ *Blessed are all who wait for the Lord.*

✦ *The day of the Lord is near: Behold, he comes to save us.*

PSALM 85   *page 412*

READING   *Matthew 9:35—10:1, 5a, 6–8*

Jesus went around to all the towns and villages, teaching in their synagogues, proclaiming the Gospel of the Kingdom, and curing every disease and illness. At the sight of the crowds, his heart was moved with pity for them because they were troubled and abandoned, like sheep without a shepherd. Then he said to his disciples, "The harvest is abundant but the laborers are few; so ask the master of the harvest to send out laborers for his harvest."

Then he summoned his Twelve disciples and gave them authority over unclean spirits to drive them out and to cure every disease and every illness.

Jesus sent out these Twelve after instructing them thus, "Go to the lost sheep of the house of Israel. As you go, make this proclamation: 'The Kingdom of heaven is at hand.' Cure the sick, raise the dead, cleanse lepers, drive out demons. Without cost you have received; without cost you are to give."

REFLECTION

How are you a "lost sheep"? Sickness, death, disease, and demons—these are intimidating concepts, indeed. Jesus comes to end all these afflictions and lead the lost and forsaken back to the embrace of the Father. Who among us is willing to reach out to the addicted, *the physically and mentally ill, the dying, the mentally and emotionally unstable, or those on destructive paths? This is the harvest for which we are needed.*

PRAYERS   *others may be added*

Aware of the lost and of the compassion of the Good Shepherd, we pray:

◆ Lord, shepherd your people.

That the Church will send out laborers to heal the sick and rescue the lost and forgotten, we pray: ◆ *That wealthy nations may reach out to empower developing nations, we pray:* ◆ *That demons of disease and evil may be cast out, we pray:* ◆ *That local ministries may be supported in efforts to assist those whose suffering is difficult to understand or acknowledge, we pray:* ◆ *That those who have died may rise again in Christ, we pray:* ◆

Our Father . . .

Healing God,
you have redeemed all sinners
through the offering of your
    own Lamb.
As you shepherd us with mercy,
may we embrace the sheep that
    remain lost.
We ask this through Christ our Lord.
Amen.

✦ *The day of the Lord is near: Behold, he comes to save us.*

✦ *The day of the Lord is near: Behold, he comes to save us.*

PSALM 85   page 412

READING   *Matthew 3: 1–6*

John the Baptist appeared, preaching in the desert of Judea and saying, "Repent, for the kingdom of heaven is at hand!" It was of him that the prophet Isaiah had spoken when he said: / *A voice of one crying out in the desert, / Prepare the way of the Lord, / make straight his paths. /* John wore clothing made of camel's hair and had a leather belt around his waist. His food was locusts and wild honey. At the time Jerusalem, all Judea, and the whole region around the Jordan were going out to him and were being baptized by him in the Jordan River as they acknowledged their sins.

REFLECTION

Do you ever feel compelled to tell the world that someday "God will take care of this mess"? What motivates this urge? Perhaps it is a yearning for true justice. To prepare for Christ, let us admit our own need for forgiveness. We are sinners, too, and we are part of this broken world. Let us pray for God's justice, tempered with loving mercy.

PRAYERS   *others may be added*

O God of endurance and encouragement, we bring our prayers before you:

◆ Reign with justice and mercy.

For the humble repentance of all believers, we pray: ◆ *For international courts of reconciliation, we pray:* ◆ *For victims of oppression and violence, we pray:* ◆ *For forgiveness between neighbors, we pray:* ◆ *For those who have died, we pray:* ◆

Our Father . . .

God of heaven and earth,
John the Baptist prepared the way for
    your Son,
and your Son proclaimed
    your kingdom.
May it come now, with justice
    and mercy.
May it come in the future, with joy
    and judgment for eternity.
Grant this through our Lord, Jesus
    Christ, your Son,
who lives and reigns with you in the
    unity of the Holy Spirit,
one God, forever and ever.
Amen.

✦ *The day of the Lord is near: Behold, he comes to save us.*

✦ *The day of the Lord is near: Behold, he comes to save us.*

PSALM 85   *page 412*

READING   *Luke 5:18–24*

And some men brought on a stretcher a man who was paralyzed; they were trying to bring him in and set him in his presence. But not finding a way to bring him in because of the crowd, they went up on the roof and lowered him on the stretcher through the tiles into the middle in front of Jesus. When Jesus saw their faith, he said, "As for you, your sins are forgiven."

Then the scribes and Pharisees began to ask themselves, "Who is this who speaks blasphemies? Who but God alone can forgive sins?" Jesus knew their thoughts and said to them in reply, "What are you thinking in your hearts? Which is easier, to say, 'Your sins are forgiven,' or to say, 'Rise and walk'? But that you may know that the Son of Man has authority on earth to forgive sins"—he said to the man who was paralyzed, "I say to you, rise, pick up your stretcher, and go home."

REFLECTION

What incredible things have you seen this week, month, or year? We often have to look closely to see the "in-breaking" of the reign of God in our chaotic world. Make a list of these events you have seen of late—a forgiving gesture, or a young person succeeding against odds. God is at work in the world around us; we only need look for him.

PRAYERS   *others may be added*

With awe before our magnificent God, we pray:

◆ Praise be to you, O God.

For the bride of Christ, the Church, that she may always delight in the splendor of the Messiah, we pray: ◆ *For scientists and philosophers, that they may give glory to God for the brilliance of his work, we pray:* ◆ *For caregivers of the sick, that their faith may sustain them and bring their loved ones peace, we pray:* ◆ *For the children of our congregation, that they may remind us of the wonder of our God, we pray:* ◆ *For those who die today, that they may slip peacefully into the arms of God, we pray:* ◆

Our Father . . .

God in the highest,
we give you glory,
and all the earth proclaims your
    power and might.
Attune our senses to your wonder
    around us;
give us glimpses of your kingdom,
where all beauty, wholeness, and
    goodness reign.
Grant this through Christ our Lord.
Amen.

✦ *The day of the Lord is near: Behold, he comes to save us.*

✚ *Blessed are all who wait for
the Lord.*

PSALM 40 — page 407

READING — *John 10:11–16*

Jesus said: "I am the good shepherd. A good shepherd lays down his life for the sheep. A hired man, who is not a shepherd and whose sheep are not his own, sees a wolf coming and leaves the sheep and runs away, and the wolf catches and scatters them. This is because he works for pay and has no concern for the sheep. I am the good shepherd, and I know mine and mine know me, just as the Father knows me and I know the Father; and I will lay down my life for the sheep. I have other sheep that do not belong to this fold. These also I must lead, and they will hear my voice, and there will be one flock, one shepherd."

REFLECTION

Call to mind all the little ones of our world—the voiceless, the powerless, the weak, and the afflicted. Our God is attending to each of them. He has great love for every sheep of the flock. He notices the pain and sorrow of everyone who is suffering and is lost. Let us rejoice in God's loving redemption and creation.

PRAYERS — *others may be added*

We bring our prayers before the Good Shepherd:

◆ Gather us into one flock.

That the Church continues the work of the Good Shepherd, advocating on behalf of the powerless, we pray: ◆
That the voices of the little ones are heard by leaders worldwide, we pray: ◆
That the sheep who have strayed are found and embraced by family, Church, and society, we pray: ◆ *That this Church family welcomes back all who have left the fold in illness, alienation, or sin, we pray:* ◆

Our Father . . .

Lord Jesus, our Good Shepherd,
you know us by name and call us
   to yourself.
May we respond to your call in faith,
leaving behind a life of sin,
transformed by your redemptive love.
You live and reign with God
   the Father
in the unity of the Holy Spirit,
one God, forever and ever.
Amen.

✚ *Blessed are all who wait for
the Lord.*

✦ *Blessed are all who wait for
the Lord.*

CANTICLE page 422

READING *Luke 1:26 – 30a,*
35b – 38b

The angel Gabriel was sent from God
to a town of Galilee called Nazareth, to
a virgin betrothed to a man named
Joseph, of the house of David, and the
virgin's name was Mary. And coming
to her, he said, "Hail, full of grace! The
Lord is with you." But she was greatly
troubled at what was said and pondered
what sort of greeting this might be.
Then the angel said to her, "Do not be
afraid, Mary . . . the Holy Spirit will
come upon you, and the power of the
Most High will overshadow you. Therefore the child to be born will be called
holy, the Son of God. And behold, Elizabeth, your relative, has also conceived
a son in her old age, and this is the sixth
month for her who was called barren;
for nothing will be impossible for God."
Mary said, "Behold, I am the handmaid
of the Lord. May it be done to me
according to your word."

REFLECTION

*Expectant parents know how long it
seems to wait for the birth of a baby. In
Mary, we see a model of patient waiting and joyful anticipation. Waiting for
a baby highlights the tenderness of that
new life; the delight in first seeing and
knowing a new person; the human and
divine work intertwined in creation.*

PRAYERS *others may be added*

*Waiting with joyful hearts, we offer
our prayers to God:*

◆ May it be done to us according to
your word.

*That the Church walks with our mother
Mary in following God's will, we pray:* ◆
*That world leaders will engage tirelessly
in peaceful efforts, we pray:* ◆ *That all
pregnant women are blessed with the
faith of Mary, we pray:* ◆ *That the new
babies among us are welcomed in love
and bring delight, we pray:* ◆

Our Father . . .

Son of Mary,
your mother's response to God
revealed her as a woman of faith
    and love.
May we imitate her faith and love
by waiting quietly to hear what God
    will do within us.
Help us to respond with a resounding
    "yes" to his call.
You live and reign with God
    the Father
in the unity of the Holy Spirit,
one God, forever and ever.
Amen.

✦ *Blessed are all who wait for
the Lord.*

✚ *The day of the Lord is near: Behold, he comes to save us.*

PSALM 85 *page 412*

READING *Matthew 11:11–15*

Jesus said to the crowds: "Amen, I say to you, among those born of women there has been none greater than John the Baptist; yet the least in the Kingdom of heaven is greater than he. From the days of John the Baptist until now, the Kingdom of heaven suffers violence, and the violent are taking it by force. All the prophets and the law prophesied up to the time of John. And if you are willing to accept it, he is Elijah, the one who is to come. Whoever has ears ought to hear."

REFLECTION

Have we over-humanized Jesus at the expense of his divinity? Do we think of him as a political wisdom figure, a compassionate pastor, or a close friend? He is greater than all those who came before him—saints, prophets, and visionaries. He is greater than all those we admire today—heroes, great speakers, teachers, and mentors. He is fully human, and fully divine. He is the answer to all our prayers, and we open our ears to the fullness of revelation in his Word.

PRAYERS *others may be added*

We open our ears, eyes, mouths, and hearts to the Lord:

◆ O God, hear us.

That the Pope and Bishops rely always on the providence of God to lead the Church, we pray: ◆ *That the great heroes and leaders of the world point beyond themselves to the source of goodness, we pray:* ◆ *That those who doubt God's power and truth may be awed by his activity in the world, we pray:* ◆ *That the saints and prophets who have inspired this parish continue to lead us to the living Christ, we pray:* ◆

Our Father . . .

Omnipotent God,
you created the mountains and
the seas;
you breathed life into every animal
and human being.
Restore our sense of wonder in your
great power,
that we might know the enormity of
the gift of your Son, Jesus.
Give us ever-greater understanding of
the truth
revealed in the Incarnation, death,
and Resurrection of your Son.
We ask this through Christ our Lord.
Amen.

✚ *The day of the Lord is near: Behold, he comes to save us.*

✚ *The day of the Lord is near: Behold, he comes to save us.*

PSALM 85 *page 412*

READING *Isaiah 48:17–19*

Thus says the LORD, your redeemer, / the Holy One of Israel: / I, the Lord, your God, / teach you what is for your good, / and lead you on the way you should go. / If you would hearken to my commandments, / your prosperity would be like a river, / and your vindication like the waves of the sea; / Your descendants would be like the sand, / and those born of your stock like its grains, / Their name never cut off / or blotted out from my presence.

REFLECTION

How do we listen to Jesus? Selectively? Inattentively? Occasionally? We are called to embrace his every word—words of forgiveness and challenge, words of familiarity and confusion. Listen. Reflect. Ask Jesus to show you where you have been inconsistent in hearing and accepting his instruction.

PRAYERS *others may be added*

With openness to the life-giving Word of God, we pray:

◆ Lord, teach us to listen.

For the Bishops, the teachers of the Church, that they are led by God in every area of their lives and ministry, we pray: ◆ *For people of all faiths, that we truly hear one another in our quest for peace, we pray:* ◆ *For those who are never satisfied, that the Word of God may bring them peace of mind and accepting hearts, we pray:* ◆ *For our community, that we stop to hear the Word of God in our midst and then obey it completely, we pray:* ◆

Our Father . . .

Good and gracious God,
you know what we need, fear,
    and desire.
Teach us to listen to your wisdom
and reject the ever-demanding voices
    of our culture.
Remind us of the truth of your Word.
May we be transformed in every way
    by your goodness.
Grant this through Christ our Lord.
Amen.

✚ *The day of the Lord is near: Behold, he comes to save us.*

✦ *The day of the Lord is near: Behold, he comes to save us.*

PSALM 85   *page 412*

READING   *Matthew 17:9a, 10–13*

As they were coming down from the mountain, the disciples asked Jesus, "Why do the scribes say that Elijah must come first?" He said in reply, "Elijah will indeed come and restore all things; but I tell you that Elijah has already come, and they did not recognize him but did to him whatever they pleased. So also will the Son of Man suffer at their hands." Then the disciples understood that he was speaking to them of John the Baptist.

REFLECTION

It is hard to put God first. It is easier to ignore God by claiming we are very busy. Even in work, "musts" and "shoulds" are not to gain priority over prayer. If we really want to strengthen our relationship with God, we must admit our excuses. We must give up the security of routines and familiar tasks. Pray this Advent for the strength to turn to God first and foremost.

PRAYERS   *others may be added*

With repentance in mind, we ask God:

◆ Be merciful, O God.

For forgiveness of our tendency to place ordinary tasks ahead of our extraordinary God, we pray: ◆ *For forgiveness of our country when it has profited at the expense of other nations and races, we pray:* ◆ *For forgiveness of our deceitful financial practices (personal or commercial) that hurt those most in need, we pray:* ◆ *For forgiveness of our internal divisions—resentments that have gone on too long, jealousy, competition, and selfishness—we pray:* ◆

Our Father . . .

God of justice and mercy,
you call us to repentance.
We know the times we have strayed
    from your path.
Remind us of our need for you;
give us the courage to ask forgiveness
    of those we have harmed;
give us the wisdom to place you
    above all else in our lives.
We ask this through Christ our Lord.
Amen.

✦ *The day of the Lord is near: Behold, he comes to save us.*

✝ *The day of the Lord is near: Behold, he comes to save us.*

PSALM 85 page 412

READING Matthew 11:2 – 6

When John the Baptist heard in prison of the works of the Christ, he sent his disciples to Jesus with this question, "Are you the one who is to come, or should we look for another?" Jesus said to them in reply, "Go and tell John what you hear and see: the blind regain their sight, the lame walk, lepers are cleansed, the deaf hear, the dead are raised, and the poor have the good news proclaimed to them. And blessed is the one who takes no offense at me."

REFLECTION

What kind of Savior do you imagine and expect? This Advent, as you wait with longing for Christ, what do you hope for in his birth? What miracles do you pray for? Be like a child and, in prayer, ask for your greatest desires for yourself, your family, and the world. Our faith allows us to dream of a Christmas that fulfills our hopes of transformation for ourselves and others. As the holidays unfold, look for signs of the actual coming of this miraculous gift.

PRAYERS others may be added

With hope in our Savior, we pray:

◆ Come, O Emmanuel.

That the Church is a witness to sight regained, hearing restored, and the dead raised, we pray: ◆ That the peaceful hopes of children all over the world are realized, we pray: ◆ That those who long for healing receive answers to their prayers, we pray: ◆ That our communal worship leads to the transformation of the world, we pray: ◆ That those who have died in Christ witness the coming of the kingdom, we pray: ◆

Our Father . . .

Prince of Peace,
you have come to set us free.
The earth rejoices at your step!
As we journey through the desert
    of life,
open our eyes to the miracles
    around us;
give us patience as we search for you;
make us bold in our hopes
    for salvation.
May we be like children,
awaiting Christmas and its promise of
    peace on earth.
You live and reign with God
    the Father
in the unity of the Holy Spirit,
one God, forever and ever.
Amen.

✝ *The day of the Lord is near: Behold, he comes to save us.*

✠ *Blessed are all who wait for the Lord.*

PSALM 40 *page 407*

READING *2 Corinthians 10:17—11:2*

Brothers and sisters: / *Whoever boasts, should boast in the Lord.* / For it is not the one who recommends himself who is approved, but the one whom the Lord recommends.

If only you would put up with a little foolishness from me! Please put up with me. For I am jealous of you with the jealousy of God, since I betrothed you to one husband to present you as a chaste virgin to Christ.

REFLECTION

Are you proud of your children? Be proud of God's gifts to them. Have you been rewarded for your job performance? Give thanks for God's blessings by sharing your gifts with others. Are you tempted to boast about your spouse's success or the happiness the two of you share? Make known the amazing grace of God. St. Lucy and all the saints remind us of where we need to be focused. Our life's accomplishments are not our own. God has blessed us in a multitude of ways, and grace alone has enabled us to become who we are today.

PRAYERS *others may be added*

Humbled and grateful, we pray:

◆ *The glory is yours, O God.*

For the growth of Christianity throughout the world, that all who believe point others to the source of life and salvation, we pray: ◆ *For just governments and the quality of life they provide, we pray:* ◆ *For educational, career, and family success, that praise is given to God for his guidance and gifts, we pray:* ◆ *For the vibrant life of our parish community, that we recognize and celebrate the Holy Spirit's work among us, we pray:* ◆

Our Father . . .

Loving God,
you have made us for yourself,
and give us sufficient grace and love.
May St. Lucy be a reminder to us of
    the truth of God in our lives,
and may we praise and honor you
    with every day.
We ask this through Christ our Lord.
Amen.

✠ *Blessed are all who wait for the Lord.*

✦ *Blessed are all who wait for the Lord.*

PSALM 40   page 407

READING   *1 Corinthians 2:1–10a*

When I came to you, brothers and sisters, proclaiming the mystery of God, I did not come with sublimity of words or of wisdom. For I resolved to know nothing while I was with you except Jesus Christ, and him crucified. I came to you in weakness and fear and much trembling, and my message and my proclamation were not with persuasive words of wisdom, but with a demonstration of spirit and power, so that your faith might rest not on human wisdom but on the power of God.

Yet we do speak a wisdom to those who are mature, but not a wisdom of this age, nor of the rulers of this age who are passing away. Rather, we speak God's wisdom, mysterious, hidden, which God predetermined before the ages for our glory, and which none of the rulers of this age knew for, if they had known it, they would not have crucified the Lord of glory.

REFLECTION

Answers to life's questions abound. Talk shows, self-help books, ongoing education, and the advice of friends offer both valid and false perspectives on life. It is human nature to seek knowledge. It is also human nature to be confounded by the array of possible truths. God's wisdom, unlike other sources, is "mysterious, hidden," and not of this world.

We must look past the obvious to find the lasting, powerful truth of Jesus Christ and the cross. When we need God—coming before him in humility—our hearts are most open to his knowing love and wise answers.

PRAYERS   *others may be added*

With hope for God, we pray:

◆ Show us your simple, yet powerful, truth.

For respected Church leaders, when their human limits of education and wisdom are reached, we pray: ◆ For political figures who feel the pressure of multiple agendas, and search for a moral compass, we pray: ◆ For those faced with important decisions, we pray: ◆ For those who have died, we pray:

Our Father . . .

Wise and loving God,
you are the source of goodness
    and light.
May all of us who struggle, who seek,
    who reach out for you
embrace our weakness, and in turn,
find ourselves in the strong, sure arms
    of your love.
We ask this through Christ our Lord.
Amen.

✦ *Blessed are all who wait for the Lord.*

✛ *The day of the Lord is near: Behold, he comes to save us.*

PSALM 85 *page 412*

READING *Luke 7:18b–23*

At that time, John summoned two of his disciples and sent them to the Lord to ask, "Are you the one who is to come, or should we look for another?" When the men came to the Lord, they said, "John the Baptist has sent us to you to ask, 'Are you the one who is to come, or should we look for another?' " At that time Jesus cured many of their diseases, sufferings, and evil spirits; he also granted sight to many who were blind. And Jesus said to them in reply, "Go and tell John what you have seen and heard: the blind regain their sight, the lame walk, lepers are cleansed, the deaf hear, the dead are raised, the poor have the good news proclaimed to them. And blessed is the one who takes no offense at me."

REFLECTION

The fruit of our faith should be visible in our families, our workplaces, our parishes, and our communities. Are our children thoughtful and generous? Are our employees/coworkers grateful and appreciated? Are our parishes places of faith and transformation? What can we do to ensure our faith is "seen and heard?"

PRAYERS *others may be added*

With trust in the one God, we pray:

◆ Come into our hearts, Lord Jesus.

That the Pope, Bishops, and clergy of the Church continue to steadfastly proclaim the truth of Jesus the Christ, we pray: ◆ *That the fruit of faith bursts forth in government practice, educational programs, generous philanthropy, and peaceful homes, we pray:* ◆ *That all those who have not heard the Good News discover the love God holds for them, we pray:* ◆ *That our witness to the goodness around us reflects the reality of our God, we pray:* ◆

Our Father . . .

Creator of all,
you made visible your power
    and glory
in the design of the world,
culminating in the gift of your Son.
We give thanks for the honor to
    collaborate in your work.
Show us ways to reflect your love and
    majesty in our good acts.
Grant this through Christ our Lord.
Amen.

✛ *The day of the Lord is near: Behold, he comes to save us.*

✦ *The day of the Lord is near.*

PSALM 85 *page 412*

READING *Luke 7:24b–30*

Jesus began to speak to the crowds about John. "What did you go out to the desert to see—a reed swayed by the wind? Then what did you go out to see? Someone dressed in fine garments? Those who dress luxuriously and live sumptuously are found in royal palaces. Then what did you go out to see? A prophet? Yes, I tell you, and more than a prophet. This is the one about whom Scripture says:

Behold, I am sending my messenger ahead of you,/he will prepare your way before you.

I tell you, among those born of women, no one is greater than John; yet the least in the Kingdom of God is greater than he." (All the people who listened, including the tax collectors, who were baptized with the baptism of John, acknowledged the righteousness of God; but the Pharisees and scholars of the law, who were not baptized by him, rejected the plan of God for themselves).

REFLECTION

How were the Israelites convinced that Jesus was the one for whom they had waited? The Gospel writers hoped to persuade various communities, including followers of John the Baptist, that Jesus was the true Messiah. They shared his message, his parables, and his miraculous deeds. It is likely that the first followers of Jesus felt something unique in his presence. What convinces you that Jesus is the Son of God, Savior of the world? Which stories or miracles make up the foundation of your faith? Hopefully, each of us has also felt the reality of Jesus in our lives and therefore has come to believe.

PRAYERS *others may be added*

God of faithful love, we pray:

◆ Lord, come and save us.

For the human hands and hearts of the Church when we doubt or falter, we pray: ◆ *For leaders of nations, that their efforts may be grounded in love of God, we pray:* ◆ *For the conversion of hearts, minds, and actions, we pray:* ◆ *For the faithful, that we are drawn ever closer to Christ and not distracted by movements that lead away from him, we pray:* ◆

Our Father . . .

Loving God,
as we prepare the way of the Lord
   this Advent,
may we remain true to our
   baptismal promises.
Renew our awe and wonder at the
   mystery of the Savior.
Draw together all people of faith
to be a light shining to all nations.
Grant this through Christ our Lord.
Amen.

✦ *The day of the Lord is near.*

✦ *The day of the Lord is near: Behold, he comes to save us.*

PSALM 85 page 412

READING Genesis 49:2, 8–10

Jacob called his sons and said to them: / "Assemble and listen, sons of Jacob, / listen to Israel, your father.

"You, Judah, shall your brothers praise / —your hand on the neck of your enemies; / the sons of father shall bow down to you. / Judah, like a lion's whelp, / you have grown up on prey, my son. / He crouches like a lion recumbent, / the king of beasts—who would dare rouse him? / The scepter shall never depart from Judah, / or the mace from between his legs, / While tribute is brought to him, / and he receives the people's homage."

REFLECTION

We may be part of a large family, or we may long to be part of a greater legacy. Extended relatives and awareness of our heritage gives us a sense of connectedness and purpose. Regardless of our earthly families or lack thereof, all of us are adopted into God's family through Baptism. These fathers and mothers listed are part of our lineage as brothers and sisters of Jesus.

PRAYERS others may be added

We come before the one who knew us from the day we were created:

◆ Father, hear us.

For the Christian family worldwide, that we can be in right relationship with one another and continually welcome new members, we pray: ◆ *For the global family, that in the suffering of all we see the face of our brother, Jesus Christ, we pray:* ◆ *For adoptive and foster families, that they may be a second chance at love for parents and children, we pray:* ◆ *For all families of this parish, that we are open and honest with one another, asking and granting forgiveness in Christian love, we pray:* ◆

Our Father . . .

Lord of our ancestors by blood and
   by faith,
you show us the love of father
   and mother.
Teach us to be good parents, children,
   siblings, and grandparents.
Teach us to welcome those beyond
   our biological families.
May we always know the comfort
   and guidance
of a loving family through you and
   your Church.
We ask this through Christ our Lord.
Amen.

✦ *The day of the Lord is near: Behold, he comes to save us.*

✦ *The day of the Lord is near.*

PSALM 85 *page 412*

READING *Matthew 1:18–21*

This is how the birth of Jesus Christ came about. When his mother Mary was betrothed to Joseph, but before they lived together, she was found with child through the Holy Spirit. Joseph her husband, since he was a righteous man, yet unwilling to expose her to shame, decided to divorce her quietly. Such was his intention when, behold, the angel of the Lord appeared to him in a dream and said, "Joseph, son of David, do not be afraid to take Mary your wife into your home. For it is through the Holy Spirit that this child has been conceived in her. She will bear a son and you are to name him Jesus, because he will save his people from their sins."

REFLECTION

"God is with us"—Emmanuel. This name describes a God who loves us so much he wanted to share in our lives, and so became flesh. He is with us in our sleeping; he is with us in our waking; he is with us in our groaning; he is with us in our laughing. He is with us in every relationship we enter. He is with us in every experience we encounter.

PRAYERS *others may be added*

Knowing our God is near, we pray:

◆ O God, be with us.

That the presence of God is known and felt in the heart of the Church: her decisions, her outreach, her prayer, and her teaching, we pray: ◆ *That meetings and interactions between governments worldwide are infused with the wisdom of God, we pray:* ◆ *That those who consider themselves unworthy become aware of God's breath and light within their daily lives, we pray:* ◆ *That our community welcomes God into our social, physical, and financial activities, we pray:* ◆

Our Father . . .

O Emmanuel,
your people have waited for you in
    patient hope.
May we see your presence in our
    daily lives
and respond with real joy, laughter,
    and action.
May our community be alive with the
    presence of God,
where you live and reign with him
in the unity of the Holy Spirit,
one God, forever and ever.
Amen.

✦ *The day of the Lord is near.*

✝ *The day of the Lord is near: Behold, he comes to save us.*

PSALM 85   page 412

READING   Matthew 1:18–23

This is how the birth of Jesus Christ came about. When his mother Mary was betrothed to Joseph, but before they lived together, she was found with child through the Holy Spirit. Joseph her husband, since he was a righteous man, yet unwilling to expose her to shame, decided to divorce her quietly. Such was his intention when, behold, the angel of the Lord appeared to him in a dream and said, "Joseph, son of David, do not be afraid to take Mary your wife into your home. For it is through the Holy Spirit that this child has been conceived in her. She will bear a son and you are to name him Jesus, because he will save his people from their sins." All this took place to fulfill what the Lord had said through the prophet: / *Behold, the virgin shall be with child and bear a son, / and they shall name him Emmanuel,* which means "God is with us."

REFLECTION

Is God asking you to do something you don't understand? Sometimes we cannot see the big picture. Sometimes the little amount of information we are privy to when we help a friend, provide support or advice, or otherwise act, leaves us confused. But if we ask in prayer for the Holy Spirit to lead us, we may be able to be part of a larger action for the good of the community.

PRAYERS   *others may be added*

With trusting hearts, we pray:

◆ May your will be done.

For the Church, that clergy, religious, and lay people, all seeing different needs of the world, work together for the good God intends, we pray: ◆ *For leaders of wealthy nations, that visits to and dialogue with rural and poverty-stricken parts of the world help them to see how we can help and learn from each other, we pray:* ◆ *For those who fear they cannot make a difference, that they entrust their small acts to God's providence, we pray:* ◆ *For the faithful of our diocese, that we can accept with faith the important needs of those in other parishes and regions around us, and find ways to effectively respond, we pray:* ◆

Our Father . . .

All-knowing and all-mighty God,
you see and know every creature
    on earth.
Help us turn to you in prayer
    and humility
as we seek direction for our Church,
    nation, schools, and businesses.
Help us to do our part to bring
    balance and meaning
to the many voices crying out in fear
    and suffering.
We ask this through Christ our Lord.
Amen.

✝ *The day of the Lord is near: Behold, he comes to save us.*

✝ *The day of the Lord is near: Behold, he comes to save us.*

PSALM 85   *page 412*

READING   *Luke 1:26 – 30a, 35b – 38b*

The angel Gabriel was sent from God to a town of Galilee called Nazareth, to a virgin betrothed to a man named Joseph, of the house of David, and the virgin's name was Mary. And coming to her, he said, "Hail, full of grace! The Lord is with you." But she was greatly troubled at what was said and pondered what sort of greeting this might be. Then the angel said to her, "Do not be afraid, Mary . . . the Holy Spirit will come upon you, and the power of the Most High will overshadow you. Therefore the child to be born will be called holy, the Son of God. And behold, Elizabeth, your relative, has also conceived a son in her old age, and this is the sixth month for her who was called barren; for nothing will be impossible for God." Mary said, "Behold, I am the handmaid of the Lord. May it be done to me according to your word."

REFLECTION   *Rev. Michael JK Fuller*

Mary's question echoes in our own hearts: How can this be? But with God nothing is impossible, not even a love that sacrifices everything. In the end, there is only one response possible, and that is the response of Mary, a simple: "May it be done to me . . ."

PRAYERS   *others may be added*

Striving to have the faith of Mary, we pray:

◆ Comfort us, O God.

For the Pope, that he may be a sign of absolute faith in a world of confusion and doubt, we pray: ◆ *For the world, that the impossible dream of peace may be the miracle of this Christmas, we pray:* ◆ *For those overcome with self-doubt, that they are called out of themselves and into living for others, we pray:* ◆ *For our teenagers, that they may dream big for us all and show us the way to make it so, we pray:* ◆

Our Father . . .

Holy, Holy, Holy Lord,
your awesome works attest to
    your greatness.
You continue to transform and
    enliven the earth with your
    creative power.
May we place our trust in you,
hoping and dreaming of miracles.
Use us, your servants, to bring about
    your kingdom on earth.
Grant this through Christ our Lord.
Amen.

✝ *The day of the Lord is near: Behold, he comes to save us.*

✦ *The day of the Lord is near: Behold, he comes to save us.*

PSALM 85   *page 412*

READING   *Luke 1:39–45*

Mary set out in those days and traveled to the hill country in haste to a town of Judah, where she entered the house of Zechariah and greeted Elizabeth. When Elizabeth heard Mary's greeting, the infant leaped in her womb, and Elizabeth, filled with the Holy Spirit, cried out in a loud voice and said, "Most blessed are you among women, and blessed is the fruit of your womb. And how does this happen to me, that the mother of my Lord should come to me? For at the moment the sound of your greeting reached my ears, the infant in my womb leaped for joy. Blessed are you who believed that what was spoken to you by the Lord would be fulfilled."

REFLECTION

The closer we come to the birth of Jesus, the more overwhelmed we are with the blessedness of believing. We see it in the sparkle of trees, the glistening of snow, the exuberance of faces around us. Joy begets joy. Life begets life. We are so blessed to receive the fulfillment of God's promises. It is time to share . . . share . . . share this gift!

PRAYERS   *others may be added*

We lift up our hearts to the Lord:

◆ Blessed are you, O God.

With gratitude for our servant leaders, the Pope, Bishops, priests, deacons, religious, lay ministers, and all volunteers who work tirelessly in Jesus' name, we pray: ◆ *With gratitude for secretaries of state, ambassadors, mediators, and translators, who strive for understanding and dialogue between all peoples, we pray:* ◆ *With gratitude for civil servants, nonprofit staffs, teachers, health care providers, and all who serve the public with their lives, we pray:* ◆ *With gratitude for one another, each time we are greeted with a smile, handshake, embrace, and genuine goodwill, we pray:* ◆

Our Father . . .

God of celebration,
you give us the capacity for joy
    and laughter.
Help us to sing, dance, play, and enjoy
    your gifts
with an enthusiasm that will fill
    all hearts
with happiness and delight.
Grant this through Christ our Lord.
Amen.

✦ *The day of the Lord is near: Behold, he comes to save us.*

✦ *The day of the Lord is near.*

PSALM 85 *page 412*

READING *Luke 1:46–55*

Mary said: "My soul proclaims the greatness of the Lord;/my spirit rejoices in God my savior./For he has looked upon his lowly servant./From this day all generations will call me blessed:/the Almighty has done great things for me,/and holy is his Name./He has mercy on those who fear him/in every generation./He has shown the strength of his arm,/and has scattered the proud in their conceit./He has cast down the mighty from their thrones/and has lifted up the lowly./He has filled the hungry with good things,/and the rich he has sent away empty./He has come to the help of his servant Israel/for he remembered his promise of mercy,/the promise he made to our fathers,/to Abraham and his children for ever."

REFLECTION

In the rush of the season, when many are overcome with gratitude for what we have, others are overwhelmed by what they lack, or are mired in depression, loneliness, or resentment. It is difficult to celebrate without loving relationships. It is hard to feel generous when faced with financial burdens. If one's heart is far from joyful, for what will one pray? O Come, O Come, Emmanuel and give the gift of which we are in most need.

PRAYERS *others may be added*

On behalf of those who struggle, we pray:

◆ O come, Emmanuel.

For Catholic Relief Services, Catholic Charities, and all organizations within the Church that reach out to those in need, that their efforts are continually supported and effective, we pray: ◆
For media that accurately and compassionately make known the needs of the oppressed, that it inspires a generous response, we pray: ◆ *For those whose hearts are breaking this season, that the love of a neighbor may bring them one step closer to healing, we pray:* ◆
For us who have been blessed, that we give thanks and proper attribution to our Lord and our God, giver of all good gifts, we pray: ◆

Our Father . . .

Merciful God,
you never forget your children.
You would not leave even one
   sheep behind.
As you are present to those in need,
may we be privileged to be your
   hands and feet:
delivering meals, opening our homes,
   embracing the lonely,
and sharing our time to improve
   others' lives.
We ask this through Christ our Lord.
Amen.

✦ *The day of the Lord is near.*

✦ *The day of the Lord is near: Behold, he comes to save us.*

PSALM 85   *page 412*

READING   *Luke 1:57–66*

When the time arrived for Elizabeth to have her child she gave birth to a son. Her neighbors and relatives heard that the Lord had shown his great mercy toward her, and they rejoiced with her. When they came on the eighth day to circumcise the child, they were going to call him Zechariah after his father, but his mother said in reply, "No. He will be called John." But they answered her, "There is no one among your relatives who has this name." So they made signs, asking his father what he wished him to be called. He asked for a tablet and wrote, "John is his name," and all were amazed. Immediately his mouth was opened, his tongue freed, and he spoke blessing God. Then fear came upon all their neighbors, and all these matters were discussed throughout the hill country of Judea. All who heard these things took them to heart, saying, "What, then, will this child be?" For surely the hand of the Lord was with him.

REFLECTION

The birth of Jesus is so near it is palpable. We anticipate acceptance, peace, closure, knowledge, and culmination. Our waiting is about to end. Our waiting has ended. Our waiting will continue until the time of the kingdom. We breathe in the air of now . . . but not yet.

PRAYERS   *others may be added*

Keeping in mind the ways of the Lord, we pray:

◆ Come, Lord Jesus.

For the apostolic Church, instrument of the Holy Spirit, that she continues the mission to share the gift of Jesus Christ to all the ends of the earth, we pray: ◆ *For the suffering of creation, that the gift of Jesus, once and always, continually draws the world closer to the time of all in all in God, we pray:* ◆ *For those who wait—for loved ones, for news, for death—that the nearness of the Christ child gives them patience and hope, we pray:* ◆ *For believers who rejoice and yet still long for the kingdom, that this coming celebration is a joyful reminder of all that is to come, we pray:* ◆

Our Father . . .

Infinite and mysterious God,
lead us on the path of peace
   and knowledge,
ever closer to you and to eternal life.
We ask this through Christ our Lord.
Amen.

✦ *The day of the Lord is near: Behold, he comes to save us.*

✦ *The day of the Lord is near.*

PSALM 85 *page 412*

READING *Luke 1:67–79*

Zechariah his father, filled with the Holy Spirit, prophesied, saying:

"Blessed be the Lord the God of Israel; / for he has come to his people and set them free. / He has raised up for us a mighty Savior, / born of the house of his servant David. / Through his prophets he promised of old / that he would save us from our enemies, / from the hands of all who hate us. / He promised to show mercy to our fathers / and to remember his holy covenant. / This was the oath he swore to our father Abraham: / to set us free from the hand of our enemies, / free to worship him without fear, / holy and righteous in his sight all the days of our life. / You, my child, shall be called the prophet of the Most High, / for you will go before the Lord to prepare his way, / to give people knowledge of salvation / by the forgiveness of their sins. / In the tender compassion of our God / the dawn from on high shall break upon us, / to shine on those who dwell in darkness and the shadow of death, / and to guide our feet into the way of peace."

REFLECTION

Spiritual darkness has ended. We don't have to wonder if God will keep his covenantal promise; we don't have to search for the answer of life; we don't have to be confused. God has revealed the light to us. We have the privilege of spending our entire lives praising him; growing in understanding and sharing the light with others.

PRAYERS *others may be added*

Blessed to be believers, we pray:

◆ Shine, O Light.

That the light of the Church may be a beacon of truth and hope, we pray: ◆ *That the light of education may lead to greater harmony between nations, we pray:* ◆ *That the light of justice may shine into the darkest corners where violence, crime, and cruelty have reigned, we pray:* ◆ *That the light of charity may pervade our community, making us generous with what we have, we pray:* ◆ *That the eternal light will lead all believers home, we pray:* ◆

Our Father . . .

God of light,
may we carry your light to others
and wait in joyful hope
for the time when we will celebrate in
    the eternal light of heaven.
We ask this through Christ our Lord.
Amen.

✦ *The day of the Lord is near.*

✦ *I proclaim to you good news of great joy: today a Savior is born for us, Christ the Lord.*

PSALM 98   *page 413*

READING   *John 1:1–5, 9–11, 14*

In the beginning was the Word, / and the Word was with God, / and the Word was God. / He was in the beginning with God. / All things came to be through him, / and without him nothing came to be. / What came to be through him was life, / and this life was the light of the human race; / the light shines in the darkness, / and the darkness has not overcome it. /
The true light, which enlightens everyone, was coming into the world. / He was in the world, / and the world came to be through him, / but the world did not know him. / He came to what was his own, / but his own people did not accept him. /
    And the Word became flesh / and made his dwelling among us, / and we saw his glory, / the glory as of the Father's only Son, / full of grace and truth.

REFLECTION

Rejoice, children of God! Our lives are forever changed this glorious morning! The Christ child brings into the world every grace and the fullness of revelation. Past, present, and future are forever touched by his birth. We praise you and thank you, O God, for this most blessed Christmas gift!

PRAYERS   *others may be added*

With the joy of children, we pray:

◆ Rejoice in the Lord!

For the people of God, that Christmas morning brings a renewed joy to their hearts, we pray: ◆ For the people of the world, that the fullness of revelation made known again today reaches every heart with love, we pray: ◆ For all children, that their natural curiosity and awe remains with them throughout their lives, we pray: ◆ For our families and friends, that the birth of Christ brings them every blessing, we pray: ◆

Our Father . . .

O God,
you who made the star that shone at
    Jesus' birth
have redeemed the world through
    your glorious love.
We give you thanks and praise.
Light our hearts on fire,
that we might transform others
by our joy and faithfulness.
We ask this through our Lord Jesus
    Christ, your Son,
who lives and reigns with you in the
    unity of the Holy Spirit,
one God, forever and ever.
Amen.

✦ *I proclaim to you good news of great joy: today a Savior is born for us, Christ the Lord.*

+ *Let the heavens be glad and the
earth rejoice!*

PSALM 98   *page 413*

READING   *Matthew 2:19–23*

When Herod had died, behold, the angel
of the Lord appeared in a dream to
Joseph in Egypt and said, "Rise, take
the child and his mother and go to the
land of Israel, for those who sought the
child's life are dead." He rose, took the
child and his mother, and went to the
land of Israel. But when he heard that
Archelaus was ruling over Judea in
place of his father Herod, he was afraid
to go back there. And because he had
been warned in a dream, he departed
for the region of Galilee. He went and
dwelt in a town called Nazareth, so that
what had been spoken through the
prophets might be fulfilled, *He shall be
called a Nazorean.*

REFLECTION

*We lift our precious families—nuclear,
extended, biological, adopted, blended—
in prayer today. Such great love exists
and is tried in the bonds of family.
Jesus, Mary, and Joseph travel together,
listening to the guidance of an angel.
May our families as well be guided by
the Spirit of the Lord.*

PRAYERS   *others may be added*

*Aware of our relationships with family
members, we pray:*

◆ Lord, hear our prayer.

*For vowed celibates, that their brother
priests and brother and sister religious
support them as family, we pray:* ◆
*For the many traditions and customs of
nations, that we may learn from one
another how to best honor and love all
our family members, we pray:* ◆ *For
families experiencing loss and division,
that the pain and grief involved may
move toward healing by the guidance of
the Holy Spirit, we pray:* ◆ *For our own
families, that we find support for our
marriages, parenting, and all stages of
life in our Church community, we pray:* ◆

Our Father . . .

O God in three persons,
you model for us right relationship
    and mutual love.
Walk with us and guide us
in our efforts to love, teach, support,
    and challenge one another.
May our families be the first place we
    find and live out our faith
as a reflection of your love.
We ask this through Christ our Lord.
Amen.

+ *Let the heavens be glad and the
earth rejoice!*

MONDAY, 27 DECEMBER 2010
FEAST OF ST. JOHN, APOSTLE, EVANGELIST

✦ *Blessed are all who wait for the Lord.*

PSALM 149 — page 421

READING — *John 20:1a and 2–8*

On the first day of the week, Mary Magdalene ran and went to Simon Peter and to the other disciple whom Jesus loved, and told them, "They have taken the Lord from the tomb, and we do not know where they put him." So Peter and the other disciple went out and came to the tomb. They both ran, but the other disciple ran faster than Peter and arrived at the tomb first; he bent down and saw the burial cloths there, but did not go in. When Simon Peter arrived after him, he went into the tomb and saw the burial cloths there, and the cloth that had covered his head, not with the burial cloths but rolled up in a separate place. Then the other disciple also went in, the one who had arrived at the tomb first, and he saw and believed.

REFLECTION

Our loving God has sent his beloved Son to us. We are loved and we love him in return. It feels so good, so right, and so inspiring to be deeply loved. God loves us in an unconditional, generous way. We, in turn, love God with all our hearts. We run to him and embrace him—in our prayer, and in the way we live. Today we are one with the beloved disciple, loving and believing in our Lord.

PRAYERS — *others may be added*

Loving God, we turn to you in prayer:

◆ *Let your love work in and through us.*

That the Church may be a great sign of the mercy, compassion, and generosity of our Lord God, we pray: ◆ *That the coming of Christ may inspire each of his followers to respond in gratitude every day and in every interaction, we pray:* ◆ *That those who feel unloved may know divine love and its earthly expressions, we pray:* ◆ *That our community of faith may be alive with the Christ child, we pray:* ◆

Our Father . . .

Lord Jesus,
our brother and saving Lord,
your birth assures us of God's
    never-ending love.
May we follow in the footsteps of
    St. John
as we love you and, in return,
    love others,
and rejoice in knowing you.
You live and reign with God
    the Father
in the unity of the Holy Spirit,
one God, forever and ever.
Amen.

✦ *Blessed are all who wait for the Lord.*

30

✠ *Blessed are all who wait for the Lord.*

PSALM 149 *page 421*

READING *Matthew 2:13–14, 16*

When the magi had departed, behold, the angel of the Lord appeared to Joseph in a dream and said, "Rise, take the child and his mother, flee to Egypt, and stay there until I tell you. Herod is going to search for the child to destroy him." Joseph rose and took the child and his mother by night and departed for Egypt.

When Herod realized that he had been deceived by the magi, he became furious. He ordered the massacre of all the boys in Bethlehem and its vicinity two years old and under, in accordance with the time he had ascertained from the magi.

REFLECTION *Saint Quodvultdeus*

The children die for Christ, though they do not know it. The parents mourn for the death of martyrs. The child makes of those as yet unable to speak fit witnesses to himself. See the kind of kingdom that is his, coming as he did in order to be this kind of king. See how the deliverer is already working deliverance, the savior already working salvation.

PRAYERS *others may be added*

Aware of real suffering and real evil, we pray:

◆ Heal us, O God.

That the Church continues to speak on behalf of the powerless, especially children, we pray: ◆ *That all governments will recognize the unique innocence of children, we pray:* ◆ *That those charged with the protection of children live this responsibility with total honesty, we pray:* ◆ *That we treat our own children with tenderness, firmness, and patience, we pray:* ◆ *That all children who have died return to the Father, we pray:* ◆

Our Father . . .

Lord Jesus,
you welcomed the little children
and continue to protect and comfort
   the smallest and weakest among us.
Remind us of our shared duty to
   protect our children.
Slow us down so that we notice these
   little souls;
help us to include them in our vision
   of the Church;
help us to listen to their wise voices.
You live and reign with God
   the Father
in the unity of the Holy Spirit,
one God, forever and ever.
Amen.

✠ *Blessed are all who wait for the Lord.*

✛ *A light will shine on us this day: the Lord is born for us.*

PSALM 98 *page 413*

READING *Luke 2:27–35*

[Simeon] came in the Spirit into the temple; and when the parents brought in the child Jesus to perform the custom of the law in regard to him, he took him into his arms and blessed God, saying:

"Lord, now let your servant go in peace; / your word has been fulfilled: / my own eyes have seen the salvation / which you prepared in the sight of every people, / a light to reveal you to the nations / and the glory of your people Israel."

The child's father and mother were amazed at what was said about him; and Simeon blessed them and said to Mary his mother, "Behold, this child is destined for the fall and rise of many in Israel, and to be a sign that will be contradicted (and you yourself a sword will pierce) so that the thoughts of many hearts may be revealed."

REFLECTION

Simeon felt such peace in the presence of the child Jesus. He felt assured of the good in the future for all people; he sensed the light of salvation. We, too, are offered this peace and assurance. As we consider our own last days, we can trust that we hold Jesus in our embrace and he, in turn, offers us eternal life.

PRAYERS *others may be added*

Resting in the arms of God, we pray:

◆ Lord, hear our prayer.

For the Church and her prophetic voice, that she may offer a challenging and welcoming path to salvation, we pray: ◆ *For leaders anxious about the future, that they find peace in the Good News of Jesus, we pray:* ◆ *For those faced with death, that fear and worry give way to assurance and peace in the embrace of Jesus, we pray:* ◆ *For ourselves as believers, that we can live out what we profess when experiencing the death of loved ones, we pray:* ◆ *For those who have died, that they may find eternal joy with God, we pray:* ◆

Our Father . . .

Lord Jesus, conqueror of death,
you prepare for us a place in the
    eternal kingdom.
Allay our fears about leaving security
    and loved ones.
Call us by name in our final hours,
that we may recognize your voice
and find peace and rest in the arms
    of God.
You live and reign with God
    the Father
in the unity of the Holy Spirit,
one God, forever and ever.
Amen.

✛ *A light will shine on us this day: the Lord is born for us.*

✦ *Let the heavens be glad and the earth rejoice!*

PSALM 98 — page 413

READING — Luke 2:36–40

There was a prophetess, Anna, the daughter of Phanuel, of the tribe of Asher. She was advanced in years, having lived seven years with her husband after her marriage, and then as a widow until she was eighty-four. She never left the temple, but worshiped night and day with fasting and prayer. And coming forward at that very time, she gave thanks to God and spoke about the child to all who were awaiting the redemption of Jerusalem.

When they had fulfilled all the prescriptions of the law of the Lord, they returned to Galilee, to their own town of Nazareth. The child grew and became strong, filled with wisdom; and the favor of God was upon him.

REFLECTION — Saint Hippolytus

The Word spoke first of all through the prophets, but because the message was couched in such obscure language that it could be only dimly apprehended, in the last days the Father sent the Word in person, commanding him to show himself openly so that the world could see him and be saved.

PRAYERS — others may be added

Rejoicing with Anna, we pray:

◆ Our hope is in you, O Lord.

For the Pope, the Bishops, and all clergy, that they continually give praise to God for the gift of his Son, we pray: ◆
For those who hope and pray for redemption from oppression, that they may live to see peace in their lands, we pray: ◆ *For those who have been waiting to speak on behalf of the Lord, that their voices cry out in praise, we pray:* ◆ *For our faithful community, that our worshipping, fasting, and praying strengthens the kingdom of God, we pray:* ◆

Our Father . . .

Teacher, Wonderful-Counselor,
    Prince of Peace,
you have come to fill the hopes of all
    holy people.
We have longed for your wisdom
    and salvation,
and now rejoice in your birth and life.
Send us forth to share the Good News
    with joyful hearts.
You live and reign with God
    the Father
in the unity of the Holy Spirit,
one God, forever and ever.
Amen.

✦ *Let the heavens be glad and the earth rejoice!*

✦ *A light will shine on us this day.*

PSALM 98   page 413

READING   *John 1:1–5, 10–14*

In the beginning was the Word, / and the Word was with God, / and the Word was God. / He was in the beginning with God. / All things came to be through him, / and without him nothing came to be. / What came to be through him was life, / and this life was the light of the human race; / the light shines in the darkness, / and the darkness has not overcome it.

He was in the world, / and the world came to be through him, / but the world did not know him. / He came to what was his own, / but his own people did not accept him.

But to those who did accept him / he gave power to become children of God, / to those who believe in his name, / who were born not by natural generation / nor by human choice nor by a man's decision / but of God.

And the Word became flesh / and made his dwelling among us, / and we saw his glory, / the glory as of the Father's only-begotten Son, / full of grace and truth.

REFLECTION

At the end of this calendar year, and not much past the beginning of the liturgical year, consider your response to Jesus. It is, in some way, a hard mystery to accept—this human and divine Jesus is our Savior and the Son of God. But if we do accept the Word Incarnate, we "become children of God." *Simply through the grace of God and our response, our identity, heritage, and destiny are transformed. What a perfect day to renew this "yes."*

PRAYERS   *others may be added*

With hearts uplifted, we pray:

◆ Make us your own, O God.

For all the children of God, that acceptance of Christ includes a daily "yes" to serve, we pray: ◆ *For people in all the countries of the world who reject Christ, that the beauty and mystery of his love may be revealed to them, we pray:* ◆ *For those who feel unworthy of God's love, that they embrace this free, undeserved and empowering gift, we pray:* ◆ *For all to be careful to see Christ in our midst, accepting his many challenges, we pray:* ◆

Our Father . . .

Lord Jesus,
Word of the Father and Light of
    the world,
you call us to be your brothers
    and sisters.
Remind us of this precious gift
and the great responsibility it brings.
You live and reign with God
    the Father
in the unity of the Holy Spirit,
one God, forever and ever.
Amen.

✦ *A light will shine on us this day.*

✚   *A light will shine on us this day.*

CANTICLE
page 422

READING
Luke 2:16–21

The shepherds went in haste to Bethlehem and found Mary and Joseph, and the infant lying in the manger. When they saw this, they made known the message that had been told them about this child. All who heard it were amazed by what had been told them by the shepherds. And Mary kept all these things, reflecting on them in her heart. Then the shepherds returned, glorifying and praising God for all they had heard and seen, just as it had been told to them.

When eight days were completed for his circumcision, he was named Jesus, the name given him by the angel before he was conceived in the womb.

REFLECTION

The Christmas season and today's solemnity are not only occasions to renew our belief in Jesus and share our joy with others, they are also occasions for quiet reflection. With Mary, sit in the winter stillness and the post-holiday quiet, and give thanks for this Christmas celebration. What was life-giving this year? What was difficult? What did you hear God speaking to you in the hushed candlelight and in the jubilant gatherings? What calls you to reflect in your heart this day?

PRAYERS
others may be added

In hushed awe, we bring our prayers to our incredible God:

◆   Give us hearts of holiness.

For our Church leaders, that they, too, may have time for retreat and reflection after this busy season, we pray: ◆ *For war-torn parts of the world, that peace and stillness may inhabit small, sacred places and bring security to those who live there, we pray:* ◆ *For those who live in noise and chaos, that they are able to find a rhythm and some sanctuary in which they come to know God, we pray:* ◆ *For all to take time to be still and know our God, we pray:* ◆

Our Father . . .

Son of Mary and Son of God,
you brought peace into the world at
    your birth—
a peace the world had never known.
Your mother accompanied and
    comforted you
throughout your earthly journey.
May she also guide and teach us
as we struggle to follow your path of
    justice and mercy,
that we might better walk in your ways.
You live and reign with God
    the Father
in the unity of the Holy Spirit,
one God, forever and ever.
Amen.

✚   *A light will shine on us this day.*

✤ *Let the heavens be glad and the earth rejoice!*

PSALM 98   *page 413*

READING   *Matthew 2:1–2, 9–12*

When Jesus was born in Bethlehem of Judea, in the days of King Herod, behold, magi from the east arrived in Jerusalem, saying, "Where is the newborn king of the Jews? We saw his star at its rising and have come to do him homage." . . . After their audience with the king they set out. And behold, the star that they had seen at its rising preceded them, until it came and stopped over the place where the child was. They were overjoyed at seeing the star, and on entering the house they saw the child with Mary his mother. They prostrated themselves and did him homage. Then they opened their treasures and offered him gifts of gold, frankincense, and myrrh. And having been warned in a dream not to return to Herod, they departed for their country by another way.

REFLECTION

Awestruck. Awesome. Awe-inspiring. It takes our breath away. Let us give thanks to the Creator of all. Think of the Magi, and the kind of awe they must have felt at seeing the night sky itself respond to the birth of this tiny child, and to lay their eyes upon the Promised One just after his birth, in the arms of his mother. We, too, revel in God's ability to overwhelm and amaze us.

PRAYERS   *others may be added*

In deep gratitude, we bring our prayers to God:

◆ Give us hearts of awe and wonder.

For all who serve the Church, that the praise, glory, and honor for all that is good is given to the Lord and Creator of all, we pray: ◆ *For those who do not know Christ, that awe at natural beauty and artistic or scientific expression causes them to look deeper into the source of this creation, we pray:* ◆ *For the depressed and despairing who have lost the ability to feel inspired, that healing may come to their hearts, we pray:* ◆ *For each of us here, that we may stop to notice the miracles around us and acknowledge their source in God, we pray:* ◆

Our Father . . .

God of majesty,
you guided the Magi to the greatest
    revelation of all time.
You chose them to witness the birth
    of Christ,
and you choose us to continually
    witness his work in the world.
Lead us to be aware of your
    ongoing presence
and to be humble enough to stand in
    awe of your power and might.
Grant this through Christ our Lord.
Amen.

✤ *Let the heavens be glad and the earth rejoice!*

✦ *A light will shine on us this day: the Lord is born for us.*

PSALM 98   *page 413*

READING   *Matthew 4:12–17*

When Jesus heard that John had been arrested, he withdrew to Galilee. He left Nazareth and went to live in Capernaum by the sea, in the region of Zebulun and Naphtali, that what had been said through Isaiah the prophet might be fulfilled:

Land of Zebulun and land of Naphtali, / the way to the sea, beyond the Jordan, / Galilee of the Gentiles, / the people who sit in darkness / have seen a great light, / on those dwelling in a land overshadowed by death light has arisen.

From that time on, Jesus began to preach and say, "Repent, for the Kingdom of heaven is at hand."

REFLECTION

Darkness and light have great meaning for us during the shortened days of this time of year. The thought of losing electricity brings us even closer to the reality of our need for light. Of course, in the time of Christ, and even in parts of the world today, darkness and light had dramatic influence over life since there was no artificial power. Sit in the darkness this evening or this morning. After a short time, light just one candle. Consider its impact on the darkness. Consider the impact of the light of Christ.

PRAYERS   *others may be added*

Yearning for the light of Christ in our lives, we pray:

◆ Shine through the darkness, Lord Jesus.

For all ministers of the Church, that they bring the light of Christ to others by their teaching, healing, and preaching, we pray: ◆ *For countries living in the darkness of poverty, famine, and war, that international aid brings the dawn of light, we pray:* ◆ *For those caught in the darkness of virtual reality and lives lived alone, that the light of day and a tangible community reaches them, we pray:* ◆ *For the deepest parts of our heart where the darkness of pain still prevails, that we allow the light of Christ to enter and heal us, we pray:* ◆

Our Father . . .

God of fulfilled promises,
you have always been faithful to
    your people.
The promised light has scattered the
    darkness in the gift of your Son.
May the whole world feel the warmth
    and clarity
offered in knowing Christ,
through whom we ask this prayer.
Amen.

✦ *A light will shine on us this day: the Lord is born for us.*

✦ *Blessed are all who wait for the Lord.*

PSALM 149 *page 421*

READING *Mark 6:34–38a*

When Jesus saw the vast crowd, his heart was moved with pity for them, for they were like sheep without a shepherd; and he began to teach them many things. By now it was already late and his disciples approached him and said, "This is a deserted place and it is already very late. Dismiss them so that they can go to the surrounding farms and villages and buy themselves something to eat." He said to them in reply, "Give them some food yourselves." But they said to him, "Are we to buy two hundred days' wages worth of food and give it to them to eat?" He asked them, "how many loaves do you have? Go and see."

REFLECTION

This saint, wife, mother, and convert to Catholicism provides a dynamic role model for American Catholics today. So many of her choices we also face: marriage or religious life, commitment to a religious tradition, where to settle and make a home, and how best to serve our God and others. As we look at a new year stretched ahead of us, let us examine where our heart, and our treasure, lies.

PRAYERS *others may be added*

Reflecting on our deepest treasure, we pray:

◆ Lead us to the kingdom, loving God.

For the Church, that she raise up men and women in the footsteps of St. Elizabeth Ann Seton, we pray: ◆ *For leaders of the world who are called by the Lord, that they serve their people with justice, mercy, and love, we pray:* ◆ *For those who serve children, the elderly, the ill and forgotten, that they draw strength from Christ, we pray:* ◆ *For we who are blessed with faith, that we rejoice in a lifetime of serving God and others, we pray:* ◆

Our Father . . .

Lord Jesus,
bringer of the kingdom,
you reveal yourself to us
and call us to recognize who you are.
May we stand before you with hearts
    of faith and eyes of wonder.
We praise you for offering us
    the treasure of eternal life;
be always with us on our
    daily journey.
You live and reign with God
    the Father
in the unity of the Holy Spirit,
one God, forever and ever.
Amen.

✦ *Blessed are all who wait for the Lord.*

✦ *Blessed are all who wait for the Lord.*

PSALM 149   page 421

READING   Mark 6:45–51

After the five thousand had eaten and were satisfied, Jesus made his disciples get into the boat and precede him to the other side toward Bethsaida, while he dismissed the crowd. And when he had taken leave of them, he went off to the mountain to pray. When it was evening, the boat was far out on the sea and he was alone on shore. Then he saw that they were tossed about while rowing, for the wind was against them. About the fourth watch of the night, he came toward them walking on the sea. He meant to pass by them. But when they saw him walking on the sea, they thought it was a ghost and cried out. They had all seen him and were terrified. But at once he spoke with them, "Take courage, it is I, do not be afraid!" He got into the boat with them and the wind died down. They were completely astounded.

REFLECTION

In prayer, stand before God. Without any people or possessions attached to you, without false adornment, present yourself to God. Ask him, "What do you see in my heart?" "How do you describe me?" "What gifts have you given me?" "Can you see the struggles and pain in my heart?" Ask God for the freedom to live simply as his child. When we recognize our God, we also recognize ourselves as his children.

PRAYERS   others may be added

Knowing ourselves as created and God as our Creator, we pray:

◆ Make us humble servants.

That leaders of the Church model for us submission to Christ's authority, we pray: ◆ *That world leaders recognize the presence of a greater power than themselves, we pray:* ◆ *That those caught up in false pretenses and deceptions find their authentic selves, we pray:* ◆ *That our parish practices honesty and humility in interactions with each other, we pray:* ◆

Our Father . . .

Lord Jesus,
by recognizing you,
we recognize the love of God
and the meaning of our lives.
As we come before you in prayer,
root us in our connection to you.
Let all other attachments fade away.
Draw us into your embrace,
where we will live forever.
You live and reign with God
   the Father
in the unity of the Holy Spirit,
one God, forever and ever.
Amen.

✦ *Blessed are all who wait for the Lord.*

✦ *Let the heavens be glad and the earth rejoice!*

PSALM 98   *page 413*

READING   *Luke 4:14–19*

[Jesus] came to Nazareth, where he had grown up, and went according to his custom into the synagogue on the sabbath day. He stood up to read and was handed a scroll of the prophet Isaiah. He unrolled the scroll and found the passage where it was written:

The Spirit of the Lord is upon me, / because he has anointed me / to bring glad tidings to the poor. / He has sent me to proclaim liberty to captives / and recovery of sight to the blind, / to let the oppressed go free, / and to proclaim a year acceptable to the Lord.

REFLECTION

Jesus names himself as the Messiah, the link between the history of the Hebrew people, and the promise of all that is to come. Understanding where we came from is important to us as human persons and as children of God. Because of Jesus, we join the Jewish people who waited for, and then saw revealed to them, the Son of God, the Savior. What Jesus proclaimed in the temple is true for us today: our God who made us, who calls us as his own, has forever sealed our future through the redemption of his human and divine Son.

PRAYERS   *others may be added*

Knowing ourselves as children of God, we pray:

◆ Help us honor our ancestors and celebrate our future.

For the Bishops of the Church, that they hold precious their apostolic birthright, living it with deep faith, we pray: ◆
For all Christians, that we recognize the faith preceding us, and continue to spread the Good News today, we pray: ◆
For all who search for identity in our fast-paced world, that they come to know themselves as made in the image and likeness of God, we pray: ◆ *For honoring all people of great faith, those known and those forever unknown, we pray:* ◆

Our Father . . .

O Anointed One of God,
you reveal to us our potential and
    our destiny.
We give thanks for all who have
    walked before us,
living faith as best they could.
May we continue this glorious
    tradition,
and invite all people to walk with us.
You live and reign with God
    the Father
in the unity of the Holy Spirit,
one God, forever and ever.
Amen.

✦ *Let the heavens be glad and the earth rejoice!*

✦ *A light will shine on us this day: the Lord is born for us.*

PSALM 98   *page 413*

READING   *Luke 5:12–16*

It happened that there was a man full of leprosy in one of the towns where Jesus was; and when he saw Jesus, he fell prostrate, pleaded with him, and said, "Lord, if you wish, you can make me clean." Jesus stretched out his hand, touched him, and said, "I do will it. Be made clean." And the leprosy left him immediately. Then he ordered him not to tell anyone, but "Go, show yourself to the priest and offer for your cleansing what Moses prescribed; that will be proof for them." The report about him spread all the more, and great crowds assembled to listen to him and to be cured of their ailments, but he would withdraw to deserted places to pray.

REFLECTION

Jesus not only enters our world, he redeems our world. He forgives, heals, and cleanses us. All our sorrow, disease, and failings are taken away in the loving sacrifice of Jesus. This innocent lamb lies down with all those who are broken by sin, who are crushed by illness, who are overwhelmed by despair, and creates a new beginning. We are healed and we are set free.

PRAYERS   *others may be added*

All of us, who are in need of healing, bring our prayers to God:

◆ May the birth of Jesus bring us to new life.

That the Church makes clear and available the loving gift of salvation, we pray: ◆ *That all who are hurting seek ways to reconcile with one another, we pray:* ◆ *That those who suffer may see the light of Jesus guiding them to fullness of life, we pray:* ◆ *That we who are forgiven continually offer forgiveness to those who have hurt us, we pray:* ◆

Our Father . . .

Lamb of God,
you take away the sin of the world.
You take on wounds of every kind
    and make us new in you.
Help us to give our hearts to you,
seek forgiveness,
and strive to follow you and sin
    no more.
You live and reign with God
    the Father
in the unity of the Holy Spirit,
one God, forever and ever.
Amen.

✦ *A light will shine on us this day: the Lord is born for us.*

✦ *A light will shine on us this day: the Lord is born for us.*

PSALM 98   *page 413*

READING   *John 3:23–30*

John was also baptizing in Aenon near Salim, because there was an abundance of water there, and people came to be baptized, for John had not yet been imprisoned. Now a dispute arose between the disciples of John and a Jew about ceremonial washings. So they came to John and said to him, "Rabbi, the one who was with you across the Jordan, to whom you testified, here he is baptizing and everyone is coming to him." John answered and said, "No one can receive anything except what has been given him from heaven. You yourselves can testify that I said that I am not the Christ, but that I was sent before him. The one who has the bride is the bridegroom; the best man, who stands and listens for him, rejoices greatly at the bridegroom's voice. So this joy of mine has been made complete. He must increase; I must decrease."

REFLECTION   *Saint Leo the Great*

No one is shut out from [the joy of Christmas]; all share the same reason for rejoicing. Our Lord, victor over sin and death, finding no man free from sin, came to free us all. Let the saint rejoice as he sees the palm of victory at hand. Let the sinner be glad as he receives the offer of forgiveness.

PRAYERS   *others may be added*

Rejoicing in Jesus and all that points the way to him, we pray:

◆ Lead me closer to you, Lord.

In thanks for parents, ministers, pastors, and teachers who serve Christ with deep faith, we pray: ◆ *In thanks for the beauty of the earth and human invention that causes us to marvel at God's handiwork, we pray:* ◆ *In thanks for friends and spouses who help us grow in self-awareness, humility, and gratitude, we pray:* ◆ *In thanks for our community of faith, in which we seek salvation, we pray:* ◆

Our Father . . .

Lord Jesus,
Bridegroom of the Church,
your coming has brought us joy
and revealed to us heaven and earth,
We give thanks for John the Baptist,
    all the saints,
and all good things that have led us to
    life in you.
May we, too, be instruments in your
    plan of salvation.
You live and reign with God
    the Father
in the unity of the Holy Spirit,
one God, forever and ever.
Amen.

✦ *A light will shine on us this day: the Lord is born for us.*

✛ *A light will shine on us this day: the Lord is born for us.*

PSALM 98   *page 413*

READING   *Matthew 3:13–17*

Jesus came from Galilee to John at the Jordan to be baptized by him. John tried to prevent him, saying, "I need to be baptized by you, and yet you are coming to me?" Jesus said to him in reply, "Allow it now, for thus it is fitting for us to fulfill all righteousness." Then he allowed him. After Jesus was baptized, he came up from the water and behold, the heavens were opened for him, and he saw the Spirit of God descending like a dove and coming upon him. And a voice came from the heavens, saying, "This is my beloved Son, with whom I am well pleased."

REFLECTION   *Saint Gregory the Great*

Christ is bathed in light; let us also be bathed in light. Christ is baptized; let us also go down with him, and rise with him. Today let us do honor to Christ's baptism and celebrate this feast in holiness. Be cleansed entirely and continue to be cleansed. . . . You are to be radiant lights as you stand beside Christ, the great light, bathed in the glory of him who is the light of heaven. You are to enjoy more and more the pure and dazzling light of the Trinity, as now you have received—though not in its fullness— a ray of its splendor, proceeding from the one God, in Christ Jesus our Lord, to whom be glory and power for ever and ever. Amen.

PRAYERS   *others may be added*

Blessed to be adopted sons and daughters of God, we turn to him in prayer:

◆ Help us share your love with others.

For those preparing to receive the sacrament of Baptism, that they will be brought to newness of life, we pray: ◆ *For missionaries abroad, that their offer of knowledge of and relationship with God is made with gentleness and received with joy, we pray:* ◆ *For those who have never known themselves as beloved, that God reveals to them their unique gifts, we pray:* ◆

Our Father . . .

God in heaven,
you looked down with pleasure at
    your Son Jesus at his baptism.
We are your adopted sons
    and daughters,
and so you rejoice in our Baptism.
May we honor and please you in
    living our Christian lives,
extending your love to those who do
    not know you,
helping them to see themselves as
    your beloved.
We ask this through our Lord Jesus
    Christ, your Son,
who lives and reigns with you in the
    unity of the Holy Spirit,
one God, forever and ever.
Amen.

✛ *A light will shine on us this day: the Lord is born for us.*

✛ *The heart of the just one is firm,
trusting in the Lord.*

PSALM 40 *page 407*

READING *Mark 1:14–20*

After John had been arrested, Jesus came to Galilee proclaiming the gospel of God: "This is the time of fulfillment. The Kingdom of God is at hand. Repent, and believe in the Gospel."

As he passed by the Sea of Galilee, he saw Simon and his brother Andrew casting their nets into the sea; they were fishermen. Jesus said to them, "Come after me, and I will make you fishers of men." Then they left their nets and followed him. He walked along a little farther and saw James, the son of Zebedee, and his brother John. They too were in a boat mending their nets. Then he called them. So they left their father Zebedee in the boat along with the hired men and followed him.

REFLECTION

At the beginning of a calendar year, our minds focus on beginnings and changes. If we consider that today Jesus calls us by name and asks us to follow him, we may be moved to change in a most important way. What "net" can you leave behind in order to respond as Jesus' disciples did? Several steps may be necessary to leave behind a "net" of significance—a harmful relationship, a job, or a destructive habit. The year is stretched out before you to take these steps with Jesus in the lead.

PRAYERS *others may be added*

Relying on God to lead us in this new year, we pray:

◆ Call us by name, Lord Jesus.

That the Son of God may be the source and inspiration for our Church leaders, we pray: ◆ *That Jesus' leadership may be a model for all who direct businesses, schools, government offices, and non-profit organizations, we pray:* ◆ *That those yearning to leave behind nets of despair and dysfunction may follow Jesus in this new year, we pray:* ◆ *That each of us may respond to Jesus without hesitation and become fishers of men, we pray:* ◆ *That those who have died, leaving behind everything familiar, may turn to God, we pray:* ◆

Our Father . . .

God of ancient promises and daily
fulfillment,
After praising you with Christmas joy,
we now look ahead to following your
Son day by day.
May we be accompanied by the
Twelve apostles,
as we repent, believe, and bring the
Good News to others.
Help us to be unafraid of leaving
behind whatever holds us back.
We ask this through Christ our Lord.
Amen.

✛ *The heart of the just one is firm,
trusting in the Lord.*

✦ *The precepts of the Lord give joy to the heart.*

PSALM 25 page 403

READING Mark 1:21–28

Jesus came to Capernaum with his followers and on the sabbath he entered the synagogue and taught. The people were astonished at his teaching, for he taught them as one having authority and not as the scribes. In their synagogue was a man with an unclean spirit; he cried out, "What have you to do with us, Jesus of Nazareth? Have you come to destroy us? I know who you are—the Holy One of God!" Jesus rebuked him and said, "Quiet! Come out of him!" The unclean spirit convulsed him and with a loud cry came out of him. All were amazed and asked one another, "What is this? A new teaching with authority. He commands even the unclean spirits and they obey him." His fame spread everywhere throughout the whole region of Galilee.

REFLECTION

How have you responded to authority figures in your life? Some automatically resist attempts by others to tell us what to do. Others admire our "elders" so much we may be disappointed to learn they are only human. How do you exert authority? Perhaps you lead with gentleness and grace, or perhaps you dictate with arrogance and humiliation. Jesus shows us authority that comes from God.

PRAYERS *others may be added*

Seeking right relationship with God and others, we pray:

◆ Root us in you, O Wise One.

For those in authority in the Church, that they exercise it with the love of Jesus, we pray: ◆ For those in authority in militaries of every nation, that they excel in mercy and justice, we pray: ◆ For those who see no need for any authority, that they learn humility before God, we pray: ◆ For any of us who hold authority over others, that we honor the dignity of every person, we pray: ◆

Our Father . . .

Omnipotent God,
you rule heaven and earth with
  merciful, generous love.
Bring us closer to you,
that we might be humbled, honored,
  and compassionate
in serving you and others.
May any authority we exercise find its
  foundation in you.
We ask this through Christ our Lord.
Amen.

✦ *The precepts of the Lord give joy to the heart.*

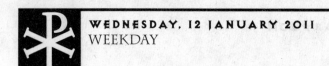

✛ *The Lord made us, we belong to him.*

PSALM 42 *page 408*

READING *Mark 1:29–34*

On leaving the synagogue Jesus entered the house of Simon and Andrew with James and John. Simon's mother-in-law lay sick with a fever. They immediately told him about her. He approached, grasped her hand, and helped her up. Then the fever left her and she waited on them.

When it was evening, after sunset, they brought to him all who were ill or possessed by demons. The whole town was gathered at the door. He cured many who were sick with various diseases, and he drove out many demons, not permitting them to speak because they knew him.

REFLECTION

Jesus came for the sick, those possessed by demons, and those who needed to hear the Word of God. If we are lucky enough to be of sound body, mind, and spirit we may consider ourselves far from "needy." It may be difficult to see that we still need something. We need to be forgiven. We all need healing of one kind or another. We must admit our need for God in order to be surprised by how he can bring us to new life.

PRAYERS *others may be added*

Aware of our deep need for a Savior, we pray:

◆ Raise us to new life, merciful God.

That the healing power of Jesus Christ is shared freely in the sacrament of the Anointing of the Sick and in all the healing ministries of the Church, we pray: ◆ *That those who seek to end abusive situations and protect human rights recognize and utilize Jesus' solidarity with all those who suffer, we pray:* ◆ *That those who are sick or dying this day may be made whole in Jesus Christ, we pray:* ◆ *That we confront our own illnesses and join in the groaning of all humanity for eternal life in God, we pray:* ◆

Our Father . . .

Lord Jesus,
healer of our every ill,
you touched eyes and brought sight;
you touched hands and cured disease;
you reached souls by bringing
    everlasting love and forgiveness.
Count us among those grasping
    at you,
hoping for your touch.
Purify our hearts, minds, and bodies
    and bring us home to you.
You live and reign with God
    the Father
in the unity of the Holy Spirit,
one God, forever and ever.
Amen.

✛ *The Lord made us, we belong to him*

✚ *The Lord made us, we belong to him.*

PSALM 42 *page 408*

READING *Mark 1:40–45*

A leper came to [Jesus] and kneeling down, begged him and said, "If you wish, you can make me clean." Moved with pity, he stretched out his hand, touched him, and said to him, "I do will it. Be made clean." The leprosy left him immediately, and he was made clean. Then, warning him sternly, he dismissed him at once. Then he said to him, "See that you tell no one anything, but go, show yourself to the priest and offer for your cleansing what Moses prescribed; that will be proof for them." The man went away and began to publicize the whole matter. He spread the report abroad so that it was impossible for Jesus to enter a town openly. He remained outside in deserted places, and people kept coming to him from everywhere.

REFLECTION

For an ancient Jew, one important component of cleanliness was the ability to rejoin the community, especially in worship. Those who were "unclean" due to illness or normal bodily functions could not enter the Temple, and therefore were excluded from a central community practice. We may have other types of ailments that prevent us from participating fully in life. In what way can you, like the leper, ask God to make you "clean" and therefore reconcile you to family, community, or the Church?

PRAYERS *others may be added*

Longing for God's cleansing waters, we pray:

◆ Reconcile us to you and one another.

That the Church may be cleansed of division, scandal, and worldly ways, we pray: ◆ *That the earth may be cleansed of pollution, overuse, and greed, we pray:* ◆ *That neighborhoods may be cleansed of drugs, crime, and vandalism, we pray:* ◆ *That our hearts may be cleansed of jealousy, fear, and control, we pray:* ◆

Our Father . . .

Loving God,
you desire for every person to be
    cleansed of sin
and returned to your love.
You continue to offer reconciliation to
    all who call upon you.
May your Word and Eucharist, your
    Spirit, and your Church
be instruments of this cleansing fire.
May we not hesitate to ask to be
    made clean,
that we may be one in you.
Grant this through Christ our Lord.
Amen.

✚ *The Lord made us, we belong to him.*

✦ *For ever I will sing the goodness of the Lord.*

PSALM 33   page 404

READING   *Mark 2:1–5, 11–12*

When Jesus returned to Capernaum after some days, it became known that he was at home. Many gathered together so that there was no longer room for them, not even around the door, and he preached the word to them. They came bringing to him a paralytic carried by four men. Unable to get near Jesus because of the crowd, they opened up the roof above him. After they had broken through, they let down the mat on which the paralytic was lying. When Jesus saw their faith, he said to him, "Child, your sins are forgiven." . . . [Jesus] said to the paralytic, "I say to you, rise, pick up your mat, and go home." He rose, picked up his mat at once, and went away in the sight of everyone. They were all astounded and glorified God, saying, "We have never seen anything like this."

REFLECTION

Are you amazed by Jesus' miracles? Look around and see what Jesus is doing in the world. We may forget to even acknowledge the possibility that God is healing and transforming people's lives. Stand in awe of how Jesus is working and is present in the lives of those you know.

PRAYERS   *others may be added*

Praising all of God's works, we pray:

◆ May your glory reign, almighty God.

In thanks for the lasting, protective, visionary role of the Church throughout history, we pray: ◆ *In thanks for peace treaties and resolutions to protect our world, we pray:* ◆ *In thanks for addictions conquered and relationships reconciled, we pray:* ◆ *In thanks for those who have touched us in our lowest and darkest moments, we pray:* ◆

Our Father . . .

God of power and might,
you made the earth
and all that is in it;
you sent your Son to redeem us,
and your Holy Spirit continues
to renew our world.
Make us instruments of your hands,
building the kingdom of love
and peace on earth.
We ask this through Christ our Lord.
Amen.

✦ *For ever I will sing the goodness of the Lord.*

✚ *The Lord made us, we belong to him.*

PSALM 130   page 418

READING   *Hebrews 4:12–16*

The word of God is living and effective, sharper than any two-edged sword, penetrating even between soul and spirit, joints and marrow, and able to discern reflections and thoughts of the heart. No creature is concealed from him, but everything is naked and exposed to the eyes of him to whom we must render an account.

Since we have a great high priest who has passed through the heavens, Jesus, the Son of God, let us hold fast to our confession. For we do not have a high priest who is unable to sympathize with our weaknesses, but one who has similarly been tested in every way, yet without sin. So let us confidently approach the throne of grace to receive mercy and to find grace for timely help.

REFLECTION
It can be difficult to be truly honest with one another, even with someone we love. Vulnerability feels uncomfortable. Yet with Jesus we can confidently bare our soul, showing him who we truly are—good and bad. We know that we will be embraced with mercy and love.

PRAYERS   *others may be added*
Revealing ourselves fully to God, we pray:

◆ See us as we truly are, and have mercy, O God.

For the leaders of the Church, whose vowed commitment is to Christ and his Church, we pray: ◆ For trust and vulnerability between collaborators for peace and justice, we pray: ◆ For raw courage and honest communication between partners in marriage, we pray: ◆ For respect for the sacredness of shared human emotion, fears, and dreams, we pray: ◆

Our Father . . .

Word of God,
may we have the courage
to ask for the grace we most need
   from you.
May we know we are loved,
even as we truly are.
We ask this through Christ our Lord.
Amen.

✚ *The Lord made us, we belong to him.*

✠ *The heart of the just one is firm, trusting in the Lord.*

PSALM 33   page 404

READING   John 1:29–34

John the Baptist saw Jesus coming toward him and said, "Behold, the Lamb of God, who takes away the sin of the world. He is the one of whom I said, 'A man is coming after me who ranks ahead of me because he existed before me.' I did not know him, but the reason why I came baptizing with water was that he might be made known to Israel." John testified further, saying, "I saw the Spirit come down like a dove from heaven and remain upon him. I did not know him, but the one who sent me to baptize with water told me, 'On whomever you see the Spirit come down and remain, he is the one who will baptize with the Holy Spirit.' Now I have seen and testified that he is the Son of God."

REFLECTION

Like John the Baptist before he knew Jesus, we are asked to believe in the Son of God based on what we have been told. We have not seen Jesus ourselves, but we have within us the voice of God, pointing us toward faith. We also have experiences, like John had, that confirm for us that the Holy Spirit is at work.

PRAYERS   *others may be added*

Testifying to what we know is true, we pray:

◆ Behold, the Lamb of God.

For the Church, which has stood the test of time and from which has come saints, miracles, conversions, and healings, we pray: ◆ *For the work of the Holy Spirit in the world, bringing people to truth, love, and reconciliation, we pray:* ◆ *For families, churches, schools, and communities coming together in love and service, we pray:* ◆ *For signs and wonders in our daily lives that reflect the goodness of God, we pray:* ◆

Our Father . . .

Lamb of God,
you came into the world in love.
We continue to know you
in our daily lives
through the Word, the sacraments,
   and the people of God.
We praise you for faith and truth.
You live and reign with God
   the Father
in the unity of the Holy Spirit,
one God, forever and ever.
Amen.

✠ *The heart of the just one is firm, trusting in the Lord.*

✛ *The heart of the just one is firm, trusting in the Lord.*

PSALM 111   page 417

READING   Ephesians 6:10–13, 18

Brothers and sisters: Draw your strength from the Lord and from his mighty power. Put on the armor of God so that you may be able to stand firm against the tactics of the Devil. For our struggle is not with flesh and blood but with the principalities, with the powers, with the world rulers of this present darkness, with the evil spirits in the heavens. Therefore, put on the armor of God, that you may be able to resist on the evil day and, having done everything, to hold your ground.

With all prayer and supplication, pray at every opportunity in the Spirit. To that end, be watchful with all perseverance and supplication for all the holy ones.

REFLECTION

When we struggle against apathy, hatred, destructiveness, and revenge, we may sense that there is more to the struggle than the one person or issue with whom we are interacting. What we sense is the force of evil, which enters into human hearts and relationships, resisting being eliminated. We are nothing against this force without the "armor of God."

PRAYERS   others may be added

Resisting evil and fighting for good, we pray:

◆ Make us vigilant and firm when faced with darkness, O God.

For the Pope, Bishops, priests, and deacons, that they may stand strong against the culture of death, we pray: ◆
For leaders of nations, that they turn away terrorists and fugitives seeking refuge within their borders, we pray: ◆
For those whose loved ones have fallen to sinful actions, that they may fight back with the courage of Jesus, we pray: ◆
For any of us, when we sense danger or sin, that we turn quickly away and lead others to do the same, we pray: ◆

Our Father . . .

Omnipotent God,
you have conquered sin and death.
Nothing can defeat us when we walk
   with you.
Give us courage and wisdom
as we resist evil in our world, nation,
   communities, and families.
Fill us with your strength
   and goodness.
Grant this through Christ our Lord.
Amen.

✛ *The heart of the just one is firm, trusting in the Lord.*

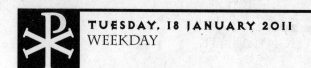
✛ *The precepts of the Lord give joy to the heart.*

PSALM 139   page 420

READING   Mark 2:23–28

As Jesus was passing through a field of grain on the sabbath, his disciples began to make a path while picking the heads of grain. At this the Pharisees said to him, "Look, why are they doing what is unlawful on the sabbath?" He said to them, "Have you never read what David did when he was in need and he and his companions were hungry? How he went into the house of God when Abiathar was high priest and ate the bread of offering that only the priests could lawfully eat, and shared it with his companions?" Then he said to them, "The sabbath was made for man, not man for the sabbath. That is why the Son of Man is lord even of the sabbath."

REFLECTION

It is hard for us to imagine such a strict Sabbath. Our Sundays may involve some sacred time—Mass—but maybe nothing further. Today, reflect on why we need the Sabbath. Why was it made for us? Implement some "Sabbath time" on Sundays, even if it is not the entire day. Try a half day or a few hours of quiet, sacred time and space, and look at the impact on your life after a few weeks.

PRAYERS   *others may be added*

In God's presence, we pray:

◆ Quiet our hearts, Lord.

For increased reverence for sacred time, on Sundays and every day, we pray: ◆ *For a universal awareness of the sacredness of the earth and those that inhabit it: vegetation, animals, and all peoples, we pray:* ◆ *For Sabbath rest for all workers, especially those in mentally and physically demanding occupations, we pray:* ◆ *For greater attentiveness and preparedness in our community for each Eucharistic celebration, we pray:* ◆

Our Father . . .

Creator God,
you rested on the seventh day
   of creation
and gave all the commandment
   to rest.
May we remember and commit
to spending time with you
in prayer and silence
on a regular basis in our everyday,
   busy lives.
Grant this through Christ our Lord.
Amen.

✛ *The precepts of the Lord give joy to the heart.*

✦ *In you, O Lord, I have found my peace.*

PSALM 130   *page 418*

READING   *Mark 3:1–6*

Jesus entered the synagogue. There was a man there who had a withered hand. They watched Jesus closely to see if he would cure him on the sabbath so that they might accuse him. He said to the man with the withered hand, "Come up here before us." Then he said to the Pharisees, "Is it lawful to do good on the sabbath rather than to do evil, to save life rather than to destroy it?" But they remained silent. Looking around at them with anger and grieved at their hardness of heart, Jesus said to the man, "Stretch out your hand." He stretched it out and his hand was restored. The Pharisees went out and immediately took counsel with the Herodians against him to put him to death.

REFLECTION

Today's reading reminds us of priests we have known who have held in balance the honor of serving the Church with daily healing, preaching, and teaching. Perhaps we know someone else, a young person, who is called to this life-giving way of following Jesus. It is up to us to encourage them to explore this vocation.

PRAYERS   *others may be added*

Calling to mind those who serve you with sincere hearts, we pray:

◆ Sustain us, Lord Jesus.

For religious brothers and sisters, priests, and Bishops of the Church, that they remain faithful to their divine call, we pray: ◆ *For young people from every nation, who are called to be priests, brothers, and sisters, we pray:* ◆ *For all who strive to integrate the holy mission of the Church with the secular workings of the world, we pray:* ◆ *For each of us to show our appreciation for those who minister in the name of Christ, we pray:* ◆

Our Father . . .

God of life,
you present to us a clear choice:
evil or good, life or destruction.
May we choose good and life,
even in the face of daily complexities.
May those called to religious life
model for us prudence, temperance,
    justice, and fortitude.
May these virtues also pervade our
    lives when we follow you.
We ask this through Christ our Lord.
Amen.

✦ *In you, O Lord, I have found my peace.*

✝   *The Lord is my light and my salvation.*

PSALM 42 *page 408*

READING *Hebrews 7:25—8:6*

Jesus is always able to save those who approach God through him, since he lives forever to make intercession for them.

It was fitting that we should have such a high priest: holy, innocent, undefiled, separated from sinners, higher than the heavens. He has no need, as did the high priests, to offer sacrifice day after day, first for his own sins and then for those of the people; he did that once for all when he offered himself. For the law appoints men subject to weakness to be high priests, but the word of the oath, which was taken after the law, appoints a son, who has been made perfect forever.

REFLECTION *St. Fulgentius of Ruspe, Bishop*

Christ is therefore the one who in himself alone embodied all that he knew to be necessary to achieve our redemption. He is at once priest and sacrifice, God and temple. He is the priest through whom we have been reconciled, the sacrifice by which we have been reconciled, the God with whom we have been reconciled. He alone is priest, sacrifice and temple because he is all these things as God in the form of a servant; but he alone is not alone as God, for he is this with the Father and the Holy Spirit in the form of God.

PRAYERS *others may be added*

Desiring to live fully for God, we pray:

◆ Open our hearts to you, O Lord.

That the Church and her preachers continue to bring the unique message of Jesus' ultimate sacrifice to the world, we pray: ◆ *That citizens of every nation give up attempts at finding solace through anything but the truth of God's astounding love, we pray:* ◆ *That all who mistakenly believe God loves them conditionally may see anew the totality of God's grace, we pray:* ◆ *That we stop tallying up our sacrifices for God and others and instead live generously in the joy of the Resurrection, we pray:* ◆

Our Father . . .

Lord,
come to us:
free us from the stain of our sins.
Help us to remain faithful to a holy way of life,
and guide us to the inheritance you have promised.
Grant this through Christ our Lord.
Amen.

✝   *The Lord is my light and my salvation.*

Optional memorials of St. Fabian, pope, martyr; St. Sebastian, martyr

✦ *The Lord is my shepherd; there is nothing I shall want.*

PSALM 37   page 406

READING   *1 Corinthians 1:26–31*

Consider your own calling, brothers and sisters. Not many of you were wise by human standards, not many were powerful, not many were of noble birth. Rather, God chose the foolish of the world to shame the wise, and God chose the weak of the world to shame the strong, and God chose the lowly and despised of the world, those who count for nothing, to reduce to nothing those who are something, so that no human being might boast before God. It is due to him that you are in Christ Jesus, who became for us wisdom from God, as well as righteousness, sanctification, and redemption, so that, as it is written, / *Whoever boasts, should boast in the Lord.* /

REFLECTION

The first Christians were not powerful, noble, or even wise by human standards, Paul tells us. Have we forgotten our origins? With a country dominated by Christianity and a world where Christianity plays a major voice, our parishes or our own attitudes may become elitist. Christianity is not only for the smart, the beautiful, or the educated. God chose, and still chooses, the outcast, the disabled, the dirty, and the despairing to be his children.

PRAYERS   *others may be added*

Shamed and reminded of our humble beginnings, we pray:

◆ May we boast only in you, O God.

For all Christians, especially those from impoverished, abusive, or neglectful situations, we pray: ◆ *For protection of the rights and needs of the underprivileged by national and international organizations, we pray:* ◆ *For those whose sense of self is built on wealth and prestige, that they may find renewed identity in Christ, we pray:* ◆ *For our parishes, that our doors may be open to our neighbors who are homebound, mentally ill, and unsuccessful, we pray:* ◆

Our Father . . .

Loving God,
you choose the lowly among us to be
      your children,
to remind the powerful that you alone
      are God.
May the little ones be welcome in
      our midst,
and may we give all glory and honor
      to you.
Grant this through Christ our Lord.
Amen.

✦ *The Lord is my shepherd; there is nothing I shall want.*

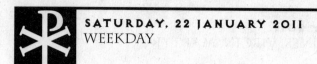

✛ *Go out to all the world, and tell the Good News.*

PSALM 25   *page 403*

READING   *Mark 3:20–21*

Jesus came with his disciples into the house. Again the crowd gathered, making it impossible for them even to eat. When his relatives heard of this they set out to seize him, for they said, "He is out of his mind."

REFLECTION

Most cultures react strongly to someone different, the one who goes against the status quo, or challenges social norms. If we follow Christ, rather than conform to our culture, we may be seen as "out of our mind" or at the very least, "weird." This should not stop us from living out our faith. Rather, a strong reaction to our honorable actions may indicate that we are challenging what people themselves know needs to change.

PRAYERS   *others may be added*

Asking for courage to follow Christ, we pray,

◆ Lord, hear our prayer.

That the Pope may remain steadfast in prayer when facing a world of criticism, we pray: ◆ *That community activists for peace may resist despair and continue to visibly demonstrate God's radical love, we pray:* ◆ *That we, members of the body of Christ, may prayerfully and lovingly support and challenge all who are called to be voices in the wilderness, we pray:* ◆ *That Christians may continue to work tirelessly on behalf of the innocent unborn, victims of genocide, the elderly, the dying, and those on death row, steadfastly insisting on the sanctity of their lives, we pray:* ◆

Our Father . . .

Lord Jesus, our teacher,
you spoke truth and confronted evil.
Show us how to be rooted in the
    community of faith when called
      to prophetic proclamation of
      the Gospel.
Help us to be passionate, committed,
    wise companions with you.
You live and reign with God
    the Father
in the unity of the Holy Spirit,
one God, forever and ever.
Amen.

✛ *Go out to all the world, and tell the Good News.*

✠ *The Lord is my light and my salvation.*

PSALM 111 *page 417*

READING *Matthew 4:13–17*

[Jesus] left Nazareth and went to live in Capernaum by the sea, in the region of Zebulun and Naphtali, that what had been said through Isaiah the prophet might be fulfilled: / *Land of Zebulun and land of Naphtali, / the way to the sea, beyond the Jordan, / Galilee of the Gentiles, / the people who sit in darkness have seen a great light, / on those dwelling in a land overshadowed by death light has arisen.* / From that time on, Jesus began to preach and say, "Repent, for the kingdom of heaven is at hand."

REFLECTION

"The people who sit in darkness have seen a great light." This sentence is the essence of Christ's life and fulfilled Isaiah's prophecy. Whenever we sense darkness and doubt, let us return to this line from scripture and remember the life and Good News of Christ. He is with us, always and forever.

PRAYERS *others may be added*

Basking in the light of Christ, we pray,

◆ Be with us, O Lord.

For teachers, preachers, and healers of the Church, that they may bring light where there is darkness, we pray: ◆ *For those working against the darkness of illiteracy, hunger, poverty, and ignorance, we pray:* ◆ *For those overcome by darkness, that they may reach for and find light in their lives, we pray:* ◆ *For each of us, that we may recognize our part in teaching and preaching about, and bringing forth the kingdom of God, we pray:* ◆

Our Father . . .

Lord Jesus Christ,
you gave your life in love for all of
  God's children.
May we be devoted in our lives to
  bringing your light to others, con-
  quering the darkness of this world
  in your name.
We do so knowing you are with us
  always, even to the end of time.
You live and reign with God
  the Father
in the unity of the Holy Spirit,
one God, forever and ever.
Amen.

✠ *The Lord is my light and my salvation.*

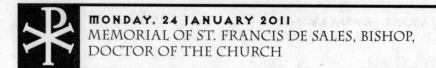

✛ *The Lord is my shepherd; there is nothing I shall want.*

PSALM 37   *page 406*

READING   *Ephesians 3:8–12*

Brothers and sisters: To me, the very least of all the holy ones, this grace was given, to preach to the Gentiles the inscrutable riches of Christ, and to bring to light for all what is the plan of the mystery hidden from ages past in God who created all things, so that the manifold wisdom of God might now be made known through the Church to the principalities and authorities in the heavens. This was according to the eternal purpose that he accomplished in Christ Jesus our Lord, in whom we have boldness of speech and confidence of access through faith in him.

REFLECTION

When we hear names like St. Frances de Sales (among other saints) given to a church, school, or organization, we rightly think highly of those saints. But we should be careful not to assume these men and women were revered because of their high stature. They were lifted up by the Church because of their devotion to serving Christ and others. They were regular people like you and me, to whom grace was given.

PRAYERS   *others may be added*

Longing for your grace, we pray:

◆ Make us your servants, O Lord.

For holy men and women who devote themselves to caring for the sick, visiting the imprisoned, feeding the hungry, and consoling the grieving, we pray: ◆ *For native people in developing nations who work tirelessly for economic improvement, greater access to education and health care, and justice, we pray:* ◆ *For young people who feel intimidated by their elders' accomplishments, that they see how they can make a difference in the world, we pray:* ◆ *For each of us, no matter how small we feel, that we recognize the grace we have been given to live for Christ, we pray:* ◆

Our Father . . .

Compassionate God,
we praise you and thank you
for the graces you have bestowed on
    your servants throughout the ages.
May St. Francis de Sales and all
    your saints
inspire us to lives of radical love
    and service.
Help us to know we are not only
    ordinary men and women,
but extraordinary servants of
    your Gospel.
Grant this through Christ our Lord.
Amen.

✛ *The Lord is my shepherd; there is nothing I shall want.*

✦ *Commit your life to the Lord, and he will help you.*

PSALM 40 *page 407*

READING *Mark 16:15–18*

Jesus appeared to the Eleven and said to them: "Go into the whole world and proclaim the Gospel to every creature. Whoever believes and is baptized will be saved; whoever does not believe will be condemned. These signs will accompany those who believe: in my name they will drive out demons, they will speak new languages. They will pick up serpents with their hands, and if they drink any deadly thing, it will not harm them. They will lay hands on the sick, and they will recover."

REFLECTION

How do we know the will of God? Is our will always to be submitted to his will? Obedience to God comes more through time in silence and prayer than in self-denigration. We do have to humble ourselves to seek out God's will, but if we grow into deep relationship with him, our own will more naturally align with God's will for us.

PRAYERS *others may be added*

Seeking the gentle, yet firm, guidance of the Father, we pray:

◆ Make us one with you, Lord Jesus Christ.

That Christians model sincere humility and relationship with Christ, rather than self-chastisement and negativity, we pray: ◆ *That national leaders spend time in prayer seeking the will of God, we pray:* ◆ *That those who have lost sight of how closely their own deepest desires are attuned to God find time for prayer, we pray:* ◆ *That our church building is a place for silent, joyful, communal, individual, and inspirational prayer, we pray:* ◆

Our Father . . .

All-knowing God,
you know what is best for us
and long for us to become one with
  you in prayer and action.
Help us make time for prayer
and to listen to your law within
  our hearts,
that we might love and serve you in
  all we do.
We ask this through our Lord Jesus
  Christ, your Son,
who lives and reigns with you in the
  unity of the Holy Spirit,
one God, forever and ever.
Amen.

✦ *Commit your life to the Lord, and he will help you.*

✠ *The Lord is my shepherd; there is nothing I shall want.*

PSALM 40   page 407

READING   *2 Timothy 1:1–8*

I am grateful to God, whom I worship with a clear conscience as my ancestors did, as I remember you constantly in my prayers, night and day. I yearn to see you again, recalling your tears, so that I may be filled with joy, as I recall your sincere faith that first lived in your grandmother Lois and in your mother Eunice and that I am confident lives also in you.

For this reason, I remind you to stir into flame the gift of God that you have through the imposition of my hands. For God did not give us a spirit of cowardice but rather of power and love and self-control. So do not be ashamed of your testimony to our Lord, nor of me, a prisoner for his sake; but bear your share of hardship for the Gospel with the strength that comes from God.

REFLECTION

Paul traces Timothy's faith to his mother and grandmother. Of course Paul also had great influence on Timothy. Many of us owe a debt of gratitude to our parents, grandparents, and all mentors for our knowledge and love of God. What more do we have to learn from these predecessors in faith?

PRAYERS   *others may be added*

Walking in the footsteps of our ancestors in faith, we pray:

◆ Lord, increase our faith.

For all Bishops, priests, deacons, religious, and lay ministers of the Church who have mentored others into deeper relationship with Christ, we pray: ◆ *For all who pass on wisdom and faith, we pray:* ◆ *For all mothers and fathers who play a unique role in forming their children's relationship to God and others, we pray:* ◆ *For a greater sense of our connectedness in faith, and our need for mentors and wise ones to companion us on the journey, we pray:* ◆

Our Father . . .

Eternal God,
the gift of faith is passed from
    generation to generation,
especially through the guidance of
    bishops like St. Timothy and
    St. Titus,
and through grandparents, parents,
    and others in our community.
May we be stewards of the gift
    of faith,
nurturing its growth in our children,
that all may praise your name.
Grant this through Christ our Lord.
Amen.

✠ *The Lord is my shepherd; there is nothing I shall want.*

✦ *Go out to all the world, and tell the Good News.*

PSALM 100 *page 414*

READING *Mark 4:21–25*

Jesus said to his disciples, "Is a lamp brought in to be placed under a bushel basket or under a bed, and not to be placed on a lampstand? For there is nothing hidden except to be made visible; nothing is secret except to come to light. Anyone who has ears to hear ought to hear." He also told them, "Take care what you hear. The measure with which you measure will be measured out to you, and still more will be given to you. To the one who has, more will be given; from the one who has not, even what he has will be taken away."

REFLECTION

From ancient times there has been a temptation to hold the message of Christ secret, accessible to only a few. But Christ came for all. Our faith, our gifts, the blessings of knowing Christ, should be shared openly and freely. If you hold anything God has given you too tightly, resolve to open it to the world.

PRAYERS *others may be added*

Opening our hearts, we pray:

◆ Send us forth, O Lord.

That the Church may be a place of welcome to newcomers, we pray: ◆ *That continued study of Christianity may increase our understanding of God's marvelous work throughout history, we pray:* ◆ *That a sense of superiority or exclusiveness in Christian groups may be eliminated, we pray:* ◆ *That we encounter others with the open arms of Christ, we pray:* ◆

Our Father . . .

Lord Jesus Christ,
you are the light of the world.
Your message of the kingdom is for
    all to hear.
May we imitate your unconditional
    offer of salvation
as we spread the news of God's mercy
    to the ends of the earth.
You live and reign with God
    the Father
in the unity of the Holy Spirit,
one God, forever and ever.
Amen.

✦ *Go out to all the world, and tell the Good News.*

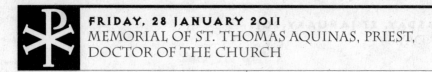

✚ *Commit your life to the Lord.*

PSALM 40 — page 407

READING — Wisdom 7:7–10, 15–16

I prayed, and prudence was given me; / I pleaded, and the spirit of Wisdom came to me. / I preferred her to scepter and throne, / And deemed riches nothing in comparison with her, / nor did I liken any priceless gem to her; / Because all gold, in view of her, is a little sand, / and before her, silver is to be accounted mire. / Beyond health and comeliness I loved her, / And I chose to have her rather than the light, / because the splendor of her never yields to sleep.

Now God grant I speak suitably / and value these endowments at their worth: / For he is the guide of Wisdom / and the director of the wise. / For both we and our words are in his hand, / as well as all prudence and knowledge of crafts.

REFLECTION

St. Thomas Aquinas devoted himself to wisdom, to knowledge, and to study and teaching of the faith. Like him, that which we are passionate about motivates and inspires us. Also like him, we must hold it in balance. God is the source and summit of all knowledge, skill, and wisdom. If we keep this in mind, we remain humble and retain our sense of awe at that which is greater than us.

PRAYERS — *others may be added*

Asking for balance between our passions and our humility, we pray:

◆ Wisdom, be our guide.

For the Pope, clergy, theologians, and all who love the Catholic faith, that they find balance between wanting to know God and resting in his mystery, we pray: ◆
For all branches and services of government, that dedication to the law is balanced by love for people, we pray: ◆
For those who love their work and love their family, that each day and week brings appropriate prioritization of both, we pray: ◆ *For our emotional attachment to our faith, way of living, or communities, that we yet remain open to growth, we pray:* ◆

Our Father . . .

O Wisdom of God,
you are the word through whom you
made the universe.
Guide us as we strive to live day
to day
in balance with the world around us
and the world we long for in
our hearts.
You live and reign with God
the Father
in the unity of the Holy Spirit,
one God, forever and ever.
Amen.

✚ *Commit your life to the Lord.*

✦ *The Lord hears the cry of the poor.*

PSALM 111   *page 417*

READING   *Hebrews 11:1–2, 8–19*

Brothers and sisters: Faith is the realization of what is hoped for and evidence of things not seen. Because of it the ancients were well attested.

By faith Abraham obeyed when he was called to go out to a place that he was to receive as an inheritance; he went out, not knowing where he was to go.

So it was that there came forth from one man, himself as good as dead, descendants as numerous as the stars in the sky and as countless as the sands on the seashore.

All these died in faith. They did not receive what had been promised but saw it and greeted it from afar and acknowledged themselves to be strangers and aliens on earth, for those who speak thus show that they are seeking a homeland.

REFLECTION

The ancient Hebrews collectively hoped for a new day for Israel. The Lord had promised; they believed, even if they knew they would not see it themselves. We are promised as well, and assured participation in the end of time. We are asked to hold onto our faith, as have our ancestors, not knowing how long we are to wait.

PRAYERS   *others may be added*

Trusting in the Lord, we pray:

◆ Remember us, O God.

For unwavering faith in God's promises by those who lead the Church, we pray: ◆ For a new creation, a new world of peace at the end of time, we pray: ◆ For those who struggle with doubt and cynicism, we pray: ◆ For that day when we will celebrate in eternal life, we hope and pray: ◆ For all those who have died in faith, we pray: ◆

Our Father . . .

God of our ancestors in faith,
your promises are true.
Abraham models for us ultimate trust
    in you.
We pray fervently for that day when
    all return to you.
Until then, may we confidently trust
    in your providence.
We ask this through Christ our Lord.
Amen.

✦ *The Lord hears the cry of the poor.*

✦ *The Lord hears the cry of the poor.*

PSALM 149 *page 421*

READING *Matthew 5:1–12a*

When [Jesus] saw the crowds, he went up the mountain, and after he had sat down, his disciples came to him. He began to teach them, saying: / "Blessed are the poor in spirit, / for theirs is the kingdom of heaven. / Blessed are they who mourn, / for they will be comforted. / Blessed are the meek, / for they will inherit the land. / Blessed are they who hunger and thirst for righteousness, / for they will be satisfied. / Blessed are the merciful, / for they will be shown mercy. / Blessed are the clean of heart, / for they will see God. / Blessed are the peacemakers, / for they will be called children of God. / Blessed are they who are persecuted for the sake of righteousness, / for theirs is the kingdom of heaven. / Blessed are you when they insult you and persecute you and utter every kind of evil against you falsely because of me. Rejoice and be glad, for your reward will be great in heaven."

REFLECTION

God has a special love for the little ones. They are favored, and easily enter heaven. Who are the poor in spirit in our world? They include the unborn, children, the abused, victims of crime and war, refugees, the homeless, the elderly, the disabled, the outcast, those on death row, the condemned, the dying, the meek, and the humble.

PRAYERS *others may be added*

Lifting up God's beloved, we pray:

◆ Remember them, O God.

For the unnoticed servants of the Church: the cloistered, women's associations, men's work groups, those who clean and decorate our sanctuaries, and the endless numbers of volunteers, we pray: ◆
For political refugees and immigrants fleeing to better lives, we pray: ◆
For those who never know life due to abortion, infanticide, genocide, and abuse, we pray: ◆ *For the special gifts brought to our community by those with mental and physical disabilities, we pray:* ◆ *For those who have died alone, we pray:* ◆

Our Father . . .

Compassionate God,
you know every little one whom you
    created in your own image.
You sent your Son especially for the
    forgotten and the despairing.
May your embrace and the support of
    the Christian community
comfort and heal those who are lost
    and suffering.
We ask this through our Lord, Jesus
    Christ, your Son,
who lives and reigns with you in the
    unity of the Holy Spirit,
one God, forever and ever.
Amen.

✦ *The Lord hears the cry of the poor.*

✦ *Commit your life to the Lord, and he will help you.*

PSALM 40   *page 407*

READING   *Philippians 4:4–9*

Brothers and sisters: Rejoice in the Lord always. I shall say it again: rejoice! Your kindness should be known to all. The Lord is near. Have no anxiety at all, but in everything, by prayer and petition, with thanksgiving, make your requests known to God. Then the peace of God that surpasses all understanding will guard your hearts and minds in Christ Jesus.

Finally, brothers and sisters, whatever is true, whatever is honorable, whatever is just, whatever is pure, whatever is lovely, whatever is gracious, if there is any excellence and if there is anything worthy of praise, think about these things. Keep on doing what you have learned and received and heard and seen in me. Then the God of peace will be with you.

REFLECTION

What if we were known for our kindness, peace, and lack of anxiety? Perhaps those who first meet us might give us one of these compliments. It is much more of a test to ask friends and family members if we meet these standards of a committed follower of Christ. Rather than trying to "keep up with the Joneses," consider making a concerted effort to have a reputation of kindness and peacefulness.

PRAYERS   *others may be added*

With hearts lifted to God, we pray:

◆ Lord, hear our prayer.

For Christians, that we may be known by our consistent gentleness, generosity, and stability in God's ways, we pray: ◆ *For believers working in commerce and competition, that they may grow a reputation of being a lamb among wolves, we pray:* ◆ *For young people carried away by frenzies, trends, and unrealistic expectations, that they may find contentment in Christ, we pray:* ◆ *For our daily driving, waiting in lines, mundane interactions, and telephone and Internet conversations, that we may bring goodness and calm, we pray:* ◆

Our Father . . .

Prince of Peace,
you walked amid the chaos and
    violence of the world
as a sign of God's love.
May we, too, seek God's peace
and bring gentleness and calm to our
    daily interactions
by practicing Christian values
and bringing peace to ourselves,
    homes, workplaces, and social
    organizations.
You live and reign with God
    the Father
in the unity of the Holy Spirit,
one God, forever and ever.
Amen.

✦ *Commit your life to the Lord, and he will help you.*

✦ *The Lord hears the cry of the poor.*

PSALM 111   *page 417*

READING   *Mark 5:22 – 24, 39–42*

One of the synagogue officials, named Jairus, came forward. Seeing [Jesus] he fell at his feet and pleaded earnestly with him, saying, "My daughter is at the point of death. Please, come lay your hands on her that she may get well and live." He went off with him and a large crowd followed him.

So he went in and said to them, "Why this commotion and weeping? The child is not dead but asleep." And they ridiculed him. Then he put them all out. He took along the child's father and mother and those who were with him and entered the room where the child was. He took the child by the hand and said to her, *"Talitha koum,"* which means, "Little girl, I say to you, arise!" The girl, a child of twelve, arose immediately and walked around.

REFLECTION

Perhaps today we simply need to endure. We may be looking for a solution. We may be dying for an answer. But perhaps today we are to endure. It may be tomorrow or the day after that we will feel Christ take our hand. God's time is not our time. Our faith and the community of the Church will carry us through.

PRAYERS   *others may be added*

In patience, we pray:

◆ Be with us, Lord.

For the deacons, priests, and Bishops of the Church, that they remain committed to fostering the healing love of Christ, we pray: ◆ *For strong and honest legislators, governors, and heads of state, that they maintain integrity and balance in their leadership, we pray:* ◆ *For caregivers of the very young and the very old, that they may be renewed in their commitment of healing love, we pray:* ◆ *For each of us when we feel tired, that we may be renewed by the touch of Christ, we pray:* ◆

Our Father . . .

Merciful Lord,
you know the cries of our hearts.
Raise us up when we are weary;
raise us up when we doubt;
and help us to walk this daily journey
    with you.
We ask this through Christ our Lord.
Amen.

✦ *The Lord hears the cry of the poor.*

✦ *The Lord is my shepherd; there is nothing I shall want.*

PSALM 40   page 407

READING   Luke 2:25–32

Now there was a man in Jerusalem whose name was Simeon. This man was righteous and devout, awaiting the consolation of Israel, and the Holy Spirit was upon him. It had been revealed to him by the Holy Spirit that he should not see death before he had seen the Christ of the Lord. He came in the Spirit into the temple; and when the parents brought in the child Jesus to perform the custom of the law in regard to him, he took him into his arms and blessed God, saying: / "Now, Master, you may let your servant go / in peace, according to your word, / for my eyes have seen your salvation, / which you prepared in sight of all the peoples: / a light for revelation to the Gentiles, / and glory for your people Israel."

REFLECTION

Simeon's words are included in the Liturgy of the Hours, or Divine Office of the Church. His words comprise the Gospel Canticle during the prayer at the close of the day, Compline or Night Prayer. Each night we hope to feel this way, that we may "go in peace," knowing the fullness of God's revelation, the fulfillment of his promises, in Christ. Pray these prayers again tonight, feeling their meaning, letting your life rest in God's hands.

PRAYERS   *others may be added*

Secure in our salvation, we pray:

◆ Embrace us, O God.

That there may be peace in the hearts of all Christians, we pray: ◆ *That the birth of every child throughout the world may be a reminder of eternal peace, we pray:* ◆ *That those who are holding onto life may find the resolution they need to go to eternal life in peace, we pray:* ◆ *That we may not be afraid of death, but welcome eternal life in God, we pray:* ◆ *That those who have died may rest in peace, we pray:* ◆

Our Father . . .

God of life and death,
beginning with Simeon and Anna,
you showed your children a
    deeper peace
when they saw your promise fulfilled
    in Jesus.
Again, with us, reveal the peace
    you offer.
Help us to say "yes" to it,
that we might rest forever in
    your arms.
We ask this through our Lord Jesus
    Christ, your Son,
who lives and reigns with you in the
    unity of the Holy Spirit,
one God, forever and ever.
Amen.

✦ *The Lord is my shepherd; there is nothing I shall want.*

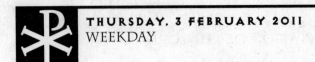
✢ *Go out to all the world, and tell the Good News.*

PSALM 25 — page 403

READING — Mark 6:7–13

Jesus summoned the Twelve and began to send them out two by two and gave them authority over unclean spirits. He instructed them to take nothing for the journey but a walking stick—no food, no sack, no money in their belts. They were, however, to wear sandals but not a second tunic. He said to them, "Wherever you enter a house, stay there until you leave from there. Whatever place does not welcome you or listen to you, leave there and shake the dust off your feet in testimony against them." So they went off and preached repentance. [The Twelve] drove out many demons, and they anointed with oil many who were sick and cured them.

REFLECTION

Teaching, preaching, and healing—this time, the apostles are called to do it. The ministry of Jesus continues today. Are we teaching—our children, and those who do not know the story of Jesus, or have questions about it? Are we preaching repentance—by our own honest stories of why we need God? Are we healing—comforting others and contributing to systemic change for good?

PRAYERS — *others may be added*

Commissioned, we pray as we set off on our journey:

◆ Lord, lift us up.

For our leaders, the Bishops, as they direct the ministries of the Church, we pray: ◆ *For teaching and preaching by Christians that includes listening to the needs and questions of those they hope to reach, we pray:* ◆ *For accountability and support among Christians, as we are sent out as disciples, "two by two," we pray:* ◆

Our Father . . .

Lord Jesus, our brother,
you summoned the Twelve and sent
   them forth.
You summon us; help us say "yes."
You send us forth; help us go
   courageously.
Help us serve you through teaching,
   preaching, and healing.
You live and reign with God
   the Father
in the unity of the Holy Spirit,
one God, forever and ever.
Amen.

✢ *Go out to all the world, and tell the Good News.*

✦ *Teach me your ways, O Lord.*

PSALM 33   page 404

READING   Hebrews 13:1–8

Let brotherly love continue. Do not neglect hospitality, for through it some have unknowingly entertained angels. Be mindful of prisoners as if sharing their imprisonment, and of the ill-treated as of yourselves, for you also are in the body. Let marriage be honored among all and the marriage bed be kept undefiled, for God will judge the immoral and adulterers. Let your life be free from love of money but be content with what you have, for he has said, */I will never forsake you or abandon you./* Thus we may say with confidence: */The Lord is my helper, / and I will not be afraid. / What can anyone do to me?*

Remember your leaders who spoke the word of God to you. Consider the outcome of their way of life and imitate their faith. Jesus Christ is the same yesterday, today, and forever.

REFLECTION   *St. Thérèse of Lisieux*

Love proves itself by deeds, so how am I to show my love? Great deeds are forbidden me. The only way I can prove my love is by scattering flowers and these flowers are every little sacrifice, every glance and word, and the doing of the least actions for love.

PRAYERS   *others may be added*

Relying on our predecessors in faith, we pray:

◆ Lead us, O Lord.

That the Christian faithful may live in confidence rather than fear, we pray: ◆ *That those in power reject the temptation to show off and make regrettable promises, we pray:* ◆ *That all who have made sinful choices return to God seeking forgiveness, we pray:* ◆ *That we may keep holy our relationships and our priorities, we pray:* ◆

Our Father . . .

Lord Jesus,
our rock and our salvation,
you are with us always.
Fixing our eyes on what is good
    and holy,
help us turn away from sin
    and temptation,
knowing it will only lead us to pain
    and guilt.
Lead us toward you, the source of
    happiness and freedom.
You live and reign with God
    the Father
in the unity of the Holy Spirit,
one God, forever and ever.
Amen.

✦ *Teach me your ways, O Lord.*

SATURDAY, 5 FEBRUARY 2011
MEMORIAL OF ST. AGATHA, VIRGIN, MARTYR

✦ *Commit your life to the Lord, and he will help you.*

PSALM 40   *page 407*

READING   *Luke 9:23–25*

[Jesus] said to all, "If anyone wishes to come after me, he must deny himself and take up his cross daily and follow me. For whoever wishes to save his life will lose it, but whoever loses his life for my sake will save it. What profit is there for one to gain the whole world yet lose or forfeit himself?"

REFLECTION

Little is known about St. Agatha, just as little is known of women who sacrifice much and worry not about themselves, but about their families. What can we learn from these women? How can we recover their stories? Jesus will reward them, indeed, but we can also grow in love and wisdom by knowing them and being inspired by them.

PRAYERS   *others may be added*

Opening our eyes to see the unnoticed, we pray:

◆ Raise them up, O God.

For holy women: saints, mothers, religious, and those unknown, we pray: ◆ *For women in service roles whose work is rarely acknowledged, we pray:* ◆ *For women living in poverty, who labor daily to feed and clothe their children, we pray:* ◆ *For the women of our community, who bring life to the mission of our parish, we pray:* ◆ *For women who have died in childbirth, giving their life for another, we pray:* ◆

Our Father . . .

Lord Jesus, our Savior,
you promised to save all who sacrifice
   everything for you.
May all women and men who,
   like St. Agatha,
have dedicated themselves to you,
be held in your embrace.
May their witness help us grow in
   understanding of faith.
You live and reign with God
   the Father
in the unity of the Holy Spirit,
one God, forever and ever.
Amen.

✦ *Commit your life to the Lord, and he will help you.*

✚ *The Lord is my light and my salvation.*

PSALM 25 *page 403*

READING *Matthew 5:13–16*

Jesus said to his disciples: "You are the salt of the earth. But if salt loses its taste, with what can it be seasoned? It is no longer good for anything but to be thrown out and trampled underfoot. You are the light of the world. A city set on a mountain cannot be hidden. Nor do they light a lamp and then put it under a bushel basket; it is set on a lampstand, where it gives light to all in the house. Just so, your light must shine before others, that they may see your good deeds and glorify your heavenly Father."

REFLECTION

How do you live and share your faith? Like salt which has lost its taste? Like a light shining on a hill? Humbly or trying to sound wise? Sharing your bread with the hungry or hiding what you have under a bushel? Today's readings offer many images of how to live one's faith. Consider which image best fits your approach to following Jesus, and how you might come closer to the ideal of a light in the darkness.

PRAYERS *others may be added*

To the Light of the world, we pray:

◆ Shine on us and through us,
Lord Jesus.

For Christians sharing the Good News, that their words may come from the power of God, we pray: ◆ *For humanitarian efforts to reach the hungry, homeless, and imprisoned, we pray:* ◆ *For those whose faith has grown stale, that they seek out new experiences of God, we pray:* ◆ *For those whose faith has been hidden, that they may be bold enough to share it with others, we pray:* ◆

Our Father . . .

Heavenly Father,
you bring light to the world
and ask us to share this light
 with others.
May we grow strong and bright in
 our faith,
remembering to live it humbly, boldly,
 generously, and gratefully.
Grant this through Christ our Lord.
Amen.

✚ *The Lord is my light and my salvation.*

✛ *For ever I will sing the goodness of the Lord.*

PSALM 33   *page 404*

READING   *Genesis 1:1–19*

In the beginning, when God created the heavens and the earth, the earth was a formless wasteland, and darkness covered the abyss, while a mighty wind swept over the waters.

Then God said, "Let there be light," and there was light. God saw how good the light was. God then separated the light from the darkness. God called the light "day," and the darkness he called "night." Thus evening came, and morning followed—the first day.

Then God said, "Let there be a dome in the middle of the waters, to separate one body of water from the other." And so it happened: God made the dome, and it separated the water above the dome from the water below it. God called the dome "the sky." Evening came, and morning followed—the second day.

REFLECTION

Rather than be threatened by advances in science, the Catholic Church welcomes the progress of human knowledge about our world. We are encouraged to use reason as people of faith, and marvel at the wonders of our God, Creator of the universe. Challenge yourself to learn something new about our solar system, the earth, or their histories, and reflect on how creation leads you to God.

PRAYERS   *others may be added*

Embracing God with our hearts and our minds, we pray:

◆ Reveal your magnificence to us, O God.

For the role of the Church in the modern world, that she is led by the Holy Spirit to balance openness to human discovery and faithfulness to divine truth, we pray: ◆ *For scientists and students of science, that they continue to use their talents to explore the world God has given us, we pray:* ◆ *For dialogue and reconciliation between opponents of science and opponents of religion, we pray:* ◆ *For each of us, that we honor and value our faith and our reason, both gifts from God, we pray:* ◆

Our Father . . .

Infinite God,
you are the Alpha and the Omega, the
    beginning and the end.
We stand in awe at the mystery of
    your handiwork,
and give thanks for the gift of
    rational thought,
which has led us today to wondrous
    discoveries about your power
    and love.
Thank you for the gift of life.
Make us perpetual learners and
    tireless seekers of you.
We ask this through Christ our Lord.
    Amen.

✛ *For ever I will sing the goodness of the Lord.*

✢ *The Lord made us, we belong to him.*

PSALM 139 *page 420*

READING *Genesis 1:24–27*

Then God said, "Let the earth bring forth all kinds of living creatures: cattle, creeping things, and wild animals of all kinds." And so it happened: God made all kinds of wild animals, all kinds of cattle, and all kinds of creeping things of the earth. God saw how good it was. Then God said: "Let us make man in our image, after our likeness. Let them have dominion over the fish of the sea, the birds of the air, and the cattle, and over all the wild animals and all the creatures that crawl on the ground."

God created man in his image; / in the divine image he created him; / male and female he created them.

REFLECTION

God establishes and secures our place in creation from the beginning. He made us uniquely in the divine image. We are meant for God. Yet, how often we distort this order! We forget God's law and follow our own. We consider ourselves less or more than our destiny.

PRAYERS *others may be added*

Knowing ourselves to be children of God, we pray:

◆ Bring us back to you, Lord.

For the leaders of the Church, that they may remain dedicated to God's commandments, we pray: ◆ *For human beings of every age, nation, and background, that they are equally treated as God's own creation, we pray:* ◆ *For those who consider themselves more important than God, that they be humbled, we pray:* ◆ *For those who consider themselves less than human, that they become aware of their dignity, we pray:* ◆

Our Father . . .

God of all peoples,
you created us in your image,
male and female, divinely inspired.
By doing so you indicate our purpose
   and destiny.
May we not be afraid of our likeness
   to you,
and may we take seriously our
   responsibility to you and to
   your creation.
Grant this through Christ our Lord.
Amen.

✢ *The Lord made us, we belong to him.*

✦ *The precepts of the Lord give joy to the heart.*

PSALM 139   *page 420*

READING   *Mark 7:14–15, 21–23*

Jesus summoned the crowd again and said to them, "Hear me, all of you, and understand. Nothing that enters one from outside can defile that person; but the things that come out from within are what defile. . . . From within the man, from his heart, come evil thoughts, unchastity, theft, murder, adultery, greed, malice, deceit, licentiousness, envy, blasphemy, arrogance, folly. All these evils come from within and they defile."

REFLECTION

There is no simple formula to follow to make us "worthy" of God. We must be careful not to get caught up in "easy fixes" or "one-shot" solutions to our relationship with him. Our words, behavior, and the desires of our heart, over time, bring us closer to or take us farther away from God. A life earnestly following Jesus and making choices to be like him is the only way we draw closer to God. It is a challenge and a joy.

PRAYERS   *others may be added*

With the desire to serve God truthfully, we pray:

◆ Give us clean hearts, all-knowing God.

For the Church, that when we come together to worship, we become aware of the journey we are on together, and our need for God, we pray: ◆ *For all Christians, that false words and false actions may be set aside in favor of genuine lives of faith, we pray:* ◆ *For those whose lives have become centered in deception or superficial impressions, that they may renew their hearts and live authentically, we pray:* ◆ *For our parish, that it may be a vibrant source of faith life, we pray:* ◆

Our Father . . .

God of truth,
you see past the superficial sacrifices
   and easy solutions
people have always used to claim
   blessing from you.
Those you favor are the pure of heart.
Those you favor are the ones who
   follow you daily.
Help us to continuously say "yes" to
   your call.
Grant this through Christ our Lord.
Amen.

✦ *The precepts of the Lord give joy to the heart.*

✦ *The Lord hears the cry of the poor.*

PSALM 130   *page 418*

READING   *Mark 7:24–30*

Jesus went to the district of Tyre. He entered a house and wanted no one to know about it, but he could not escape notice. Soon a woman whose daughter had an unclean spirit heard about him. She came and fell at his feet. The woman was a Greek, a Syrophoenician by birth, and she begged him to drive the demon out of her daughter. He said to her, "Let the children be fed first. For it is not right to take the food of the children and throw it to the dogs." She replied and said to him, "Lord, even the dogs under the table eat the children's scraps." Then he said to her, "For saying this, you may go. The demon has gone out of your daughter." When the woman went home, she found the child lying in bed and the demon gone.

REFLECTION

God responds to those in need. He saw Adam's need for a companion. He saw the Syrophoenician woman's need for healing of her daughter. Feeling compassion for all of creation, God sent Christ to Israel and offered salvation to all. We can be sure that God sees and hears our needs.

PRAYERS   *others may be added*

At the feet of the Lord, we pray:

◆ Hear us, O God.

That God responds with compassion to the prayers of the Church, we pray: ◆
That the needs of warring peoples may bring them together in the hope of fulfillment in Christ, we pray: ◆ *That our need for intimate relationships is met with love and respect, we pray:* ◆
That we turn to God when we see a need for his healing touch, we pray: ◆

Our Father . . .

Compassionate God,
you give us a world that meets
    our needs,
yet our deepest need is for you.
Show us how to find you in the gifts
    around us,
and lift us up when we cry out
    in pain.
May we all be reconciled to you in
    Jesus Christ,
who lives and reigns with you in the
    unity of the Holy Spirit,
one God, forever and ever.
Amen.

✦ *The Lord hears the cry of the poor.*

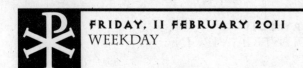
✢ *The heart of the just one is firm.*

PSALM 100   *page 414*

READING   *Mark 7:31–37*

Jesus left the district of Tyre and went by way of Sidon to the Sea of Galilee, into the district of the Decapolis. And people brought to him a deaf man who had a speech impediment and begged him to lay his hand on him. He took him off by himself away from the crowd. He put his finger into the man's ears and, spitting, touched his tongue; then he looked up to heaven and groaned, and said to him, "*Ephphatha!*" (that is, "Be opened!") And immediately the man's ears were opened, his speech impediment was removed, and he spoke plainly. He ordered them not to tell anyone. But the more he ordered them not to, the more they proclaimed it. They were exceedingly astonished and they said, "He has done all things well. He makes the deaf hear and the mute speak."

REFLECTION

Spend some time with this command of Jesus: "Be opened!" What do you feel opening within yourself? Perhaps your eyes are open to the suffering and the needs of those around you; perhaps your ears are open to the call from your community to use your gifts; perhaps your hands are open to be generous with your time and treasure; perhaps your mouth is open to speak the Word of God; perhaps your heart is open to see your own sin and need for God.

PRAYERS   *others may be added*

With trust in God, we pray:

◆ Be opened!

For the ministers of the Church, that they know and respond to the will of God, we pray: ◆ *For the ears of leaders of all nations, to hear the needs of their people, we pray:* ◆ *For the eyes of those blinded by selfishness, to see how they affect others, we pray:* ◆ *For the mouths on behalf of the voiceless, to call out for justice, we pray:* ◆ *For the hands within our parish, to serve, give, and not count the cost, we pray:* ◆

Our Father . . .

Lord Jesus, miracle-worker,
you opened the eyes of the blind and
    the mouths of the mute.
You make all things possible.
Open our very beings;
wash away obstacles, sin, and refusal
    to acknowledge truth.
May your Holy Spirit blow like wind
    through us,
opening us to your work in the world.
You live and reign with God
    the Father
in the unity of the Holy Spirit,
one God, forever and ever.
Amen.

✢ *The heart of the just one is firm.*

✦ *For ever I will sing the goodness of the Lord.*

PSALM 42   *page 408*

READING   *Mark 8:2–9*

[Jesus said], "My heart is moved with pity for the crowd, because they have been with me now for three days and have nothing to eat. If I send them away hungry to their homes, they will collapse on the way, and some of them have come a great distance." His disciples answered him, "Where can anyone get enough bread to satisfy them here in this deserted place?" Still he asked them, "How many loaves do you have?" They replied "Seven," they replied. He ordered the crowd to sit down on the ground. Then, taking the seven loaves he gave thanks, broke them, and gave them to his disciples to distribute, and they distributed them to the crowd. They also had a few fish. He said the blessing over them and ordered them distributed also. They ate and were satisfied. They picked up the fragments left over—seven baskets. There were about four thousand people.

REFLECTION

Popular diet and health gurus advise knowing the feeling of satiation, of being full. When was the last time your soul felt "satisfied"—at rest in God? Listen to your hunger for God. What will fill it? Find prayer time, companions in faith, participation in the sacraments, and inspirational stories of holy men and women to meet your need for closeness to God.

PRAYERS   *others may be added*

Seeking the bread that truly satisfies, we pray:

◆ Fill us, O God.

That the Eucharistic feast continues to be offered generously to fill the hunger of the people of God, we pray: ◆ *That international organizations may succeed in meeting the world's primary needs for nutrition, health, and safety so that people may be free to seek God, we pray:* ◆ *That those who think their hunger for God can be filled with worldly answers may seek him anew, we pray:* ◆ *That we practice our faith daily in order to know our own rhythms of hunger for and resting in God, we pray:* ◆

Our Father . . .

Lord Jesus, Bread of Life,
you provided real food for those who
    were hungry
and offered real substance for those
    who sought God.
Be the bread that forever fills us;
help us to notice our hunger and fill it
    with your love,
leading us to your eternal banquet.
You live and reign with God
    the Father
in the unity of the Holy Spirit,
one God, forever and ever.
Amen.

✦ *For ever I will sing the goodness of the Lord.*

✦ *In you, O Lord, I have found
my peace.*

PSALM 100   page 414

READING   *Matthew 5:21–22a,
27–28, 33–34a, 37*

[Jesus said to his disciples:] "You have
heard that it was said to your ancestors, /
*You shall not kill; and whoever kills will
be liable to judgment.* / But I say to you,
whoever is angry with his brother will
be liable to judgment.

"You have heard that it was said, / *You
shall not commit adultery.* / But I say to
you, everyone who looks at a woman
with lust has already committed adultery with her in his heart.

"Again you have heard that it was
said to your ancestors, / *Do not take a
false oath,* / *but make good to the Lord
all that you vow.* / But I say to you, do
not swear at all. Let your 'Yes' mean
'Yes,' and your 'No' mean 'No.' Anything more is from the evil one."

REFLECTION

*The commandments and practices of
our faith lead us to God. We cannot
dismiss these righteous teachings. But
even before we live them, we must live
out Jesus' commandment to love. Jesus
asks even more of us than God asked
of the Hebrew people. Every act of worship must be preceded by acts of justice
and reconciliation with our families
and neighbors, or the worship and laws
are worthless.*

PRAYERS   *others may be added*

*Inspired by God's expectations of us,
we pray:*

◆ Reconcile us to one another and
to you.

*For faithfulness in our worship and
Christian lives, we pray:* ◆ *For love of
neighbor as the basis for every civil law,
we pray:* ◆ *For continuity between our
faith practices and our personal lives,
we pray:* ◆ *For conversion of every
hypocritical tendency among us,
we pray:* ◆

Our Father . . .

Lord Jesus, our teacher,
you revealed the law and the prophets
to us,
and fulfilled and surpassed their
understanding of God's will.
Lead us first in love and second in
obedience to the law.
Make us like you.
You live and reign with God
the Father
in the unity of the Holy Spirit,
one God, forever and ever.
Amen.

✦ *In you, O Lord, I have found
my peace.*

✝ *The heart of the just one is firm, trusting in the Lord.*

PSALM   page 417

READING   Mark 8:11–13

The Pharisees came forward and began to argue with Jesus, seeking from him a sign from heaven to test him. He sighed from the depth of his spirit and said, "Why does this generation seek a sign? Amen, I say to you, no sign will be given to this generation." Then he left them, got into the boat again, and went off to the other shore.

REFLECTION

God has been present from the beginning of time. His handiwork can be seen in all of creation. The Old Testament testifies to his omnipresence with the chosen people in a multitude of ways. Still, people in Jesus' time and people today ask for more evidence of God. What is underlying our desire for a "sign?" Is it fear we could be wrong? Are we simply procrastinating on what we know we must do? Let us pray instead for the gift of faith that overcomes all obstacles.

PRAYERS   *others may be added*

With faith that overcomes doubt, we pray:

◆ May your grace lead us forward.

For preachers and teachers of the faith that know, love, and explain well the work of God in human history, we pray: ◆
For attentiveness to the movement of God in history across cultures and religions, we pray: ◆ *For trust in communal revelation by those intent on personal revelation, we pray:* ◆
For children, elderly, immigrants, and the poor who bear witness with an unfaltering faith, we pray: ◆

Our Father . . .

Lord God,
you revealed yourself to Israel
     through signs, wonders,
     and prophets.
You revealed yourself completely
     in your Son, Jesus Christ.
Help us to participate in the
     community of faith
and let go of a selfish need for
     personal signs and miracles.
Grant this through Christ our Lord.
Amen.

✝ *The heart of the just one is firm, trusting in the Lord.*

✤ *The Lord is my light and my salvation.*

PSALM 139 page 420

READING Mark 8:14–21

The disciples had forgotten to bring bread, and they had only one loaf with them in the boat. Jesus enjoined them, "Watch out, guard against the leaven of the Pharisees and the leave of Herod." They concluded among themselves that it was because they had no bread. When he became aware of this he said to them, "Why do you conclude that it is because you have no bread? Do you not yet understand or comprehend? Are your hearts hardened? Do you have eyes and not see, ears and not hear? And do you not remember, when I broke the five loaves for the five thousand, how many wicker baskets full of fragments you picked up?" They answered him, "Twelve." "When I broke the seven loaves for the four thousand, how many full baskets of fragments did you pick up?" They answered him, "Seven." He said to them, "Do you still not understand?"

REFLECTION

The disciples talked among themselves and felt they found the answer, but how wrong they were! We sometimes need to be reminded how wrong we can be about God or ourselves, especially in isolation. Community provides a start- ing place for reflection, but it helps to have the guidance of teachers, mentors, and spiritual leaders. Let us remember to seek the guidance and wisdom of God through others and the Church.

PRAYERS *others may be added*

Desiring deeper understanding of you, O God, we pray:

◆ Wisdom of God, enlighten us.

That the inspired, historical interplay between Word, tradition, and the faithful be continually guided by the Holy Spirit, we pray: ◆ *That heads of state seek the counsel of advisory bodies in making decisions that affect thousands of lives, we pray:* ◆ *That dialogue between believers may lead to greater understanding of God through wise and trustworthy spiritual leaders, we pray:* ◆ *That we do not become so headstrong in our thinking that we cannot see when we are wrong, we pray:* ◆

Our Father . . .

Lord Jesus, our brother,
human stubbornness, pride,
    and confusion
certainly must lead you to
    disappointment in us.
Send us your Holy Spirit at all times
    to inspire and lead us.
Direct and support the insights of
    our leaders,
that they might be shepherds of your
    gift for all the faithful.
You live and reign with God
    the Father
in the unity of the Holy Spirit,
one God, forever and ever.
Amen.

✤ *The Lord is my light and my salvation.*

✦ *For ever I will sing the goodness of the Lord.*

PSALM 130 — page 418

READING — Mark 8:22–26

When Jesus and his disciples arrived at Bethsaida, people brought to him a blind man and begged Jesus to touch him. He took the blind man by the hand and led him outside the village. Putting spittle on his eyes he laid his hands on the man and asked, "Do you see anything?" Looking up the man replied, "I see people looking like trees and walking." Then he laid hands on the man's eyes a second time and he saw clearly; his sight was restored and he could see everything distinctly. Then he sent him home and said, "Do not even go into the village."

REFLECTION

Our God is a God of second chances. God washed away wickedness in the flood but offered Noah and his family a second chance. The blind man could see after Jesus laid hands on him a second time. We might feel we cannot turn to God a second time with our fears and sin if we have failed to respond to his first offer of forgiveness and healing. But we can. God wants to restore our sight, forgive our sins, and transform us right now—despite the number of times we have asked him before.

PRAYERS — *others may be added*

Bringing our prayers to a merciful God, we pray:

◆ Heal us, O Lord.

For priests and ministers of the Church who cannot forgive themselves of sin, we pray: ◆ For those who could not see truth when it was presented the first time, we pray: ◆ For any who consider their sins impossible to overcome, we pray: ◆ For the generosity to offer second chances to others as God does to us, we pray: ◆

Our Father . . .

God of heaven and earth,
you washed the earth clean and
    promised Noah and his family a
    new beginning.
We, too, need a second chance.
When we have turned away and
    refused offers of grace,
welcome us back when we finally are
    ready to accept your mercy.
We ask this through Christ our Lord.
Amen.

✦ *For ever I will sing the goodness of the Lord.*

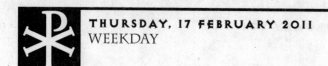
✛ *For ever I will sing the goodness of the Lord.*

PSALM 111
page 417

READING
Genesis 9:8–13

God said to Noah and to his sons with him: "See, I am now establishing my covenant with you and your descendants after you and with every living creature that was with you: all the birds, and the various tame and wild animals that were with you and came out of the ark. I will establish my covenant with you, that never again shall all bodily creatures be destroyed by the waters of a flood; there shall not be another flood to devastate the earth." God added: "This is the sign that I am giving for all ages to come, of the covenant between me and you and every living creature with you: I set my bow in the clouds to serve as a sign of the covenant between me and the earth."

REFLECTION

First the rainbow; later, the cross. These signs of God's love and covenant surround us. God's promises to his people are lasting and complete. The Old Testament tells the story of the covenant with Israel. The New Testament gives the account of the covenant offered to all people. See yourself as the chosen people, loved by God. See yourself as the recipient of the offer of eternal life. Look for the rainbow, the cross, and other signs in our daily lives that remind us of God's tremendous, forgiving love.

PRAYERS
others may be added

With gratitude for our loving God, we pray:

◆ Lord, hear our prayer.

For the signs and symbols of the Roman Catholic Church, that they reveal to all the awesome, generous love of God, we pray, ◆ *For the signs of nature, that they lead people everywhere closer to God, we pray:* ◆ *For artists who display, explore, and expand signs and symbols, provoking us to greater awareness of God, we pray:* ◆ *For the courage to display signs of God's love in our own homes and on our own persons, in ways that convey meaning to us and others, we pray:* ◆

Our Father . . .

Omnipotent God,
you put signs in the heavens, on earth,
    and around us,
indicating your radical love for us.
Direct our minds to these signs,
and inspire us to reflect on them;
thus, reflecting more deeply on your
    saving love.
Grant this through Christ our Lord.
Amen.

✛ *For ever I will sing the goodness of the Lord.*

✚ *The precepts of the Lord give joy to the heart.*

PSALM 42   *page 408*

READING   *Mark 8:34—9:1*

Jesus summoned the crowd with his disciples and said to them, "Whoever wishes to come after me must deny himself, take up his cross, and follow me. For whoever wishes to save his life will lose it, but whoever loses his life for my sake and that of the Gospel will save it. What profit is there for one to gain the whole world and forfeit his life? What could one give in exchange for his life? Whoever is ashamed of me and of my words in this faithless and sinful generation, the Son of Man will be ashamed of when he comes in his Father's glory with the holy angels."

He also said to them, "Amen, I say to you, there are some standing here who will not taste death until they see that the Kingdom of God has come in power."

REFLECTION

What does it mean to deny oneself? How do we avoid becoming so sure of ourselves and our own authority? Think about what activities humble you. Spending time with those who possess far less wealth and power than ourselves can be one way. If we only spend time with others like ourselves in a privileged world, we will become very smug indeed. Seek out those who make you uncomfortable and reveal your own need for pride, security, and control.

PRAYERS   *others may be added*

Asking to be humbled, we pray:

◆ Lead us, O Lord.

That all Christians honestly look for places, people, and conditions that challenge them to rely more on Christ and less on familiar privilege, we pray: ◆
That all people of the world become more willing to enter dialogue with those they consider different from themselves, we pray: ◆ *That those with wealth, higher education, and powerful occupations be extremely sensitive to the advantages they have over others, we pray:* ◆ *That we open our eyes to see our arrogance and assumptions, making room for humility in our lives, we pray:* ◆

Our Father . . .

Lord Jesus,
we want to come after you,
and enter the kingdom of heaven.
We know that as of now we are
   not prepared.
Strip us of our certainty and authority
   if you see fit,
and open us to the humble path
   to you.
You live and reign with God
   the Father
in the unity of the Holy Spirit,
one God, forever and ever.
Amen.

✚ *The precepts of the Lord give joy to the heart.*

✚ *In you, O Lord, I have found my peace.*

PSALM 111 *page 417*

READING *Hebrews 11:1–3, 6–7*

Brothers and sisters: Faith is the realization of what is hoped for and evidence of things not seen. Because of it the ancients were well attested. By faith we understand that the universe was ordered by the word of God, so that what is visible came into being through the invisible. But without faith it is impossible to please him, for anyone who approaches God must believe that he exists and that he rewards those who seek him. By faith Noah, warned about what was not yet seen, with reverence built an ark for the salvation of his household. Through this, he condemned the world and inherited the righteousness that comes through faith.

REFLECTION

By faith, through the stories passed down to us, we believe in what we cannot see. The faith of children in their parents makes possible belief in the future, themselves, and Santa Claus. We, too, can believe falsely based on trust in others, but it is only through genuine trust in Jesus Christ that we have faith at all.

PRAYERS *others may be added*

Looking to the prophets and disciples in faith, we pray:

◆ Lord, hear our prayer.

For the trustworthiness of our deacons, priests, and Bishops who inspire us in our faith, we pray: ◆ *For a worldwide hope for peace, we pray:* ◆ *For parents who inspire trust from their children, we pray:* ◆ *For a celebration of innocence and leaps of faith, we pray:* ◆

Our Father . . .

God of the visible and invisible,
your people Israel held faith in you
    through thousands of years
    of history,
and, even today, through
    unspeakable suffering.
May we be inspired by their faith,
    hope, and trust in you.
Give us hearts of unimaginable faith,
unbreakable trust,
and unending hope.
We ask this through our Lord Jesus
    Christ, your Son,
who lives and reigns with you in the
    unity of the Holy Spirit,
one God, forever and ever.
Amen.

✚ *In you, O Lord, I have found my peace.*

✚ *In you, O Lord, I have found
my peace.*

PSALM 130   *page 418*

READING   *Matthew 5:38–48*

Jesus said to his disciples: "You have heard that it was said, / *An eye for an eye and a tooth for a tooth.* / But I say to you, offer no resistance to one who is evil. When someone strikes you on your right cheek, turn the other one as well. If anyone wants to go to law with you over your tunic, hand over your cloak as well. Should anyone press you into service for one mile, go for two miles. Give to the one who asks of you, and do not turn your back on one who wants to borrow.

"You have heard that it was said, / *You shall love your neighbor and hate your enemy.* / But I say to you, love your enemies and pray for those who persecute you, that you may be children of your heavenly Father, for he makes his sun rise on the bad and the good, and causes rain to fall on the just and the unjust. For if you love those who love you, what recompense will you have? Do not the tax collectors do the same? And if you greet your brothers only, what is unusual about that? Do not the pagans do the same? So be perfect, just as your heavenly Father is perfect."

REFLECTION

Think of someone you love for whom you have been praying. You have probably asked that God guide, protect, heal, and comfort this person. Think of someone who persecutes you or whom you consider an enemy. Hold the one whom you struggle with in this same type of loving prayer. What feelings arise? Talk this over with God.

PRAYERS   *others may be added*

    We come before God, and pray:

◆ Lord, hear our prayer.

For those who persecute and undermine the Church, we pray in love: ◆ *For those who slaughter innocents and plot destruction, we pray in love:* ◆ *For those who abuse partners, children, or the elderly, we pray in love:* ◆ *For those who have hurt us and with whom we are angry, we pray in love:* ◆

Our Father . . .

O God,
you make the sun rise on the bad and
    the good.
We lift up those whom we do not
    understand and find it hard to love,
praying that you reach them with your
    healing, comforting touch.
We ask this through Christ our Lord.
Amen.

✚ *In you, O Lord, I have found
my peace.*

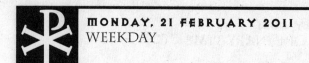
✜ *The Lord is my light and my salvation.*

PSALM 42 *page 408*

READING *Sirach 1:1, 4–10*

All wisdom comes from the LORD and with him it remains forever, and is before all time . . . . The word of God on high is the fountain of wisdom and her ways are everlasting. To whom has wisdom's root been revealed? Who knows her subtleties? To whom has the discipline of wisdom been revealed? And who has understood the multiplicity of her ways? There is but one, wise and truly awe-inspiring, seated upon his throne:

There is but one, Most High all-powerful creator-king and truly awe-inspiring one, seated upon his throne and he is the God of dominion. It is the Lord; he created her through the Holy Spirit, has seen her and taken note of her. He has poured her forth upon all his works, upon every living thing according to his bounty; he has lavished her upon his friends.

REFLECTION

The wisdom of God comes to us through Jesus Christ and the Holy Spirit. When we have known a deep truth in prayer, when we have felt the peace of God in a decision, when the Holy Spirit has led us to a strong conviction—this is the wisdom of God at work in us. Look back over the last weeks of prayer and notice when God's wisdom has been with you.

PRAYERS *others may be added*

Giving thanks for God's gift of wisdom, we pray:

◆ Glory to you, O God.

In thanks for wisdom in the tradition and leadership of the Church, we pray: ◆ *In thanks for the outpouring of wisdom upon the world, we pray:* ◆ *In thanks for the fountain of wisdom accessible through catechesis, education, and experiential learning, we pray:* ◆ *In thanks for the wisdom of God within each of us, undergirding our faith, we pray:* ◆

Our Father . . .

Awe-inspiring God,
wisdom was with you in the creation
    of the world;
wisdom came to us in your
    Son, Jesus;
and wisdom remains with us, offering
    us knowledge and truth.
May we recognize our gifts
and continue to increase in our
    understanding of your ways.
We ask this through Christ our Lord.
Amen.

✜ *The Lord is my light and my salvation.*

✚ *Commit your life to the Lord.*

PSALM 40 *page 407*

READING *Matthew 16:13–19*

When Jesus went into the region of Caesarea Philippi he asked his disciples, "Who do people say that the Son of Man is?" They replied, "Some say John the Baptist, others Elijah, still others Jeremiah or one of the prophets." He said to them, "But who do you say that I am?" Simon Peter said in reply, "You are the Christ, the Son of the living God." Jesus said to him in reply, "Blessed are you, Simon son of Jonah. For flesh and blood has not revealed this to you, but my heavenly Father. And so I say to you, you are Peter, and upon this rock I will build my Church, and the gates of the netherworld shall not prevail against it. I will give you the keys to the Kingdom of heaven. Whatever you bind on earth shall be bound in heaven; and whatever you loose on earth shall be loosed in heaven."

REFLECTION

A significant issue at the end of life is raised here by Jesus: what binds or frees us so that we may or may not enter into eternal paradise. Jesus entrusts this important ministry—forgiveness and reconciliation—to Peter and to his successors. What a sacred role: to hold people accountable for their lives and actions, and to assure them of God's loving mercy and unconditional welcome to eternal life.

PRAYERS *others may be added*

As humans in need of divine guidance, we pray:

◆ Lord, hear our prayer.

For the Pope, the successor to St. Peter, that his deep relationship with Jesus guides him as he leads the Church in showing justice and mercy to all, we pray: ◆ *For all priests, who in the sacrament of Reconciliation, represent the whole Church and God's love, offering the liberating gift of absolution of sins, we pray:* ◆ *For all who make the sacrament of Reconciliation, that they make a genuine confession, make amends for their wrongdoing, and rejoice in being forgiven, we pray:* ◆ *For all who are chained to guilt, denial, and sin, that they may open their hearts to the freedom that comes with conversion, we pray:* ◆

Our Father . . .

God of wisdom,
you know the human heart,
and its need for accountability,
   responsibility, and justice.
You also know our need to be loved
   and forgiven.
We praise you for your mercy,
in allowing your representatives
   on earth
to offer in a tangible way the gift of
   your grace.
We ask this through Christ our
   Lord. Amen.

✚ *Commit your life to the Lord.*

✛ *For ever I will sing the goodness of the Lord.*

PSALM 100   *page 414*

READING   *Mark 9:38–40*

John said to Jesus, "Teacher, we saw someone driving out demons in your name, and we tried to prevent him because he does not follow us." Jesus replied, "Do not prevent him. There is no one who performs a mighty deed in my name who can at the same time speak ill of me. For whoever is not against us is for us."

REFLECTION

Goodness is rooted in love. Love is God. We can trust goodness and truth, for when we encounter them in others and in the world, we know that they are ultimately from God. We need not concern ourselves with judgment. Those who love wisdom and serve God's law find favor with him.

PRAYERS   *others may be added*

Allowing ourselves to be guided by wisdom, we pray:

◆ May God's goodness spread throughout the world.

For unity of mind and heart between all Christians, we pray: ◆ *For collaboration between those who seek justice and peace in all religions, we pray:* ◆ *For greater trust between political parties, ethnic groups, and social classes, we pray:* ◆ *For a welcoming and non-judgmental attitude to those whom we encounter, we pray:* ◆

Our Father . . .

Most Holy God,
your wisdom pervades all that
    is good.
The earth and all who dwell on it are
    made for you.
May we work toward that end,
seeking shared truth and goodness
    with all those of integrity.
May all be all in you at the end
    of time.
Grant this through Christ our Lord.
Amen.

✛ *For ever I will sing the goodness of the Lord.*

✚ *The heart of the just one is firm,*
trusting in the Lord.

PSALM 51   *page 409*

READING   *Mark 9:42–50*

[Jesus said to his disciples:] "Whoever causes one of these little ones who believe in me to sin, it would be better for him if a great millstone were put around his neck and he were thrown into the sea. If your hand causes you to sin, cut it off. It is better for you to enter into life maimed than with two hands to go into Gehenna, into the unquenchable fire. And if your foot causes you to sin, cut if off. It is better for you to enter into life crippled than with two feet to be thrown into Gehenna. And if your eye causes you to sin, pluck it out. Better for you to enter into the Kingdom of God with one eye than with two eyes to be thrown into Gehenna, where *their worm does not die, and the fire is not quenched.*

REFLECTION

Do not deny the gravity of your own sin. It is easy for us to rationalize away our sins, or be overly confident of God's mercy. Think of sins you have been trying to ignore, put off, or avoid. If we dismiss our need for repentance, we allow sin to further control our lives, as well as run the risk of leading others into sin. Let us humbly admit our sin, and vow to forsake it.

PRAYERS   *others may be added*

Hoping in the Lord, we pray:

◆ Lead us, O God.

For all Christians, that we readily admit our own sin and seek forgiveness, we pray: ◆ *For greater accountability and reparation within government, we pray:* ◆ *For voices to speak out against false prophets, we pray:* ◆ *For honest appraisal of any practices or habits that lead us into sin, we pray:* ◆

Our Father . . .

Merciful and just God,
you offer abundant love and
    perfect justice.
You sent your Son Jesus to call us
    to repentance;
may we heed his commands.
Help us to make difficult choices,
which lead us away from sin and into
    your arms.
We ask this through Christ our Lord.
Amen.

✚ *The heart of the just one is firm,*
trusting in the Lord.

✦ *The precepts of the Lord give joy to the heart.*

PSALM 149   *page 421*

READING   *Sirach 6:5–7, 14–17*

A kind mouth multiplies friends and appeases enemies, / and gracious lips prompt friendly greetings. / Let your acquaintances be many, / but one in a thousand your confidant. / When you gain a friend, first test him, / and be not too ready to trust him. / A faithful friend is a sturdy shelter; / he who finds one finds a treasure. / A faithful friend is beyond price, / no sum can balance his worth. / A faithful friend is a life-saving remedy, / such as he who fears God finds; / For he who fears God behaves accordingly, / and his friend will be like himself.

REFLECTION

Our deepest relationships—friendships and marriages—enrich our lives by reflecting and enhancing our relationship with God. Be grateful today for any relationships you have that meet these criteria. Name them, lift them in prayer. Consider how to nurture relationships that could grow. Reflect on ending any relationships that lead you away from God. Take an honest look at people who are subtly changing the priorities and values of your life.

PRAYERS   *others may be added*

Together with our friends, we pray:

◆ Be with us, Lord.

For those who have taken a vow of celibacy, that faithful friends support their relationship with God, we pray: ◆ *For cross-cultural friendships and marriages, that unity in God allows mutual learning and respect, we pray:* ◆ *For all married couples, that patience, trust, and faithfulness lead them in love to God, we pray:* ◆ *For lifelong friendships and friendships just beginning, that God be always present with them, we pray:* ◆

Our Father . . .

Lord Jesus,
you are a friend to us like no other,
present in our relationships if we open
    ourselves to you.
Show us how to be loyal,
    compassionate, listening,
    loving friends.
Remind us of your everlasting
    friendship.
You live and reign with God
    the Father
in the unity of the Holy Spirit,
one God, forever and ever.
Amen.

✦ *The precepts of the Lord give joy to the heart.*

✦ *For ever I will sing the goodness of the Lord.*

PSALM 100   *page 414*

READING   *Mark 10:13–16*

People were bringing children to Jesus that he might touch them, but the disciples rebuked them. When Jesus saw this he became indignant and said to them, "Let the children come to me; do not prevent them, for the Kingdom of God belongs to such as these. Amen, I say to you, whoever does not accept the Kingdom of God like a child will not enter it." Then he embraced the children and blessed them, placing his hands on them.

REFLECTION

Jesus has loved us since we were small children. He has known us through infancy, childhood, adolescence, adulthood, middle age, and our wisdom years. He has blessed us abundantly with gifts to use in this life. He has made a promise to walk with us. If we rest in this loving presence, we can greet each day like a child—eager, passionate, optimistic, and with arms open to love.

PRAYERS   *others may be added*

Modeling our hearts after those of children, we pray:

◆ Listen to us, O God.

That our Church may be blessed with God's loving guidance and presence, we pray: ◆ *That our world may be filled with peace, justice, and equality, we pray:* ◆ *That any who are suffering or are alone may be comforted, we pray:* ◆ *That each of us may use the gifts given us wisely, we pray:* ◆

Our Father . . .

Loving Creator,
you made us in your own image
and welcome us in our most pure,
    innocent form.
Help us strip away cynicism and fear,
finding within ourselves our dignity
    as your son or daughter,
longing for you and longing to share
    love with the world.
We ask this through our Lord Jesus
    Christ, your Son,
who lives and reigns with you
in the unity of the Holy Spirit,
one God, forever and ever.
Amen.

✦ *For ever I will sing the goodness of the Lord.*

✦ *The Lord made us, we belong to him.*

PSALM 25   *page 403*

READING   *Matthew 6:24–34*

Jesus said to his disciples: "No one can serve two masters. He will either hate one and love the other, or be devoted to one and despise the other. You cannot serve God and mammon.

"Therefore I tell you, do not worry about your life, what you will eat or drink, or about your body, what you will wear. Is not life more than food and the body more than clothing? Look at the birds in the sky; they do not sow or reap, they gather nothing into barns, yet your heavenly Father feeds them. Are not you more important than they? Can any of you by worrying add a single moment to your life-span? Why are you anxious about clothes? Learn from the way the wild flowers grow. They do not work or spin. But I tell you that not even Solomon in all his splendor was clothed like one of them. If God so clothes the grass of the field, which grows today and is thrown into the oven tomorrow, will he not much more provide for you, O you of little faith? So do not worry and say, 'What are we to eat?' or 'What are we to drink?' or 'What are we to wear?' All these things the pagans seek. Your heavenly Father knows that you need them all. But seek first the kingdom of God and his righteousness, and all these things will be given you besides."

REFLECTION

Nurturing, protecting, feeding, consoling, sheltering—we have known these caring acts in mothers, fathers, grandparents, spouses, and friends. God's love surpasses the love of all those we have known. Imagine a god who knows your every need and tenderly cares for you. This God is real.

PRAYERS   *others may be added*

Awed by God's love, we pray:

◆ May we rest in your embrace.

That every believer knows the real, loving touch of our Creator, we pray: ◆ *That the body of Christ, the Church, extends God's loving touch throughout the world, we pray:* ◆ *That those who heal, nurture, console, and feed others do so in genuine love, we pray:* ◆ *That all who have not felt tender love may experience the love of God, we pray:* ◆

Our Father . . .

O God,
our ruler and protector,
you watch out for us with a
    father's love,
nurturing us with a mother's love.
We give thanks for this overwhelming
    providence.
Keep us from ever doubting this love.
We ask this through Christ our Lord.
Amen.

✦ *The Lord made us, we belong to him.*

✦ *The Lord is my light and my salvation.*

PSALM 139   page 420

READING   Mark 10:17–21

As Jesus was setting out on a journey, a man ran up, knelt down before him, and asked him, "Good teacher, what must I do to inherit eternal life?" Jesus answered him, "Why do you call me good? No one is good but God alone. You know the commandments: / *You shall not kill; / you shall not commit adultery; you shall not steal; / you shall not bear false witness; / you shall not defraud; / honor your father and your mother."* / He replied and said to him, "Teacher, all of these I have observed from my youth." Jesus, looking at him, loved him and said to him, "You are lacking in one thing. Go, sell what you have, and give to the poor and you will have treasure in heaven; then come, follow me."

REFLECTION

If this saying makes us uncomfortable or afraid, we need to listen. Rather than solely feeling guilty, how can we actually repent and follow Jesus? What wealth can we give away? What wealth can we share? What wealth can we detach from ourselves? Let us bring our possessions and our privilege before God, asking how we can put them into his service.

PRAYERS   *others may be added*

Hoping in God who makes all things possible, we pray:

◆ Make us rich in faith.

For all who follow the commandments, that we may be inspired to give completely of ourselves to Jesus, we pray: ◆ *For ears to hear the challenging words of Jesus when we are not aware of our excess, we pray:* ◆ *For creative sharing, use, and donation of our possessions, we pray:* ◆ *For astonishment, rather than despair, as we repent and follow Jesus, we pray:* ◆

Our Father . . .

O God,
with you, nothing is impossible.
Give us courage to look at our
     own wealth;
give us strength to prioritize our love
     for you
over our attachment to possessions.
May we always be filled with
     your love
and the joy of sharing in your
     saving work.
Grant this through Christ our Lord.
Amen.

✦ *The Lord is my light and my salvation.*

✦ *In you, O Lord, I have found
my peace.*

PSALM 25 page 403

READING Mark 10:28–31

Peter began to say to Jesus, "We have given up everything and followed you." Jesus said, "Amen, I say to you, there is no one who has given up house or brothers or sisters or mother or father or children or lands for my sake and for the sake of the Gospel who will not receive a hundred times more now in this present age: houses and brothers and sisters and mothers and children and lands, with persecutions, and eternal life in the age to come. But many that are first will be last, and the last will be first."

REFLECTION

It's a scary feeling—rejecting the security and offers of happiness in this world, and relying on the promise of life in Christ. We can be honest with God about how vulnerable we feel, and how much we need his assurance. He will embrace us, in turn, and promise us we are never alone as we journey toward eternal life. The more we practice trusting him, the more comfortable we will become in leaning on him first and foremost.

PRAYERS *others may be added*

In desperate need of God, we pray:

◆ Give us your peace, O Lord.

That Christians inspire and support each other as we courageously follow Christ, we pray: ◆ *That those who face life-threatening persecution for their Christian faith may sense God's closeness to them, we pray:* ◆ *That those who dare to risk everything for Christ be most richly rewarded, we pray:* ◆ *That those among us who have made sacrifices for Christ inspire all of us to live our faith boldly, we pray:* ◆ *That all those who have died in faith may find the embrace of God, we pray:* ◆

Our Father . . .

O God, most high,
you ask much of us
and you promise us much.
May we rise to the occasion,
serving as disciples with integrity
and bravery.
May we wait eagerly for the day when
we will live with you,
forever at rest and in peace.
We ask this through Christ our Lord.
Amen.

✦ *In you, O Lord, I have found
my peace.*

✢ *For ever I will sing the goodness of the Lord.*

PSALM 111   *page 417*

READING   *Sirach 36:1, 4–5a, 14–17*

Come to our aid, O God of the universe, / look upon us, show us the light of your mercies, / and put all the nations in dread of you! / Thus they will know, as we know, / that there is no God but you, O Lord.

Give new signs and work new wonders.

Give evidence of your deeds of old; / fulfill the prophecies spoken in your name, / Reward those who have hoped in you, / and let your prophets be proved true. / Hear the prayer of your servants, / for you are ever gracious to your people; / and lead us in the way of justice. / Thus it will be known to the very ends of the earth / that you are the eternal God.

REFLECTION

This fervent prayer of the Old Testament is wondrously fulfilled in Jesus! Who could imagine a Savior who came to serve? Who could comprehend the Son of God, not wanting to be glorified, but wanting to give his life? Jesus is a sign and wonder unlike any other. Our God's love amazes and transforms the world.

PRAYERS   *others may be added*

Longing for signs and wonders, we pray:

◆ May your goodness, O God, renew the earth.

That the Pope and Bishops signify to the world the uniqueness of Jesus, who served and gave his life for all, we pray: ◆ That civil leaders and corporate CEOs startle their colleagues by modeling servant leadership, we pray: ◆ That those who, by profession, care for others, may be signs of Jesus' healing love, we pray: ◆ That we who look for signs may become the sign ourselves by the way we live our lives, we pray: ◆

Our Father . . .

O God of the universe,
your wonders are many.
Your most perfect revelation in Jesus
surpasses any sign for which we
    might have hoped.
May we see his life-giving love
    reflected in your Church, in
    each other,
and in our own hearts.
We ask this through Christ our Lord.
Amen.

✢ *For ever I will sing the goodness of the Lord.*

✛ *Commit your life to the Lord.*

PSALM 40   *page 407*

READING   *Matthew 25:31–40*

Jesus said to his disciples: "When the Son of Man comes in his glory, and all the angels with him, he will sit upon his glorious throne, and all the nations will be assembled before him. And he will separate them one from another, as a shepherd separates the sheep from the goats. He will place the sheep on his right and the goats on his left. Then the king will say to those on his right, 'Come, you who are blessed by my Father. Inherit the kingdom prepared for you from the foundation of the world. For I was hungry and you gave me food, I was thirsty and you gave me drink, a stranger and you welcomed me, naked and you clothed me, ill and you cared for me, in prison and you visited me.' Then the righteous will answer him and say, 'Lord, when did we see you hungry and feed you, or thirsty and give you drink? When did we see you a stranger and welcome you, or naked and clothe you? When did we see you ill or in prison, and visit you?' And the king will say to them in reply, 'Amen, I say to you, whatever you did for one of the least brothers of mine, you did for me.'"

Optional memorial of St. Katharine Drexel, virgin. Today's reading is from the Common of Holy Men and Women: for Virgins, Lectionary #736, 2.

REFLECTION

Today we honor St. Katharine Drexel. This American saint responded to the needs she saw around her: the education and welfare of Native American Indians and former slaves. Our devotion to Christ, our dedication to prayer, and dedication to Eucharist should also lead us to be sensitive to needs around us. Aware of these needs, we respond as though it were to Christ himself.

PRAYERS   *others may be added*

Looking for Christ in the faces of those in need, we pray:

◆ Make us your hands in the world, Lord God.

For religious communities and offices of the Church that are devoted to serving the oppressed, we pray: ◆ *For world relief organizations that feed the hungry, care for the sick, provide shelter, and welcome refugees, we pray:* ◆ *For all who continue to overcome enslavement and persecution, we pray:* ◆

Our Father . . .

Lord God,
open our eyes to the suffering of
    people around us.
Make us responsive servants, like St.
    Katharine.
Use our hands to feed, welcome,
    clothe, and visit those in need.
We ask this through Christ our Lord.
Amen.

✛ *Commit your life to the Lord.*

✤ *Go out to all the world, and tell the Good News.*

PSALM 139 *page 420*

READING *Mark 11:15–17*

[Jesus and his disciples] came to Jerusalem, and on entering the temple area he began to drive out those selling and buying there. He overturned the tables of the money changers and the seats of those who were selling doves. He did not permit anyone to carry anything through the temple area. Then he taught them saying, "Is it not written: / *My house shall be called a house of prayer for all peoples? / But you have made it a den of thieves." /*

REFLECTION

We have ancestors who show us faithfulness, and we have ancestors who show us misuse of faith, as the moneychangers in the temple in today's Gospel. We are like a tree that can either bear fruit or be useless. Jesus implores us to have strong faith in God. If we do, we can do great things in his name.

PRAYERS *others may be added*

Trusting in God, we pray:

◆ Make us fruitful, Lord.

For religious vocations, service to the poor, and conversions to Christianity, we pray: ◆ *For resolutions for peace, relief for the hungry, and advances in human rights, we pray:* ◆ *For strong schools, welcoming churches, and neighborly actions, we pray:* ◆ *For forgiveness, love, and openness to God's call in our families, we pray,* ◆ *For unity of mind and heart between all Christians, we pray:* ◆ *For collaboration between those who seek justice and peace in all religions, we pray:* ◆ *For greater trust between political parties, ethnic groups, and social classes, we pray:* ◆ *For a welcoming and non-judgmental attitude to those whom we encounter, we pray:* ◆

Our Father . . .

God of the harvest,
your covenant with Israel reaped a
    faithful people;
your covenant in Jesus reaped eternal
    life for all of us.
May our faith produce fruit,
and our response to you allow you to
    reach the hearts of all nations.
Grant this through Christ our Lord.
Amen.

✤ *Go out to all the world, and tell the Good News.*

✛ *The heart of the just one is firm.*

PSALM 42 *page 408*

READING *Mark 11:27–33*

Jesus and his disciples returned once more to Jerusalem. As he was walking in the temple area, the chief priests, the scribes, and the elders approached he and said to him, "By what authority are you doing these things? Or who gave you this authority to do them?" Jesus said to them, "I shall ask you one question. Answer me, and I will tell you by what authority I do these things. Was John's baptism of heavenly or of human origin? Answer me." They discussed this among themselves and said, "If we say, 'Of heavenly origin,' he will say, 'Then why did you not believe him?' But shall we say, 'Of human origin'?"—they feared the crowd, for they all thought John really was a prophet. So they said to Jesus in reply, "We do not know." Then Jesus said to them, "Neither shall I tell you by what authority I do these things."

REFLECTION

Who are you, O Christ? How is it that my relationship with you brings me inner peace? Why is it that as I spend more time with you, the other things in my life fall into place? Perhaps I do not need to fully understand. As long as I see the truth of who you are in my life—the good effects upon my relationships, my work, my self-identity, I know that you are the ultimate answer to my life's questions.

PRAYERS *others may be added*

Thanking God for his blessings, we pray:

◆ May your greatness be known to all who trust in you.

For the presence of Christ in the ministries of the Church, we pray: ◆
For the work of the Holy Spirit across the face of the earth, we pray: ◆ *For the impact of Christ's message on those in prison, refugee camps, and those facing inner loneliness, we pray:* ◆ *For the gift of faith given to us by our families, teachers, and God, we pray:* ◆

Our Father . . .

Lord Jesus, Son of God,
the mystery of your time and presence
    on earth
no doubt left many followers
    in confusion.
We also feel overwhelmed by the
    unique gift you are to us.
Help us to trust the spirit of love
    and peace
that comes to us in seeking you.
May we rest in your guidance
    and wisdom.
You live and reign with God
    the Father
in the unity of the Holy Spirit,
one God, forever and ever.
Amen.

✛ *The heart of the just one is firm.*

✝ *The Lord is my light and my salvation.*

PSALM 100 page 414

READING *Matthew 7:24–27*

[Jesus said to his disciples:] "Everyone who listens to these words of mine and acts on them will be like a wise man who built his house on rock. The rain fell, the floods came, and the winds blew and buffeted the house. But it did not collapse; it had been set solidly on rock. And everyone who listens to these words of mine but does not act on them will be like a fool who built his house on sand. The rain fell, the floods came, and the winds blew and buffeted the house. And it collapsed and was completely ruined."

REFLECTION

Jesus depicts the "fool" as prophesying, driving out demons, and doing mighty deeds in Christ's name. This type of believer is caught up in self-importance and attention-getting behavior. The wise one listens to God in prayer and responds with solid actions. Take a solid step today toward the foundation of your life.

PRAYERS *others may be added*

Seeking your wisdom, we pray:

◆ Root us in you, Rock of Life.

For wise leaders to continue to build the body of Christ, we pray: ◆ *For wisdom among those who hear the foolish preachers using Christ's name, we pray:* ◆ *For new beginnings for all who have built their lives on foolish promises, we pray:* ◆ *For support and guidance when we have to discern between wise and foolish choices, we pray:* ◆

Our Father . . .

Lord God,
you sent your Son to be the
    master builder.
We hope that we will always heed
    his direction
when we mistakenly build our lives
    on sand.
When we wisely build our lives
    on rock,
rejoice in our return.
We ask this through our Lord Jesus
    Christ, your Son,
who lives and reigns with you
in the unity of the Holy Spirit,
one God, forever and ever.
Amen.

✝ *The Lord is my light and my salvation.*

✦ *In you, O Lord, I have found*
my peace.

PSALM 25 *page 403*

READING *Mark 12:1b–8*

[Jesus said:] "A man planted a vineyard, put a hedge around it, dug a wine press, and built a tower. Then he leased it to tenant farmers and left on a journey. At the proper time he sent a servant to the tenants to obtain from them some of the produce of the vineyard. But they seized him, beat him, and sent him away empty-handed. Again he sent them another servant. And that one they beat over the head and treated shamefully. He sent yet another whom they killed. So, too, many others; some they beat, others they killed. He had one other to send, a beloved son. He sent him to them last of all, thinking, 'They will respect my son.' But those tenants said to one another, 'This is the heir. Come, let us kill him, and the inheritance will be ours.' So they seized him and killed him, and threw him out of the vineyard."

REFLECTION

How do we react to messages we don't want to hear? How do we react to the messenger? Can we graciously respond to and accept a boss's constructive criticism? Can we, at the suggestion of a teacher, acknowledge room for our child to grow? Can we see God speaking to us in a difficult confrontation with our spouse?

PRAYERS *others may be added*

Coming to the Lord who knows us best, we pray:

◆ Open our ears, O God.

For congregations listening to challenging homilies and preachers faced with difficult questions, we pray: ◆
For local and regional leaders confronted with new models and suggestions for improving civil services, we pray: ◆
For students, employees, and mentees given constructive criticism by mentors, supervisors, and teachers, we pray: ◆
For families unaware of each other's needs, hopes, and concerns, we pray: ◆

Our Father . . .

Loving God,
you send us holy men and women to
   help us see your light.
May we recognize your love and
   guidance in truth that returns to us
   again and again.
May we be open to change and
   correction,
knowing it will ultimately prepare us
   for life with you.
Grant this through Christ our Lord.
Amen.

✦ *In you, O Lord, I have found*
my peace.

✛ *The Lord made us, we belong to him.*

PSALM 42   page 408

READING   Mark 12:13–17

Some Pharisees and Herodians were sent to Jesus to ensnare him in his speech. They came and said to him, "Teacher, we know that you are a truthful man and that you are not concerned with anyone's opinion. You do not regard a person's status but teach the way of God in accordance with the truth. Is it lawful to pay the census tax to Caesar or not? Should we pay or should we not pay?" Knowing their hypocrisy he said to them, "Why are you testing me? Bring me a denarius to look at." They brought one to him and he said to them, "Whose image and inscription is this?" They replied to him, "Caesar's." So Jesus said to them, "Repay to Caesar what belongs to Caesar and to God what belongs to God." They were utterly amazed at him.

REFLECTION

The Israelites were unsure how to classify Jesus; understandably, they limited him. The Israelites saw him as a political savior, an earthly king. Time and again he tried to explain the limitless nature of his Father's kingdom, and his role in saving all people, for all time. How might we be limiting our understanding of the Messiah?

PRAYERS   *others may be added*

Alternately confused and awed, we come before God:

◆ Reveal your truth to us, O God.

For a clarity of purpose and belief by Church leaders in a world murky with indistinction, we pray: ◆ For balance between work for earthly justice and trust in God's heavenly reward, we pray: ◆ For new hope when we feel lost in the mystery of God's saving work on earth, we pray: ◆ For clear minds when we read scripture, hear preaching and receive the sacraments, we pray: ◆

Our Father . . .

God of love and mercy,
we struggle to make sense of living a
    Christian life in a chaotic world.
May the words and presence of Jesus
    bring light and insight to our faith.
We ask this through Christ our Lord.
Amen.

✛ *The Lord made us, we belong to him.*

Optional memorial of St. John of God, religious

✦ *Be merciful, O Lord.*

PSALM 51 *page 409*

READING *Matthew 6:1–4*

Jesus said to his disciples: "Take care not to perform righteous deeds in order that people may see them; otherwise, you will have no recompense from your heavenly Father. When you give alms, do not blow a trumpet before you, as the hypocrites do in the synagogues and in the streets to win the praise of others. Amen, I say to you, they have received their reward. But when you give alms, do not let your left hand know what your right is doing, so that your almsgiving may be secret. And your Father who sees in secret will repay you."

REFLECTION

Whether you have been anticipating Lent or have stumbled into it, now is the moment. We are urged to seize this time with contrite hearts. Take time today, without procrastinating, to consider how God is calling you back to him. In what ways have we grown apart from God? What is keeping us from his love? And how best can we make an act of contrition and journey closer to Jesus during these holy days? The purpose of Lent is spiritual conversion, not for the sake of other's impressions or opinions.

PRAYERS *others may be added*

Humbled and repentant, we pray:

◆ Bring us back to you, God.

That the Church returns to God in every way and at every level, we pray: ◆ *That a healthy sense of inadequacy and awe before God stirs the hearts of world leaders, we pray:* ◆ *That those who suffer know how close they are to the heart of God and are comforted, we pray:* ◆ *That we as a parish community challenge each other to make authentic strides in our prayer life, we pray:* ◆ *That those who have died return to the love of the Father, we pray:* ◆

Our Father . . .

Heavenly Father,
you see the innermost parts of
  our hearts
and continue to love and reach out
  to us.
Help us to focus on the journey each
  of us must make through
  the desert,
undeterred by distractions and
  temptations,
that on Easter morning we may
  rejoice with new hearts.
We ask this through our Lord Jesus
  Christ, your Son,
who lives and reigns with you in the
  unity of the Holy Spirit,
one God, forever and ever.
Amen.

✦ *Be merciful, O Lord.*

✚ *Be merciful, O Lord.*

PSALM 51   page 409

READING   Luke 9:22–25

Jesus said to his disciples, "The Son of Man must suffer greatly and be rejected by the elders, the chief priests, and the scribes, and be killed and on the third day be raised."

Then he said to all, "If anyone wishes to come after me, he must deny himself and take up his cross daily and follow me. For whoever wishes to save his life will lose it, but whoever loses his life for my sake will save it. What profit is there for one to gain the whole world yet lose or forfeit himself?"

REFLECTION

In what ways do we try to "save" our lives, rather than deny or lose them? Do we hoard money in our retirement plans rather than give more generously to those in need? Do we protect our homes with security systems and our relationships with exclusionary practices, rather than risk vulnerability? Do we obsess about nutrition and exercise excessively, rather than "waste" time with someone who feels lonely? Where is the line between living a life for Christ and living a life for ourselves?

PRAYERS   *others may be added*

Seeking guidance, we pray:

◆ Heal us, O Lord.

For Bishops, priests, deacons, religious, lay ministers, and all believers who are persecuted because of their faith, that they continue to be a sign of the love of God in the midst of violence and hatred, we pray: ◆ *For political and business leaders who have developed an inflated sense of self, that they may return to a balanced view of their need for God, we pray:* ◆ *For victims of war and oppression, those who have lost their lives, dignity, and sense of security, that with Christ as their center they may have the determination to move forward, we pray:* ◆ *For all the faithful, struggling daily with small and large crosses, that we may find strength in God and each other, we pray:* ◆

Our Father . . .

God of wisdom,
you offer us clear direction on how to
    live our lives
grounded in you and in true happiness,
yet, we still lose our way.
Forgive us for our selfish habits
    and fears
and lead us in the path of humility
    and life.
We ask this through Christ our Lord.
Amen.

✚ *Be merciful, O Lord.*

✦ *I am the resurrection and the life,*
says the Lord; whoever believes in
me will never die.

PSALM 51   *page 409*

READING   *Matthew 9:14–15*

The disciples of John approached Jesus and said, "Why do we and the Pharisees fast much, but your disciples do not fast?" Jesus answered them, "Can the guests mourn as long as the bridegroom is with them? The days will come when the bridegroom is taken away from them, and then they will fast."

REFLECTION

Jesus tells us that fasting is a type of mourning; it is a recognition of loss and lack of wholeness. When we fast, we remember the lack of food, shelter, security, peace, and love in so many people's lives—today and in the past. We are in solidarity with those who suffer. In doing so, we honor our brother Jesus, who suffered once and suffers still from the pain in the world. We unite with him, crying out for the wholeness of every child, woman, and man.

PRAYERS   *others may be added*

Aware of so many needs, we pray:

◆ May Christ increase in us.

That our fasting will bring forth greater desire for Christian unity, we pray: ◆ *That politicians and social leaders will be aware of the needs of the voiceless, we pray:* ◆ *That all will have stronger interest in treating each other with gentleness, we pray:* ◆ *That we may be willing to see our flaws and biases and become determined to change them, we pray:* ◆

Our Father . . .

Lord Jesus, our brother,
we look back in astonishment
at the time when you walked
     among us.
You know the pain and sin of this
     world, as well as its potential.
Help us to be brave enough to fast
and to open our eyes to all those
     fasting with us,
intentionally and by circumstance.
Stir in our hearts a fire to bring your
     love to all.
You live and reign with God
     the Father
in the unity of the Holy Spirit,
one God, forever and ever.
Amen.

✦ *I am the resurrection and the life,*
says the Lord; whoever believes in
me will never die.

✦ *Even now, says the LORD, return to me with your whole heart; for I am gracious and merciful.*

PSALM 51   *page 409*

READING   *Luke 5:27–32*

Jesus saw a tax collector named Levi sitting at the customs post. He said to him, "Follow me." And leaving everything behind, he got up and followed him. Then Levi gave a great banquet for him in his house, and a large crowd of tax collectors and others were at table with them. The Pharisees and their scribes complained to his disciples, saying, "Why do you eat and drink with tax collectors and sinners?" Jesus said to them in reply, "Those who are healthy do not need a physician, but the sick do. I have not come to call the righteous but sinners."

REFLECTION

"I've got nothing to lose." Can we say this catchphrase when asked to follow Christ? To what are we clinging too tightly? Why is it that a "sinner" like Levi could leave everything to embrace Jesus? Does he recognize more readily his need for Christ, his need for something more meaningful? Sometimes we can take other things besides Christ too seriously. We can become obsessed with schedules, social groups, family traditions, or hobbies. We need to be ready to drop everything when Christ calls.

PRAYERS   *others may be added*

Jesus, our healer, we pray:

◆ Lead us to you.

For the health and energy of our Pope, Bishops, priests, deacons, religious, and lay ministers, we pray: ◆ *For an end to corruption and partisanship among our country's legislators, we pray:* ◆ *For the wholeness of body and spirit for those in hospitals and hospice, we pray:* ◆ *For the safety and health of all those we love, we pray:* ◆

Our Father . . .

Lord Jesus,
conqueror of sin and death,
you are more powerful than any
    illness, addiction, or evil.
You welcome us no matter how
    tormented or torn apart we are.
May we respond with leaps of faith,
and may we leave behind the false
    promises of health and happiness
in favor of your living Word and
    Sacrament.
You live and reign with God
    the Father
in the unity of the Holy Spirit,
one God, forever and ever.
Amen.

✦ *Even now, says the LORD, return to me with your whole heart; for I am gracious and merciful.*

✦ *Be merciful, O Lord.*

PSALM 51 page 409

READING Matthew 4:1–4

At the time Jesus was led by the Spirit into the desert to be tempted by the devil. He fasted for forty days and forty nights, and afterwards he was hungry. The tempter approached and said to him, "If you are the Son of God, command that these stones become loaves of bread." He said in reply, "It is written: / One does not live by bread alone, / but by every word that comes forth / from the mouth of God."

REFLECTION

What are you tempted by? The lure of a little more money? Infidelity? Gossip? Grudges? Blaming others? Depression? We cannot ignore or pretend temptations do not exist. We must be honest with ourselves and try to understand why we have particular weaknesses. We also need to be actively involved in growing in our faith—through study, community support, prayer, and/or mentors. Let us give ourselves completely to the Son of God.

PRAYERS others may be added

Grateful for the providence of our God, we pray:

◆ Make us firm in faith.

For the Church to return to God in every way and at every level, we pray: ◆
For international courts and peace and reconciliation tribunals, that justice may be done and forgiveness begin, we pray: ◆ *For those tempted by addictions to gambling, pornography, drugs, and deception, that denial may end and restitution begin, we pray:* ◆ *For those who have died drawn more to evil than to good, that they may be open to God's call, even after death, we pray:* ◆

Our Father . . .

Lord Jesus,
you resisted temptation by
    faithfulness to the Father.
Walk with us when we are distracted
    by and attracted to sinful ways.
Help us return to you on the path of
    goodness and truth;
show us the happiness you offer
    in salvation;
and help us to say "yes" again and
    again to your life-giving love.
You live and reign with God
    the Father
in the unity of the Holy Spirit,
one God, forever and ever.
Amen.

✦ *Be merciful, O Lord.*

✛ *Be merciful, O Lord.*

PSALM 51   *page 409*

READING   *Leviticus 19:1–2, 11–18*

The LORD said to Moses, "Speak to the whole assembly of the children of Israel and tell them: Be holy, for I, the LORD, your God, am holy.

"You shall not steal. You shall not lie or speak falsely to one another. You shall not swear falsely by my name, thus profaning the name of your God. I am the LORD.

"You shall not defraud or rob your neighbor. You shall not withhold overnight the wages of your day laborer. You shall not curse the deaf, or put a stumbling block in front of the blind, but you shall fear your God. I am the LORD.

"You shall not act dishonestly in rendering judgment. Show neither partiality to the weak nor deference to the mighty, but judge your fellow men justly. You shall not go about spreading slander among your kin; nor shall you stand by idly when your neighbor's life is at stake. I am the LORD.

"You shall not bear hatred for your brother in your heart. Though you may have to reprove him, do not incur sin because of him. Take no revenge and cherish no grudge against your fellow countrymen. You shall love your neighbor as yourself. I am the LORD."

REFLECTION

"Nor shall you stand by idly when your neighbor's life is at stake." The lack of doing something for those who are hungry, thirsty, alone, or in need is a sin of omission. We cannot say that we did not do anything to hurt the victims of the sex trade in Asia, the war casualties in the Middle East, the AIDS orphans in Africa, the sweatshop laborers in Latin America. When we ignore those in need, we are ignoring Jesus.

PRAYERS   *others may be added*

The Lord leads us to holiness,
and so we pray:

◆ Help us act with justice, O Lord.

For the Church, that she may be a model of assistance and support for those in need and those searching for a way to help, we pray: ◆ *For the United Nations and its efforts to provide assistance and aid, that countries may continue to come together to alleviate suffering in parts of the world experiencing crisis and chaos, we pray:* ◆ *For the forgotten ones of all nations, the elderly, children, and the imprisoned, that their plight may be known and supplies may reach them, we pray:* ◆

Our Father . . .

O most holy God,
open our eyes to the many
who are hungry in our world, locally
    and globally.
We ask this through Christ our Lord.
Amen.

✛ *Be merciful, O Lord.*

✦ *I am the resurrection and the life, says the Lord; whoever believes in me will never die.*

PSALM 130 *page 418*

READING *Matthew 6:7–15*

Jesus said to his disciples: "In praying, do not babble like the pagans, who think that they will be heard because of their many words. Do not be like them. Your Father knows what you need before you ask him.

"This is how you are to pray:

Our Father who art in heaven, / hallowed be thy name, / thy Kingdom come, / thy will be done, / on earth as it is in heaven. / Give us this day our daily bread; / and forgive us our trespasses, / as we forgive those who trespass against us; / and lead us not into temptation, / but deliver us from evil.

"If you forgive men their transgressions, your heavenly Father will forgive you. But if you do not forgive men, neither will your Father forgive your transgressions."

REFLECTION

With so many elements to the Lord's Prayer, it can be hard to know how to pray "correctly." The key comes at the end of Jesus' explanation: we are to forgive others or God will not respond to us. Our prayer must be transformative. If it is just words or if we expect God to do all the work, it is ineffective. Authentic prayer changes us—our attitudes, our expectations, our behavior.

PRAYERS *others may be added*

With the Holy Spirit as our guide, we pray:

◆ Forgive us as we forgive others.

That our leaders in the Church model for us prayers of praise, petition, submission, and transformation, we pray: ◆ *That the will of God be done throughout the earth, we pray:* ◆ *That the daily bread necessary for all is plentiful, we pray:* ◆ *That forgiveness defines our relationships at home, at work, and in Church, we pray:* ◆

Our Father . . .

Lord Jesus, our teacher,
you make the way to the Father clear
   to us.
Be with us as we continue to learn
   to pray,
transform our hearts that we may
   trust in him,
and love one another as you did.
You live and reign with God
   the Father
in the unity of the Holy Spirit,
one God, forever and ever.
Amen.

✦ *I am the resurrection and the life, says the Lord; whoever believes in me will never die.*

✦ *Even now, says the LORD, return to me with your whole heart; for I am gracious and merciful.*

PSALM 138
page 419

READING
Luke 11:29–32

While still more people gathered in the crowd Jesus said to them, "This generation is an evil generation; it seeks a sign, but no sign will be given it, except the sign of Jonah. Just as Jonah became a sign to the Ninevites, so will the Son of Man be to this generation. At the judgment the queen of the south will rise with the men of this generation and she will condemn them, because she came from the ends of the earth to hear the wisdom of Solomon, and there is something greater than Solomon here. At the judgment the men of Nineveh will arise with this generation and condemn it, because at the preaching of Jonah they repented, and there is something greater than Jonah here."

REFLECTION

Sometimes we say, "I'm waiting for a sign." We may speak in jest, but if not, we need to stop waiting. Our God has given us signs throughout history, and in Jesus, the fullness of revelation. When Jesus laid down his very life for us with love, this action contained all the wisdom, explanation, and direction we would ever need. If we doubt or struggle in our faith, we can return to the story of God's people and to the moment of the Crucifixion and Resurrection in prayer, study, and action.

PRAYERS
others may be added

Following in the steps of our ancestors in faith, we pray:

◆ Show us again the sign of Jesus.

For the Pope, Bishops, and clergy, that they may they show us the path of repentance, we pray: ◆ *For nations in desperate need of change and a return to God's ways, we pray:* ◆ *For those waiting to change their lives, that they may see Jesus as the fullness of God's revelation, we pray:* ◆ *For this community, that we continue our journey of repentance this Lent with eyes fixed upon the sign of the cross, we pray:* ◆

Our Father . . .

O merciful God,
you forgave the Ninevites when they
 repented and returned to you.
Open wide your mercy to us and to
 all our generation,
for we so desperately need your
 loving forgiveness.
Help us cast out violence, greed,
 and selfishness,
that we may live peacefully,
 generously, and in unity.
Grant this through Christ our Lord.
Amen.

✦ *Even now, says the LORD, return to me with your whole heart; for I am gracious and merciful.*

✛ *The Lord is gracious and merciful.*

PSALM 138 *page 419*

READING *Matthew 7:7–12*

Jesus said to his disciples: "Ask and it will be given to you; seek and you will find; knock and the door will be opened to you. For everyone who asks, receives; and the one who seeks, finds; and to the one who knocks, the door will be opened. Which one of you would hand his son a stone when he asked for a loaf of bread, or a snake when he asks for a fish? If you, who are wicked, know how to give good things to your children, how much more will your heavenly Father give good things to those who ask him.

"Do to others whatever you would have them do to you. This is the law and the prophets."

REFLECTION

God's goodness overwhelms us. Think of the many times God has blessed you with what you dreamed of—more than what you asked for—or a surprise beyond your imagination. Perhaps the gift of your spouse, a long marriage, surviving a tragedy, the miracle of a child, or an opportunity that changed your life comes to mind. When we are attentive to prayer and to God's movement in our lives, gratitude is the prevalent feeling.

PRAYERS *others may be added*

With raised hearts, we pray:

◆ We thank you, heavenly Father.

For our Pope, Bishops, clergy, religious, and lay ministers and the unique gifts they bring to the life of the Church, we pray: ◆ *For wise visionaries and bold peacemakers in leadership positions of all nations, we pray:* ◆ *For those with disabilities, illnesses, and burdens who have overcome obstacles through faith, we pray:* ◆ *For the founders, supporters, and new members of our parish, we pray:* ◆

Our Father . . .

God of ages past,
you have been faithful to all who call
    upon you.
We praise you for your goodness
    and mercy
and give thanks for your love and
    generosity.
You are holy!
You are mighty!
You are our God!
Strengthen and guide us as we live as
    your disciples.
We ask this through our Lord Jesus
    Christ, your Son,
who lives and reigns with you
in the unity of the Holy Spirit,
one God, forever and ever.
Amen.

✛ *The Lord is gracious and merciful.*

✤ *Commit your life to the Lord.*

PSALM 103 page 415

READING Matthew 5:20–24

Jesus said to his disciples: "I tell you, unless your righteousness surpasses that of the scribes and Pharisees, you will not enter into the Kingdom of heaven.

"You have heard that it was said to your ancestors,/*You shall not kill; and whoever kills will be liable to judgment./* But I say to you, whoever is angry with his brother will be liable to judgment, and whoever says to his brother, *Raqa*, will be answerable to the Sanhedrin, and whoever says, 'You fool,' will be liable to fiery Gehenna. Therefore, if you bring your gift to the altar, and there recall that your brother has anything against you, leave your gift there at the altar, go first and be reconciled with your brother, and then come and offer your gift."

REFLECTION

Life is short. We cannot put off mending the broken relationships in our lives. If we sense the time of judgment coming, we will be prompted to ask for and grant forgiveness. If there is someone against whom we are holding a grudge, or someone we have hurt, Lent is the time to make amends. Make a call; send a note; plan to get together for lunch. Nothing is too big or too small to ignore. God has promised us forgiveness; we need only ask.

PRAYERS others may be added

As sinners, we come before God:

◆ Lord, unite us in you.

For dialogue between all those in the Church who are angry with one another, or distrust the faith of the other, we pray: ◆ *For Godspeed and peacemaking skills for ambassadors and mediators between governments, we pray:* ◆ *For effective working relationships between unions and corporations that protect the rights and needs of all, we pray:* ◆ *For openness and civility between cliques and groups in our community, we pray:* ◆

Our Father . . .

Prince of Peace,
in you the lion and the lamb lie
    down together.
You came to reconcile all of
    humanity.
May your Word work among us,
bring forth peaceful dialogue,
    reconciliation,
and new beginnings.
You live and reign with God
    the Father
in the unity of the Holy Spirit,
one God, forever and ever.
Amen.

✤ *Commit your life to the Lord.*

✦ *Commit your life to the Lord and he will help you.*

PSALM 40 *page 407*

READING *Matthew 1:18–21, 24a*

Now this is how the birth of Jesus Christ came about. When his mother Mary was betrothed to Joseph, but before they lived together, she was found with child through the Holy Spirit. Joseph her husband, since he was a righteous man, yet unwilling to expose her to shame, decided to divorce her quietly. Such was his intention when, behold, the angel of the Lord appeared to him in a dream and said, "Joseph, son of David, do not be afraid to take Mary your wife into your home. For it is through the Holy Spirit that this child has been conceived in her. She will bear a son and you are to name him Jesus, because he will save his people from their sins." When Joseph awoke, he did as the angel of the Lord had commanded him and took his wife into his home.

REFLECTION

Surely Joseph was surprised at his role in the plan of salvation. Are we, too, surprised at our role? Do we try to respectfully decline? Does God offer us uncomfortably bold opportunities to serve? Joseph can be our model and inspiration at accepting our responsibilities in the plan of salvation. We can enter situations fraught with danger and turmoil confident that Jesus' earthly father has walked before us.

PRAYERS *others may be added*

Allowing God to surprise us, we pray:

◆ Lead us, O Lord.

For our pastors, that they may bravely say "yes" to the challenges God brings before them, we pray: ◆ *For our legislators, that they may courageously rise to the new and uncharted battles before them to protect the common good, we pray:* ◆ *For those with disabilities, that the Church may call them forward to teach us all, we pray:* ◆ *For our local community, that we may see how our actions transform lives around us every day, we pray:* ◆

Our Father . . .

Almighty God,
your plan of salvation history has
    been laid out through time.
Your sons and daughters in every age
    have accepted your call
to bring forth the revelation of
    your love.
May we, too, cooperate in your work
    in the world
by our "yes" to all that you ask of us.
May St. Joseph be our model:
a worker and father who listened to
    your voice in his heart.
We ask this through Christ our Lord.
Amen.

✦ *Commit your life to the Lord and he will help you.*

✠ *Be merciful, O Lord.*

PSALM 51 page 409

READING Matthew 17:1–5

Jesus took Peter, James, and John his brother, and led them up a high mountain by themselves. And he was transfigured before them; his face shone like the sun and his clothes became white as light. And behold, Moses and Elijah appeared to them, conversing with him. Then Peter said to Jesus in reply, "Lord, it is good that we are here. If you wish, I will make three tents here, one for you, one for Moses, and one for Elijah." While he was still speaking, behold, a bright cloud cast a shadow over them, then from the cloud came a voice that said, "This is my beloved Son, with whom I am well pleased; listen to him."

REFLECTION

Today's reading is full of tangible details: the height of a mountain, dazzling light, the shadow of a cloud, a voice from heaven, the disciples lying on the ground, and the touch of Jesus. The disciples experienced Jesus with their human senses. Our Catholic faith engages our senses as well, believing that we, too, experience him through human means. We smell incense, taste bread and wine, reach out and touch our brothers and sisters in the sign of peace, and feel water every time we renew our Baptism. This Lent, be aware of experiencing Jesus through all your senses.

PRAYERS others may be added

Awed by our God permeating every aspect of our lives, we pray:

◆ Be present in each experience of life today, Jesus.

For the Roman Catholic Church, that she continues to promote a sacramental way of life in which we taste, touch, and hear the presence of the Lord, we pray: ◆
For the earth: its land, water, wind and fire, which make up the life in which we experience God, we pray: ◆ *For our places of worship, that we tend to their sights, sounds and smells, so as to enhance our experience of prayer, we pray:* ◆ *For those who have never had or have lost one of their senses, that their life may be enriched in other ways, through God's grace, we pray:* ◆

Our Father . . .

Lord Jesus,
Son of God and Son of Man,
help us to believe in you,
and to bring the hope of transformation to this world.
May your Holy Spirit infuse our daily living in its most concrete elements, leading all to you.
You live and reign with God the Father
in the unity of the Holy Spirit,
one God, forever and ever.
Amen.

✠ *Be merciful, O Lord.*

✝ *Even now, says the LORD, return to me with your whole heart; for I am gracious and merciful.*

PSALM 103   page 415

READING   Luke 6:36–38

Jesus said to his disciples: "Be merciful, just as your Father is merciful.

"Stop judging and you will not be condemned. Stop condemning and you will not be condemned. Forgive and you will be forgiven. Give and gifts will be given to you; a good measure, packed together, shaken down, and overflowing, will be poured into your lap. For the measure with which you measure will in return be measured out to you."

REFLECTION

Stop judging. How? How can I look at people and not judge? I must try to have the mind of God. I must see them each as a child of God. I must take time to pray for them, to offer their intentions, to love them. And then when I see them, I will be moved with compassion and not spend needless time trying to "figure them out," or worrying about what they have or have not done.

PRAYERS   *others may be added*

Giving thanks for God's mercy, we pray:

◆ Make us merciful, O Lord.

That all Christians may be known by their mercy, not their judgment, we pray: ◆ *That judges, employers, and all who hold power over others do not condemn, but forgive, we pray:* ◆ *That our prison system may become a place of rehabilitation, we pray:* ◆ *That our petty nature gives way to loving compassion this Lent, we pray:* ◆

Our Father . . .

Merciful Father,
you show us unconditional,
    forgiving love.
May we, in return, show mercy and
    compassion to all others.
Forgive us when we forget your
    abundant grace.
Grant this through Christ our Lord.
Amen.

✝ *Even now, says the LORD, return to me with your whole heart; for I am gracious and merciful.*

✠ *The Lord is gracious and merciful.*

PSALM 34 *page 405*

READING *Matthew 23:1–12*

Jesus spoke to the crowds and to his disciples, saying, "The scribes and the Pharisees have taken their seat on the chair of Moses. Therefore, do and observe all things whatsoever they tell you, but do not follow their example. For they preach but they do not practice. They tie up heavy burdens hard to carry and lay them on people's shoulders, but they will not lift a finger to move them. All their works are performed to be seen. They widen their phylacteries and lengthen their tassels. They love places of honor at banquets, seats of honor in synagogues, greetings in marketplaces, and the salutation 'Rabbi.' As for you, do not be called 'Rabbi.' You have but one teacher, and you are all brothers. Call no one on earth your father; you have but one Father in heaven. Do not be called 'Master'; you have but one master, the Christ. The greatest among you must be your servant. Whoever exalts himself will be humbled; but whoever humbles himself will be exalted."

REFLECTION

We can become very caught up in pointing fingers at leaders and "role models" who do not live up to standards. We may be looking for or waiting for a "perfect" leader at work, at home, or in politics. The truth is, none of us is perfect. We can still learn from our elders and authority figures, even if their behavior is humanly flawed. For we, too, are imperfect. As we humble ourselves and strive to follow Christ, we then set an example for all who follow us, even if we "mess up."

PRAYERS *others may be added*

Humbled by Christ's love, we pray:

◆ Be in our words and actions, Lord.

For all ordained and lay ministers of the Church, we pray: ◆ *For all heads of state, we pray:* ◆ *For all who give honor to God, we pray:* ◆ *For all of us when we are tempted by arrogance, we pray:* ◆

Our Father . . .

Lord Jesus Christ,
we model our lives after you.
Help us to serve in humility,
to repent when we have strayed,
and to live our faith in the best
   way possible.
You live and reign with God
   the Father
in the unity of the Holy Spirit,
one God, forever and ever.
Amen.

✠ *The Lord is gracious and merciful.*

✦ *Behold, now is a very acceptable time; behold, now is the day of salvation.*

PSALM 103 *page 415*

READING *Matthew 20:25–28*

Jesus summoned [his disciples] and said, "You know that the rulers of the Gentiles lord it over them, and the great ones make their authority over them felt. But it shall not be so among you. Rather, whoever wishes to be great among you shall be your servant; whoever wishes to be first among you shall be your slave. Just so, the Son of Man did not come to be served but to serve and to give his life as a ransom for many."

REFLECTION

Our communities of faith are called to be examples of servant leadership, equal shares in responsibility and power, and loving service to others. Do we do this? Do we work to overcome boundaries of income, status, gender, and age in our parishes? Do we greet one another warmly no matter who we are, and do welcome each to take an important role? When we do, we show the world a new model of effectiveness—and even more, we reveal the kingdom of God.

PRAYERS *others may be added*

Longing for wisdom, we pray:

◆ May God's reign be revealed.

That the Church may embody Christ who laid down his life for others, we pray: ◆ *That communities all over the world work together to help those in need, we pray:* ◆ *That our civic community may open its doors of commerce and success to people of all backgrounds, we pray:* ◆ *That our parish community may find new ways to offer hospitality to longtime members as well as inquiring faces, we pray:* ◆

Our Father . . .

Lord Jesus, Son of God,
you came and showed us a radically
    new way of love and sacrifice.
May we continue to lay down our
    time, talent, and treasure for the
    good of others.
May your Holy Spirit guide us as we
    prayerfully respond to your
    commands.
We look forward to the coming of the
    kingdom of God,
where you live and reign forever
    and ever.
Amen.

✦ *Behold, now is a very acceptable time; behold, now is the day of salvation.*

✦ *Be merciful, O Lord.*

PSALM 51   *page 409*

READING   *Luke 16:19–26*

Jesus said to the Pharisees: "There was a rich man who dressed in purple garments and fine linen and dined sumptuously each day. And lying at his door was a poor man named Lazarus, covered with sores, who would gladly have eaten his fill of the scraps that fell from the rich man's table. Dogs even used to come and lick his sores. When the poor man died, he was carried away by angels to the bosom of Abraham. The rich man also died and was buried, and from the netherworld, where he was in torment, he raised his eyes and saw Abraham far off and Lazarus at his side. And he cried out, 'Father Abraham, have pity on me. Send Lazarus to dip the tip of his finger in water and cool my tongue, for I am suffering torment in these flames.' Abraham replied, 'My child, remember that you received what was good during your lifetime while Lazarus likewise received what was bad; but now he is comforted here, whereas you are tormented. Moreover, between us and you a great chasm is established to prevent anyone from crossing who might wish to go from our side to yours or from your side to ours.'"

REFLECTION

If we have gone this far in Lent without a sense of repentance or awareness of how we need to grow, surely this Gospel shames us. "Lazarus" is all around us—in the developing countries of the world and even in our own country. This is the reading that keeps us up at night. There is no easy answer for us, the rich—rich in education, power, possessions, and wealth. How can we repent for our sin?

PRAYERS   *others may be added*

With deep gratitude, we pray:

◆ Lord, hear our prayer.

For the gift of our Catholic faith passed on to us by our families, our schools, and our Church leaders, we pray: ◆ *For the gift of the freedom we enjoy due to the sacrifices of our founders, our civil leaders, and our military, we pray:* ◆ *For the gift of education we have received from countless teachers, administrators, and benefactors, we pray:* ◆

Our Father . . .

Lord Jesus,
help us to repent for the times we
    have not acknowledged
or shared our rich blessings.
You live and reign with God
    the Father
in the unity of the Holy Spirit,
one God, forever and ever.
Amen.

✦ *Be merciful, O Lord.*

✠ *Commit your life to the Lord.*

CANTICLE
page 422

READING
Luke 1:26–33

The angel Gabriel was sent from God to a town of Galilee called Nazareth, to a virgin betrothed to a man named Joseph, of the house of David, and the virgin's name was Mary. And coming to her, he said, "Hail, full of grace! The Lord is with you." But she was greatly troubled at what was said and pondered what sort of greeting this might be. Then the angel said to her, "Do not be afraid, Mary, for you have found favor with God. Behold, you will conceive in your womb and bear a son, and you shall name him Jesus. He will be great and will be called Son of the Most High, and the Lord God will give him the throne of David his father, and he will rule over the house of Jacob forever, and of his Kingdom there will be no end."

REFLECTION

This sign of hope and God's love interrupts our season of repentance with the promise of redemption. When we despair that there is no way we can reverse our sinful ways, God reminds us of his loving plan. A Savior, who will sacrifice his life for our selfish choices, gives us the chance of eternal life with God. The miracle of the Annunciation draws us forward toward the miracle of the Resurrection.

PRAYERS
others may be added

Buoyed by hope, we have the courage to pray:

◆ Lord, fill us with hope.

For all the faithful who rely on Mary for strength and comfort, that they may feel her presence and be called forth by her "yes," we pray: ◆ *For all devout women from humble means, that they may hear God's call to be instruments of his saving work, we pray:* ◆ *For all religious orders who honor Mary as their inspiration, that this solemnity will renew them and invigorate their important ministries, we pray:* ◆

Our Father . . .

Lord Jesus,
your mother carried you into
    this world,
that we might not despair,
but rather find hope and life in you.
May she carry us until we burst forth,
proclaiming the Good News.
You live and reign with God
    the Father
in the unity of the Holy Spirit,
one God, forever and ever.
Amen.

✠ *Commit your life to the Lord.*

✛ *Be merciful, O Lord.*

PSALM 103   page 415

READING   Luke 15:11a, 13b, 14a, 14c, 20a, 20f – 22a, 23b – 24, 25, 28, 29, 31–31

[Jesus said:] "A man had two sons . . . the younger son collected all his belongings and set off to a distant country where he squandered his inheritance on a life of dissipation. When he had freely spent everything. . . he found himself in dire need. . . . Coming to his senses. . . he got up and went back to his father. While he was still a long way off, his father. . . ran to his son, embraced him, and kissed him. His son said to him, 'Father, I have sinned against heaven and against you; I no longer deserve to be called your son.' But his father ordered his servants . . . 'let us celebrate with a feast, because this son of mine was dead, and has come to life again; he was lost, and has been found.' . . . Now the older son had been out in the field and, on his way back, as he neared the house, he heard the sound of music and dancing. . . He became angry. . . He said to his father in reply, 'Look, all these years I served you and not once did I disobey your orders; yet you never gave me even a young goat to feast on with my friends. . . .' [His father] said to him, 'My son, you are here with me always; everything I have is yours. But now we must celebrate and rejoice, because your brother was dead and has come to life again; he was lost and has been found.' "

REFLECTION

Whether we identify with the elder or younger son, don't we long to be embraced by our God? Don't we yearn to hear that we are loved, forgiven, and accepted as we are? Today we rest in the embrace of God. We hear God telling us that we are loved and precious and always welcome in his house.

PRAYERS   *others may be added*

Wrapped in God's love, we pray:

◆ May we place our trust in you, Lord.

That Christians who have lost their way may return home to the community of faith, we pray: ◆ *That those who lead and are weary find renewal at the banquet of the Lord, we pray:* ◆
That sons and daughters of God who have squandered their gifts hear their loving Father calling them home, we pray: ◆ *That all who labor for Christ may be nurtured and comforted by God, we pray:* ◆

Our Father . . .

Merciful God,
you shepherd both your followers and
    those who stray.
May we who sin recognize your
    endless love for us
and make a return to you.
Grant this, Christ our Lord.
Amen.

✛ *Be merciful, O Lord.*

✦ *Behold, now is a very acceptable time; behold, now is the day of salvation.*

PSALM 138 page 419

READING John 4:6–10

Jesus, tired from his journey, sat down there at the well. It was about noon.

A woman of Samaria came to draw water. Jesus said to her, "Give me a drink." His disciples had gone into the town to buy food. The Samaritan woman said to him, "How can you, a Jew, ask me, a Samaritan woman, for a drink?" . . . Jesus answered and said to her, "If you knew the gift of God and who is saying to you, 'Give me a drink,' you would have asked him and he would have given you living water."

REFLECTION

Our faith must be our own—not that of our parents, our school teachers, nor even that of our pastor. When we are face to face with Jesus, as was the Samaritan woman, we must be able to ask him our questions, open our hearts for him to see, and affirm who he is in our own words. When he responds, affirming our faith, what great joy will fill us!

PRAYERS others may be added

Standing face to face with Jesus, we pray:

◆ We declare our faith in you, O Lord.

For those teachers and pastors who lead others to Jesus, opening the door to a personal profession of faith, we pray: ◆ *For philosophers and seekers who raise questions and pursue truth in the journey of faith, we pray:* ◆ *For those who have not heard the story of salvation, we pray:* ◆ *For every personal experience of seeing, hearing, and touching Jesus, we pray:* ◆

Our Father . . .

Lord Jesus Christ,
you are our Savior and Lord.
We have known you in the Word and
    in the breaking of the bread,
and in the working of the Holy Spirit
    in our lives.
May we stand confidently in our
    relationship with you.
You live and reign with God
    the Father
in the unity of the Holy Spirit,
one God, forever and ever.
Amen.

✦ *Behold, now is a very acceptable time; behold, now is the day of salvation.*

✛ *Commit your life to the Lord.*

PSALM 51 *page 409*

READING *Luke 4:24–30*

[Jesus said:] "Amen, I say to you, no prophet is accepted in his own native place. Indeed, I tell you, there were many widows in Israel in the days of Elijah when the sky was closed for three and a half years and a severe famine spread over the entire land. It was to none of these that Elijah was sent, but only to a widow in Zarephath in the land of Sidon. Again, there were many lepers in Israel during the time of Elisha the prophet; yet not one of them was cleansed, but only Naaman the Syrian." When the people in the synagogue heard this, they were all filled with fury. They rose up, drove him out of the town, and led him to the brow of the hill on which their town had been built, to hurl him down headlong. But he passed through the midst of them and went away.

REFLECTION

We do not want to share "our Jesus." We want to hear his message when it fits our world. We want to limit him to the confines of our box. It is hard for us to think outside our culture, our traditions, our habits. Yet our Church is global, responding to the call to go out to all the world with the Good News. It is good for us to think about Jesus from the perspectives of many cultures and to learn more about Jesus being sent to all people.

PRAYERS *others may be added*

Opening our hearts to God's work throughout the world, we pray:

◆ Show us your face, O Lord.

For Bishops, priests, deacons, and all holy men and women, we pray: ◆ *For greater inter-cultural dialogue between the East and the West, we pray:* ◆ *For recognition and celebration of members of our faith community with different ethnicities, we pray:* ◆ *For opening of our minds to images of God and depictions of faith in Christianity from countries other than our own, we pray:* ◆

Our Father . . .

God of many nations, languages, and peoples,
your message began in Israel and has now reached the ends of the earth.
May our faith in you and our participation in the Church
bring us out of our limited perspectives
and open our eyes to the face of Jesus in all peoples.
We ask this through Christ our Lord. Amen.

✛ *Commit your life to the Lord.*

✦ *If today you hear his voice, harden not your hearts.*

PSALM 103 *page 415*

READING *Matthew 18:21–22*

Peter approached Jesus and said to him, "Lord, if my brother sins against me, how often must I forgive him? As many as seven times?" Jesus answered, "I say to you, not seven times but seventy-seven times."

REFLECTION

From whom are we withholding forgiveness or generosity of spirit? As we repent, we must look to those around us who have asked for a fresh start and receive them with reconciled hearts. Perhaps a teenager who has earned the right to be trusted again; perhaps a spouse who has taken steps to think of the other; perhaps a former convict looking for a rehabilitated life; perhaps a neighbor who has been too busy for us but now seeks friendship. Let us allow Jesus to support new beginnings by being instruments of forgiveness.

PRAYERS *others may be added*

With gentleness, we pray:

◆ Forgive us as we forgive others.

That all who seek a new beginning in their faith are welcomed by the people of God, we pray: ◆ *That all nations who sincerely seek negotiations are given a genuine fresh start, we pray:* ◆ *That all family members seeking to regain trust and love may be supported in their efforts, we pray:* ◆ *That our repentance and promises to change may be true from the depth of our hearts, we pray:* ◆

Our Father . . .

Loving God,
you have been patient with us so
    many times.
Thank you for your kindness
    and mercy.
May we shower your generous love on
    all those who seek forgiveness
    from us,
and may new beginnings be the mark
    of a faithful Christian.
We ask this through Christ our Lord.
Amen.

✦ *If today you hear his voice, harden not your hearts.*

✚ *I am the resurrection and the life, says the Lord; whoever believes in me will never die.*

PSALM 23   page 402

READING   Matthew 5:17–19

Jesus said to his disciples: "Do not think that I have come to abolish the law or the prophets. I have come not to abolish but to fulfill. Amen, I say to you, until heaven and earth pass away, not the smallest letter or the smallest part of a letter will pass from the law, until all things have taken place. Therefore, whoever breaks one of the least of these commandments and teaches others to do so will be called least in the Kingdom of heaven. But whoever obeys and teaches these commandments will be called greatest in the Kingdom of heaven."

REFLECTION

Unlike many of Christ's challenging sayings, here we find words of comfort. For the Jews, and for us, Christ assures that living a life following the laws and commandments of God does indeed bring us closer to God. Although Christ may challenge us by surpassing what we know and expect, he will not disregard our human efforts at following his teaching.

PRAYERS   others may be added

Challenged and comforted, we pray:

◆ Fulfill our hopes, Lord God.

For leaders of the Church who inspire and teach us about our faith, we pray: ◆ *For those who tirelessly follow their faith in places of persecution, we pray:* ◆ *For those who struggle, feeling they can never do enough in following Christ, we pray:* ◆ *For our parents and grandparents who showed us a life lived in faith, we pray:* ◆ *For each of us, that we may be strengthened in our efforts to live like Christ, we pray:* ◆ *For all who have died faithfully following the Lord, we pray:* ◆

Our Father . . .

Loving Father,
you sent your Son to call us to repentance
and to offer us eternal life.
When we are overwhelmed by the challenges and surprises in our life,
give us your love and your grace.
We ask this through our Lord Jesus Christ, your Son,
who lives and reigns with you in the unity of the Holy Spirit,
one God, forever and ever.
Amen.

✚ *I am the resurrection and the life, says the Lord; whoever believes in me will never die.*

✦ *If today you hear his voice, harden not your hearts.*

PSALM 51 *page 409*

READING *Luke 11:14–20*

Jesus was driving out a demon that was mute, and when the demon had gone out, the mute man spoke and the crowds were amazed. Some of them said, "By the power of Beelzebul, the prince of demons, he drives out demons." Others, to test him, asked him for a sign from heaven. But he knew their thoughts and said to them, "Every kingdom divided against itself will be laid waste and house will fall against house. And if Satan is divided against himself, how will his kingdom stand? For you say that it is by Beelzebul that I drive out demons. If I, then, drive out demons by Beelzebul, by whom do your own people drive them out? Therefore they will be your judges. But if it is by the finger of God that I drive it demons, then the Kingdom of God has come upon you."

REFLECTION

Do we realize how serious it is when we turn away from God? Do we recognize that our hard-heartedness is no small matter? We may think of indifference, selfishness, or laziness as "mild" sins, but Christ points out that our apathy is in fact a choice against him.

PRAYERS *others may be added*

Wanting to be with you, O God, we pray:

◆ Hold us close to you.

That Christians may turn away from indifference and apathy and choose to respond to God in daily life, we pray: ◆
That all those who ride the fence of agnosticism may choose Christ, we pray: ◆
That hearts hardened with anger, fear, and habit may soften, we pray: ◆
That we hold one another accountable to our commitment to discipleship, we pray: ◆

Our Father . . .

Sovereign God,
you see clearly those who choose to
    follow you
and those who have turned away.
You call each of us back to you,
to a life of love and service.
May our daily response to you be a
    joyful "yes!"
Grant this through Christ our Lord.
Amen.

✦ *If today you hear his voice, harden not your hearts.*

✦ *Be merciful, O Lord.*

PSALM 130   *page 418*

READING   *Mark 12:28–33*

One of the scribes, came to Jesus and asked him, "Which is the first of all the commandments?" Jesus replied, "The first is this:/*Hear, O Israel!/The Lord our God is Lord alone!/You shall love the Lord your God with all your heart, with all your soul,/with all your mind,/and with all your strength.* The second is this: *You shall love your neighbor as yourself./*There is no other commandment greater than these." The scribe said to him, "Well said, teacher. You are right in saying,/*He is One and there is no other than he./And to love him with all your heart,/with all your understanding,/ with all your strength, and to love your neighbor as yourself/* is worth more than all burnt offerings and sacrifices."

REFLECTION

How do you love God? Consider how you love another person. You spend time with that person, you learn more about him or her, you consider his or her needs and desires, you share joy and sorrow with him or her, you laugh and talk together, and you offer your love to the world together. Can you do these things with God? How will they be the same or different? Think of how you spend time with God. Consider what it feels like to collaborate in God's love and care for the world.

PRAYERS   *others may be added*

Loving you, O God, we pray:

◆ Lord, hear our prayer.

That the love the saints have for God be a model and inspiration for all the faithful, we pray: ◆ *That those from other nations may not be judged, persecuted, or discriminated, but treated lovingly as neighbor, we pray:* ◆ *That as people of faith, we mature in our love of God, we pray:* ◆ *That children who grow up not knowing the love of a parent may find true, unselfish love from another adult, we pray:* ◆ *That our love for our spouses, children, and friends may be enriched by and reflective of our love for God, we pray:* ◆

Our Father . . .

O Lord, our God,
you have been faithful to your people
     for all time.
Our love for you is our first priority.
May we be caught up in a total,
     committed, intoxicating love
     for you,
that, in loving you, we will be called
     forth to love others.
We ask this through Christ our Lord.
Amen.

✦ *Be merciful, O Lord.*

✠ *Even now, says the LORD, return to me with your whole heart; for I am gracious and merciful.*

PSALM 138 *page 419*

READING *Luke 18:9–14*

Jesus addressed this parable to those who were convinced of their own righteousness and despised everyone else. "Two people went up to the temple area to pray; one was a Pharisee and the other was a tax collector. The Pharisee took up his position and spoke this prayer to himself, 'O God, I thank you that I am not like the rest of humanity— greedy, dishonest, adulterous—or even like this tax collector. I fast twice a week, and I pay tithes on my whole income.' But the tax collector stood off at a distance and would not even raise his eyes to heaven but beat his breast and prayed, 'O God, be merciful to me a sinner.' I tell you, the latter went home justified, not the former; for everyone who exalts himself will be humbled, and the one who humbles himself will be exalted."

REFLECTION

God knows our needs. Do you know which message you need to hear? Consider your own heart and imagine the version of this parable Jesus might deliver to you. What kind of prayer do you make? From whose prayer could you learn? You may not be like the Pharisee or the tax collector. Ask God to show you what you need to grow closer to him.

PRAYERS *others may be added*

Humbly seeking God, we pray:

◆ Reveal to us your ways, O God.

For sincerity and humility of heart among our Church leaders, we pray: ◆ *For a bold conversion among the self-righteous, we pray:* ◆ *For confidence through God among the self-hating, we pray:* ◆ *For awareness of our own gifts and sins among our community, we pray:* ◆

Our Father . . .

Omniscient God,
you reward the lowly ones
and bring low the arrogant.
Show us where we truly stand
    before you.
Give us the courage to see our
    own sin
and thank you for the opportunity to
    return to you.
We ask this through Christ our Lord.
Amen.

✠ *Even now, says the LORD, return to me with your whole heart; for I am gracious and merciful.*

✦ *The Lord is gracious and merciful.*

PSALM 130 *page 418*

READING *John 9:1–3, 5–7*

As Jesus passed by he saw a man blind from birth. His disciples asked him, "Rabbi, who sinned, this man or his parents, that he was born blind?" Jesus answered, "Neither he nor his parents sinned; it is so that the works of God might be made visible through him." When he had said this, he spat on the ground and made clay with the saliva, and smeared the clay on his eyes, and said to him, "Go wash in the Pool of Siloam" — which means Sent. — So he went and washed, and came back able to see.

REFLECTION

In this scripture reading, Jesus gives the gift of sight—literally and figuratively—to an unlikely figure. A man born blind, shunned by the community, who is also quite young, is suddenly flush with insight into Jesus' identity. God does not only choose the likely, recognizable leaders to carry his message. Many of us who feel insignificant or incapable of being disciples are also called to believe, worship, and share the Good News of Jesus Christ.

PRAYERS *others may be added*

With eyes open in faith, we pray:

◆ Raise up the lowly.

For young people in the Church who have been given the vocation to serve, that they respond in joy, we pray: ◆ *For unlikely leaders to rise up in communities of poverty, war, and injustice, we pray:* ◆ *For hearers of God's Word who feel unworthy to be called, we pray:* ◆ *For sensitivity to those whom God may have given the Good News with which to instruct us, we pray:* ◆

Our Father . . .

Lord God,
you call the lowly, the blind, and the
    lame to serve you.
May we be inspired by their response
    and their wisdom
to listen to their words and follow you
    with our hearts.
We ask this through Christ our Lord.
Amen.

✦ *The Lord is gracious and merciful.*

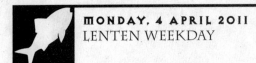

✠ *I am the resurrection and the life, says the Lord; whoever believes in me will never die.*

PSALM 23   page 402

READING   John 4:46–53

[Jesus] returned to Cana in Galilee, where he had made the water wine. Now there was a royal official whose son was ill in Capernaum. When he heard that Jesus had arrived in Galilee from Judea, he went to him and asked him to come down and heal his son, who was near death. Jesus said to him, "Unless you people see signs and wonders, you will not believe." The royal official said to him, "Sir, come down before my child dies." Jesus said to him, "You may go; your son will live." The man believed what Jesus said to him and left. While the man was on his way back, his slaves met him and told him that his boy would live. He asked them when he began to recover. They told him, "The fever left him yesterday, about one in the afternoon." The father realized that just at that time Jesus had said to him, "Your son will live," and he and his whole household came to believe.

REFLECTION

God hears our prayers and cries for help. He does not turn a deaf ear or ask us to simply "suffer through." God is compassionate, longing for the day when the world is reconciled to him and there is no more crying. Be assured that God wants fullness of life for us and our loved ones.

PRAYERS   *others may be added*

Longing for wholeness, we pray:

◆ Lift us up, Lord.

For the body of Christ, the Church, tha she may be an instrument of healing and reconciliation, we pray: ◆ *For the abused, neglected, oppressed, and hungry of our world, that God may rescue, heal, and fill them, we pray:* ◆ *For those who endure chronic illness, that God may bring an end to their pain, we pray:* ◆ *For all people of faith who long for miracles, that God's kingdom may come, we pray:* ◆

Our Father . . .

Compassionate God,
you hear the groaning of the earth
and the pleas of your children
   who suffer.
You promise to be with us until the
   end of time,
when the little ones will be raised up
and peace will eternally reign.
May you sustain us until that
∶   joyful day.
Grant this through Christ our Lord.
Amen.

✠ *I am the resurrection and the life, says the Lord; whoever believes in me will never die.*

✦ *I am the resurrection and the life, says the Lord; whoever believes in me will never die.*

PSALM 138 page 419

READING John 5:2–9

Now there is in Jerusalem at the Sheep Gate a pool called in Hebrew Bethesda, with five porticoes. In these lay a large number of ill, blind, lame, and crippled. One man was there who had been ill for thirty-eight years. When Jesus saw him lying there and knew that he had been ill for a long time, he said to him, "Do you want to be well?" The sick man answered him, "Sir, I have no one to put me into the pool when the water is stirred up; while I am on my way, someone else gets down there before me." Jesus said to him, "Rise, take up your mat, and walk." Immediately the man became well, took up his mat, and walked.

REFLECTION

What would it mean for us to immediately become well? What healing can you imagine coursing through your body? What kind of mental, physical, and emotional wounds would disappear? What spiritual reconciliation would take place? Imagine yourself lying at the side of a pool of healing waters, waiting for Jesus.

PRAYERS *others may be added*

Asking for healing, we pray:

◆ Hear our cries, O Lord.

For the Pope, Bishops, and servants of the Church, that their physical, mental, and emotional wounds may be healed, we pray: ◆ *For the physical, emotional, and mental health of our civil leaders, we pray:* ◆ *For those too weak to reach out for help, that the pool of healing waters washes over them, we pray:* ◆ *For prayerful reflection on our need for Jesus and acceptance of his healing touch, we pray:* ◆

Our Father . . .

Healing God,
you make the lame walk, the blind
  see, and the deaf hear.
Touch us with your saving love and
  heal our wounds.
We ask this through Christ our Lord.
Amen.

✦ *I am the resurrection and the life, says the Lord; whoever believes in me will never die.*

✦ *The Lord is gracious and merciful.*

PSALM 138 *page 419*

READING *John 5:24–25*

[Jesus said,] "Amen, amen, I say to you, whoever hears my word and believes in the one who sent me has eternal life and will not come to condemnation, but has passed from death to life. Amen, amen, I say to you, the hour is coming and is now here when the dead will hear the voice of the Son of God, and those who hear will live."

REFLECTION

Our Christian faith holds that Father, Son, and Spirit are inextricably and inexplicably one God and yet three persons. If we find ourselves more drawn to or comfortable with our relationship with God the Father, the Creator, we may learn by realizing everything Jesus does is from the Father, and in this way, learn more about God. Conversely, if we are more connected with God the Son, Jesus, we may grow by deepening our understanding of what Jesus reveals about the Father/Creator. If we are moved by a sense of God as Holy Spirit, we can grow by focusing from time to time on the mystery of the Father and the Son. Reflection on the relationship between Father, Son, and Holy Spirit will strengthen our relationship with all.

PRAYERS *others may be added*

Seeking wisdom and understanding, we pray:

◆ Wisdom of God, lead us deeper into you.

For the holy Church, teacher of the mystery of God, we pray: ◆ *For fathers, mothers, artists, and innovators, that their creative drive begins with and returns to the one source of all, we pray:* ◆ *For preachers, storytellers, healers, and teachers, that their charisma and influence draws upon and walks with Jesus, we pray:* ◆ *For each of us, that this Lent we may grow in our understanding of our Trinitarian God—Father, Son and Spirit, we pray:* ◆

Our Father . . .

God our Father,
your Son came to us to reveal your
   plan of salvation.
He is in you and you are in him.
Your Spirit remains with us, uniting
   us forever with your love.
May we enter into the mystery of
   your relationship
and prayerfully respond to your
   one will.
We ask this through Christ our Lord.
Amen.

✦ *The Lord is gracious and merciful.*

✠ *Commit your life to the Lord and he will help you.*

PSALM 40 *page 407*

READING *Matthew 18:1–5*

The disciples approached Jesus and said, "Who is the greatest in the Kingdom of heaven?" He called a child over, placed it in their midst, and said, "Amen, I say to you, unless you turn and become like children, you will not enter the Kingdom of heaven. Whoever humbles himself like this child is the greatest in the Kingdom of heaven. And whoever receives one child such as this in my name receives me."

REFLECTION

St. John Baptist de la Salle was a reformer and champion of elementary schools, and especially of poor children's access to these schools. Take time today to learn a little more about Catholic, private, and public schools, and their most pressing needs today. Education is a right of all children, and we have a responsibility to support it. Let us be part of receiving God's children in the various ways we prioritize access to and excellence in education.

PRAYERS *others may be added*

In the spirit of Saint John Baptist de la Salle, we call to mind all children:

◆ Give us courage to do what is right.

For Catholic schools, that they may strive for academic excellence, accessibility to those in need, and ultimately, formation of students as followers of Christ, we pray: ◆ *For public schools, that legislators and administrators come together to offer the best possible education to all children, we pray:* ◆ *For private schools that respond to unique needs in the educational community, that their creativity may inspire others and their dedication to students may never waver, we pray:* ◆ *For schools and educators serving children with special needs, that the Holy Spirit may be at work in giving access to the basic human need to learn and grow, we pray:* ◆

Our Father . . .

Lord Jesus,
may our society and our Church
always recognize the unique value of
   our children.
You live and reign with God
   the Father
in the unity of the Holy Spirit,
one God, forever and ever.
Amen.

✠ *Commit your life to the Lord and he will help you.*

Optional memorial of St. John Baptist de la Salle, priest; Today's reading is from the memorial, Lectionary #549.

✦ *I will get up and go to my father and say to him: Father, I have sinned against heaven and against you.*

PSALM 103 page 415

READING John 7:25–30

Some of the inhabitants of Jerusalem said, "Is he not the one they are trying to kill? And look, he is speaking openly and they say nothing to him. Could the authorities have realized that he is the Christ? But we know where he is from. When the Christ comes, no one will know where he is from." So Jesus cried out in the temple area as he was teaching and said, "You know me and also know where I am from. Yet I did not come on my own, but the one who sent me, whom you do not know, is true. I know him, because I am from him, and he sent me." So they tried to arrest him, but no one laid a hand upon him, because his hour had not yet come.

REFLECTION

When do we attack the good—the presence of God—and try to deny it? Can we admit that sometimes we are faced with the truth and it makes us uncomfortable? That this good challenges us? Do we turn away and ignore it? Goodness might come in the words of a small child, or of a parent or close friend. It might be in the guilt we feel over our own sinful actions. Let us call upon God to save us from our fearful, cowardly ways.

PRAYERS *others may be added*

Turning toward truth, we pray:

◆ Lay bare our sins and the path back to you, O God.

For radical honesty among Christians, with each other, and in challenging the world, we pray: ◆ *For courage among elected officials, to root out corruption and serve with justice, we pray:* ◆ *For integrity among those tempted to ignore or deny sin and wrongdoing, we pray:* ◆ *For careful examination of guilt to determine whether it points to truth, we pray:* ◆

Our Father . . .

Lord Jesus, Prince of Truth,
you proclaimed the reign of God
in the light of day and in the dark
   of night.
May truth be our battle shield in the
   fight against sin and evil,
and may we have the courage to see
   our own sin
and our complicity in the sin
   of others.
Show us the way of repentance,
leading us back to the Father.
You live and reign with God
   the Father
in the unity of the Holy Spirit,
one God, forever and ever.
Amen.

✦ *I will get up and go to my father and say to him: Father, I have sinned against heaven and against you.*

✦ *If today you hear his voice, harden not your hearts.*

PSALM 138 *page 419*

READING *John 7:40–46*

Some in the crowd who heard these words of Jesus said, "This is truly the Prophet." Others said, "This is the Christ." But others said, "The Christ will not come from Galilee, will he? Does not scripture say that the Christ will be of David's family and come from Bethlehem, the village where David lived?" So a division occurred in the crowd because of him. Some of them even wanted to arrest him, but no one laid hands on him.

So the guards went to the chief priests and Pharisees, who asked them, "Why did you not bring him?" The guards answered, "Never before has anyone spoken like this man."

REFLECTION

We all can be blinded by prejudices and assumptions. We may jump to conclusions about families, neighbors, or people of different ages, cultures, or races. We need to see the face of Christ in every person, and ask ourselves what would surprise us the most to find out about that person, and then act accordingly.

PRAYERS *others may be added*

Unearthing our biases, we pray:

◆ Show us the image and likeness of God.

That Christians may show their love by seeing the face of Christ in every neighbor, we pray: ◆ *That partisanship and accusations in politics may be replaced by genuine collaboration, we pray:* ◆ *That those never given a chance at inclusion or success because of their appearance may be surprised by open minds and opportunities, we pray:* ◆ *That each of us may reach out to others of whom we have the lowest expectations, we pray:* ◆

Our Father . . .

Lord Jesus,
you came from Nazareth and humble beginnings
with a mission from God unlike any before you.
You call the poor and lowly to be your followers.
May we be surprised and delighted by your work in the world around us,
especially in those least likely to be recognized by society.
You live and reign with God the Father
in the unity of the Holy Spirit,
one God, forever and ever.
Amen.

✦ *If today you hear his voice, harden not your hearts.*

✝ *Behold, now is a very acceptable time; behold, now is the day of salvation.*

PSALM 23 — page 402

READING — John 11:17, 20–23

When Jesus arrived, he found that Lazarus had already been in the tomb for four days. Now Bethany was near Jerusalem, only about two miles away. And many of the Jews had come to Martha and Mary to comfort them about their brother. When Martha heard that Jesus was coming, she went to meet him; but Mary sat at home. Martha said to Jesus, "Lord, if you had been here, my brother would not have died. But even now I know that whatever you ask of God, God will give you." Jesus said to her, "Your brother will rise."

REFLECTION

Today Jesus calls us as well. Come out! Come out of your sadness! Come out of your fears! Come out of your self-defeat! Come out of your obsessions! Come out and into the Lord's arms! Rest in Jesus and start anew a life without death.

PRAYERS — others may be added

Rejoicing in God's healing mercy, we pray:

◆ Lead us into the light.

For Eucharistic rejoicing in the Church today and every day, we pray: ◆ *For signs and wonders to bring hope to cynics, we pray:* ◆ *For unreasonable joy and gratitude in hospitals, nursing homes, and places of mourning, we pray:* ◆ *For unshakable confidence in God when the world tries to defeat us, we pray:* ◆

Our Father . . .

Merciful God,
you know our pain and sadness.
You sent us your Son to give us hope.
May we hold fast to your promise of
    eternal life in you,
that today will be the day we leave
    behind our sins and brokenness
and walk in the marvelous light of
    the Lord.
We ask this through our Lord Jesus
    Christ, your Son,
who lives and reigns with you in the
    unity of the Holy Spirit,
one God, forever and ever.
Amen.

✝ *Behold, now is a very acceptable time; behold, now is the day of salvation.*

✢ *Even now, says the LORD, return to me with your whole heart; for I am gracious and merciful.*

PSALM 51   *page 409*

READING   *John 8:3–11*

The scribes and the Pharisees brought [to Jesus] a woman who had been caught in adultery and made her stand in the middle. They said to him, "Teacher, this woman was caught in the very act of committing adultery. Now in the law, Moses commanded us to stone such women. So what do you say?" They said this to test him, so that they could have some charge to bring against him. Jesus bent down and began to write on the ground with his finger. But when they continued asking him, he straightened up and said to them, "Let the one among you who is without sin be the first to throw a stone at her." Again he bent down and wrote on the ground. And in response, they went away one by one, beginning with the elders. So he was left along with the woman before him. Then Jesus straightened up and said to her, "Woman, where are they? Has no one condemned you?" She replied, "No one, sir." Jesus said, "Neither do I condemn you. Go, and from now on do not sin any more."

REFLECTION

God does not want us to be burdened by guilt and shame, thereby giving up our lives of light. We are not condemned for our sins; we are forgiven and challenged to start anew in our quest to follow Jesus. Today we place our sins in the hands of Jesus, allowing him to wash them away, leading us to a new beginning.

PRAYERS   *others may be added*

Ready to be transformed, we pray:

◆ Take away our sins, Lord, so we may follow you.

That the Church is guided by the Holy Spirit to ever-deeper faithfulness to her mission in the world, we pray: ◆ *That those who have been condemned in the court of public opinion may be given second chances, we pray:* ◆ *That those who have hurt family and friends may be prompted by efforts of reconciliation, we pray:* ◆ *That those burdened by sin may be lifted from their despair, we pray:* ◆

Our Father . . .

Forgiving God,
you forgive us our sins.
May we respond in gratitude
by promising our lives of faithfulness
    to you.
We ask this through Christ our Lord.
Amen.

✢ *Even now, says the LORD, return to me with your whole heart; for I am gracious and merciful.*

✦ *I am the resurrection and the life, says the Lord; whoever believes in me will never die.*

PSALM 138   page 419

READING   John 8:23–30

[Jesus said to the Pharisees:] "You belong to what is below, I belong to what is above. You belong to this world, but I do not belong to this world. That is why I told you that you will die in your sins. For if you do not believe that I AM, you will die in your sins." So they said to him, "Who are you?" Jesus said to them, "What I told you from the beginning. I have much to say about you in condemnation. But the one who sent me is true, and what I heard from him I tell the world." They did not realize that he was speaking to them of the Father. So Jesus said to them, "When you lift up the Son of Man, then you will realize that I AM, and that I do nothing on my own, but I say only what the Father taught me. The one who sent me is with me. He has not left me alone, because I always do what is pleasing to him." Because he spoke this way, many came to believe in him.

REFLECTION

It certainly was difficult for those surrounding Jesus, and it continues to be challenging today, to understand the relationship between the Son and the Father. Jesus tells us what we know about God, and yet we are still lacking in much understanding. Our hearts reach out in faith to trust in Jesus.

PRAYERS   *others may be added*

Awed by God, we pray:

◆ Give us faith that surpasses understanding.

That the Church's teachers convey a sense of the wideness and depth of God's love, we pray: ◆ *That the majesty of God and his works provides a humbling perspective to worldly leaders, we pray:* ◆ *That the mysteries of the faith are not a deterrent but an inspiration to skeptics, we pray:* ◆ *That our faith may be humbled, grateful, and intrigued by the greatness of God, we pray:* ◆

Our Father . . .

God the Father, Son, and Holy Spirit, you are the Alpha and the Omega, the beginning and the end. All time and all seasons belong to you. You inspire us with faith in your holy and enduring presence. May we rest in peace with you, grow in understanding of you; but even more, may we grow in faith, and live with you forever. We ask this through Christ our Lord. Amen.

✦ *I am the resurrection and the life, says the Lord; whoever believes in me will never die.*

✦ *I am the resurrection and the life, says the Lord; whoever believes in me will never die.*

PSALM 103   *page 415*

READING   *John 8:31–38*

Jesus then said to those Jews who believed in him, "If you remain in my word, you will truly be my disciples, and you will know the truth, and the truth will set you free." They answered him, "We are descendants of Abraham and have never been enslaved to anyone. How can you say, 'You will become free'?" Jesus answered them, "Amen, amen, I say to you, everyone who commits sin is a slave of sin. A slave does not remain in a household forever, but a son always remains. So if a son frees you, then you will truly be free. I know that you are descendants of Abraham. But you are trying to kill me, because my word has no room among you. I tell you what I have seen in the Father's presence; then do what you have heard from the Father."

REFLECTION

Freedom is when we are released from our tortured habits and tendencies. Freedom is when we allow God to lead us from our fixed frameworks of thinking and acting. Freedom is when we confess our inadequacies, inabilities, and fears, and allow him to take control. When we fully trust in God, we are free from how sin binds us.

PRAYERS   *others may be added*

Longing to be free, we pray:

◆ Help us to trust in you, O God.

For the Pope, Bishops, and all ministers of the Church, that their commitment to prayer allows them to serve in freedom, we pray: ◆ For all those living under oppressive regimes, that their faith may bring them inner freedom, we pray: ◆ For addicts, the controlling, and the fearful, that they may choose real freedom, we pray: ◆ For an increase in faith, so that we might grow in the freedom Christ offers us, we pray: ◆ For a sense of freedom in the time of death, we pray: ◆

Our Father . . .

Lord Jesus, Son of God,
your faithfulness to God despite
    suffering is a model for us.
The closer we follow you, the freer,
    by grace, we become.
Bring us to total freedom at the end
    of time.
Until then, show us how to trust
    in you.
You live and reign with God
    the Father
in the unity of the Holy Spirit,
one God, forever and ever.
Amen.

✦ *I am the resurrection and the life, says the Lord; whoever believes in me will never die.*

✦ *Behold, now is a very acceptable time; behold, now is the day of salvation.*

PSALM 130   page 418

READING   John 8:51–55a, 56–59

Jesus said to the Jews: "Amen, amen, I say to you, whoever keeps my word will never see death." So the Jews said to him, "Now we are sure that you are possessed. Abraham died, as did the prophets, yet you say, 'Whoever keeps my word will never taste death.' Are you greater than our father Abraham, who died? Or the prophets, who died? Who do you make yourself out to be?" Jesus answered, "If I glorify myself, my glory is worth nothing; but it is my Father who glorifies me, of whom you say, 'He is our God.' You do not know him, but I know him. Abraham your father rejoiced to see my day; he saw it and was glad." So the Jews said to him, "You are not yet fifty years old and you have seen Abraham?" Jesus said to them, "Amen, amen, I say to you, before Abraham came to be, I AM." So they picked up stones to throw at him; but Jesus hid and went out of the temple area.

REFLECTION

Jesus fulfills the Old Covenant. He surpasses anything Abraham's people could have hoped for. He is the New Covenant, the new promise from God to his people. How blessed are we by a god who fulfills his promises and offers us a future beyond our dreams.

PRAYERS   *others may be added*

With faith in God, we pray:

◆ Lord Jesus, lead us from promise to fulfillment.

For a continuation of God's promise that Abraham's descendants would be as numerous as the stars, we pray: ◆ *For the fulfillment of God's promise to lead all his people out of suffering, we pray:* ◆ *For a rejoicing in God's promise to give us a future full of hope, we pray:* ◆ *For confidence in God's promise to be with us until the end of time, we pray:* ◆

Our Father . . .

Lord God,
your Son Jesus showed us love,
fulfilling your promise of salvation.
May we be your sons and daughters,
and may your promises carry us in
   times of doubt,
and the time of fulfillment bring us
   great rejoicing.
We ask this through Christ our Lord.
Amen.

✦ *Behold, now is a very acceptable time; behold, now is the day of salvation.*

✦ *I am the resurrection and the life, says the Lord; whoever believes in me will never die.*

PSALM 138 · page 419

READING · *Jeremiah 20:10–13*

I hear the whisperings of many: / "Terror on every side! / Denounce! let us denounce him!" / All those who were my friends / are on the watch for any misstep of mine. / "Perhaps he will be trapped; then we can prevail, / and take our vengeance on him." / But the LORD is with me, like a mighty champion: / my persecutors will stumble, they will not triumph. / In their failure they will be put to utter shame, / to lasting, unforgettable confusion. / O LORD of hosts, you who test the just, / who probe mind and heart, / Let me witness the vengeance you take on them, / for to you I have entrusted my cause. / Sing to the LORD, / praise the LORD, / For he has rescued the life of the poor / from the power of the wicked!"

REFLECTION

Wouldn't it be wonderful to have a sports, political, or career "idol" or hero with you as you went about your daily tasks? This person would surely inspire you, raise you to new heights of achievement, and be an exciting companion. Christ offers to be that hero if we make our task to live the Gospel. Think of how much stronger and more confident you will be with Christ at your side.

PRAYERS · *others may be added*

Imagining our undefeatable Lord at our side, we pray:

◆ Be with us, Lord.

That every Christian may feel the daily presence of Christ, our friend and brother, we pray: ◆ *That professionals in their fields may look to Christ for their ultimate inspiration, we pray:* ◆ *That youths who look up to heroes may find models of integrity, we pray:* ◆ *That we may find support and companionship in one another as we do the difficult work of bringing about the kingdom, we pray:* ◆

Our Father . . .

Jesus Christ, our Redeemer,
you know the tasks and challenges
that face us in daily life.
You walk with us, especially when we
are weak.
May we know you in prayer,
community, and in the sacraments
that fortify us.
You live and reign with God
the Father
in the unity of the Holy Spirit,
one God, forever and ever.
Amen.

✦ *I am the resurrection and the life, says the Lord; whoever believes in me will never die.*

✢ *Be merciful, O Lord.*

PSALM 51 *page 409*

READING *John 11:46–53*

Some of [the Jews] went to the Pharisees and told them what Jesus had done. So the chief priests and the Pharisees convened the Sanhedrin and said, "What are we going to do? This man is performing many signs. If we leave him alone, all will believe in him, and the Romans will come and take away both our land and our nation." But one of them, Caiaphas, who was high priest that year, said to them, "You know nothing, nor do you consider that it is better for you that one man should die instead of the people, so that the whole nation may not perish." He did not say this on his own, but since he was high priest for that year, he prophesied that Jesus was going to die for the nation, and not only for the nation, but also to gather into one the dispersed children of God. So from that day on they planned to kill him.

REFLECTION

Even Caiaphas, the high priest, sees that Jesus has the potential to bring unity among all God's children by his life and death. What is so threatening about this unity? It has the potential to overcome corrupt power with good. We still know and do not know the potential force for good that we can be as Christians. We continue to divide among ourselves and therefore diminish Jesus' message and Holy Spirit.

PRAYERS *others may be added*

Desiring unity, we pray:

◆ Lord, hear our prayer.

For progress in ecumenical dialogue, we pray: ◆ *For advances in international discussions for peace, we pray:* ◆ *For the use of peaceful words and resolutions instead of weapons to resolve conflict, we pray:* ◆ *For reconciliation among estranged friends and family, we pray:* ◆

Our Father . . .

Prince of Peace,
may your love for all God's children
inspire us to work for the
     common good.
There is a power held in the bonds
     of Christianity
that remains yet unseen.
Show us how to abandon divisions
     and work together
toward the reign of God.
You live and reign with God
     the Father
in the unity of the Holy Spirit,
one God, forever and ever.
Amen.

✢ *Be merciful, O Lord.*

✦ *Be merciful, O Lord.*

PSALM 22 *page 401*

READING *Matthew 21:1–11*

When Jesus and the disciples drew near Jerusalem and came to Bethphage on the Mount of Olives, Jesus sent two disciples, saying to them, "Go into the village opposite you, and immediately you will find an ass tethered, and a colt with her. Untie them and bring them here to me. And if anyone should say anything to you, reply, 'The master has need of them.' Then he will send them at once." This happened so that what had been spoken through the prophet might be fulfilled: / *Say to daughter Zion, / "Behold, your king comes to you, / meek and riding on an ass, / and on a colt, the foal of a beast of burden." /* The disciples went and did as Jesus had ordered them. They brought the ass and the colt and laid their cloaks over them, and he sat upon them. The very large crowd spread their cloaks on the road, while others cut branches from the trees and strewed them on the road. The crowds preceding him and those following kept crying out and saying: / "Hosanna to the Son of David; / blessed is he who comes in the name of the Lord; / hosanna in the highest." / And when he entered Jerusalem the whole city was shaken and asked, "Who is this?" And the crowds replied, "This is Jesus the prophet, from Nazareth in Galilee."

REFLECTION

We remember Jesus' suffering in our prayer today. We give him thanks and praise for his sacrifice. We pray that we might be able to take on just one other person's pain and sorrow this week— one who is ill, dying, destitute, adrift, or mourning. We journey with them, following in the footsteps of Jesus on the way of the cross.

PRAYERS *others may be added*

In solidarity with all who suffer, we pray:

◆ Lord, hear our prayer.

For Christian ministries of healing, we pray: ◆ *For victims of war and genocide, we pray:* ◆ *For those who are sick, in pain, and are alone, we pray:* ◆ *For those who mourn, we pray:* ◆ *For those who have died, we pray:*

Our Father . . .

Compassionate God,
you sent your Son to heal the world.
May we offer our lives as a sacrifice
 of praise.
May we be your embrace
and your helping hands lifting up all
 who are in need.
We ask this through our Lord Jesus
 Christ, your Son,
who lives and reigns with you
in the unity of the Holy Spirit,
one God, forever and ever.
Amen.

✦ *Be merciful, O Lord.*

✝ *I am the resurrection and the life, says the Lord; whoever believes in me will never die.*

PSALM 22 — page 401

READING — John 12:1–8

Six days before Passover Jesus came to Bethany, where Lazarus was, whom Jesus had raised from the dead. They gave a dinner for him there, and Martha served, while Lazarus was one of those reclining at table with him. Mary took a liter of costly perfumed oil made from genuine aromatic nard and anointed the feet of Jesus and dried them with her hair; the house was filled with the fragrance of the oil. Then Judas the Iscariot, one of his disciples, and the one who would betray him, said, "Why was this oil not sold for three hundred days' wages and given to the poor?" He said this not because he cared about the poor but because he was a thief and held the money bag and used to steal the contributions. So Jesus said, "Leave her alone. Let her keep this for the day of my burial. You always have the poor with you, but you do not always have me."

REFLECTION

We, too, want to praise and glorify Jesus for who he is. We know of his miracles, his healings, his insightful and challenging teachings. We see how he has changed us and so many others. We feel the power of his presence and the possibility that the world might be redeemed. May we each praise and glorify him in our own way today.

PRAYERS — *others may be added*

Praising and thanking God, we pray:

◆ Lord, hear our prayer.

For the gift of the apostolic Church, its wisdom and guidance throughout time, we pray: ◆ *For the blessing of so many holy men and women who have been faithful to Jesus and called each of us to follow him, we pray:* ◆ *For the myriad ways Jesus has touched our hearts and changed our lives, we pray:* ◆ *For the goodness and love of Jesus to be felt to all the ends of the earth, we pray:* ◆ *For the transforming of all of creation at the end of time, we pray:* ◆

Our Father . . .

Almighty God,
we know you in your Son, our Lord,
who amazes us with his miracles
    and love.
We praise you and thank you
for the gift of his life, death,
    and Resurrection.
We wait in hope for the reconciliation
    of the world in you,
where you live and reign with him
in the unity of the Holy Spirit,
one God, forever and ever.
Amen.

✝ *I am the resurrection and the life, says the Lord; whoever believes in me will never die.*

✠ *I am the resurrection and the life, says the Lord; whoever believes in me will never die.*

PSALM 22   *page 401*

READING   *John 13:21b–27*

Jesus was deeply troubled and testified, "Amen, amen, I say to you, one of you will betray me." The disciples looked at one another, at a loss as to whom he meant. One of his disciples, the one whom Jesus loved, was reclining at Jesus' side. So Simon Peter nodded to him to find out whom he meant. He leaned back against Jesus' chest and said to him, "Master, who is it?" Jesus answered, "It is the one to whom I hand the morsel after I have dipped it." So he dipped the morsel and took it and handed it to Judas, son of Simon the Iscariot. After he took the morsel, Satan entered him. So Jesus said to him, "What you are going to do, do quickly."

REFLECTION

As we approach the death of Jesus, who are we like at the table with him? Are we Peter, ever curious, trying to make sense of who Jesus is and what happens to him? Are we the beloved disciple, drawing ever closer to our Lord and teacher? Are we Judas, feeling guilty and avoiding the entire scene? Or perhaps are we another disciple; what do we feel and see as we are drawn into the final days of Jesus' life?

PRAYERS   *others may be added*

Reflecting on Jesus' final days, we pray:

◆ May the faith of the apostles live in us today.

For our Pope, who follows in the footsteps of Peter, we pray: ◆ *For all disciples of Jesus, who meet him in prayer and walk with him in life, we pray:* ◆ *For those who feel unwelcome at the table of the Lord, that there may be mending of hearts and relationships to bring them home, we pray:* ◆ *For all who have felt beloved by Jesus and love him with all their hearts, we pray:* ◆

Our Father . . .

O most holy Lord Jesus,
you sat with your disciples in your
    final hours,
sharing what you could and preparing
    for your death.
May we spend some time with you
    this week,
sharing what we can and preparing
    for our life with you.
You live and reign with God
    the Father
in the unity of the Holy Spirit,
one God, forever and ever.
Amen.

✠ *I am the resurrection and the life, says the Lord; whoever believes in me will never die.*

✠ *I am the resurrection and the life, says the Lord; whoever believes in me will never die.*

PSALM 22   *page 401*

READING   *Matthew 26:14–16*

One of the Twelve, who was called Judas Iscariot, went to the chief priests and said, "What are you willing to give me if I hand him over to you?" They paid him thirty pieces of silver, and from that time on he looked for an opportunity to hand him over.

REFLECTION

How have we, like Judas, betrayed Christ? When have we chosen the world over our friend and Savior? We need to be honest with God about what tempts us away from life as a disciple. We need to consider the choices that led Judas to make such a terrible decision, and recognize our own potential to do the same.

PRAYERS   *others may be added*

Searching our hearts, we pray:

◆ Lord, hear our prayer.

For our priests and leaders, that temptation may be conquered by faithfulness to Christ, we pray: ◆ *For betrayers of countries, of promises, of families, and of friendships, that they may repent and return to lives of integrity, we pray:* ◆ *For strength in moments of temptation, we pray:* ◆ *For forgiveness of our own past sins and of those who sin against us, we pray:* ◆ *For those who have died in a state of sin, we pray:* ◆

Our Father . . .

Lord Jesus, our brother,
you knew your betrayer,
and you also know us
when we betray and hurt you.
Forgive us our sins,
and lead us into a life of faith.
You live and reign with God
    the Father
in the unity of the Holy Spirit,
one God, forever and ever.
Amen.

✠ *I am the resurrection and the life, says the Lord; whoever believes in me will never die.*

✝ *I am the resurrection and the life, says the Lord; whoever believes in me will never die.*

PSALM 34   page 405

READING   John 13:2–4

During supper, fully aware that the Father had put everything into his power and that he had come from God and was returning to God, [Jesus] rose from supper and took off his outer garments. He took a towel and tied it around his waist. Then he poured water into a basin and began to wash the disciples' feet and dry them with the towel around his waist.

REFLECTION

Every time we say "yes" by saying "Amen" when receiving the Body and Blood of Christ in Eucharist, we agree to share in his life. In the Gospel according to John, Jesus shows us tangibly how we are to follow in his steps: by washing the feet of others. Find a way during the Paschal Triduum to say "yes" to God through humble and loving service toward others.

PRAYERS   others may be added

Rejoicing in the call to follow you, Lord, we pray:

◆ May we share in your life, Lord Jesus.

For the leaders of the Church, that they serve in Jesus' name and footsteps, we pray: ◆ For the leaders of nations, that they bow down to the poorest among them, hearing their pleas, and working for the common good, we pray: ◆ For teachers and parents, that they model leadership in humility and love, we pray: ◆ For each of us, that we lower ourselves in love and honor of those around us, we pray: ◆ For those who have died serving others, we pray: ◆

Our Father . . .

Lord Jesus,
you humbled yourself in love,
washing the feet of those you came
    to serve.
Be with us in these holy days,
as we remember your suffering
    and sacrifice.
Lead us to serve and love in
    your name.
You live and reign with God
    the Father
in the unity of the Holy Spirit,
one God, forever and ever.
Amen.

✝ *I am the resurrection and the life, says the Lord; whoever believes in me will never die.*

✚ *I am the resurrection and the life, says the Lord; whoever believes in me will never die.*

PSALM 22 *page 401*

READING *Isaiah 52:13—53:12*

Though he was harshly treated, he submitted / and opened not his mouth; / like a lamb led to the slaughter / or a sheep before the shearers, / he was silent and opened not his mouth. / Oppressed and condemned, he was taken away, / and who would have thought any more of his destiny? / When he was cut off from the land of the living, / and smitten for the sin of his people, / a grave was assigned him among the wicked / and a burial place with evildoers, / though he had done no wrong / nor spoken any falsehood. / But the LORD was pleased / to crush him in infirmity.

If he gives his life as an offering for sin, / he shall see his descendants in a long life, / and the will of the LORD shall be accomplished through him.

REFLECTION

Any time we feel alone, when our pain and suffering is unbearable, or we lose faith in God's presence, this is the passage we should read. The Passion of our Lord shows us the incredible strength, love, and mercy of our Savior. He knows our pain; he knows our loneliness; he knows our despair. No matter how alone or despairing we may feel, he is there. He took on our suffering in order to conquer it forever.

PRAYERS *others may be added*

In mourning for you and for all who have died in pain, we pray:

◆ Lord, hear our prayer.

For the martyrs and saints of the Church, who gave their very lives out of love for you and their brothers and sisters, we pray: ◆ For victims of genocide, war, natural disasters, torture, and rape, we pray: ◆ For the weakest and smallest among us: the unborn, the elderly, and children, we pray: ◆ For all we love who have died, and all who suffer, we pray: ◆

Our Father . . .

Merciful God,
pain seems too great to bear,
yet your Son bore it all for
    our salvation.
May we enter into solidarity with all
    who suffer,
longing for the peace and joy of
    eternal life.
May all suffering end, and God's
    reign last forever.
We ask this through Christ our Lord.
Amen.

✚ *I am the resurrection and the life, says the Lord; whoever believes in me will never die.*

✝ *I am the resurrection and the life, says the Lord; whoever believes in me will never die.*

PSALM 138   *page 419*

READING   *Isaiah 54:7, 9–10*

For a brief moment I abandoned you, / but with great tenderness I will take you back. / In an outburst of wrath, for a moment / I hid my face from you; / but with an enduring love I take pity on you, / says the LORD, your redeemer. / This is for me like the days of Noah, when I swore that the waters of Noah / should never again deluge the earth; / so I have sworn not to be angry with you, / or to rebuke you. / Though the mountains leave their place / and the hills be shaken, / my love shall never leave you / nor my covenant of peace be shaken, / says the LORD, who has mercy on you.

REFLECTION

We are part of a long line of God's people. He has been with us through dangers, battles, darkness, and confusion. God has taken us back time after time when we have wandered, sinned, and lost our way. This Easter night we trace our story as children of God. In the Incarnation, we know we are deeply loved. In the Crucifixion, we know we will never be alone. In the Resurrection of our Lord, we know that we will never die, but instead we will live with God forever. Rejoice!

PRAYERS   *others may be added*

Looking back on salvation history, we pray:

◆ God of mercy, raise us to new life.

For the faithful, who, despite many trials, continue to follow God, we pray: ◆ For humanity, that the wisdom and compassion of God may wash over all people, we pray: ◆ For those who enter the Church this night, that the light of Christ may burn brightly in their lives, we pray: ◆ For all the baptized, that we may rejoice in our destiny as children of God, we pray: ◆ For all who have died, that they may be reunited with the love of God in heaven, we pray: ◆

Our Father . . .

God of Moses, Abraham, Isaiah, and David,
you walked with your people throughout all of history.
You sent your Son into the world to show us your love.
By his cross and Resurrection we are saved from sin and death.
We rejoice in your glorious love and grace.
We ask this through our Lord Jesus Christ, your Son,
who lives and reigns with you in the unity of the Holy Spirit,
one God, forever and ever.
Amen.

✝ *I am the resurrection and the life, says the Lord; whoever believes in me will never die.*

✛ *I am the resurrection and the life, says the Lord; whoever believes in me will never die.*

PSALM 66   *page 410*

READING   *John 20:1–8*

On the first day of the week, Mary of Magdala came to the tomb early in the morning, while it was still dark, and saw the stone removed from the tomb. So she ran and went to Simon Peter and to the other disciple whom Jesus loved, and told them, "They have taken the Lord from the tomb, and we don't know where they put him." So Peter and the other disciple went out and came to the tomb. They both ran, but the other disciple ran faster than Peter and arrived at the tomb first; he bent down and saw the burial cloths there, but did not go in. When Simon Peter arrived after him, he went into the tomb and saw the burial cloths there, and the cloth that had covered his head, not with the burial cloths but rolled up in a separate place. Then the other disciple also went in, the one who had arrived at the tomb first, and he saw and believed.

REFLECTION

What is this death that Christ has conquered? The disciples feared it, and we fear it. It is emptiness, nothingness, and loneliness. Instead, Christ gives us fullness of life, meaning, and eternal happiness in the community of heaven. It is our richest dreams and imaginations fulfilled. It is joy and peace beyond what we know in this life.

PRAYERS   *others may be added*

Awed by God's miraculous love, we pray:

◆ Risen Lord, hear our prayer.

For deeper understanding throughout the Church of the meaning of the Resurrection of Jesus the Christ, we pray: ◆ For the triumph of life over death throughout the world, we pray: ◆ For all who fear death, and for all who fear life, that peace is found in Christ, we pray: ◆ For our community, that we create and extend a culture of life and meaning, we pray: ◆ For all who have died, that they celebrate today in heaven, we pray: ◆

Our Father . . .

Risen Lord,
your cross and Resurrection have
    saved us from death,
offering us eternal life.
May we steep our lives in the joy and
    promise of you
and turn our backs to the culture
    of death.
We cry out in joy, Alleluia!
You live and reign with God
    the Father
in the unity of the Holy Spirit,
one God, forever and ever.
Amen.

✛ *I am the resurrection and the life, says the Lord; whoever believes in me will never die.*

✚ *Rejoice, O hearts that seek the Lord.*

PSALM 66   *page 410*

READING   *Matthew 28:8–10*

Mary Magdalene and the other Mary went away quickly from the tomb, fearful yet overjoyed, and ran to announce the news to his disciples. And behold, Jesus met them on their way and greeted them. They approached, embraced his feet, and did him homage. Then Jesus said to them, "Do not be afraid. Go tell my brothers to go to Galilee, and there they will see me."

REFLECTION

The joy and mystery of the Resurrection requires that we spread the Good News to others. We can easily forget to do this; instead, we complain, vent, or speak ill of people. Today let us share bits of Good News with friends and family, reflecting the greater light of the love and mercy of God. Let us imagine our hearts "fearful and overjoyed" like Mary Magdalene and the other Mary, bursting with the news.

PRAYERS   *others may be added*

Eager to praise God and to share his glory with others, we pray:

◆ Make us joyful servants of the Lord.

That the Church and her leaders radiate the joy and glory of God to all the world, we pray: ◆ That the news of being loved and offered life in Christ reaches to all the ends of the earth, we pray: ◆ That all who are holding grudges, resentments, or bitterness may be set free by the news of the Resurrection, we pray: ◆ That we as a community celebrate each other's joys and happiness, giving the honor and glory to God, we pray: ◆

Our Father . . .

Risen Lord,
you inspired awe and joy in your
    disciples
by your life, death, and Resurrection.
Inspire us, too, to be your disciples,
sharing your news with those
    around us.
Help us to be continual beacons of
    light and goodness,
that we might more accurately reflect
    your love.
You live and reign with God the
    Father
in the unity of the Holy Spirit,
one God, forever and ever.
Amen.

✚ *Rejoice, O hearts that seek the Lord.*

✦ *Rejoice, O hearts that seek the Lord.*

PSALM 66 *page 410*

READING *John 20:11–17*

Mary Magdalene stayed outside the tomb weeping. And as she wept, she bent over into the tomb and saw two angels in white sitting there, one at the head and one at the feet where the Body of Jesus had been. And they said to her, "Woman, why are you weeping?" She said to them, "They have taken my Lord, and I don't know where they laid him." When she had said this, she turned around and saw Jesus there, but did not know it was Jesus. Jesus said to her, "Woman, why are you weeping? Whom are you looking for?" She thought it was the gardener and said to him, "Sir, if you carried him away, tell me where you laid him, and I will take him." Jesus said to her, "Mary!" She turned and said to him in Hebrew, "Rabbouni," which means Teacher. Jesus said to her, "Stop holding on to me, for I have not yet ascended to the Father. But go to my brothers and tell them, 'I am going to my Father and your Father, to my God and your God.'"

REFLECTION

Sometimes we need to be directly and sharply called by name by our Lord. We may be caught up in mourning, in despair, or by distractions. We forget that as Christians, this is a life of rejoicing. No matter what weighs us down, we have the gift of faith. We have confidence in a God that has been with us for all time and will call us home at the end of our earthly lives. Imagine Jesus calling your name today and from what he calls you away.

PRAYERS *others may be added*

Saddened and worried, we bring our prayers to our God:

◆ Call us by name, Lord Jesus.

For Christians, when we have lost sight of Jesus or doubt in his presence, that we may be filled with Easter joy, we pray: ◆
For visionaries and leaders who despair at the brokenness in the world, that they may be filled with Easter hope, we pray: ◆
For all who mourn, that they may be filled with Easter life, we pray: ◆ *For all those who have died, that they may glory in the Resurrection, we pray:* ◆

Our Father . . .

Risen Lord,
you call us by name and redirect us
    toward what is important.
Help us to listen to Mary's
    proclamation of the Good News
and cease to despair or be distracted.
Rejoice and dance with us
as we celebrate your unending love
    and companionship
throughout all the challenges of life.
You live and reign with God
    the Father
in the unity of the Holy Spirit,
one God, forever and ever.
Amen.

✦ *Rejoice, O hearts that seek the Lord.*

✦ *Athirst is my soul for the living God.*

PSALM 66 page 410

READING Luke 24:28–32

As [the disciples] approached the village to which they were going, [Jesus] gave the impression that he was going on farther. But they urged him, "Stay with us, for it is nearly evening and the day is almost over." So he went in to stay with them. And it happened that, while he was with them at table, he took bread, said the blessing, broke it, and gave it to them. With that their eyes were opened and they recognized him, but he vanished from their sight. Then they said to each other, "Were not our hearts burning within us while he spoke to us on the way and opened the Scriptures to us?"

REFLECTION

When we look back on our lives, especially the most difficult and most beautiful moments, we see that God was present, burning within our hearts, reaching out to us in pain and in joy. Perhaps we responded or perhaps we turned away. This Easter season, we renew our promise to be children of God, attentive to the Holy Spirit's presence in our daily lives. We will look for Christ's face around us and notice when he knocks on the door of our hearts. We will listen when he reveals himself and God's wisdom to us in the Word, the sacraments, and the community of the faithful.

PRAYERS *others may be added*

We turn to the risen Christ, who walks with us, as we pray:

◆ Burn in our hearts, risen Lord.

That the Pope, Bishops, and all servants of the Church will feel the nearness of Christ this Easter season, we pray: ◆
That those in pain will be comforted by the hope of Resurrection, we pray: ◆
That those who walk in difficult times will recognize God walking with them, we pray: ◆ *That we do not take God's presence for granted, but rejoice and give thanks, we pray:* ◆

Our Father . . .

Lord Jesus,
you are always with us,
burning within our hearts.
Sometimes we forget you are there,
but you conquered death in order to
    be with us forever.
May all who feel your presence turn
    to you,
confessing their faith and rejoicing
    in gratitude.
You live and reign with God
    the Father
in the unity of the Holy Spirit,
one God, forever and ever.
Amen.

✦ *Athirst is my soul for the living God.*

✦ *Everyone who believes in the Son has eternal life, and I shall raise him on the last day, says the Lord.*

PSALM 66 *page 410*

READING *Luke 24:35–40*

The disciples of Jesus recounted what had taken place along the way and how they had come to recognize him in the breaking of the bread.

While they were still speaking about this, he stood in their midst and said to them, "Peace be with you." But they were startled and terrified and thought that they were seeing a ghost. Then he said to them, "Why are you troubled? And why do questions arise in your hearts? Look at my hands and my feet, that it is I myself. Touch me and see, because a ghost does not have flesh and bones as you can see I have." And as he said this, he showed them his hands and his feet.

REFLECTION

When we are gripped by fear or over-whelmed with confusion, we, too, may not recognize Christ and the peace he offers us. Even in our greatest despair, Easter joy is available to us. Christ invites us to reach out and touch him, and to accept his peace.

PRAYERS *others may be added*

Awed by the gift of the Resurrection, we pray:

◆ Prince of Peace, walk with us.

For the Church when she struggles or is divided, that the peace of Christ may triumph, we pray: ◆ *For miraculous moments of peace and security in the world amid war and violence, we pray:* ◆ *For anyone who is overcome by fear, that they may choose happiness, we pray:* ◆ *For each of us, that we may be carriers of Christ's peace in places of fear and confusion, we pray:* ◆

Our Father . . .

Jesus Christ, our brother,
you came to your apostles after your
   Resurrection
and offered them true peace.
May we accept and embrace your
   invitation to be at peace,
no matter what is happening in
   our lives
or in the world around us.
You live and reign with God
   the Father
in the unity of the Holy Spirit,
one God, forever and ever.
Amen.

✦ *Everyone who believes in the Son has eternal life, and I shall raise him on the last day, says the Lord.*

✦ *Everyone who believes in the Son has eternal life, and I shall raise him on the last day, says the Lord.*

PSALM 66 *page 410*

READING *John 21:1–7a*

Jesus revealed himself again to his disciples at the Sea of Tiberias. He revealed himself in this way. Together were Simon Peter, Thomas called Didymus, Nathanael from Cana in Galilee, Zebedee's sons, and two others of his disciples. Simon Peter said to them, "I am going fishing." They said to him, "We also will come with you." So they went out and got into the boat, but that night they caught nothing. When it was already dawn, Jesus was standing on the shore; but the disciples did not realize that it was Jesus. Jesus said to them, "Children, have you caught anything to eat?" They answered him, "No." So he said to them, "Cast the net over the right side of the boat and you will find something." So they cast it, and were not able to pull it in because of the number of fish. So the disciple whom Jesus loved said to Peter, "It is the Lord."

REFLECTION

Is today's message that if we obey God, we will be rewarded with wealth? The Christ we know in scripture and in the Church does not promise us worldly success. Rather, he reveals himself to us in the face of adversity. He promises to be with us in Eucharist, and to reward us—not in wealth but in abundant life.

PRAYERS *others may be added*

In gratitude, we pray:

◆ Lord, hear our prayer.

That Christians eagerly await God's presence and guidance, not riches, we pray: ◆ *That God-fearing nations seek the kingdom of God, not a kingdom of power or wealth, we pray:* ◆ *That those who struggle financially may be led by God to stability, good choices, and gratitude, we pray:* ◆ *That we turn over to God our greed and live anew in his sufficient love, we pray:* ◆

Our Father . . .

Lord God,
you care for each of the "fishermen" among us, searching for success.
Show us how to find happiness by faith, trust, and gratitude,
and to reject false messages of material wealth.
You fill our nets with all that we need.
We ask this through Christ our Lord.
Amen.

✦ *Everyone who believes in the Son has eternal life, and I shall raise him on the last day, says the Lord.*

✝ *Rejoice, O hearts that seek the Lord.*

PSALM 16 *page 400*

READING *Mark 16:9–15*

When Jesus had risen, early on the first day of the week, he appeared first to Mary Magdalene, out of whom he had driven seven demons. She went and told his companions who were mourning and weeping. When they heard that he was alive and had been seen by her, they did not believe.

After this he appeared in another form to two of them along on their way to the country. They returned and told the others; but they did not believe them either.

But later, as the Eleven were at table, he appeared to them and rebuked them for their unbelief and hardness of heart because they had not believed those who saw him after he had been raised. He said to them, "Go into the whole world and proclaim the Gospel to every creature."

REFLECTION

If we have seen the unbelievable, heard the unthinkable, and experienced the risen Christ, we cannot hold back our astonishment. When joy and faith fill us, we are compelled to share it with others. Easter faith spills over into the rest of our lives.

PRAYERS *others may be added*

Rejoicing, we pray:

◆ Send us forth with gladness.

For Christian preachers, that joy pervades their proclamation this Easter, we pray: ◆ *For the Good News to travel the whole world through personal stories of joy, we pray:* ◆ *For those who most desperately need the Gospel message of love and joy to hear it this Easter, we pray:* ◆ *For our community to be a witness to the peace and celebration of the Resurrection, we pray:* ◆

Our Father . . .

Risen Lord,
you fill us with such awe and hope;
it cannot be contained.
Be with us as we share the story
of how your death and Resurrection
    have renewed our lives.
You live and reign with God
    the Father
in the unity of the Holy Spirit,
one God, forever and ever.
Amen.

✝ *Rejoice, O hearts that seek the Lord.*

✢ *Athirst is my soul for the living God.*

PSALM 66   *page 410*

READING   *John 20:24–29*

Thomas, called Didymus, one of the Twelve, was not with them when Jesus came. So the other disciples said to him, "We have seen the Lord." But he said to them, "Unless I see the mark of the nails in his hands and put my finger into the nailmarks and put my hand into his side, I will not believe."

Now a week later his disciples were again inside and Thomas was with them. Jesus came, although the doors were locked, and stood in their midst and said, "Peace be with you." Then he said to Thomas, "Put your finger here and see my hands, and bring your hand and put it into my side, and do not be unbelieving, but believe." Thomas answered and said to him, "My Lord and my God!" Jesus said to him, "Have you come to believe because you have seen me? Blessed are those who have not seen and have believed."

REFLECTION

It is good to be with our brothers and sisters in Christ. The disciples gathered after the Crucifixion, united by fear, confusion, and passion. We, too, have a need to gather with others in faith, so that we can share our questions, joys, and concerns. When we do this, Christ stands in our midst.

PRAYERS   *others may be added*

With Christ beside us, we pray:

◆ May we be the body of Christ in the world.

That all Christians, including our leaders, may gather in groups for prayer, discussion, and service, we pray: ◆
That international and interreligious dialogue brings all people to greater knowledge and understanding of God and one another, we pray: ◆ *That anyone living faith in solitude may find a community in which to grow, we pray:* ◆
That our parish may find ways to gather in small groups and welcome Christ into our midst, we pray: ◆

Our Father . . .

Risen Lord,
you are with us,
as you were with the disciples.
Your Holy Spirit continues to work
    among us,
especially when we gather together in
    your name.
Thank you for every opportunity to
    walk in faith with one another.
You live and reign with God
    the Father
in the unity of the Holy Spirit,
one God, forever and ever.
Amen.

✢ *Athirst is my soul for the living God.*

✦ *The Lord is my shepherd; there is nothing I shall want.*

PSALM 40 {page 407}

READING {Matthew 10:22–25}

Jesus said to the Twelve: "You will be hated by all because of my name, but whoever endures to the end will be saved. When they persecute you in one town, flee to another. Amen, I say to you, you will not finish the towns of Israel before the Son of Man comes. No disciple is above his teacher, no slave above his master. It is enough for the disciple that he become like the teacher, and the slave that he become like the master. If they have called the master of the house Beelzebub, how much more those of his household!"

REFLECTION

St. Athanasius, who shaped the core of our understanding of Jesus as both human and divine, is an extraordinary example of endurance. He did not live to see the full confirmation of the faith he defended. When we cannot see the fruit of our labor, or the end results of our persistence in faith, we can ask for St. Athanasius to be our model and companion.

PRAYERS {others may be added}

Inspired, we pray:

◆ May it be enough to know we are doing your will, O God.

For Bishops and theologians, who preserve and teach the faith in parallel ways, to be inspired by the example of St. Athanasius, we pray: ◆ *For civil servants and humanitarians, who labor without seeing success, we pray:* ◆ *For those who wake each day to trial and turbulence, that they may persevere, we pray:* ◆ *For hope and confidence when we walk by faith without reward of evidence by sight, we pray:* ◆

Our Father . . .

Lord Jesus,
you inspired St. Athanasius to give
    you glory by his work and
    his persistence.
May we also glorify you by our
    untiring efforts in this life,
so as to rejoice with you in the next.
May your love and blessing be enough
    for us
when our own times and contexts do
    not value our faith.
You live and reign with God
    the Father
in the unity of the Holy Spirit,
one God, forever and ever.
Amen.

✦ *The Lord is my shepherd; there is nothing I shall want.*

✦ *Commit your life to the Lord.*

PSALM 40 page 407

READING John 14:8–14

Philip said to [Jesus], "Master, show us the Father, and that will be enough for us." Jesus said to him, "Have I been with you for so long a time and you still do not know me, Philip? Whoever has seen me has seen the Father. How can you say, 'Show us the Father'? Do you not believe that I am in the Father and the Father is in me? The words that I speak to you I do not speak on my own. The Father who dwells in me is doing his works. Believe me that I am in the Father and the Father is in me, or else, believe because of the works themselves. Amen, amen, I say to you, whoever believes in me will do the works that I do, and will do greater ones than these, because I am going to the Father. And whatever you ask in my name, I will do, so that the Father may be glorified in the Son. If you ask anything of me in my name, I will do it."

REFLECTION

This reading is comforting. Even the apostle Philip could fail to understand Jesus' identity. We may not feel we really know Jesus, or we may struggle with questions of faith. Our tradition has a rich history of developing theology in response to questions. And yet, Jesus asks us to believe by faith. We are asked to follow him daily, and to do his will by proclaiming the kingdom and serving those most in need.

PRAYERS *others may be added*

Needing guidance, we pray:

◆ Grace us with wisdom and faith, O God.

For the people of God, who walk by faith, despite sometimes feeling lost or unsure, we pray: ◆ *For the people of the world who do not have faith, that they may see how God has been with them throughout time, we pray:* ◆ *For anyone who is searching for answers, that they proceed toward God with pure hearts, prayers, and acts of service, we pray:* ◆ *For humility among all of us, since, despite the gift of faith, we still do not fully understand, we pray:* ◆

Our Father . . .

Loving Lord,
you know us well,
as you knew your apostles.
You are not shocked by our failings,
but teach us and lead us again
    and again.
May we follow you even when we are
    unsure, through your grace.
You live and reign with God
    the Father
in the unity of the Holy Spirit,
one God, forever and ever.
Amen.

✦ *Commit your life to the Lord.*

✦ *God so loved the world that he gave his only-begotten Son.*

PSALM 149 *page 421*

READING *John 3:16–21*

God so loved the world that he gave his only-begotten Son, so that everyone who believes in him might not perish but might have eternal life. For God did not send his Son into the world to condemn the world, but that the world might be saved through him. Whoever believes in him will not be condemned, but whoever does not believe has already been condemned, because he has not believed in the name of the only-begotten Son of God. And this is the verdict, that the light came into the world, but people preferred darkness to light, because their works were evil. For everyone who does wicked things hates the light and does not come toward the light, so that his works might not be exposed. But whoever lives the truth comes to the light, so that his works may be clearly seen as done in God.

REFLECTION

John 3:16: *What is it about this verse that prompts people and organizations to post it on billboards, posters at professional sporting games, bumper stickers, and T-shirts? What impacts us the most about this verse? Is it the mystery of a God who loves us as much as his own Son, or himself? Is it the joy at realizing we are offered eternal life despite our flaws, sin, and brokenness? What about this verse gives it power?*

PRAYERS *others may be added*

With love for God, we pray:

✦ Lord, hear our prayer.

That the Church may strive to foster and help people realize the never-ending love of God, we pray: ◆ *That the people of God may understand that his love is truly for all, we pray:* ◆ *That any lost soul, broken heart, or fearful mind may be comforted by the message of God's love, we pray:* ◆ *That our lives of faith may carry the same power as the Word of God, we pray:* ◆

Our Father . . .

Loving God,
you love us with a love unlike any
    other we have known,
and want us to choose the happiness
    you offer us now and forever.
May we embrace your love and return
    it by sharing it with others.
Grant this through Christ our Lord.
Amen.

✦ *God so loved the world that he gave his only-begotten Son.*

✚ *The Holy Spirit will teach you everything and remind you of all I told you.*

PSALM 16 *page 400*

READING *Acts 5:27–33*

When the court officers had brought the Apostles in and made them stand before the Sanhedrin, the high priest questioned them, "We gave you strict orders did we not, to stop teaching in that name. Yet you have filled Jerusalem with your teaching and want to bring this man's blood upon us." But Peter and the Apostles said in reply, "We must obey God rather than men. The God of our ancestors raised Jesus, though you had him killed by hanging him on a tree. God exalted him at his right hand as leader and savior to grant Israel repentance and forgiveness of sins. We are witnesses of these things, as is the Holy Spirit whom God has given to those who obey him."

When they heard this, they became infuriated and wanted to put them to death.

REFLECTION

If you see a car accident, you are required to give testimony to the police. If you observe an astonishing performance of talent, you feel impelled to tell others. The apostles witnessed the death and Resurrection of Jesus. Think of the responsibility they must have felt to bear witness. We are their legacy; we have inherited their mission.

PRAYERS *others may be added*

Honored to be called, we pray:

◆ Holy Spirit, lead us.

For Bishops, successors to the apostles, that their witness may be true and bold, we pray: ◆ *For witnesses to crimes, genocide, and unethical action, that they may have courage to respond in justice, we pray:* ◆ *For witnesses to hidden abilities and unknown opportunities, that they may bring them forward to be shared with the world, we pray:* ◆ *For our parish, to carry seriously our responsibility to bring the mission of the Church to the world, we pray:* ◆

Our Father . . .

Lord Jesus,
the apostles were the chosen
   witnesses
to carry your message to the world.
We are blessed to be called to carry
   on their work.
Give us courage, confidence,
   and gentleness
as we live as witnesses to your life,
   death, and Resurrection.
You live and reign with God
   the Father
in the unity of the Holy Spirit,
one God, forever and ever.
Amen.

✚ *The Holy Spirit will teach you everything and remind you of all I told you.*

✛ *Remain in me, as I remain in you,*
says the Lord; whoever remains in
me will bear much fruit.

PSALM 66   *page 410*

READING   *Acts 5:34–42*

A Pharisee in the Sanhedrin named Gamaliel, a teacher of the law, respected by all the people, stood up, ordered the Apostles to be put outside for a short time, and said to the Sanhedrin, "Fellow children of Israel, be careful what you are about to do to these men. Some time ago, Theudas appeared, claiming to be someone important, and about four hundred men joined him, but he was killed, and all those who were loyal to him were disbanded and came to nothing. After him came Judas the Galilean at the time of the census. He also drew people after him, but he too perished and all who were loyal to him were scattered. So now I tell you, have nothing to do with these men, and let them go. For if this endeavor or this activity is of human origin, it will destroy itself. But if it comes from God, you will not be able to destroy them; you may even find yourselves fighting against God." They were persuaded by him.

REFLECTION

How true that evil often destroys itself. What is good, survives. It may be small and weak, but it will persist. We can trust in the power of God to persevere through time, and for that which is unworthy or untrue to fade away.

PRAYERS   *others may be added*

With trust in God, we pray:

◆ May all that is good grow strong.

That the Church will persist through God's grace, we pray: ◆ *That violence, destruction, and false gods will fade away, we pray:* ◆ *That those who speak in God's name will be strengthened, we pray:* ◆ *That those who trust in God will lead us toward truth and away from misleading human efforts, we pray:* ◆

Our Father . . .

God of power and might,
you are present with all who believe
    in you.
You do not choose the strong,
but you make strong those whom
    you choose.
Make us aware of your lasting truth
    around us,
helping us follow the good.
We ask this through Christ our Lord.
Amen.

✛ *Remain in me, as I remain in you,*
says the Lord; whoever remains in
me will bear much fruit.

✚ *Athirst is my soul for the living God.*

PSALM 66 *page 410*

READING *John 6:16–21*

When it was evening, [Jesus'] disciples went down to the sea, embarked in a boat, and went across the sea to Capernaum. It had already grown dark, and Jesus had not yet come to them. The sea was stirred up because a strong wind was blowing. When they had rowed about three or four miles, they saw Jesus walking on the sea and coming near the boat, and they began to be afraid. But he said to them, "It is I. Do not be afraid." They wanted to take him into the boat, but the boat immediately arrived at the shore to which they were heading.

REFLECTION

For the apostles, to see Jesus as stronger than the forces of nature upset their worldview. What might upset our worldview? We understand so much more of science and nature. Still, the ability to conquer death eludes us. And this is something Jesus still offers us. Jesus walks toward us, crushing death, and offering eternal life.

PRAYERS *others may be added*

Awed by the Lord Jesus, we pray:

◆ Renew our faith in your power.

For all clergy and lay ministers of the Church, that their eyes are open to daily miracles, we pray: ◆ *For nations still overwhelmed by the forces of nature, that improvements in infrastructure keep them from being at the mercy of storms, floods, and drought, we pray:* ◆ *For those afraid of death, that the mystery of eternal life be revealed to them, we pray:* ◆ *For each of us, that we may not be afraid, but instead rejoice and trust when Jesus walks toward us, we pray:* ◆

Our Father . . .

Lord Jesus, miracle-worker,
you are stronger than death
and greater than any knowledge.
May we accept your miracles
and rejoice in the life you offer to us.
We long for you, above all things.
You live and reign with God
    the Father
in the unity of the Holy Spirit,
one God, forever and ever.
Amen.

✚ *Athirst is my soul for the living God.*

✦ *Rejoice, O hearts that seek the Lord.*

PSALM 66 *page 410*

READING *Luke 24:13–15, 30–32*

That very day, the first day of the week, two of Jesus' disciples were going to a village seven miles from Jerusalem called Emmaus, and they were conversing about all the things that had occurred. And it happened that while they were conversing and debating, Jesus himself drew near and walked with them. And it happened that, while he was with them at table, he took bread, said the blessing, broke it, and gave it to them. With that their eyes were opened and they recognized him, but he vanished from their sight. Then they said to each other, "Were not our hearts burning within us while he spoke to us on the way and opened the Scriptures to us?"

REFLECTION

Our understanding of Jesus' death and Resurrection must include a historical, cultural, and religious foundation from the Old Testament. It begins with the story of the Lord and his covenant with the Jewish people. It includes his promise to lead them to freedom and to always be faithful to them. Through this lens, we can begin to comprehend the depth of the meaning of Messiah. Prayerfully we enter into the ancient scripture stories to come to know our Savior more deeply.

PRAYERS *others may be added*

Aware of our ancestors in faith, we pray:

◆ Reveal your truth to us, O Savior.

For the Church, who continues to explore the liberating story and sacrifice of Jesus, and its meaning for all people, we pray: ◆ *For all students of faith, who read scripture, engage in worship, and participate in the community of faith, we pray:* ◆ *For the Jewish people, the first to hear the Word of God, we pray:* ◆ *For greater understanding of ancient Jewish customs, language, and people, we pray:* ◆

Our Father . . .

Lord Jesus, our Messiah,
you came to us in a concrete time
    and place,
revealing God through a particular
    religious tradition.
May we grow in understanding of
    the signs and symbols you
    transformed,
growing deeper in knowledge of and
    faith in you.
You live and reign with God
    the Father
in the unity of the Holy Spirit,
one God, forever and ever.
Amen.

✦ *Rejoice, O hearts that seek the Lord.*

✠ *Remain in me, as I remain in you, says the Lord; whoever remains in me will bear much fruit.*

PSALM 16   page 400

READING   John 6:24–29

[The crowds] came to Capernaum looking for Jesus. And when they found him across the sea they said to him, "Rabbi, when did you get here?" Jesus answered them and said, "Amen, amen, I say to you, you are looking for me not because you saw signs but because you ate the loaves and were filled. Do not work for food that perishes but for the food that endures for eternal life, which the Son of Man will give you. For on him the Father, God, has set his seal." So they said to him, "What can we do to accomplish the works of God?" Jesus answered and said to them, "This is the work of God, that you believe in the one he sent."

REFLECTION

Throughout this passage, the people are focused on earthly, practical work and results, naturally. Jesus is trying to refocus their eyes on faith in God and God's "work." We, too, are likely drawn to human works—our schools, our buildings, funding, "programs." Have we lost sight of or failed to understand the most important goal—the "bread" of eternal life, the "work" of faith in God?

PRAYERS   *others may be added*

Lifting our hearts and minds in prayer, we come before God:

◆ May your work be done.

For all who labor in the Church, that their sights are set on the kingdom of God, we pray: ◆ *For nourishment of bodies with real bread, and of souls with eternal fulfillment, we pray:* ◆ *For anyone overly focused on earthly works, that God may remind him or her of a greater purpose, we pray:* ◆ *For growth in understanding as followers of Jesus, we pray:* ◆

Our Father . . . .

Lord Jesus, our teacher,
you drew people out of their daily
    concerns
and pointed them toward
the highest purpose of their lives: life
  in God.
Remind us to take time in prayer,
refocusing our minds and hearts
on the bread that gives
    everlasting life.
You live and reign with God
    the Father
in the unity of the Holy Spirit,
one God, forever and ever.
Amen.

✠ *Remain in me, as I remain in you, says the Lord; whoever remains in me will bear much fruit.*

✦ *God so loved the world that he gave his only-begotten Son.*

PSALM 149 *page 421*

READING *John 6:30–35*

The crowd said to Jesus: "What sign can you do, that we may see and believe in you? What can you do? Our ancestors ate manna in the desert, as it is written: / *He gave them bread from heaven to eat.*" / So Jesus said to them, "Amen, amen, I say to you, it was not Moses who gave the bread from heaven; my Father gives you the true bread from heaven. For the bread of God is that which comes down from heaven and gives life to the world."

So they said to him, "Sir, give us this bread always." Jesus said to them, "I am the bread of life; whoever comes to me will never hunger, and whoever believes in me will never thirst."

REFLECTION

Jesus is the ultimate sign and symbol for which people—of the past and of the present—have been waiting. We have been given this sign once and for all. It is offered to us again and again through the sacraments and through our relationship with Jesus. We know him by the calming of our minds and the fulfillment of our hearts. We hear of him through the Word. We know him in Baptism and in Eucharist. When our hunger is satisfied and our thirst is quenched, it will be because we have fully embraced God in the gift of Jesus Christ.

PRAYERS *others may be added*

Receiving and rejoicing in the bread of life, we pray:

◆ Lord Jesus, feed us.

For the Pope, Bishops, clergy, and all ministers of the Church, that their hungers are filled and their thirsts are quenched by the bread of life, we pray: ◆ *For the joy of Christians to permeate the world and be a sign of God's love, we pray:* ◆ *For weary and lost souls, broken and battered hearts, that the love of God touches them, we pray:* ◆ *For recognition of answered prayers among our community, we pray:* ◆ *For those who have entered into eternal rest, we pray:* ◆

Our Father . . .

Lord Jesus, Bread of Life,
you know our hunger and our thirst.
May we rejoice in receiving your
    Body and Blood
and hearing your Word that forever
    fill us.
You live and reign with God
    the Father
in the unity of the Holy Spirit,
one God, forever and ever.
Amen.

✦ *God so loved the world that he gave his only-begotten Son.*

✦ *Let us rejoice and be glad!*

PSALM 66 *page 410*

READING *John 6:44-51*

[Jesus said,] "No one can come to me unless the Father who sent me draw him, and I will raise him on the last day. It is written in the prophets: /*They shall all be taught by God.* / Everyone who listens to my Father and learns from him comes to me. Not that anyone has seen the Father except the one who is from God; he has seen the Father. Amen, amen, I say to you, whoever believes has eternal life. I am the bread of life. Your ancestors ate the manna in the desert but they died; this is the bread that comes from heaven so that one may eat it and not die. I am the living bread that came down from heaven; whoever eats this bread will live forever; and the bread that I will give is my Flesh for the life of the world."

REFLECTION

Does Jesus really mean "everyone"? Are there no exceptions to salvation? In the scripture itself we hear the story of St. Paul, who was once Saul, a Pharisee who persecuted Christians. Saul took on the name Paul, the great missionary to the Gentiles. If God's mercy extends even to those who doubt him, surely no one is exempt from the possibility of forgiveness. What amazing hope we can have for every person to be saved! Persecutors, tormentors, evildoers, anyone—including ourselves— are called by Jesus.

PRAYERS *others may be added*

Bringing our prayers before God, we pray:

◆ Lord, lead us to new life.

For those who persecute the Church, Christians, and any who live by faith, we pray: ◆ *For corrupt dictators, warlords, and terrorists, we pray:* ◆ *For slave traffickers, drug dealers, and all who profit by the suffering of others, we pray:* ◆ *For all who have sinned and come before God, we pray:* ◆

Our Father . . .

Merciful God,
your love is unending;
your will is that not even one should
    be lost.
We give you thanks and praise
for your amazing compassion.
Bring each of us,
even the most desperate,
straight into your fold.
We ask this through our Lord Jesus
    Christ, your Son,
who lives and reigns with you
in the unity of the Holy Spirit,
one God, forever and ever.
Amen.

✦ *Let us rejoice and be glad!*

✦ *Rejoice, O hearts that seek the Lord.*

PSALM 66 *page 410*

READING
Acts 8:27b, 28–31, 35–36, 38

Now there was an Ethiopian eunuch, a court official of the Candace, that is, the queen of the Ethiopians, in charge of her entire treasury, who had come to Jerusalem to worship, and was returning home. Seated in his chariot, he was reading the prophet Isaiah. The Spirit said to Philip, "Go and join up with that chariot." Philip ran up and heard him reading Isaiah the prophet and said, "Do you understand what you are reading?" He replied, "How can I, unless someone instructs me?" So he invited Philip to get in and sit with him. Then Philip opened his mouth and, beginning with this Scripture passage, he proclaimed Jesus to him. As they traveled along the road they came to some water, and the eunuch said, "Look, there is water. What is to prevent my being baptized?" Then he ordered the chariot to stop, and Philip and the eunuch both went down into the water, and he baptized him.

REFLECTION

The Ethiopian eunuch would have faced lifelong exclusion for his deformity. No wonder he asks to be baptized once he understands what Jesus offers him—life, inclusion, and joy. We all crave these things, and we can accept them from Jesus, as well as offer them to others.

PRAYERS
others may be added

Full of joy, we pray:

◆ **Change our hearts, O Lord.**

That every Christian may see the Gospel's offer of total inclusion, a full life, and lasting joy, we pray: ◆ *That every seeker may find the Good News through the Word, the sacraments, and a community of faith, we pray:* ◆ *That all who are excluded from fullness of life by disability, illness, ethnicity, or gender may be welcomed to share their gifts in community, we pray:* ◆ *That our parish may be a model of inclusion and joy, we pray:* ◆ *That all who have died feeling alone or excluded may be embraced at the heavenly banquet, we pray:* ◆

Our Father . . .

God of compassion,
you know the human heart's longing
  to be in relationship,
and sent your Son to unite all people
  in your love.
May we continue to proclaim this
  joyful news to all,
especially those at the margins of
  our society.
Grant this through Christ our Lord.
Amen.

✦ *Rejoice, O hearts that seek the Lord.*

✝ *Christ is risen, who made all things; he has shown mercy on all people.*

PSALM 16   *page 400*

READING   *Acts 9:10–19*

There was a disciple in Damascus named Ananias, and the Lord said to him in a vision, "Ananias." He answered, "Here I am, Lord." The Lord said to him, "Get up and go to the street called Straight and ask at the house of Judas for a man from Tarsus named Saul. He is there praying, and in a vision he has seen a man named Ananias come in and lay his hands on him, that he may regain his sight." But Ananias replied, "Lord, I have heard from many sources about this man, what evil things he has done to your holy ones in Jerusalem. And here he has authority from the chief priests to imprison all who call upon your name." But the Lord said to him, "Go, for this man is a chosen instrument of mine to carry my name before Gentiles, kings, and children of Israel, and I will show him what he will have to suffer for my name." So Ananias went and entered the house; laying his hands on him, he said, "Saul, my brother, the Lord has sent me, Jesus who appeared to you on the way by which you came, that you may regain your sight and be filled with the Holy Spirit." Immediately things like scales fell from his eyes and he regained his sight. He got up and was baptized.

REFLECTION

Imagine Ananias's fear at the Lord's command to go to Saul and lay hands on him. God may use us in ways we do not understand to witness to our faith in challenging circumstances. He may ask us to speak for him in front of our peers; he may ask us to treat someone we dislike as a sister or brother; he may ask us to reach out in love to someone we fear will reject us.

PRAYERS   *others may be added*

Seeking courage, we pray:

◆ Make us your instruments, Lord.

For those who hear God calling them to do what is right, we pray: ◆ *For police officers, negotiators, and mediators called into conflict, trusting in a higher plan, we pray:* ◆ *For peacemakers who risk their own pride, alliances, or personal safety for the sake of another, we pray:* ◆ *For those used by God to bring faith and happiness to another, we pray;* ◆

Our Father . . .

God of miracles,
we cannot know your divine plan,
and can only serve this plan through
    humble faith.
Make use of our hands, feet, and
    hearts as it is your will.
We ask this through Christ our Lord.
Amen.

✝ *Christ is risen, who made all things; he has shown mercy on all people.*

✦ *The Lord is my shepherd; there is nothing I shall want.*

PSALM 40   *page 407*

READING   *John 15:12–17*

[Jesus said to his disciples,] "This is my commandment: love one another as I love you. No one has greater love than this, to lay down one's life for one's friends. You are my friends if you do what I command you. I no longer call you slaves, because a slave does not know what his master is doing. I have called you friends, because I have told you everything I have heard from my Father. It was not you who chose me, but I who chose you and appointed you to go and bear fruit that will remain, so that whatever you ask the Father in my name he may give you. This I command you: love one another."

REFLECTION

Ideally, a child is born into a loving and secure relationship. We can fully trust that we have been created and are held in the love of God. Just as children explore and challenge the limits of their parents' love, we have to learn for ourselves what it means to know, trust, and remain in God's love.

PRAYERS   *others may be added*

In awe of God's love, we pray:

◆ Lord, hear our prayer.

For the people of God, that trial and error leads them to choose the lasting, all-encompassing embrace of God, we pray: ◆ For opportunities within families, schools, parishes, and faith organizations to safely explore and understand the nature of God and his unconditional love, we pray: ◆ For children who are born into chaos, that God may give them the strength and courage to overcome the many obstacles to trust, we pray: ◆ For foster and adoptive parents and communities, who welcome children and adults who have not been given unconditional love, we pray: ◆

Our Father . . .

Heavenly Father,
we thank you for earthly families
    whose love leads us to you.
We pray for all those who have not
    known human care and trust.
May each of us in our own way come
    to know your great love
and devote ourselves to whatever
    it takes,
to remain in your arms until the end
    of time.
Grant this through Christ our Lord.
Amen.

✦ *The Lord is my shepherd; there is nothing I shall want.*

✙ *God so loved the world, that he gave his only-begotten Son, so that everyone who believes in him might have eternal life.*

PSALM 66   page 410

READING   John 10:7–10

Jesus said again, "Amen, amen, I say to you, I am the gate for the sheep. All who came before me are thieves and robbers, but the sheep did not listen to them. I am the gate. Whoever enters through me will be saved, and will come in and go out and find pasture. A thief comes only to steal and slaughter and destroy; I came so that they might have life and have it more abundantly."

REFLECTION

Throughout John's account of the Gospel, Jesus emphasizes that the path to salvation—the way to the Father—is through him. The writer of the Gospel account wants to establish the uniqueness of Jesus the Messiah against other prophets and teachers—good or deceitful. The Church continues to assert this teaching despite pluralistic views of religion. It is a challenging task for the Church today.

PRAYERS   *others may be added*

Longing for truth, we pray:

◆ Show us the way.

When the Church tries to be faithful to the Word and also interact with the realities of modern life, we pray: ◆
When members of different religions and faiths come together to understand one another and the meaning of life, we pray: ◆
When we are overwhelmed by the variety of values held up by science, history, cultures, and religion, we pray: ◆
When we read scripture and listen for your wisdom, we pray: ◆

Our Father . . .

God of all creation,
you are bigger and more mysterious
    than we can imagine:
the ground of all being
and the center of every human heart.
As we follow you, guide us in
    understanding the unique
    revelation
found in your Son's life, death,
    and Resurrection.
Welcome us through the gate to
    pasture in your presence,
where you live and reign with your
    Son Jesus Christ, our Lord,
in the unity of the Holy Spirit,
one God, forever and ever.
Amen.

✙ *God so loved the world, that he gave his only-begotten Son, so that everyone who believes in him might have eternal life.*

✦ *Athirst is my soul for the living God.*

PSALM 130   *page 418*

READING   *John 10:11–17*

Jesus said: "I am the good shepherd. A good shepherd lays down his life for the sheep. A hired man, who is not a shepherd and whose sheep are not his own, sees a wolf coming and leaves the sheep and runs away, and the wolf catches and scatters them. This is because he works for pay and has no concern for the sheep. I am the good shepherd, and I know mine and mine know me, just as the Father knows me and I know the Father; and I will lay down my life for the sheep. I have other sheep that do not belong to this fold. These also I must lead, and they will hear my voice, and there will be one flock, one shepherd. This is why the Father loves me, because I lay down my life in order to take it up again."

REFLECTION

Allow yourself to imagine the sheep, shepherd, hired man, wolf, and gate as a set of children's toys. Imagine this passage acted out. Who are you in the story? How does it feel when the danger comes? What is the most inspiring part of the story to you? Who would you like to become? Pray after reflecting on these questions, and ask for God to help you see who you are today and who you may become in the future.

PRAYERS   *others may be added*

Like a child, we bring our prayers before God:

◆ Lord, hear us.

For the shepherds of the Church, named and unnamed, who attend to each sheep, especially the lost sheep and the sheep who do not belong to the fold, we pray: ◆
For religious education of children, which allows them to develop a relationship with God, we pray: ◆
For those who identify with the lost sheep, the sheep afraid of the wolf, or the sheep abandoned by the hired man, that the true shepherd may care for and protect them always, we pray: ◆
For imaginative prayer, which opens us to seeing God, ourself, and others in new ways, we pray: ◆

Our Father . . .

O Good Shepherd,
you give us identity, security, and
    hope in you.
May we be unafraid when we follow
    your lead.
Make us like children,
trusting in your goodness and care,
ready to go wherever you are.
You live and reign with God
    the Father
in the unity of the Holy Spirit,
one God, forever and ever.
Amen.

✦ *Athirst is my soul for the living God.*

✦ *The Holy Spirit will teach you everything and remind you of all I told you.*

PSALM 16 page 400

READING Acts 11:19–24

Those who had been scattered by the persecution that arose because of Stephen went as far as Phoenicia, Cyprus, and Antioch, preaching the word to no one but Jews. There were some Cypriots and Cyrenians among them, however, who came to Antioch and began to speak to the Greeks as well, proclaiming the Lord Jesus. The hand of the Lord was with them and a great number who believed turned to the Lord. The news about them reached the ears of the Church in Jerusalem, and they sent Barnabas to go to Antioch. When he arrived and saw the grace of God, he rejoiced and encouraged them all to remain faithful to the Lord in firmness of heart, for he was a good man, filled with the Holy Spirit and faith. And a large number of people was added to the Lord.

REFLECTION

When was the last time you took your faith outside your comfort zone? The first followers of Jesus who shared the Good News with the Greeks, not only the Jews, were delighted at the responsiveness of the people. With which people, and in what places, do you assume your faith is not welcome or needed?

PRAYERS *others may be added*

Asking for the hand of the Lord to be with us, we pray:

◆ Lead us, O Lord.

For Christians sent into inner cities, remote settlements, and hostile territories to bring the Gospel where it may be most needed, we pray: ◆
For confidence in sharing the story of Christianity and its unique gift in any part of the world, we pray: ◆
For ministries to the most overlooked of our world—the uneducated, the isolated, the rebellious, we pray: ◆
For the courage to share our faith and the love of Jesus no matter where we journey, we pray: ◆

Our Father . . .

Lord Jesus, our Shepherd,
you proclaimed God's kingdom to
    Jews and Gentiles,
breaking down assumptions about
    who could be saved.
Lead us to carry your love
    and forgiveness
into every corner of the world that
    aches for you.
You live and reign with God
    the Father
in the unity of the Holy Spirit,
one God, forever and ever.
Amen.

✦ *The Holy Spirit will teach you everything and remind you of all I told you.*

✦ *Rejoice, O hearts that seek the Lord.*

PSALM 66 — page 410

READING — *John 12:44–50*

Jesus cried out and said, "Whoever believes in me believes not only in me but also in the one who sent me, and whoever sees me sees the one who sent me. I came into the world as light, so that everyone who believes in me might not remain in darkness. And if anyone hears my words and does not observe them, I do not condemn him, for I did not come to condemn the world but to save the world. Whoever rejects me and does not accept my words has something to judge him: the word that I spoke, it will condemn him on the last day, because I did not speak on my own, but the Father who sent me commanded me what to say and speak. And I know that his commandment is eternal life. So what I say, I say as the Father told me."

REFLECTION

Such a vivid image of light and darkness! Even little children are drawn toward light. Who among us is not uplifted by the increasing daylight in the spring? We can pray with the image of Christ as a light reaching into every corner of our lives and into every molecule of our very selves. The more we welcome him and the Good News into every part of who we are, the more we will feel ourselves filled with light and goodness.

PRAYERS — *others may be added*

Giving glory and praise to God, we pray:

◆ Fill us with your light, Lord.

For the Church, that her leaders, ministries, places of worship, and offices be flooded with the light of Christ, we pray: ◆ *For the entire world, that every nation, city, countryside, jungle, desert, ocean, and mountain be open to the light of Christ, we pray:* ◆ *For all who live in darkness of any kind may turn their faces to the light of Christ, we pray:* ◆ *For each of us, that we may always be drawn to and reflective of Christ's marvelous light, we pray:* ◆

Our Father . . .

Christ, our Light,
you came into the world and shattered
    the darkness forever.
May we recognize and respond to
    your light in our lives.
Filled with this overflowing and
    joyful light,
may we offer its loving rays to all
    who walk in darkness.
You live and reign with God
    the Father
in the unity of the Holy Spirit,
one God, forever and ever.
Amen.
✦ *Rejoice, O hearts that seek the Lord.*

✦ *Remain in me, as I remain in you, says the Lord; whoever remains in me will bear much fruit.*

PSALM 16   *page 400*

READING   *John 13:16–20*

When Jesus had washed the disciples' feet, he said to them: "Amen, amen, I say to you, no slave is greater than his master nor any messenger greater than the one who sent him. If you understand this, blessed are you if you do it. I am not speaking of all of you. I know those whom I have chosen. But so that the Scripture might be fulfilled,/*The one who ate my food has raised his heel against me.*/From now on I am telling you before it happens, so that when it happens you may believe that I AM. Amen, amen, I say to you, whoever receives the one I send receives me, and whoever receives me receives the one who sent me."

REFLECTION

Who has Jesus sent into our lives? Perhaps an old friend has resurfaced. Maybe a neighbor is asking for help. It could be that one we thought we couldn't connect with is longing for friendship. Which people have been able to reveal Jesus to us in unique ways? How have we responded to and treated those people? They may not be the typical messengers of God; they may be small, humble, even peculiar disciples of the Lord.

PRAYERS   *others may be added*

With thanks to God, we pray:

◆ O God, hear us.

That parents, teachers, mentors, children, and simple ones who have inspired us in our faith may be welcomed in our homes and communities, we pray: ◆ *That those who show faith, courage, and integrity may be respected and honored by our society, we pray:* ◆ *That we may not easily dismiss or oppress messengers who bring difficult challenges from God, we pray:* ◆ *That our community may recognize its prophets, servants, and faithful disciples who give glory to God, we pray:* ◆

Our Father . . .

Lord Jesus,
you come to us in the faces and hearts
    of people in our lives.
Help us to treat them with the respect
    and love we want to show you.
Make us aware of your presence
    with us,
revealing God's being by the work,
    words, and wisdom
of your chosen servants.
You live and reign with God
    the Father
in the unity of the Holy Spirit,
one God, forever and ever.
Amen.

✦ *Remain in me, as I remain in you, says the Lord; whoever remains in me will bear much fruit.*

✢ *Christ is risen, who made all things;*
he has shown mercy on all people.

PSALM 66 *page 410*

READING *John 14:1–6*

Jesus said to his disciples, "Do not let your hearts be troubled. You have faith in God; have faith also in me. In my Father's house there are many dwelling places. If there were not, would I have told you that I am going to prepare a place for you? And if I go and prepare a place for you, I will come back again and take you to myself, so that where I am you also may be. Where I am going you know the way." Thomas said to him, "Master, we do not know where you are going; how can we know the way?" Jesus said to him, "I am the way and the truth and the life. No one comes to the Father except through me."

REFLECTION

There is great comfort in the image of the Father's house with its many rooms prepared for each of us. Jesus promises us a dwelling place with him. We know that those we have loved who have died have also been offered this eternal path. When we miss those who have passed on, we can allow ourselves to imagine the reunions that will take place after death in the heavenly kingdom. Our compassionate God will provide for our aching hearts and our desire to be with our beloved.

PRAYERS *others may be added*

With trust in God, we pray:

◆ Lord, comfort us.

For the saints, Popes, Bishops, and servants of the Church who have died, that they find their dwelling place for all eternity, we pray: ◆ For believers across all times and places, that they find hope and joy in knowing Jesus' promise to bring them to himself, we pray: ◆ For those who have lost loved ones and fear for their future home, we pray: ◆ For us, when we fear the uncertainty of death, that we may take refuge in the loving words of Jesus, we pray: ◆ For all who have died, especially those whom we loved, we pray: ◆

Our Father . . .

Lord Jesus,
you are the Way, the Truth, and
    the Life.
May we trust in your goodness
    and mercy
as we dream of the day when we will
    join you in your Father's house of
    many rooms.
May we look forward to the day of
    reuniting with loved ones
and all who have loved their God.
You live and reign with God the
    Father
in the unity of the Holy Spirit,
one God, forever and ever.
Amen.

✢ *Christ is risen, who made all things;*
he has shown mercy on all people.

✝ *The Holy Spirit will teach you everything and remind you of all I told you.*

PSALM 16 — page 400

READING — Acts 13:44–52

On the following sabbath almost the whole city gathered to hear the word of the Lord. When the Jews saw the crowds, they were filled with jealousy and with violent abuse contradicted what Paul said. Both Paul and Barnabas spoke out boldly and said, "It was necessary that the word of God be spoken to you first, but since you reject it and condemn yourselves as unworthy of eternal life, we now turn to the Gentiles. For so the Lord has commanded us, / *I have made you a light to the Gentiles, that you may be an instrument of salvation to the ends of the earth.*"

REFLECTION

Paul and Barnabas "spoke out boldly," and were then persecuted and expelled. Yet they were able to shake the dust from their feet and be filled with joy and the Holy Spirit. When we do the will of God, no matter the consequences that may befall us in the world, may we feel deeply the presence of God within us and be filled with unshakable joy.

PRAYERS — *others may be added*

As disciples, confident in God, we pray:

◆ Be with us, Holy Spirit.

For the Pope and Bishops who speak boldly on behalf of the Church, despite opposition, we pray: ◆ *For those who seek justice and face persecution and exile from their homelands, we pray:* ◆ *For all who speak in a voice of courage for what is right, we pray:* ◆ *For a community filled with a faith that cannot be overcome, we pray:* ◆

Our Father . . .

God of light and salvation,
you give us the gifts of faith, service,
    and leadership.
Walk with us as we seek justice
    and truth,
and fill us with joy on our journey.
When the road is difficult, may we
    not grow weary.
Help us to "shake the dust from
    our feet"
and continue to follow the path
    of Jesus.
We ask this through our Lord Jesus
    Christ, your Son,
who lives and reigns with you
in the unity of the Holy Spirit,
one God, forever and ever.
Amen.

✝ *The Holy Spirit will teach you everything and remind you of all I told you.*

✚ *Everyone who believes in the Son has eternal life, and I shall raise him on the last day, says the Lord.*

PSALM 66   *page 410*

READING   *John 14:1–12*

Jesus said to his disciples: "Do not let your hearts be troubled. You have faith in God; have faith also in me. In my Father's house there are many dwelling places. If there were not, would I have told you that I am going to prepare a place for you? And if I go and prepare a place for you, I will come back again and take you to myself, so that where I am you also may be. Where I am going you know the way." Thomas said to him, "Master, we do not know where you are going; how can we know the way?" Jesus said to him, "I am the way and the truth and the life. No one comes to the Father except through me. If you know me, then you will also know my Father. From now on you do know him and have seen him."

REFLECTION   *St. Augustine*

Faith is to believe what we do not see; the reward of this faith is to see what we believe.

PRAYERS   *others may be added*

Longing to understand, we pray:

◆ Be our way, truth, and life, O Lord.

That theologians and teachers of the faith may spark our minds with wisdom, we pray: ◆ *That music, art, science, and drama may lead us to new ways of knowing God, we pray:* ◆ *That laughter and life experiences may dislodge the rigid restrictions we place upon God and open our eyes in renewed faith, we pray:* ◆ *That our parish may be a safe and supportive place to explore our relationship with God, we pray:* ◆

Our Father . . .

Gracious God,
you sent your Son as the clearest,
most tangible revelation of yourself
   and your love.
Each day is an opportunity to come to
   know you better
in hearing your Word and receiving
   your sacraments.
Continue to lead us to you through
   our Lord Jesus Christ, your Son,
who is with us in our daily lives,
and who lives and reigns with you
in the unity of the Holy Spirit,
one God, forever and ever.
Amen.

✚ *Everyone who believes in the Son has eternal life, and I shall raise him on the last day, says the Lord.*

✦ *Athirst is my soul for the living God.*

PSALM 130 *page 418*

READING *Acts 14:9 – 12, 14–15*

[The crippled man] listened to Paul speaking, who looked intently at him, saw that he had the faith to be healed, and called out in a loud voice, "Stand up straight on your feet." He jumped up and began to walk about. When the crowds saw what Paul had done, they cried out in Lycaonian, "The gods have come down to us in human form." They called Barnabas "Zeus" and Paul "Hermes," because he was the chief speaker.

The Apostles Barnabas and Paul tore their garments when they heard this and rushed out into the crowd, shouting, "Men, why are you doing this? We are of the same nature as you, human beings. We proclaim to you good news that you should turn from these idols to the living God, / *who made heaven and earth and sea and all that is in them.*

REFLECTION

We often idolize people rather than remain centered on God. We compliment them, think we can never live up to their example, and we think of them as set apart from humanity. We can then be deeply disappointed by their sin and failure. We need to realize the presence of the Holy Spirit among us, as well as God's distance from us, holy and set apart. No human is a god. God alone is the true source of power, love, and mercy.

PRAYERS *others may be added*

Alive in the Spirit, we pray:

◆ We praise you, O God.

That Christian leaders defer praise and thanks given to them, and instead point others to the true God, we pray: ◆
That civic leaders inspire every person to use his or her own gifts, we pray: ◆
That disappointment in our mentors does not lead us to despair but to renewed commitment to our own baptismal call, we pray: ◆ *That our community may be the Body of Christ on earth, valuing every member with equal appreciation, we pray:* ◆

Our Father . . .

Living and true God,
we are tempted to idolize what we
   can see and hear.
May we return to you,
giver of life and spirit of truth.
Inspire us to share equally in the
   mission to bring all people to you.
May we worship you alone.
Grant this through Christ our Lord.
Amen.

✦ *Athirst is my soul for the living God.*

✚ *Rejoice, O hearts that seek the Lord.*

PSALM 66   *page 410*

READING   *Acts 14:21–27*

After [the disciples] had proclaimed the good news to that city and made a considerable number of disciples, they returned to Lystra and to Iconium and to Antioch. They strengthened the spirits of the disciples and exhorted them to persevere in the faith, saying, "It is necessary for us to undergo many hardships to enter the Kingdom of God." They appointed presbyters for them in each Church and, with prayer and fasting, commended them to the Lord in whom they had put their faith. Then they traveled through Pisidia and reached Pamphylia. After proclaiming the word at Perga they went down to Attalia. From there they sailed to Antioch, where they had been commended to the grace of God for the work they had now accomplished. And when they arrived, they called the Church together and reported what God had done with them and how he had opened the door of faith to the Gentiles.

REFLECTION

There is a shortage of good news in our lives. No wonder, then, that we often enjoy so intensely the visit of a missionary to our parish, or the opportunity to bless a young person heading off on a service trip. In a big church, we can lose sight of the many amazing stories of healing and conversion happening among us. We must bring stories of evangelization, miracles, and God's faithfulness before the community. In them, we will be renewed in faith and the desire to serve our God.

PRAYERS   *others may be added*

Listening for the Good News today, we pray:

◆ Lord, hear our prayer.

That the universal Church continues to prioritize mass communication of the good work being done in the name of Jesus, we pray: ◆ That opportunities are created and utilized to gather together with others and share what God has done, we pray: ◆ That we demand good news from our media outlets, we pray: ◆ That Christians who serve daily also find time and means to share their stories with the larger community, we pray: ◆

Our Father . . .

God of power and might,
you are at work in numerous and
    miraculous ways.
May our Church recognize, support,
    and encourage
all who go forth serving you,
especially by sharing and celebrating
    the stories of your hand at work.
Open our eyes and ears and hearts to
    these opportunities to praise you.
Grant this through Christ our Lord.
Amen.

✚ *Rejoice, O hearts that seek the Lord.*

✦ *Remain in me, as I remain in you, says the Lord; whoever remains in me will bear much fruit.*

PSALM 66   page 410

READING   John 15:4–8

[Jesus said to his disciples,] "Remain in me, as I remain in you. Just as a branch cannot bear fruit on its own unless it remains on the vine, so neither can you unless you remain in me. I am the vine, you are the branches. Whoever remains in me and I in him will bear much fruit, because without me you can do nothing. Anyone who does not remain in me will be thrown out like a branch and wither; people will gather them and throw them into a fire and they will be burned. If you remain in me and my words remain in you, ask for whatever you want and it will be done for you. By this is my Father glorified, that you bear much fruit and become my disciples."

REFLECTION

This reading calls to mind the ways we need to stay connected to God in order to be fruitful in our lives. We do this through prayer, the sacraments, and the community of faith. Our families, schools, parishes, and communities also desperately need the vine to be nourished. What feeds these institutions? In what ways are groups and organizations refreshed in order to bear fruit? We consider how we can connect them to the true vine.

PRAYERS   *others may be added*

Recognizing our need for the vine, we pray:

♦ God, nourish us.

That parishes take time to reflect upon their growth and discern ways to improve, we pray: ♦ *That our schools—public and parochial—have the most effective and consistent support they need to maintain strong education, we pray:* ♦ *That our communities are blessed with responsible leaders who evaluate change and how to respond to it, we pray:* ♦ *That our families make time for each other, for recreation, and for grounding in faith, we pray:* ♦

Our Father . . .

Heavenly Father,
you provide us with all that we need,
so long as we remain in you.
Alert us when we have become cut
    off from you
and need to return to the source of
    our life and happiness.
May we remain strong in you so as to
    help others and groups
in which we participate to be rooted
    in you.
We ask this through Christ our Lord.
Amen.

✦ *Remain in me, as I remain in you, says the Lord; whoever remains in me will bear much fruit.*

Optional memorials of St. Bede the Venerable, priest, doctor of the Church; St. Gregory VII, pope; St. Mary Magdalene de 'Pazzi, virgin

✤ *Commit your life to the Lord and he will help you.*

PSALM 40   *page 407*

READING   *John 17:20–24*

[Jesus prayed, saying:] "I pray not only for them, but also for those who will believe in me through their word, so that they may all be one, as you, Father, are in me and I in you, that they also may be in us, that the world may believe that you sent me. And I have given them the glory you gave me, so that they may be one, as we are one, I in them and you in me, that they may be brought to perfection as one, that the world may know that you sent me, and that you loved them even as you loved me. Father, they are your gift to me. I wish that where I am they also may be with me, that they may see my glory that you gave me, because you loved me before the foundation of the world."

REFLECTION

A true lover of souls, St. Philip Neri was devoted to the care of others and to the good of the Church. Priests are called by God to tend to his flock, seeing every person as a precious child of God. Many are called by God to care for others. On this memorial, let us lovingly accept the people God has given us to love and serve in our own way.

PRAYERS   *others may be added*

With Jesus as our example, we pray:

◆ May we be one in you, God.

For priests, deacons, and all ministers of the Church, that they be filled with love for the flock, we pray: ◆ *For physicians, nurses, and all health care providers, that they may be motivated by the desire to heal, we pray:* ◆ *For teachers, that they value the unique gifts of every student, we pray:* ◆ *For parents, that they treasure their children and give them freedom, we pray:* ◆

Our Father . . .

Lord God,
with St. Philip Neri,
we pray for all people,
especially those who serve others.
May we be one in Christ Jesus, no
     matter our role,
and see one another as a child of God.
We ask this through the same Christ
     our Lord.
Amen.

✤ *Commit your life to the Lord and he will help you.*

✦ *Christ is risen, who made all things; he has shown mercy on all people.*

PSALM 16   *page 400*

READING   *John 15:12–17*

Jesus said to his disciples: "This is my commandment: love one another as I love you. No one has greater love than this, to lay down one's life for one's friends. You are my friends if you do what I command you. I no longer call you slaves, because a slave does not know what his master is doing. I have called you friends, because I have told you everything I have heard from my Father. It was not you who chose me, but I who chose you and appointed you to go and bear fruit that will remain, so that whatever you ask the Father in my name he may give you. This I command you: love one another."

REFLECTION

Think of a friend you love dearly. Think of the ways you share your life, resources, and time with this friend. Think of sacrifices you have gladly made to help your friend. Jesus asks us to love like this every day. We are to open ourselves in great love to all our brothers and sisters.

PRAYERS   *others may be added*

In love, we pray:

◆ Lord, hear our prayer.

That Christians may love others in a unique way that inspires others to love, we pray: ◆ *That the United States of America may share its resources with other nations in love, we pray:* ◆ *That our friendships may be lasting and life-giving, we pray:* ◆ *That we may be inspired by the loving acts of our friends, we pray:* ◆

Our Father . . .

Lord Jesus, our teacher,
you gave us love
and taught us to care for one another
with the sacrificial love of a
    true friend.
Bless our friends,
and bless all those to whom we are
    called to be friend.
May you provide compassion
    and mercy
through our gentle hands and hearts.
You live and reign with God
    the Father
in the unity of the Holy Spirit,
one God, forever and ever.
Amen.

✦ *Christ is risen, who made all things; he has shown mercy on all people.*

✦ *God so loved the world that he gave his only-begotten Son, so that everyone who believes in him might have eternal life.*

PSALM 149   page 421

READING   John 15:18–21

Jesus said to his disciples, "If the world hates you, realize that it hated me first. If you belonged to the world, the world would love its own; but because you do not belong to the world, and I have chosen you out of the world, the world hates you. Remember the word I spoke to you, 'No slave is greater than his master.' If they persecuted me, they will also persecute you. If they kept my word, they will also keep yours. And they will do all these things to you on account of my name, because they do not know the one who sent me."

REFLECTION

Imagine a parent saying this to a child: "You do not belong to the world, and I have chosen you out of the world." The underlying message is that the child is precious, beloved, and created by God for a purpose. Our God speaks to us with deep love in these very words. God is our protective, nurturing, and attentive parent who reminds us of our eternal destiny. Rest in the embrace of God.

PRAYERS   *others may be added*

In gratitude, we pray:

◆ Show us your love.

That Christian parents instill a sense of dignity and purpose in their children, we pray: ◆ That God's Word guides leaders of nations to works of charity, justice, and mercy, we pray: ◆ That children without parents come to know themselves as children of God, we pray: ◆ That workers know their eternal purpose beyond their earthly work, we pray: ◆ That all members of our community know that they are uniquely and wonderfully made in the image of God, we pray: ◆

Our Father . . .

Loving God,
you chose us for yourself
and redeemed the world from sin.
May we attend to our
     highest purpose,
undeterred by the distractions of the
     secular life.
May your great love surround and
     embrace us.
Grant this through Christ our Lord.
Amen.

✦ *God so loved the world that he gave his only-begotten Son, so that everyone who believes in him might have eternal life.*

✦ *The Holy Spirit will teach you everything and remind you of all I told you.*

PSALM 149   *page 421*

READING   *John 14:15–17*

Jesus said to his disciples: "If you love me, you will keep my commandments. And I will ask the Father, and he will give you another Advocate to be with you always, the Spirit of truth, whom the world cannot accept, because it neither sees nor knows him. But you know him, because he remains with you, and will be in you."

REFLECTION

Does loneliness keep you from a full life and relationship with God? Jesus says the Holy Spirit will "be with you always," "remains with you," and "will be in you." Loneliness can be overwhelming or deeply saddening. It may be hard to turn to prayer when feeling so desolate. A gentle reminder to open the Word, attend the Mass, or open your hearts to a true Christian friend may help. A note on the mirror, a plaque on the wall, or a small crucifix around our neck or in the car can be that reminder. Jesus will never leave us and has sent the Holy Spirit to support and inspire. God's love is right there when we reach for it.

PRAYERS   *others may be added*

Admitting our loneliness, we pray:

◆ May we be in you and you in us, Lord.

For our priests and religious, who face loneliness in unique ways as celibates, that the Holy Spirit may always lead them to fullness of life and friendship, we pray: ◆ *For unhappy married couples, who experience loneliness in the presence of another, that the Holy Spirit may reopen their hearts to one another, we pray:* ◆ *For those longing for children and facing difficulties, that the Holy Spirit may comfort them and give them life in unexpected ways, we pray:* ◆ *For all of us, that we remember to turn to God in our loneliest hours, we pray:* ◆

Our Father . . .

Lord Jesus, our brother,
you knew loneliness as you walked
   the earth,
misunderstood and persecuted.
You promise to be with us always by
   sending your Holy Spirit.
May we always turn to you when we
   ache with loneliness.
You live and reign with God
   the Father
in the unity of the Holy Spirit,
one God, forever and ever.
Amen.

✦ *The Holy Spirit will teach you everything and remind you of all I told you.*

✚ *The Holy Spirit will teach you everything and remind you of all I told you.*

PSALM 16   page 400

READING   *John 15:26—16:4a*

Jesus said to his disciples: "When the Advocate comes whom I will send you from the Father, the Spirit of truth who proceeds from the Father, he will testify to me. And you also testify, because you have been with me from the beginning.

"I have told you this so that you may not fall away. They will expel you from the synagogues; in fact, the hour is coming when everyone who kills you will think he is offering worship to God. They will do this because they have not known either the Father or me. I have told you this so that when their hour comes you may remember that I told you."

REFLECTION

Jesus warns the disciples that it's going to get bad. Would you have been "tough enough" to stick around, knowing violent persecution lay ahead? Can we expect rough times in our lives and in our faith, but commit to staying in the race? Think through the persecutions or obstacles you have faced. What has been the key to making it through them? Has the Holy Spirit been behind, within, and around you? Pray for that grace in the future.

PRAYERS   *others may be added*

Honest in our fears, we come to God for courage and pray:

◆ Be behind us. Be within us. Be around us, O Lord.

When our Pope and Bishops are maligned for their teachings on peace, justice, and respect for life, we pray: ◆ *When our country faces war and division, poverty and inequality, we pray:* ◆ *When others hurt us by their words or actions, we pray:* ◆ *When our personal faith undergoes the greatest challenges it can face, we pray:* ◆ *When we face death and the fears of the unknown, we pray:* ◆

Our Father . . .

Lord Jesus,
you show us how to be strong in the
    face of adversity.
May we always be courageous in faith
when we are attacked personally
    and communally.
Send us your Holy Spirit
to be our guide and source
    of strength.
You live and reign with God
    the Father
in the unity of the Holy Spirit,
one God, forever and ever.
Amen.

✚   *The Holy Spirit will teach you everything and remind you of all I told you.*

✝ *Blessed is the Virgin Mary, who kept the Word of God and pondered it in her heart.*

CANTICLE   page 422

READING   Luke 1:39–45

Mary set out and traveled to the hill country in haste to a town of Judah, where she entered the house of Zechariah and greeted Elizabeth. When Elizabeth heard Mary's greeting, the infant leaped in her womb, and Elizabeth, filled with the Holy Spirit, cried out in a loud voice and said, "Blessed are you among women, and blessed is the fruit of your womb. And how does this happen to me, that the mother of my Lord should come to me? For at the moment the sound of your greeting reached my ears, the infant in my womb leaped for joy. Blessed are you who believed that what was spoken to you by the Lord would be fulfilled."

REFLECTION

If you invited Mary into your home today, what would you serve her? How would you make time for her? Think of all the ways you treat a special guest. Notice your reaction to being selected for her visit. Do you feel humbled, honored, or do you rise to the occasion with greater faithfulness and commitment to God than you had the day before? What could you learn from her? Make an effort to develop a relationship with her and see her as family, as someone sent to help you become closer to God. Listen to all she has to teach you in prayer.

PRAYERS   others may be added

Welcoming Mary into our hearts, we pray:

◆ Lead us, Lord.

For the Church, that Mary may be our model of faith and service, we pray: ◆ For refugees in camps and foreign lands, that they may feel the companionship of Mary, we pray: ◆ For travelers and visitors to our homes, that we may welcome them as did Elizabeth, we pray: ◆ For open hearts among us, that we may learn from Mary and Elizabeth, we pray:◆

Our Father . . .

God of providence,
you filled Mary with faith
and blessed her among all women.
We are honored to have her example
and to know she intercedes on
    our behalf.
May we walk in her footsteps of faith.
We ask this through Christ our Lord.
Amen.

✝ *Blessed is the Virgin Mary, who kept the Word of God and pondered it in her heart.*

✦ *Commit your life to the Lord and he will help you.*

PSALM 40 page 407

READING John 12:24–26

Jesus said to his disciples: "Amen, amen, I say to you, unless a grain of wheat falls to the ground and dies, it remains just a grain of wheat; but if it dies, it produces much fruit. Whoever loves his life loses it, and whoever hates his life in this world will preserve it for eternal life. Whoever serves me must follow me, and where I am, there also will my servant be. The Father will honor whoever serves me."

REFLECTION

When we sense an obstacle or difficulty coming in our lives, our inclination may be to avoid it. We want to detour from the path we set out on, or try to make the work as easy as possible. However, the only way God can work through us is if we are open to growth. Transformation—sanctification—occurs when we "die" to our failures, our sins, our loneliness, our despair. This means we should welcome the obstacles, follow the hard road when it opens up in front of us, for it is in these experiences of "dying" that the life of Christ can grow in us.

PRAYERS *others may be added*

Open to death, we pray:

◆ We put our lives in your hands, God.

That the witness of St. Justin is the paradigm for the witness of all Christians, we pray: ◆ *That our nation's leaders do not avoid difficult negotiations, but face them headfirst, we pray:* ◆ *That families and friends will let go of grudges, cease to avoid conflict, and choose direct dialogue, we pray:* ◆ *That we may willingly choose to lay down our lives, our pride, and our fear so that God may work through us, we pray:* ◆ *That all those who have died know the joy of new life at the heavenly banquet, we pray:* ◆

Our Father . . .

Lord Jesus, our Messiah,
you showed us that the path to
    eternal life
goes through the process of
    death—natural death and death
    to sin.
Your servant, Justin, gave glory to
    you in his life and in his death.
May we, too, risk everything in order
    to grow closer to you.
Make us willing to follow you,
    even to death.
You live and reign with God
    the Father
in the unity of the Holy Spirit,
one God, forever and ever.
Amen.

✦ *Commit your life to the Lord and he will help you.*

✦ *Rejoice, O hearts that seek the Lord.*

PSALM 66 *page 410*

READING *Matthew 28:16–20*

The eleven disciples went to Galilee, to the mountain to which Jesus had ordered them. When they saw him, they worshiped, but they doubted. Then Jesus approached and said to them, "All power in heaven and on earth has been given to me. Go, therefore, and make disciples of all nations, baptizing them in the name of the Father, and of the Son, and of the Holy Spirit, teaching them to observe all that I have commanded you. And behold, I am with you always, until the end of the age."

REFLECTION

This reading highlights the pinnacle of the disciples' understanding of Jesus as divine, one with God. Just before this moment "they worshiped, but they doubted." Their message to us is this: throughout the time we knew Jesus, we saw and heard many amazing things, especially his Resurrection from the dead. We were confused, unsure, and grasping at understanding as we followed him. In the end, they tell us, we knew him as king of heaven and earth.

PRAYERS *others may be added*

In awe of Jesus the Lord, we pray:

◆ Glory to you, O God.

For the divine nature of the Church, which guides all Christian people, we pray: ◆ *For earthly kings and rulers, who hold great power yet still need wisdom, we pray:* ◆ *For angels, saints, tranquil spaces, and hallowed ground, we pray:* ◆ *For the privilege of faith, which carries us even through doubt, we pray:* ◆ *For the moment of death, when we will see God face to face, we pray:* ◆

Our Father . . .

Risen Lord,
you revealed the truth of God's
    kingdom in every way you could.
Your disciples strained to know and
    understand you and your message;
still, our understanding
    remains limited.
We give you glory and praise
for a foretaste of the magnificence of
    your reign.
Lead us to that day when all will be
    one with you.
You live and reign with God
    the Father
in the unity of the Holy Spirit,
one God, forever and ever.
Amen.

✦ *Rejoice, O hearts that seek the Lord.*

✦ *Commit your life to the Lord and he will help you.*

PSALM 40   *page 407*

READING   *Matthew 5:1–12a*

When [Jesus] saw the crowds, he went up the mountain, and after he had sat down, his disciples came to him. He began to teach them, saying: / "Blessed are the poor in spirit, / for theirs is the Kingdom of heaven. / Blessed are they who mourn, / for they will be comforted. / Blessed are the meek, / for they will inherit the land. / Blessed are they who hunger and thirst for righteousness, / for they will be satisfied. / Blessed are the merciful, / for they will be shown mercy. / Blessed are the clean of heart, / for they will see God. / Blessed are the peacemakers, / for they will be called children of God. / Blessed are they who are persecuted for the sake of righteousness, / for theirs is the Kingdom of heaven. / Blessed are you when they insult you and persecute you and utter every kind of evil against you falsely because of me. Rejoice and be glad, for your reward will be great in heaven."

REFLECTION

Lives of radical accountability and honesty seem rare today. The Beatitudes speak of a radical way of life that is counter-cultural, counter-intuitive, and remarkable. The martyrs St. Charles Lwanga and his companions faced temptation and persecution. Their response—and that of other recognized Christians—was to follow the radical way of the Beatitudes. These brave Ugandan faithful should inspire every decision we make to live with unashamed purity.

PRAYERS   *others may be added*

With deep commitment to living our faith, we pray:

◆ Make our hearts clean, O God.

For the Pope, Bishops, and priests who represent our faith, that they take seriously their responsibility to be honest, we pray: ◆ *For political figures who maintain a balanced, healthy work ethic, we pray:* ◆ *For those out of work, depressed, or ill, we pray:* ◆ *For serious consideration of our roles and responsibilities to God and others, we pray:* ◆

Our Father . . .

Loving God,
bless and reward those who live
humbly and courageously.
We ask this through Christ our Lord.
Amen.

✦ *Commit your life to the Lord and he will help you.*

✠ *Rejoice, O hearts that seek the Lord.*

PSALM 16   page 400

READING   *Acts 18:23–28*

A Jew named Apollos, a native of Alexandria, an eloquent speaker, arrived in Ephesus. He was an authority on the Scriptures. He had been instructed in the Way of the Lord and, with ardent spirit, spoke and taught accurately about Jesus, although he knew only the baptism of John. He began to speak boldly in the synagogue; but when Priscilla and Aquila heard him, they took him aside and explained to him the Way of God more accurately. And when he wanted to cross to Achaia, the brothers encouraged him and wrote to the disciples there to welcome him. After his arrival he gave great assistance to those who had come to believe through grace. He vigorously refuted the Jews in public, establishing from the Scriptures that the Christ is Jesus.

REFLECTION

The description of Apollos sharing the truth of Jesus as the Christ lays out the balance between faith and reason. Converts had come to believe "through grace" but were still interested in giving their faith a rational foundation in scripture. We, too, feel the tug between faith and reason, and our Church encourages us to develop both elements of our discipleship.

PRAYERS   *others may be added*

Grateful for our faith and our intellect, we pray:

◆ Lord, hear our prayer.

For all teachers of the faith, that priority is given to God's grace working in a person, and also respect for the desire to understand, we pray: ◆ *For Catholic universities, that they exemplify excellence in scholarship and commitment to the longing of the soul for God, we pray:* ◆ *For all Christian congregations to encourage a balance between faith of the heart and faith of the mind, we pray:* ◆ *For reading, discussion, speakers, retreats, and continuing education in the faith in our faith communities, we pray:* ◆

Our Father . . .

All-knowing God,
you work by grace in the hearts of
    your followers,
and in the gifts of our intellect
    and creativity.
Show us the balance between faith
    in you
and rational exploration to understand
    the meaning of Christianity.
We ask this through Christ our Lord.
Amen.

✠ *Rejoice, O hearts that seek the Lord.*

✜ *Everyone who believes in the Son has eternal life, and I shall raise him on the last day, says the Lord.*

PSALM 66 page 410

READING John 17:1–5

Jesus raised his eyes to heaven and said, "Father, the hour has come. Give glory to your son, so that your son may glorify you, just as you gave him authority over all people, so that your son may give eternal life to all you gave him. Now this is eternal life, that they should know you, the only true God, and the one whom you sent, Jesus Christ. I glorified you on earth by accomplishing the work that you gave me to do. Now glorify me, Father, with you, with the glory that I had with you before the world began."

REFLECTION

We have much to learn from those who received the sacraments at Easter. Consider meeting with and listening to the newly initiated. What is their story: from their identity as children of God, to their acceptance of Jesus as Savior, to their study and comprehension of the fullness of faith? How did they first come to the Christian and Catholic faith? How are they sustained in these beliefs? What hopes do they have for their future life in Christ Jesus?

PRAYERS others may be added

With the new members of God's flock in mind, we pray:

◆ We belong to you, God.

For candidates and catechumens who came into the Church this past Easter, that their faith may be a light to us all, we pray: ◆ *For non-believers searching for meaning, understanding, and community, we pray:* ◆ *For those who do not realize they have lost their way, we pray:* ◆ *For all Christians, that their faith is reawakened and renewed by the witness of the newly initiated, we pray:* ◆

Our Father . . .

Christ, our light,
you showed us the way to the Father,
and will not rest until we belong
    to him.
We praise you for your
    loving sacrifice,
which opened the doors of heaven
    to us.
May we be inspired by those
who have recently committed to life
    in you.
You live and reign with God
    the Father
in the unity of the Holy Spirit,
one God, forever and ever.
Amen.

✜ *Everyone who believes in the Son has eternal life, and I shall raise him on the last day, says the Lord.*

✦ *The Holy Spirit will teach you everything and remind you of all I told you.*

PSALM 16   page 400

READING   *Acts 19:1–7*

While Apollos was in Corinth, Paul traveled through the interior of the country and down to Ephesus where he found some disciples. He said to them, "Did you receive the Holy Spirit when you became believers?" They answered him, "We have never even heard that there is a Holy Spirit." He said, "How were you baptized?" They replied, "With the baptism of John." Paul then said, "John baptized with a baptism of repentance, telling the people to believe in the one who was to come after him, that is, in Jesus." When they heard this, they were baptized in the name of the Lord Jesus. And when Paul laid his hands on them, the Holy Spirit came upon them, and they spoke in tongues and prophesied. Altogether there were about twelve men.

REFLECTION

Unlike the disciples in this story who were baptized by John, we who were baptized in Christ Jesus do not have any excuse for not living in the Holy Spirit. Our faith asks us to repent and believe. We cannot only ask forgiveness. We also are to live our faith and share the gifts the Holy Spirit has given us.

PRAYERS   *others may be added*

Alive in our faith in Christ Jesus, we pray:

◆ May the Holy Spirit be upon us.

That all Christians are aware that the Holy Spirit has anointed them, we pray: ◆
That the Holy Spirit will come upon all nations and their leaders, we pray: ◆
That those who doubt they have gifts and suffer from low self-esteem will be aware of the gifts the Holy Spirit has given them, we pray: ◆ *That the Holy Spirit will raise up all those who have died in the Lord, we pray:* ◆

Our Father . . .

Generous God,
you not only forgive our sins
and offer us eternal life,
but you invite us to share in the joy
and wonder of this life,
by the grace of your Holy Spirit,
who gives us every gift we need
to be your servants in the world.
May we respond joyfully with a
   resounding "yes!"
We ask this through Christ our Lord.
Amen.

✦ *The Holy Spirit will teach you everything and remind you of all I told you.*

✦ *Commit your life to the Lord.*

PSALM 16   *page 400*

READING   *Acts 20:19–27*

[Paul said:] "I served the Lord with all humility and with the tears and trials that came to me because of the plots of the Jews, and I did not at all shrink from telling you what was for your benefit, or from teaching you in public or in your homes. I earnestly bore witness for both Jews and Greeks to repentance before God and to faith in our Lord Jesus. But now, compelled by the Spirit, I am going to Jerusalem. What will happen to me there I do not know, except that in one city after another the Holy Spirit has been warning me that imprisonment and hardships await me. Yet I consider life of no importance to me, if only I may finish my course and the ministry that I received from the Lord Jesus, to bear witness to the Gospel of God's grace.

REFLECTION

God calls for change. We may have served God in one capacity for many years—faithfully, humbly, earnestly— just as St. Paul. Still, God may call us to something new and unknown. We can look back on our service with a sense of satisfaction that we gave of our whole selves. Then, we must let go of that community and follow God where he leads.

PRAYERS   *others may be added*

Trusting God, we pray:

◆ Show us the way.

That pastors reassigned, parishes or schools that have closed, and religious communities that have merged may continue to be signs of faithful service, we pray: ◆ *That nations in political upheaval or change in regime find peace, we pray:* ◆ *That all who face retirement may look back fondly and look forward hopefully, we pray,* ◆ *That unexpected changes in our lives may lead us to lean on God, we pray:* ◆ *That all who have died will be received at the heavenly banquet, we pray:* ◆

Our Father . . .

Compassionate God,
you know the faithful service of
   your children.
Comfort those letting go of the past
   and experiencing change.
Open our eyes and hearts to the
   future you have prepared for us,
and reassure us of your love
   and protection.
We ask this through Christ our Lord.
Amen.

✦ *Commit your life to the Lord.*

✦ *Remain in me, as I remain in you, says the Lord; whoever remains in me will bear much fruit.*

PSALM 16   *page 400*

READING   *John 17:14–19*

[Jesus prayed, saying:] "I gave them your word, and the world hated them, because they do not belong to the world any more than I belong to the world. I do not ask that you take them out of the world but that you keep them from the Evil One. They do not belong to the world any more than I belong to the world. Consecrate them in the truth. Your word is truth. As you sent me into the world, so I sent them into the world. And I consecrate myself for them, so that they also may be consecrated in truth."

REFLECTION   *Pope Benedict XVI*

To consecrate something or someone means, therefore, to give that thing or person to God as his property, to take it out of the context of what is ours and to insert it in his milieu, so that it no longer belongs to our affairs, but is totally of God. Consecration is thus a taking away from the world and a giving over to the living God. The thing or person no longer belongs to us, or even to itself, but is immersed in God. Such a giving up of something in order to give it over to God, we also call a sacrifice.

PRAYERS   *others may be added*

Guided by the Holy Spirit, we pray:

◆ Bless us and send us, O God.

That the Church carries out her mission to bring the light of Christ to all the world, we pray: ◆ *That Christians in every walk of life recognize that they have been consecrated by God and live in holiness, we pray:* ◆ *That those who defile their bodies and spirits may return to their baptismal promises, we pray:* ◆ *That our community of faith may take seriously its responsibility to live as holy men and women, we pray:* ◆

Our Father . . .

O Holy God,
you have blessed and sanctified us by
    your grace.
Show us how to live in holiness,
through prayer, reconciliation,
    forgiveness, service, humility,
    and love.
May our example lead others to lives
    of holiness and happiness.
Grant this through Christ our Lord.
Amen.

✦ *Remain in me, as I remain in you, says the Lord; whoever remains in me will bear much fruit.*

✦ *Christ is risen. Alleluia.*

PSALM 149 *page 421*

READING *Acts 23:6–11*

Paul was aware that some were Sadducees and some Pharisees, so he called out before the Sanhedrin, "My brothers, I am a Pharisee, the son of Pharisees; I am on trial for hope in the resurrection of the dead." When he said this, a dispute broke out between the Pharisees and Sadducees, and the group became divided. A great uproar occurred, and some scribes belonging to the Pharisee party stood up and sharply argued, "We find nothing wrong with this man. Suppose a spirit or an angel has spoken to him?" The dispute was so serious that the commander, afraid that Paul would be torn to pieces by them, ordered his troops to go down and rescue Paul from their midst and take him into the compound. The following night the Lord stood by him and said, "Take courage. For just as you have borne witness to my cause in Jerusalem, so you must also bear witness in Rome."

REFLECTION

Yes, life can be hard. We may go through one trial, only to undergo another. It doesn't seem fair that if we are faithful in difficult times, we may be presented with yet another challenge. God does not promise us an easy life. But, God does promise to stand by us and to provide us with the courage and strength we need to persevere.

PRAYERS *others may be added*

In times of trouble, we pray:

◆ Give us courage, O God.

For Christians who witness to God's love despite illness, financial distress, and deep sadness, we pray: ◆ *For our national leaders who experience great stress in the responsibility of protecting and determining the future of our country, we pray:* ◆ *For the despairing, who have been dealt many crises and have limited support, we pray:* ◆ *For our spiritual path, that it might provide us with opportunities to persevere in Jesus' name, we pray:* ◆

Our Father . . .

Provident God,
you were at the side of your
    servant Paul
through persecution and
    imprisonment.
You promise to be with us in every
    trial we experience,
yet we must look within ourselves
and to our faith to carry on with
    fortitude and grace.
May we not be discouraged by trials,
but know that you give us the courage
    we need.
We ask this through Christ our Lord.
Amen.

✦ *Christ is risen. Alleluia.*

✤ *Everyone who believes in the Son has eternal life, and I shall raise him on the last day, says the Lord.*

PSALM 16   page 400

READING   *John 21:15–17*

[Jesus] said to Simon Peter, "Simon, son of John, do you love me more than these?" He said to him, "Yes, Lord, you know that I love you." He said to him, "Feed my lambs." He then said to him a second time, "Simon, son of John, do you love me?" He said to him, "Yes, Lord, you know that I love you." He said to him, "Tend my sheep." He said to him the third time, "Simon, son of John, do you love me?" Peter was distressed that he had said to him a third time, "Do you love me?" and he said to him, "Lord, you know everything; you know that I love you." Jesus said to him, "Feed my sheep."

REFLECTION

Read today's Gospel account with your name in place of Simon's, and your parent's names in the place of John's name. Hear Jesus ask you if you love him. Hear Jesus plead with you to feed his lambs. Hear Jesus ask you to tend his sheep. Hear Jesus entrust to you his ministry, his love, and his mercy. Listen to his words, and open your heart to the message he has for you.

PRAYERS   *others may be added*

With love for Jesus, we pray:

◆ Make us shepherds like you.

For all disciples, that we hear God calling us by name to love and serve others, we pray: ◆ For the social service programs in our country that feed children, tend to the elderly and disabled, and help the disadvantaged gain education and skills, we pray: ◆ For consumers, that we make decisions which will have a more gentle impact on our earth and its creatures, we pray: ◆ For each parishioner, young and old, that we hear Jesus' unique message for us of how we can tend to his sheep, we pray: ◆

Our Father . . .

Lord Jesus, our Good Shepherd,
you showed us the greatest love there
    is by giving up your life.
Make us loving shepherds in whatever
    way we can best serve you,
as feeders, tenders, and caregivers of
    your flock.
May our love for you impel us to care
    for others.
You live and reign with God
    the Father
in the unity of the Holy Spirit,
one God, forever and ever.
Amen.

✤ *Everyone who believes in the Son has eternal life, and I shall raise him on the last day, says the Lord.*

✤ *The Lord is my shepherd; there is nothing I shall want.*

PSALM 40 *page 407*

READING *Matthew 10:7–13*

Jesus said to the Twelve: "As you go, make this proclamation: 'The Kingdom of heaven is at hand.' Cure the sick, raise the dead, cleanse the lepers, drive out demons. Without cost you have received; without cost you are to give. Do not take gold or silver or copper for your belts; no sack for the journey, or a second tunic, or sandals, or walking stick. The laborer deserves his keep. Whatever town or village you enter, look for a worthy person in it, and stay there until you leave. As you enter a house, wish it peace. If the house is worthy, let your peace come upon it; if not, let your peace return to you."

REFLECTION

The joy of serving as a disciple is an outcome of a gift freely given. God's grace, healing, and forgiveness are given to us for free, and we in turn offer these gifts to others with delight. We should not impose expectations, judgments, or burdens on others, but rejoice in their faith and the goodness of God in their lives.

PRAYERS *others may be added*

With joy and peace, we pray:

◆ We praise you, gracious God.

For the faith of children and adults who have entered the Church this Easter season, we pray: ◆ *For civil servants who have been inspired by Christ to spend their lives for the good of all, we pray:* ◆ *For personal stories of God's mercy and love at work in people's lives, we pray:* ◆ *For the freedom to greet our brothers and sisters as beloved children of God, we pray:* ◆ *For a sense of peace and contentment for those who have died in Christ, we pray:* ◆

Our Father . . .

Lord Jesus, our brother,
you sent out the disciples to proclaim
   the kingdom
without asking for anything in return.
You also send us forth with the joy
   of faith,
to cure, cleanse, and heal,
leaving judgment and mercy to God.
May we freely accept your gifts
and freely share them with others.
You live and reign with God
   the Father
in the unity of the Holy Spirit,
one God, forever and ever.
Amen.

✤ *The Lord is my shepherd; there is nothing I shall want.*

✦ *Rejoice, O hearts that seek the Lord.*

PSALM 104 *page 416*

READING *John 20:19–23*

On the evening of that first day of the week, when the doors were locked, where the disciples were, for fear of the Jews, Jesus came and stood in their midst and said to them, "Peace be with you." When he had said this, he showed them his hands and his side. The disciples rejoiced when they saw the Lord. Jesus said to them again, "Peace be with you. As the Father has sent me, so I send you." And when he had said this, he breathed on them and said to them, "Receive the Holy Spirit. Whose sins you forgive are forgiven them, and whose sins you retain are retained."

REFLECTION

Marketers spend countless hours and dollars segmenting populations according to their differences. We can be grouped by gender, income, race, lifestyle, geographical location, and personal preferences. It is extraordinary that, by the power of the Holy Spirit, the disciples (and the Church today) were graced with a diversity of gifts in order to reach people all over the world. May we celebrate our uniqueness and rejoice in our common source and destiny: our provident and loving God.

PRAYERS *others may be added*

Awed by God's magnificence, we pray:

◆ Fill us with your Holy Spirit.

For Christians of every age, gender, race, profession, and personality, we pray: ◆ *For all peoples and all nations, we pray:* ◆ *For the wealthy, the middle class, the poor, and the destitute, we pray:* ◆ *For unity within our communities of faith, family, work, and living, we pray:* ◆ *For those who have died from every background and way of life, that they may be one in eternal life, we pray:* ◆

Our Father . . .

Risen Lord,
may the mystery of your truth and
    love continue to be
evident and compelling to people in
    every walk of life.
As we find you in our unique ways,
may we also find one another through
    what we hold in common.
You live and reign with God
    the Father
in the unity of the Holy Spirit,
one God, forever and ever.
Amen.

✦ *Rejoice, O hearts that seek the Lord.*

✝ *Lord, open my lips and my mouth shall proclaim your praise.*

PSALM 40   page 407

READING   Luke 6:43–45

Jesus said to his disciples: "A good tree does not bear rotten fruit, nor does a rotten tree bear good fruit. For every tree is known by its own fruit. For people do not pick figs from thorn bushes, nor do they gather grapes from brambles. A good person out of the store of goodness in his heart produces good, but an evil person out of a store of evil produces evil; for from the fullness of the heart the mouth speaks."

REFLECTION

"I didn't really mean to say that." What we say and do reveals who we are. We may try to deny something we said or did previously, but the fact remains that our words come from within. We have no one to blame them on but ourselves. Make a list of your actions and words from one day. Be mindful that your heart is revealed within these words and behaviors.

PRAYERS   *others may be added*

Attending to the good or evil deep within us, we pray:

◆ May our hearts and mouths be full of your goodness.

For Christians, that our speech and conduct reflect our deep faith, we pray: ◆ For orators and speech writers who hold the potential to inspire millions to action, we pray: ◆ For those prone to gossip and envy, we pray: ◆ For each of us to think before we speak, we pray: ◆ For the humility to ask for forgiveness when our words and actions have hurt others, we pray: ◆

Our Father . . .

One and true God,
your Son revealed your goodness
through his words and actions.
May we, like St. Anthony of Padua,
speak from the fullness of our hearts.
We ask this through Christ our Lord.
Amen.

✝ *Lord, open my lips and my mouth shall proclaim your praise.*

✚ *Commit your life to the Lord.*

PSALM 139   *page 420*

READING   *2 Corinthians 8:1–2, 7–9*

We want you to know, brothers and sisters, of the grace of God that has been given to the churches of Macedonia, for in a severe test of affliction, the abundance of their joy and their profound poverty overflowed in a wealth of generosity on their part. Now as you excel in every respect, in faith, discourse, knowledge, all earnestness, and in the love we have for you, may you excel in this gracious act also. I say this not by way of command, but to test the genuineness of your love by your concern for others. For you know the gracious act of our Lord Jesus Christ, that for your sake he became poor although he was rich, so that by his poverty you might become rich.

REFLECTION

We have Jesus' example before us—he gave the ultimate sacrifice, his life for the salvation of all. Can we love like he did? If we were tested, would we show that we have concern for others? Would we sacrifice our very self? As followers of Jesus, we should respond to one in pain, no matter if they are stranger, friend, or foe. Our concern for others should extend to the poor and marginalized, not just our loved ones. Excuses abound, but genuine love acts. Let us love and respond to the needs of others.

PRAYERS   *others may be added*

Inspired to love, we pray:

◆ Lord, hear our prayer.

For the health, strength, and happiness of our Bishops, priests, deacons, and lay ministers, we pray: ◆ *For the safety, success, and endurance of government leaders who promote and foster peace around the world, we pray:* ◆ *For living wages, accessible health care, and strong schools for all our neighbors, we pray:* ◆ *For peace and healing for all those who have asked us to pray for them, we pray:* ◆

Our Father . . .

Lord Jesus,
you suffered and died for all
    God's children.
May we respond in gratitude and love.
Show us the needs of all those
    around us,
and help us to act on their behalf.
You live and reign with God
    the Father
in the unity of the Holy Spirit,
one God, forever and ever.
Amen.

✚ *Commit your life to the Lord.*

✝ *The Lord is my light and my salvation.*

PSALM 16 *page 400*

READING *Matthew 6:16–18*

[Jesus said:] "When you pray, do not be like the hypocrites, who love to stand and pray in the synagogues and on street corners so that others may see them. Amen, I say to you, they have received their reward. But when you pray, go to your inner room, close the door, and pray to your Father in secret. And your Father who sees in secret will repay you.

"When you fast, do not look gloomy like the hypocrites. They neglect their appearance, so that they may appear to others to be fasting. Amen, I say to you, they have received their reward. But when you fast, anoint your head and wash your face, so that you may not appear to others to be fasting, except to your Father who is hidden. And your Father who sees what is hidden will repay you."

REFLECTION

Let what we give to God be freely offered. Christian prayer, generosity, and love should not be tallied in order to determine if we have lived by a "holy" standard. We should not expect recognition or reward for our faith-filled lives. We are to humbly and joyfully follow Jesus simply because we cannot imagine living otherwise.

PRAYERS *others may be added*

With generous hearts, we pray:

◆ May we follow Lord Jesus.

For religious women and men, who for centuries have sowed their very lives on behalf of others, we pray, ◆ *For relief agencies, that they inspire generosity among their donors, we pray:* ◆ *For the poor who give so freely from their own meager existence, we pray:* ◆ *For our communities of faith, that our bountiful giving may transform those around us, we pray:* ◆

Our Father . . .

Generous God,
your grace is everywhere.
May we say "yes" to your call
and follow you with authenticity,
not for reward or recognition.
We eagerly await the fruit of our
    cooperation with your work.
Grant this through Christ our Lord.
Amen.

✝ *The Lord is my light and my salvation.*

✝ *The Lord made us, we belong to him.*

PSALM 111 page 417

READING *Matthew 6:9–15*

[Jesus said to his disciples:] This is how you are to pray:

'Our Father who art in heaven / hallowed be thy name, / thy Kingdom come, / thy will be done, / on earth as it is in heaven. / Give us this day our daily bread; / and forgive us our trespasses, / as we forgive those who trespass against us; / and lead us not into temptation, / but deliver us from evil.'

"If you forgive others their transgressions, your heavenly Father will forgive you. But if you do not forgive others, neither will your Father forgive your transgressions."

REFLECTION *St. Augustine*

Great are you, O Lord, and exceedingly worthy of praise; your power is immense, and your wisdom beyond reckoning. And so we humans, who are part of your creation, long to praise you—we who carry our mortality about with us, carry the evidence of our sin and with it the proof that you thwart the proud. Yet these humans, due part of your creation as they are, still long to praise you. You arouse us so that praising you may bring us joy, because you have made us and drawn us to yourself, and our heart is unquiet until it rests in you.

PRAYERS *others may be added*

With the Holy Spirit as our guide, we pray:

◆ Forgive us as we forgive others.

That our leaders in the Church model for us prayers of praise, petition, submission, and transformation, we pray: ◆ *That the will of God be done throughout the earth, we pray:* ◆ *That the daily bread necessary for all is plentiful, we pray:* ◆ *That forgiveness defines our relationships at home, at work, and in Church, we pray:* ◆

Our Father . . .

Lord Jesus, our teacher,
you make the way to the Father clear
    to us.
Be with us as we continue to learn
    to pray;
transform our hearts that we may
    trust in God
and love one another as you did.
You live and reign with God the
    Father
in the unity of the Holy Spirit,
one God, forever and ever.
Amen.

✝ *The Lord made us, we belong to him.*

✦ *The Lord hears the cry of the poor.*

PSALM 149 page 421

READING 2 Corinthians 11:18, 24–30

Brothers and sisters: Since many boast according to the flesh, I too will boast. To my shame I say that we were too weak!

Five times at the hands of the Jews I received forty lashes minus one. Three times I was beaten with rods, once I was stoned, three times I was shipwrecked, I passed a night and a day on the deep; on frequent journeys, in dangers from rivers, dangers from robbers, dangers from my own race, dangers from Gentiles, dangers in the city, dangers in the wilderness, dangers at sea, dangers among false brothers; in toil and hardship, through many sleepless nights, through hunger and thirst, through frequent fastings, through cold and exposure. And apart from these things, there is the daily pressure upon me of my anxiety for all the churches. Who is weak, and I am not weak? Who is led to sin, and I am not indignant?

If I must boast, I will boast of the things that show my weakness.

REFLECTION

What aspects of life disappoint you? What causes you to despair? Your career, your retirement fund, your looks, your personal goals for success? Perhaps you procrastinate, deny your flaws, criticize others, lose your temper, or wait for others to take initiative? Rejoice! It is only when we are weak or let go that God can be strong. He will heal our brokenness and use us to build his kingdom.

PRAYERS *others may be added*

Vulnerable before God, we pray:

◆ Hear us, O Lord.

That Church ministries suffering from change and disinterest may be transformed by God for new work, we pray: ◆ *That failing efforts to end hunger, war, and poverty may be redirected by the Holy Spirit, we pray:* ◆ *That the weakest and smallest voices may teach us all, we pray:* ◆ *That those filled with doubt and despair may find new hope, we pray:* ◆

Our Father . . .

Almighty God,
bring forth a new day,
that we may rejoice and give thanks
    for your saving power.
We ask this through Christ our
    Lord. Amen.

✦ *The Lord hears the cry of the poor.*

✛ *In you, O Lord, I have found
my peace.*

PSALM 42 *page 408*

READING *2 Corinthians 12:5–10*

[Brothers and sisters:] About this man I will boast, but about myself I will not boast, except about my weaknesses. . . . Therefore, that I might not become too elated, a thorn in the flesh was given to me, an angel of Satan, to beat me, to keep me from being too elated. Three times I begged the Lord about this, that it might leave me, but he said to me, "My grace is sufficient for you, for power is made perfect in weakness." I will rather boast most gladly of my weaknesses, in order that the power of Christ may dwell with me. Therefore, I am content with weaknesses, insults, hardships, persecutions, and constraints, for the sake of Christ; for when I am weak, then I am strong.

REFLECTION

We don't know the nature of Paul's "thorn," but it continually reminded him of his need for God. What "thorn" have you asked God to take from you? Could it be that without this fear or problem you would no longer remember your need for God? When life's thorns arise, call to mind God's unfailing love, support, and providence. Look for ways to allow obstacles and difficulties to lead you to God rather than despair.

PRAYERS *others may be added*

Accepting the challenges God has set before us, we pray:

◆ Turn our hearts to you, O God.

For Christians seeking perfection, that the lack of perfection be a reminder of the world to come, we pray: ◆ *For the world's poor, who continually show us how far we have to go in extending God's love and mercy, we pray:* ◆ *For those who cannot escape mental illness, that medical healing may come to them, we pray:* ◆ *For the nagging concern, difficulty, or challenge in our lives that prompts us to return to God, we pray:* ◆

Our Father . . .

Omniscient God,
you see and know all for all eternity.
We struggle to understand this life
and long for the one to come.
We thank you for the blessings and
    obstacles you have given us.
May your grace grow in us as we
    allow life to teach us,
that we may be strengthened in
    our weakness.
Grant this through Christ our Lord.
Amen.

✛ *In you, O Lord, I have found
my peace.*

✦ *For ever I will sing the goodness of the Lord.*

PSALM 100 — page 414

READING — John 3:16–18

God so loved the world that he gave his only Son, so that everyone who believes in him might not perish but might have eternal life. For God did not send his Son into the world to condemn the world, but that the world might be saved through him. Whoever believes in him will not be condemned, but whoever does not believe has already been condemned, because he has not believed in the name of the only Son of God.

REFLECTION — *St. Catherine of Siena*

O eternal Trinity, You are a deep sea in which the more I seek the more I find, and the more I find, the more I seek to know You. You fill us insatiably, because the soul, before the abyss which You are, is always famished; and hungering for You, O eternal Trinity, it desires to behold truth in Your light. As the thirsty hart pants after the fount of living water, so does my soul long to leave this gloomy body and see You as You are, in truth.

PRAYERS — *others may be added*

In gratitude, we pray:

◆ Lord, hear our prayer.

For those living religious and single vocations, that celibacy empowers them to reach out in love in radical ways, we pray: ◆ *For those living the vocation to married life, that shared love overflows into service to the community, we pray:* ◆ *For those who have given the gift of life as parents, that they sacrifice their own needs at times for what their children most need, we pray:* ◆ *For those searching to hear God's call, that when it comes, they may say "yes" without reservation, we pray:* ◆ *For those who have died, giving their lives to God and others, we pray:* ◆

Our Father . . .

O God of mystery,
your very being is the source and end
of all love.
You show us love as Creator, Word,
and Eternal Spirit.
May our lives reflect your love in
every relationship.
We ask this through our Lord Jesus
Christ, your Son,
who lives and reigns with you in the
unity of the Holy Spirit,
one God, forever and ever.
Amen.

✦ *For ever I will sing the goodness of the Lord.*

✦ *The precepts of the Lord give joy to the heart.*

PSALM 51 *page 409*

READING *Matthew 7:1–5*

Jesus said to his disciples: "Stop judging, that you may not be judged. For as you judge, so will you be judged, and the measure with which you measure will be measured out to you. Why do you notice the splinter in your brother's eye, but do not perceive the wooden beam in your own eye? How can you say to your brother, 'Let me remove that splinter from your eye,' while the wooden beam is in your eye? You hypocrite, remove the wooden beam from your eye first; then you will see clearly to remove the splinter from your brother's eye."

REFLECTION

Did you ever secretly give your sibling less dessert than you gave yourself? Did you ever criticize your spouse for something you had also done? What makes us stingy in our "measures"? If we can give the benefit of the doubt to others, if we can be generous donors, if we can put trust in others, then we can rest in knowing God will judge us gently as well. The next time a "stingy nature" rises up in us, may we silence it with Jesus' words.

PRAYERS *others may be added*

With generous hearts, we pray:

◆ Forgive us and help us forgive.

For those we have doubted or criticized in their Christian lifestyles, we pray: ◆ *For those whose reputation we have maligned, we pray:* ◆ *For those whose sincerity or integrity we have questioned, we pray:* ◆ *For those we have treated as less than ourselves, we pray:* ◆

Our Father . . .

Merciful God,
your generosity completely ignores
    what we truly deserve.
May we be forgiven for our greedy
    and judgmental actions,
and start again with a bountiful
    measure and a loving heart.
Grant this through Christ our Lord.
Amen.

✦ *The precepts of the Lord give joy to the heart.*

✝ *The Lord is my shepherd, there is nothing I shall want.*

PSALM 40   page 407

READING   *Matthew 22:34–40*

When the Pharisees heard that Jesus had silenced the Sadducees, they gathered together, and one of them a scholar of the law, tested him by asking, "Teacher, which commandment in the law is the greatest?" Jesus said to him, "You shall love the Lord, your God, with all your heart, with all your soul, and with all your mind. This is the greatest and the first commandment. The second is like it: You shall love your neighbor as yourself. The whole law and the prophets depend on these two commandments."

REFLECTION

Brilliant, wealthy young people are presented with so many opportunities in life—travel, business investments, fame, and the very best education. What could possibly move one to choose a life for others? Christian mentors, schools, and universities often persuade the young people of just that. Lucky is the young person who chooses the uniquely rewarding path of following Christ.

PRAYERS   *others may be added*

Inspired by those who choose faith over worldly success, we pray:

◆ Renew us with your love, O God.

For young people saying "yes" to religious life, volunteer service, and missionary work, we pray: ◆ For schools, colleges, universities, campus ministries, and Newman Centers that work to form young people as Catholic Christians, we pray: ◆ For young people destroyed by wealth and overindulgence, we pray: ◆ For each of us who may inspire a young person by our witness to Christ, we pray: ◆ For young men and women who have died in their most promising years, we pray: ◆

Our Father . . .

Lord Jesus, our Savior,
you offer all God's children a life of
    true happiness.
Help young people to see the
    promise contained
in faithfulness, service, and prayer.
Strengthen those who follow you
    despite the world's temptations.
You live and reign with God
    the Father
in the unity of the Holy Spirit,
one God, forever and ever.
Amen.

✝ *The Lord is my shepherd, there is nothing I shall want.*

✦ *The precepts of the Lord give joy to the heart.*

PSALM 139   page 420

READING   Matthew 7:15–20

Jesus said to his disciples: "Beware of false prophets, who come to you in sheep's clothing, but underneath are ravenous wolves. By their fruits you will know them. Do people pick grapes from thornbushes, or figs from thistles? Just so, every good tree bears good fruit, and a rotten tree bears bad fruit. A good tree cannot bear bad fruit, nor can a rotten tree bear good fruit. Every tree that does not bear good fruit will be cut down and thrown into the fire. So by their fruits you will know them."

REFLECTION

We can look back on our lives and trace our legacy. There may be times when we were faithful to God and our lives bore fruit. There may be times when we distanced ourselves from God and in turn, our lives were unfruitful. Reflect and make the connections: What ways of being faithful to God led to what kinds of fruitfulness? What nurturing do we need to do at this time in our lives in order to produce more "fruit"?

PRAYERS   *others may be added*

Examining the tree of life, we pray:

◆ May we bear your fruit, O God.

For courageous, hard-working servants of the Church, from whose efforts came the legacy of Catholic relief agencies, Catholic hospitals, Catholic schools, and parishes of empowered disciples, we pray: ◆ *For "behind-the-scenes" policy makers who have brought about improvements in education, health care, and international bridge building, we pray:* ◆ *For those wondering why they keep repeating unhappy patterns, that they will look to God for a new beginning, we pray:* ◆ *For prayerful attention to our choices and the outcomes, we pray:* ◆

Our Father . . .

Lord God,
you made a covenant with your
    beloved people.
May we uphold our promises to you,
living as faithful disciples.
We ask this through Christ our Lord.
Amen.

✦ *The precepts of the Lord give joy to the heart.*

Optional memorials of St. Paulinus of Nola, bishop; St. John Fisher, bishop, martyr; and St. Thomas More, martyr

✝ *The Lord hears the cry of the poor.*

PSALM 111 *page 417*

READING *Genesis 16:1–4, 6b–11*

Abram's wife Sarai had borne him no children. . . . Thus, after Abram had lived ten years in the land of Canaan, his wife Sarai took her maid, Hagar the Egyptian, and gave her to her husband Abram to be his concubine. He had intercourse with her, and she became pregnant. When she became aware of her pregnancy, she looked on her mistress with disdain. Sarai then abused her so much that Hagar ran away from her.

The LORD's messenger found her by a spring in the wilderness, the spring on the road to Shur, and he asked, "Hagar, maid of Sarai, where have you come from and where are you going?" She answered, "I am running away from my mistress, Sarai." But the LORD's messenger told her: "Go back to your mistress and submit to her abusive treatment. I will make your descendants so numerous," added the LORD's messenger, "that they will be too many to count. Besides," the LORD's messenger said to her:/"You are now pregnant and shall bear a son;/you shall name him Ishmael,/For the LORD has heard you,/God has answered you."

REFLECTION

Think of the ways God has fulfilled the deepest desires of your heart. Recognize prayers answered. Close friends, spouse, children, the ability to use your gifts— these are signs of God keeping his promises to you. Rejoice and praise our faithful God!

PRAYERS *others may be added*

With gratitude, we pray:

◆ We praise you, faithful God.

That Christians rejoice in the gifts of the Word, the community of faith, the sacraments and the opportunities to serve God, we pray: ◆ That those whose prayers have been answered give glory to God, we pray: ◆ That those who wait for the fulfillment of a holy desire may continue to have faith, we pray: ◆ That those who have died may be given the gift of eternal life, we pray: ◆

Our Father . . .

Generous and faithful God,
you heard the cries of your people
    from of old;
and you hear the cries of our
    own hearts.
Grant those desires that will lead us
    closer to you.
We ask this through Christ our Lord.
Amen.

✝ *The Lord hears the cry of the poor.*

✠ *The Lord is my shepherd, there is nothing I shall want.*

PSALM 40   page 407

READING   *Luke 1:57–63*

When the time arrived for Elizabeth to have her child she gave birth to a son. Her neighbors and relatives heard that the Lord had shown his great mercy toward her, and they rejoiced with her. When they came on the eighth day to circumcise the child, they were going to call him Zechariah after his father, but his mother said in reply, "No. He will be called John." But they answered her, "There is no one among your relatives who has this name." So they made signs, asking his father what he wished him to be called. He asked for a tablet and wrote, "John is his name," and all were amazed.

REFLECTION

Most of us celebrate the birth of a baby with gifts, happiness, and support of the family. Do we celebrate other answers to prayers with our friends and neighbors? Do we support families whose members have made radical choices to serve and love others? Our community has a responsibility to celebrate these brave Christians.

PRAYERS   *others may be added*

Opening our eyes to saints in our midst, we pray:

◆ Let us celebrate in joy.

For those who choose religious life, that they may be affirmed in their response to God, we pray: ◆ *For those who volunteer in service programs such as the Peace Corps, volunteer corps of religious orders, and other outreach programs, we pray:* ◆ *For those who live out their faith in Catholic auxiliary organizations, thereby diversifying and strengthening the community of the Church, we pray:* ◆ *For a celebration of each child's Baptism as a calling forth of a new disciple, we pray:* ◆

Our Father . . .

Loving God,
your servant St. John the Baptist
was called from an early age to
    proclaim the kingdom.
His family, too, served an
    important role
by giving him life, examples of faith,
    and support for his journey.
May we also call forth our
    community members
to lives of radical faith and service.
We ask this through our Lord Jesus
    Christ, your Son,
who lives and reigns with you in the
    unity of the Holy Spirit,
one God, forever and ever.
Amen.

✠ *The Lord is my shepherd, there is nothing I shall want.*

Today's reading is from the Mass during the Day, Lectionary #587.

SATURDAY, 25 JUNE 2011
WEEKDAY

✛ *The heart of the just one is firm,*
trusting in the Lord.

PSALM 42   page 408

READING   *Genesis 18:1– 2, 9–15*

The LORD appeared to Abraham by the Terebinth of Mamre, as Abraham sat in the entrance of his tent, while the day was growing hot. Looking up, he saw three men standing nearby.

They asked him, "Where is your wife Sarah?" He replied, "There in the tent." One of them said, "I will surely return to you about this time next year, and Sarah will then have a son." Sarah was listening at the entrance of the tent, just behind him. Now Abraham and Sarah were old, advanced in years, and Sarah had stopped having her womanly periods. So Sarah laughed to herself and said, "Now that I am so withered and my husband is so old, am I still to have sexual pleasure?" But the LORD said to Abraham: "Why did Sarah laugh and say, 'Shall I really bear a child, old as I am?' Is anything too marvelous for the LORD to do? At the appointed time, about this time next year, I will return to you, and Sarah will have a son." Because she was afraid, Sarah dissembled, saying, "I didn't laugh." But he replied, "Yes you did."

PRAYERS .   *others may be added*

Struggling between our rational world and the faith of our hearts, we pray:

◆ Fill us with faith.

In thanks for the guidance of the Pope and the teachers of the Church who offer us understanding of faith and reason, we pray: ◆ *In thanks for science and medicine, which make health more possible than ever, we pray:* ◆ *In thanks for people of little education, little money, and little power, who instruct us in great faith, we pray:* ◆ *In hope of wisdom, to know God and his miraculous ways, we pray:* ◆

Our Father . . .

Almighty God,
for thousands of years
you have touched the lives of
   humanity with love.
We struggle to understand your role
in a changing and increasingly
   secular world.
Give us faith that rises above division,
and emphasizes your love, your
   mercy, and your eternal promises.
Grant this through Christ our Lord.
Amen.

✛ *The heart of the just one is firm,*
trusting in the Lord.

✢ *I am the living bread that came down from heaven, says the Lord; whoever eats this bread will live forever.*

PSALM 42   *page 408*

READING   *John 6:52–54*

The Jews quarreled among themselves, saying, "How can this man give us his flesh to eat?" Jesus said to them, "Amen, amen, I say to you, unless you eat the flesh of the Son of Man and drink his blood, you do not have life within you. Whoever eats my flesh and drinks my blood has eternal life, and I will raise him on the last day."

REFLECTION

If you have received the Body and Blood of Christ in Eucharist hundreds of times, you can be sure that it has formed who you are. Your hunger for Christ keeps you coming back, and the transformation you experience in being one with Christ keeps you hungry for the kingdom of God. If you feel weary in waiting for the day when your deepest hungers will be fulfilled, you may be sure that Christ is alive within you.

PRAYERS   *others may be added*

Fed, yet hungry, we pray:

◆ Transform us with the Bread of Life.

For increased participation in Eucharist by all Catholics, we pray: ◆ For an end to world hunger, we pray: ◆ For progress toward one Christian table of the Eucharist, we pray: ◆ For thoughtfulness given to our deepest hunger for God, we pray: ◆ For attentiveness to how our hunger for Christ leads us to ever greater hunger for peace, justice, and the reign of God, we pray: ◆

Our Father . . .

Christ Jesus,
our Bread of Life,
we long to receive you each time we
    come to Eucharist.
Your Body and Blood renew us,
    sustain us,
and open for us a deeper hunger for
    the coming of God's kingdom.
May we return daily or weekly to
    your table,
entering into the mystery in order to
    be sent forth, hungry again.
You live and reign with God
    the Father
in the unity of the Holy Spirit,
one God, forever and ever.
Amen.

✢ *I am the living bread that came down from heaven, says the Lord; whoever eats this bread will live forever.*

✦ *I have found my peace.*

PSALM 25   *page 403*

READING   *Genesis 18:20–25, 32–33*

Then the LORD said: "The outcry against Sodom and Gomorrah is so great, and their sin so grave, that I must go down and see whether or not their actions fully correspond to the cry against them that comes to me. I mean to find out."

While the two men walked on farther toward Sodom, the LORD remained standing before Abraham. Then Abraham drew nearer to him and said: "Will you sweep away the innocent with the guilty? Suppose there were fifty innocent people in the city; would you wipe out the place, rather than spare it for the sake of the fifty innocent people within it? Far be it from you to do such a thing, to make the innocent die with the guilty, so that the innocent and the guilty would be treated alike! Should not the judge of all the world act with justice?"

But he still persisted: "Please, let not my Lord grow angry if I speak up this last time. What if there are at least ten there?" He replied, "For the sake of those ten, I will not destroy it."

REFLECTION

We whisper our deepest fears to God: despair, the state of the world, loss of a loved one, unconquerable sin, being alone. We plead with him for mercy. We cannot help but imagine the worst. Then, we wait for God's response. As with Abraham, no matter how desperate our pleas and fears, God responds with loving mercy.

PRAYERS   *others may be added*

Aware of our fears, we pray:

◆ Hold us in your mercy, Lord.

For the Church, when it seems she may be overcome by the violence and apathy of the world, we pray: ◆ *For the world, at times and in places consumed by war, hatred, and destruction, we pray:* ◆ *For the lost, caught up in sin and darkness, we pray:* ◆ *For each of us, sinners, when we lose faith in God, we pray:* ◆

Our Father . . .

Merciful God,
hear our whispered prayers,
hear our anxious hearts,
and soothe us with your
   loving embrace.
We ask this through Christ our Lord.
Amen.

✦ *I have found my peace.*

✢ *Commit your life to the Lord, and he will help you.*

PSALM 40   page 407

READING   *John 17:20–26*

[Jesus said:] "Holy Father, I pray not only for these, but also for those who will believe in me through their word, so that they may all be one, as you, Father, are in me and I in you, that they also may be in us, that the world may believe that you sent me. And I have given them the glory you gave me, so that they may be one, as we are one, I in them and you in me, that they may be brought to perfection as one, that the world may know that you sent me, and that you loved them even as you loved me. Father, they are your gift to me. I wish that where I am they also may be with me, that they may see my glory that you gave me, because you loved me before the foundation of the world. Righteous Father, the world also does not know you, but I know you, and they know that you sent me. I made known to them your name and I will make it known, that the love with which you loved me may be in them and I in them."

REFLECTION

The early Christians honored and venerated their Bishops and martyrs after death. These holy men and women so loved Christ that they devoted their lives, even to the point of death, to serving him. We are reminded that our deep love for Christ should be our greatest motivation in all that we do.

PRAYERS   *others may be added*

Pondering our love for Christ, we pray:

◆ Make us like Christ.

For all Bishops of the Church, that shepherding their flocks may always be an exercise of love, we pray: ◆
For missionaries who share the Word of God, that their own love for Christ may shine through them, we pray: ◆ *For those who follow Christ even to the point of death—physical or by reputation or isolation—that they may know his love forever, we pray:* ◆ *For our community of faith, that we may be joyfully committed to making God's name known in all we do, we pray:* ◆

Our Father . . .

Everlasting God,
your Son Jesus gave thanks and praise
    to you
and asked that we might share in your
    mercy and love.
We, too, plead before you, with
    St. Irenaeus at our side,
that we might be on fire with love
    for you
and bring glory to your name.
We ask this through our Lord Jesus
    Christ, your Son,
who lives and reigns with you
in the unity of the Holy Spirit,
one God, forever and ever.
Amen.

Commit your life to the Lord, and he will help you.

Today's reading is from the memorial, Lectionary #589.

WEDNESDAY, 29 JUNE 2011
SOLEMNITY OF ST. PETER AND ST. PAUL, APOSTLES

✦ *Commit your life to the Lord.*

PSALM 40   *page 407*

READING   *John 21:17c–19*

Jesus said to [Simon Peter], "Feed my sheep. Amen, amen, I say to you, when you were younger, you used to dress yourself and go where you wanted; but when you grow old, you will stretch out your hands, and someone else will dress you and lead you where you do not want to go." He said this signifying by what kind of death he would glorify God. And when he had said this, he said to him, "Follow me."

REFLECTION

St. Peter was a rock-solid foundation for the Church because he knew Jesus as the Christ. St. Paul made a radical conversion to faith in Christ, and went on to lead the Church in bringing the Gospel to the Gentiles. The underpinnings of our Catholic tradition rest on the faith, prayers, and devotion of those who carried on the apostolic tradition. May we maintain the worthiness of this tradition, by the grace of God. We who call ourselves Christians, and especially those we recognize as descendants of the apostles, hold a great responsibility.

PRAYERS   *others may be added*

Clinging to the rock of our tradition, we pray:

◆ Lord, hear our prayer.

For the Pope, successor to St. Peter, that he may grow strong in faith, hope, and love, we pray: ◆ *For the Church in the world, that she may be a sign of God's love by her concrete actions on behalf of all the poor and the voiceless, we pray:* ◆ *For all people of great faith, that their example may inspire more men and women to follow the Catholic tradition, we pray:* ◆ *For all humble servants, that we may follow Christ, despite our sin and failings, we pray:* ◆

Our Father . . .

Almighty God,
you chose your servants St. Peter and St. Paul
to be a cornerstone for the Church.
We give thanks for all faithful leaders who have built up the Catholic tradition in Jesus' name.
May our current Pope and Bishops lead us all as we strive to be a rock of love, mercy,
and proclamation of the Gospel to the world.
We ask this through our Lord, Jesus Christ, your Son,
who lives and reigns with you in the unity of the Holy Spirit,
one God forever and ever.
Amen.

✦ *Commit your life to the Lord.*

214   Today's reading is from the vigil Mass, Lectionary #590.

✝ *Go out to all the world, and tell the Good News.*

PSALM 42   page 408

READING   Matthew 9:1–8

After entering a boat, Jesus made the crossing, and came into his own town. And there people brought to him a paralytic lying on a stretcher. When Jesus saw their faith, he said to the paralytic, "Courage, child, your sins are forgiven." At that, some of the scribes said to themselves, "This man is blaspheming." Jesus knew what they were thinking, and said, "Why do you harbor evil thoughts? Which is easier, to say, 'Your sins are forgiven,' or to say, 'Rise and walk'? But that you may know that the Son of Man has authority on earth to forgive sins"—he then said to the paralytic, "Rise, pick up your stretcher, and go home." He rose and went home. When the crowds saw this they were struck with awe and glorified God who had given such authority to men.

REFLECTION

What would inspire more awe in you: seeing a person physically healed or knowing a person was made whole through God's forgiveness? Which would mean more if it happened to you? Which kind of pain is more debilitating, more entrenched, or more resistant to new life? Jesus reaches through both kinds of suffering and offers a complete answer.

PRAYERS   *others may be added*

Awed by Jesus' touch, we pray:

◆ Make us whole, Lord God.

For those who minister in the Church, bringing forth Jesus' healing, we pray: ◆ *For all diseases cured, broken bones set, physical suffering eased, and emotional illnesses eased, we pray:* ◆ *For all sins forgiven, relationships mended, broken souls reborn, we pray:* ◆ *For this community, who celebrates daily the great love of God, we pray:* ◆ *For the peace and eternal life offered to those who have died, we pray:* ◆

Our Father . . .

Lord Jesus, our brother,
you understood the pain of illness
and the suffering of sin.
You reached out to offer healing
   and forgiveness.
May we turn to you when we are
   broken in mind, body, or spirit.
You live and reign with God
   the Father
in the unity of the Holy Spirit,
one God, forever and ever.
Amen.

✝ *Go out to all the world, and tell the Good News.*

✤ *The Lord made us; we belong to him.*

PSALM 149 *page 421*

READING *Matthew 11:28–30*

[Jesus exclaimed:] "Come to me, all you who labor and are burdened, and I will give you rest. Take my yoke upon you and learn from me, for I am meek and humble of heart; and you will find rest for yourselves. For my yoke is easy, and my burden light."

REFLECTION

In times of distress, it may be difficult to feel an easy yoke or a light burden. In these times, Jesus walks very closely with us, offering to share the load, to direct our gaze heavenward, and to strengthen our faith. We admit how desperately we need him, and he responds with abundant love.

PRAYERS *others may be added*

Yearning for Jesus, we pray:

◆ Be with us, O Lord.

For all Christians who long for rest, that they are led by the heart of Jesus, we pray: ◆ For laborers who are weary, that the heart of Jesus reaches them with love, we pray: ◆ For those who are burdened, that Jesus shows them how to make their hearts light, we pray: ◆ For each of us, when we doubt Jesus is near, that we may know his love, we pray: ◆

Our Father . . .

Lord Jesus,
you are good and loving,
bearing a great burden and wearing a
    heavy yoke.
Your love for the Father and for us
allowed you to act with joy and
    lightness of heart.
Show us the way to follow you
when life seems heavy and
    unbearable.
You live and reign with God
    the Father
in the unity of the Holy Spirit,
one God, forever and ever.
Amen.

✤ *The Lord made us; we belong to him.*

✦ *Blessed is the Virgin Mary, who kept the word of God and pondered it in her heart.*

CANTICLE
page 422

READING
Luke 2:43–51

After three days [Jesus' parents] found him in the temple, sitting in the midst of the teachers, listening to them and asking them questions, and all who heard him were astounded at his understanding and his answers. When his parents saw him, they were astonished, and his mother said to him, "Son, why have you done this to us? Your father and I have been looking for you with great anxiety." And he said to them, "Why were you looking for me? Did you not know that I must be in my Father's house?" But they did not understand what he said to them. He went down with them and came to Nazareth, and was obedient to them; and his mother kept all these things in her heart.

REFLECTION

We can learn from Mary how to handle struggles as parents, spouses, children, and friends. We may not always understand the others in our lives, no matter how much we love them. Mary "kept all these things in her heart." If we follow her example, we practice patience and calm upon first hearing upsetting news. Then we take time for quiet reflection and prayer. Only then do we act or speak in love and truth.

PRAYERS
others may be added

With Mary at our side, we pray:

◆ Give us hearts of patience.

For pastors facing parish crises, divisions, and daily stress, we pray: ◆
For parents and teenagers, when love for one another is overwhelmed by struggles for independence, control, and better communication, we pray: ◆ *For friends and family members worried about loved ones, we pray:* ◆ *For any of us when we are tempted to speak or act before prayerful consideration, we pray:* ◆

Our Father . . .

God, Creator of us all,
Mary is the model of Christian
  discipleship.
May she guide and teach us
as we struggle to follow your path of
  justice and mercy.
When we face difficulty and pain,
send Mary to our side
to give us patience and love.
We ask this through our Lord Jesus
  Christ, your Son,
who lives and reigns with you
in the unity of the Holy Spirit,
one God, forever and ever.
Amen.

✦ *Blessed is the Virgin Mary, who kept the word of God and pondered it in her heart.*

✦ *The precepts of the Lord give joy to the heart.*

PSALM 33 *page 404*

READING *Matthew 11:25–27*

Jesus exclaimed: "I give praise to you, Father, Lord of heaven and earth, for although you have hidden these things from the wise and the learned you have revealed them to little ones. Yes, Father, such has been your gracious will. All things have been handed over to my Father. No one knows the Son except the father, and no one knows the Father except the Son and anyone to whom the Son wishes to reveal him."

REFLECTION

Consider which news sources and "experts" you trust. We can become caught up in worldly wisdom and authorities. If God is asking us to listen to the "little ones," we must explore who these little ones are and then seek them out in order to hear their insights. We might know someone who lives simply, honestly, and humbly, not boasting of credentials, but trusting in God. We may learn a great deal from seeking this one's wisdom.

PRAYERS *others may be added*

Opening ourselves to the voices of the lowly, we pray:

◆ May we have ears that hear.

For the growing Church in Africa, Asia, and Latin America, that we may hear her prophetic voice, we pray: ◆ *For strong women all over the world, that we may learn from their struggle to survive, we pray:* ◆ *For the unborn, newly born, and young children, that their innocence may shake us to our core when setting priorities, we pray:* ◆ *For the elderly and the sick, that their age-old wisdom may be treasured, we pray:* ◆

Our Father . .

Provident God,
you have given us all we need,
but have hidden knowledge
    and wisdom
within those we easily dismiss
    and ignore.
Turn our stubborn ways upside down.
Send us prophets from the young, the
    old, and the downtrodden,
and make us listen to the message
    they proclaim from you.
Grant this through Christ our Lord.
Amen.

✦ *The precepts of the Lord give joy to the heart.*

✦ *Go out to all the world, and tell the Good News.*

PSALM 33 page 404

READING Genesis 1:26–28

God said: "Let us make man in our image, after our likeness. Let them have dominion over the fish of the sea, the birds of the air, and the cattle, and over all the wild animals and all the creatures that crawl on the ground."

God created man in his image; / in the divine image he created him; / male and female he created them.

God blessed them, saying: "Be fertile and multiply; fill the earth and subdue it. Have dominion over the fish of the sea, the birds of the air, and all the living things that move on the earth."

REFLECTION

Our country, so richly blessed, has a special responsibility in its care of the earth. We must hold in balance what is good for the community of humans, animals, plants, and the earth itself. We must remember that we are made in the image of God: the creator, sustainer, and redeemer of life.

PRAYERS others may be added

With respect for our birthright, civil and heavenly, we pray:

◆ Fill the world with your grace, O God.

That the United States Conference of Catholic Bishops may continue to take an active role in calling for gentle and responsible stewardship of the earth, we pray: ◆ *That Christians may take part in caring for the earth in their homes, jobs, and community, we pray:* ◆ *That hikers, hunters, nature lovers, and artists may continue to remind all of us of the beauty and sacredness of the wildlife around us, we pray:* ◆ *That we may prioritize our Christian commitments, we pray:* ◆

Our Father . . .

Creator God,
you blessed humanity with a world of
    life and beauty,
and you blessed this country with
    extraordinary riches.
May we of faith use our
    resources wisely
and treasure them as your gifts.
We ask this through our Lord Jesus
    Christ, your Son,
who lives and reigns with you
in the unity of the Holy Spirit,
one God, forever and ever.
Amen.

✦ *Go out to all the world, and tell the Good News.*

Optional memorial of St. Elizabeth of Portugal. Today's reading is from the optional proper Mass for Independence Day, Lectionary #882.

✤ *Go out to all the world, and tell the Good News.*

PSALM 42   *page 408*

READING   *Matthew 9:35–38*

Jesus went around to all the towns and villages, teaching in their synagogues, proclaiming the Gospel of the Kingdom, and curing every disease and illness. At the sight of the crowds, his heart was moved with pity for them because they were troubled and abandoned, like sheep without a shepherd. Then he said to his disciples, "The harvest is abundant but the laborers are few; so ask the master of the harvest to send out laborers for his harvest."

REFLECTION

There are many in need of a shepherd today, just as in Jesus' time. Youth search for true friends. Children need reliable parents. Students seek wise teachers. The vulnerable soul within all of us hopes for a loving guide. With God's guidance, we can be one step, as laborers, in leading others to the shepherd whom they truly seek. We can live up to expectations and take our commitments seriously. In this way, we bring others to God.

PRAYERS   *others may be added*

Offering ourselves as laborers, we pray:

◆ Send us forth, O Lord.

That all Christians may, by their presence and love, help others find their way to God, we pray: ◆ That all parents strive to be trustworthy, all friends genuine, and all teachers wise, we pray: ◆ That all who are troubled and abandoned find the Good Shepherd, we pray: ◆ That we are not overwhelmed by the great need for laborers and the enormity of the harvest, we pray: ◆

Our Father . . .

Lord God,
your heart is full of compassion for
   your children.
You call us to cooperate in your plan
   of salvation,
by being best friends, parents,
   teachers, and servants of others.
May we always show others your love
   and lead them to you.
We ask this through Christ our Lord.
Amen.

✤ *Go out to all the world, and tell the Good News.*

✛ *Go out to all the world, and tell the Good News.*

PSALM 111   page 417

READING   *Matthew 10:1, 5–7*

Jesus summoned his Twelve disciples and gave them authority over unclean spirits to drive them out and to cure every disease and every illness.

Jesus sent out these Twelve after instructing them thus, "Do not go into pagan territory or enter a Samaritan town. Go rather to the lost sheep of the house of Israel. As you go, make this proclamation: 'The Kingdom of heaven is at hand.'"

REFLECTION

The Gospel writers were concerned with the story of Jesus as it related to the history of the people of Israel. Like us, they wanted to know what would happen to their ancestors, their relatives, and their descendants. God's instruction to reach out to the "lost sheep" shows a God who forgives all and welcomes all into the fold. Later Christians came to understand that our God reaches out to all ethnicities, nationalities, religions, and races.

PRAYERS   *others may be added*

Grateful for the wideness of God's mercy, we pray:

◆ Bring home all the lost sheep, Good Shepherd.

For the Pope, Bishops, and servants of the Church, that their physical, mental, and emotional wounds may be healed, we pray: ◆ For a proclamation of the Gospel to people of all nations, we pray: ◆ For dialogue and mutual respect between Christians and Jews, we pray: ◆ For the physical, emotional, and mental health of our civil leaders, we pray: ◆ For positive discussion of faith and religion within families and between friends, we pray: ◆ For those too weak to reach out for help, that the pool of healing waters washes over them, we pray: ◆ For prayerful reflection on our need for Jesus and acceptance of his healing touch, we pray: ◆ For a return to the flock by all who have fallen away from the Catholic family, we pray: ◆

Our Father . . .

Faithful God,
you never abandoned your child Israel,
but sought out every lost sheep.
May you always call us home.
We ask this through Christ our Lord.
Amen.

✛ *Go out to all the world, and tell the Good News.*

Optional memorial of St. Maria Goretti, virgin, martyr   **221**

✦ *I have found my peace.*

PSALM 139   *page 420*

READING   *Matthew 10:7–14*

Jesus said to his Apostles: "As you go, make this proclamation: 'The Kingdom of heaven is at hand.' Cure the sick, raise the dead, cleanse the lepers, drive out demons. Without cost you have received; without cost you are to give. Do not take gold or silver or copper for your belts; no sack for the journey, or a second tunic, or sandals, or walking stick. The laborer deserves his keep. Whatever town or village you enter, look for a worthy person in it, and stay there until you leave. As you enter a house, wish it peace. If the house is worthy, let your peace come upon it; if not, let your peace return to you. Whoever will not receive you or listen to your words—go outside that house or town and shake the dust from your feet."

REFLECTION   *Gaudium et Spes, 27*

In our times a special obligation binds us to make ourselves the neighbor of absolutely every person, and of actively helping him when he comes across our path, whether he be an old person abandoned by all, a foreign laborer unjustly looked down upon, a refugee, a child born of an unlawful union and wrongly suffering for a sin he did not commit, or a hungry person who disturbs our conscience by recalling the voice of the Lord: "As long as you did it for one of these, the least of my brethren, you did it for me" (Matt. 25:40).

PRAYERS   *others may be added*

Following in Jesus' footsteps, we pray:

◆ Fill us with your peace.

For a Church that offers peace to the world at every chance, never becoming demanding or negative, we pray: ◆ For those who work for peace and justice, that they model the joyful freedom of following Christ, we pray: ◆ For people full of bitterness and anger, that negative feelings will be replaced with love, we pray: ◆ For all of us, that we do not become caught up in concern over those who will not listen to God's Word, but continue reaching out to those who do hear, we pray: ◆

Our Father . . .

Prince of Peace,
calm our fears,
and open our hearts to your love.
As we remain in that serenity,
may we offer it to others,
You live and reign with God
   the Father
in the unity of the Holy Spirit,
one God, forever and ever.
Amen.

✦ *I have found my peace.*

✦ *The heart of the just one is firm,
trusting in the Lord.*

PSALM 16   page 400

READING   Matthew 10:16–20

Jesus said to his Apostles: "Behold, I am sending you like sheep in the midst of wolves; so be shrewd as serpents and simple as doves. But beware of men, for they will hand you over to courts and scourge you in their synagogues, and you will be led before governors and kings for my sake as a witness before them and the pagans. When they hand you over, do not worry about how you are to speak or what you are to say. You will be given at that moment what you are to say. For it will not be you who speak but the Spirit of your Father speaking through you."

REFLECTION

We may feel like sheep among wolves in trying to live our Christian faith in a secular, sometimes violent world. Christ's message of love seems battered by messages of revenge, competition, and narcissistic attitudes. Christ asks us to think strategically about how to proclaim the kingdom, while remaining focused in our hearts on the simple, powerful news of God's love.

PRAYERS   *others may be added*

Balancing faith and reason, we pray:

◆ Give us courage in the world.

For Christians to proclaim the Gospel in word and deed, we pray: ◆ *For the gentle souls of the world, so easily buffeted about by war, violence, and corruption, we pray:* ◆ *For those who have been hurt or killed for their faith, we pray:* ◆ *For the courage and wisdom to use our talents for the good of our beliefs, we pray:* ◆

Our Father . . .

Son of God and Son of Man,
you walked among the wolves as
    the most innocent lamb.
May we never fear the obstacles or
    threats around us.
May we give thanks for our
    unique gifts
and always utilize these gifts for the
    sake of Gospel.
You live and reign with God
    the Father
in the unity of the Holy Spirit,
one God, forever and ever.
Amen.

✦ *The heart of the just one is firm,
trusting in the Lord.*

✛ *I have found my peace.*

PSALM 111 *page 417*

READING *Genesis 50:22–26*

Joseph remained in Egypt, together with his father's family. He lived a hundred and ten years. He saw Ephraim's children to the third generation, and the children of Manasseh's son Machir were also born on Joseph's knees.

Joseph said to his brothers: "I am about to die. God will surely take care of you and lead you out of this land to the land that he promised on oath to Abraham, Isaac and Jacob." Then, putting the sons of Israel under oath, he continued, "When God thus takes care of you, you must bring my bones up with you from this place." Joseph died at the age of a hundred and ten.

REFLECTION

Allow God to speak to you about the plan he has for your life. Listen in stillness to the stories of your ancestors, for whom God provided. Ask family members to share memories of how they survived in difficult times, and what graces carried them. Be silent and hear what God has promised you, your family, and all who follow him.

PRAYERS *others may be added*

Trusting God, we pray:

◆ Lead us on your path of life.

For the future of the Church in a changing world, we pray: ◆ *For the future of all nations embracing peace and prosperity, we pray:* ◆ *For young people unsure of their vocation, we pray:* ◆ *For each of us when we worry, we pray:* ◆ *For the people of God, who walk by faith, despite sometimes feeling lost or unsure, we pray:* ◆ *For the people of the world, who do not have faith, that they may see how God has been with them throughout time, we pray:* ◆ *For anyone who is searching for answers, that they proceed toward God with pure hearts, prayers, and acts of service, we pray:* ◆ *For humility among all of us, since, despite the gift of faith, we still do not fully understand, we pray:* ◆

Our Father . . .

Provident God,
you led your people out of Egypt
to a future full of hope.
Surely your hand is guiding our lives,
abiding with us, and giving us all
    we need.
May you always be with us.
May we always be faithful to you.
We ask this through Christ our Lord.
Amen.
✛ *I have found my peace.*

Optional memorials of St. Augustine Zhao Rong, priest, martyr, and companions, martyrs; Blessed Virgin Mary

✤ *The Lord is my light and my salvation.*

PSALM 33   page 404

READING   Matthew 13:1–9

On that day, Jesus went out of the house and sat down by the sea. Such large crowds gathered around him that he got into a boat and sat down, and the whole crowd stood along the shore. And he spoke to them at length in parables, saying: "A sower went out to sow. And as he sowed, some seed fell on the path, and birds came and ate it up. Some fell on rocky ground, where it had little soil. It sprang up at once because the soil was not deep, and when the sun rose it was scorched, and it withered for lack of roots. Some seed fell among thorns, and the thorns grew up and choked it. But some seed fell on rich soil and produced fruit, a hundred or sixty or thirtyfold. Whoever has ears ought to hear."

REFLECTION   *Rev. Michael J. K. Fuller*

There is a great medieval story about how Mary became pregnant with Christ. Monks decided that Christ had to enter into Mary through her ear—this is how they perceived his conception to have occurred. Now this may seem silly and obviously erroneous, but there is a greater theological truth to this belief. If we are going to take seriously what Christ is telling us in this parable, we need to ask ourselves just exactly how do we take the Word of God to heart? How do we become the rich soil in which the word takes root and produces a bountiful harvest? And, of course, the
answer is through the ear. We need, therefore, to make it a practice to listen to the Word of God as often as we can.

PRAYERS   others may be added

As gardeners for God, we pray:

◆ Bring us harvest joy.

For new members of the Christian community, who are the fruit of so much nurture, we pray: ◆ *For parents, catechists, pastors, and mentors who plant the seeds of faith, we pray:* ◆ *For consistent donations to Church services and ministries that allow the continued watering and feeding of young efforts for Christ, we pray:* ◆ *For rejoicing in our community at each successful effort to bring about God's kingdom on earth, we pray:* ◆ *For those who have died having lived a full and fruitful life, we pray:* ◆

Our Father . . .

God of earth and sky,
you brought forth all life by your
    great love.
You offer growth and life to
    every person.
May we be rich soil for that growth,
rejoicing in every flower and every
    fruit that gives you glory.
We ask this through Christ our Lord.
Amen.

✤ *The Lord is my light and my salvation.*

✝ *Commit your life to the Lord, and he will help you.*

PSALM 40   *page 407*

READING   *John 15:1–8*

[Jesus said:] "I am the true vine, and my Father is the vine grower. He takes away every branch in me that does not bear fruit, and everyone that does he prunes so that it bears more fruit. You are already pruned because of the word that I spoke to you. Remain in me, as I remain in you. Just as a branch cannot bear fruit on its own unless it remains on the vine, so neither can you unless you remain in me. I am the vine, you are the branches. Whoever remains in me and I in him will bear much fruit, because without me you can do nothing. Anyone who does not remain in me will be thrown out like a branch and wither; people will gather them and throw them into a fire and they will be burned. If you remain in me and my words remain in you, ask for whatever you want and it will be done for you. By this is my Father glorified, that you bear much fruit and become my disciples."

REFLECTION

Religious men and women commit to their communities in a unique way in order to be steadfastly tied to Christ. They live as one body, dedicated to Christ according to a particular charism. They model for lay Christians a way to think about commitment and community. All Christians need others to "remain" in Christ.

PRAYERS   *others may be added*

As branches clinging to the vine of Christ, we pray:

◆ Nourish us, Lord.

For all religious communities of men and women, especially those of the Order of St. Benedict, that they find support and love from one another, we pray: ◆
For all Christians to realize we need one another to best follow Christ, we pray: ◆
For our desire for the common good to surpass our selfish tendencies, we pray: ◆
For those who are truly alone, that the Church provides the family they seek, we pray: ◆ *For those who have died connected to us, that they remain as part of our branches, as saints in heaven, we pray:* ◆

Our Father . . .

Lord Jesus,
you are the vine and we are
    the branches.
may we live our faith through
    relationship with one another,
inspired by St. Benedict to remain in
    you always.
You live and reign with God
    the Father
in the unity of the Holy Spirit,
one God, forever and ever.
Amen.

✝ *Commit your life to the Lord, and he will help you.*

✛ *For ever I will sing the goodness of the Lord.*

PSALM 100   *page 414*

READING   *Exodus 3:4b–6, 9–10*

God called out to [Moses] from the bush, "Moses! Moses!" He answered, "Here I am." God said, "Come no nearer! Remove the sandals from your feet, for the place where you stand is holy ground. I am the God of your father," he continued, "the God of Abraham, the God of Isaac, the God of Jacob. The cry of the children of Israel has reached me, and I have truly noted that the Egyptians are oppressing them. Come, now! I will send you to Pharaoh to lead my people, the children of Israel, out of Egypt."

REFLECTION

God is nearer than we know. God is at work within us, calling us to greater roles than we expect. Realizing God's presence, Moses removed his sandals. To acknowledge God within us, behind us, and surrounding us, we honor our bodies and make sacred our homes. Then we interact gently with others and recognize God dwelling in our daily lives.

PRAYERS   *others may be added*

Acknowledging the Holy One, we pray:

◆ May we realize your presence, O God.

For the domestic Church, that this honor and responsibility may be taken very seriously, we pray: ◆ *For experiences of the Word, breaking bread, and the movement of the Spirit in ordinary life, we pray:* ◆ *For those who feel God calling them, that they muster a strong "yes!" we pray:* ◆ *For awareness of how we reverence God in Church, and for an extension of that honor to all the places God is present in our lives, we pray:* ◆

Our Father . . .

God of Israel,
you existed before time and exist until the end of time.
You are present in all places.
May we see and know you in more ways in our lives.
We ask this through Christ our Lord. Amen.

✛ *For ever I will sing the goodness of the Lord.*

✤ *The Lord is my shepherd, there is nothing I shall want.*

PSALM 40 page 407

READING Matthew 25:1–13

Jesus told his disciples this parable: "The Kingdom of heaven will be like ten virgins who took their lamps and went out to meet the bridegroom. Five of them were foolish and five were wise. The foolish ones, when taking their lamps, brought no oil with them, but the wise brought flasks of oil with their lamps. Since the bridegroom was long delayed, they all became drowsy and fell asleep. At midnight, there was a cry, 'Behold, the bridegroom! Come out to meet him!' Then all those virgins got up and trimmed their lamps. The foolish ones said to the wise, 'Give us some of your oil, for our lamps are going out.' But the wise ones replied, 'No, for there may not be enough for us and you. Go instead to the merchants and buy some for yourselves.' While they went off to buy it, the bridegroom came and those who were ready went into the wedding feast with him. Then the door was locked. Afterwards the other virgins came and said, 'Lord, Lord, open the door for us!' But he said in reply, 'Amen, I say to you, I do not know you.' Therefore, stay awake, for you know neither the day nor the hour."

REFLECTION

Being "ready" for heaven may require of us great courage and perseverance. At times, God asks of us even more than we think we can endure. Bl. Kateri Tekawitha, a young Native American girl, resisted the pressures of her culture, era, and circumstances, and became a Christian. She inspires us and walks with us when we need strength.

PRAYERS others may be added

Before God, we pray:

◆ Lord, hear our prayer.

For Christian men and women who remain ethical, chaste, and honorable through the trials of life, we pray: ◆
For all women and men who survive the violation of their bodies, we pray: ◆
For young people preserving their virginity for marriage or religious vocation, we pray: ◆ *For resistance to our culture's devaluation of human dignity, we pray:* ◆

Our Father . . .

Loving God,
bring comfort and tenderness to all
   who are suffering.
Make us strong enough to be "ready"
   for life with you.
We ask this through Christ our Lord.
Amen.

✤ *The Lord is my shepherd, there is nothing I shall want.*

Today's reading is from the Common of Virgins, Lectionary #736, 2.

229

FRIDAY, 15 JULY 2011
MEMORIAL OF ST. BONAVENTURE, BISHOP, DOCTOR OF THE CHURCH

✦ *Commit your life to the Lord, and he will help you.*

PSALM 40   *page 407*

READING   *Matthew 12:1–8*

Jesus was going through a field of grain on the sabbath. His disciples were hungry and began to pick the heads of grain and eat them. When the Pharisees saw this, they said to him, "See, your disciples are doing what is unlawful to do on the sabbath." He said to them, "Have you not read what David did when he and his companions were hungry, how he went into the house of God and ate the bread of offering, which neither he nor his companions but only the priests could lawfully eat? Or have you not read in the law that on the sabbath the priests serving in the temple violate the sabbath and are innocent? I say to you, something greater than the temple is here. If you knew what this meant, / *I desire mercy, not sacrifice*, you would not have condemned these innocent men. For the Son of Man is Lord of the sabbath."

REFLECTION

We all can be leaders in some capacity—at home, at work, at school, at church, or even among our friends and neighbors. When we lead, we can profoundly affect others by our type of leadership. Leaders who follow Christ turn expectations upside down by serving others. Christian leaders are willing to do the smallest task, the dirtiest job, or the longest hours rather than sitting back and watching others do the work.

PRAYERS   *others may be added*

Aspiring to be servant-leaders, we pray:

◆ Guide us, Lord.

That leaders of the Church see their role as serving the poor and the lowly, we pray: ◆ *That civil servants maintain a sense of the common good as their goal, we pray:* ◆ *That our bountiful giving may transform those around us, we pray:* ◆ *That any time we lead others we also serve others in the spirit of Christ, we pray:* ◆

Our Father . . .

Lord Jesus,
faithful servant,
your obedience to God and love for
    the little ones
shook expectations of the Messiah.
Rather than ruling like royalty,
you sacrificed everything for us
and took the role of a servant.
We are honored to follow you,
leading by serving those around us.
You live and reign with God
    the Father
in the unity of the Holy Spirit,
one God, forever and ever.
Amen.

✦ *Commit your life to the Lord, and he will help you.*

230

✚ *For ever I will sing the goodness of the Lord.*

PSALM 111 *page 417*

READING *Exodus 12:37–42*

The children of Israel set out from Rameses for Succoth, about six hundred thousand men on foot, not counting the little ones. A crowd of mixed ancestry also went up with them, besides their livestock, very numerous flocks and herds. Since the dough they had brought out of Egypt was not leavened, they baked it into unleavened loaves. They had rushed out of Egypt and had no opportunity even to prepare food for the journey.

The time the children of Israel had stayed in Egypt was four hundred and thirty years. At the end of four hundred and thirty years, all the hosts of the LORD left the land of Egypt on this very date. This was a night of vigil for the LORD, as he led them out of the land of Egypt; so on this same night all the children of Israel must keep a vigil for the LORD throughout their generations.

REFLECTION

Such an image of the love of the Lord for his people! We know that God has kept vigil with other peoples in their suffering, escape, and journey into new life. We call to mind those who need the Lord's protective watching over at this time. We, too, wait prayerfully with them.

PRAYERS *others may be added*

With trust in God, we pray:

◆ Be with us, Lord.

For the Pope, Bishops, and all clergy, that the Holy Spirit will guide pastoral decisions, teaching statements, and leadership appointments, we pray: ◆ *For heads of state, as they make choices about national security and steps toward war, we pray:* ◆ *For refugees and those emigrating from home, as they wait for acceptance into a new land, we pray:* ◆ *For those awaiting the end of life on death row, we pray:* ◆ *For women expecting the birth of a child, we pray:* ◆

Our Father . . .

Lord God,
you kept watch
as you waited through your children's
    escape from slavery.
You are always with those who wait
    for new life.
May our prayers strengthen all those
    who wait in darkness and despair.
Grant this through Christ our Lord.
Amen.

✚ *For ever I will sing the goodness of the Lord.*

✠ *The heart of the just one is firm, trusting in the Lord.*

PSALM 100 *page 414*

READING *Exodus 14:10–14*

Pharaoh was already near when the children of Israel looked up and saw that the Egyptians were on the march in pursuit of them. In great fright they cried out to the LORD. And they complained to Moses, "Were there no burial places in Egypt that you had to bring us out here to die in the desert? Why did you do this to us? Why did you bring us out of Egypt? Did we not tell you this in Egypt, when we said, 'Leave us alone. Let us serve the Egyptians'? Far better for us to be the slaves of the Egyptians than to die in the desert." But Moses answered the people, "Fear not! Stand your ground, and you will see the victory the LORD will win for you today. These Egyptians whom you see today you will never see again. The LORD himself will fight for you; you have only to keep still."

REFLECTION

"Why did you do this to us?" We may plea to God in these very words. We may not understand why God has brought us to a particular situation in life. Perhaps we are afraid. Perhaps we doubt God's goodness. Moses' words provide comfort. "Fear not! Stand your ground, and you will see the victory the LORD *will win for you today." God's reasons and plan will become clear to us with time.*

PRAYERS *others may be added*

Bringing our prayers before God, we pray:

◆ May we trust in you.

For an understanding of change in the Church, we pray: ◆ *For a victory in the campaign for world peace, we pray:* ◆ *For trust in God when all seems lost, we pray:* ◆ *For the wisdom to know our questions and the courage to bring them to God, we pray:* ◆

Our Father . . .

Infinite God,
your ways are beyond our
    understanding.
We cannot see the end of time or the
    end of our journeys.
Help us to come to you in our fears
    and doubts.
Help us to trust in you despite
    evidence to the contrary.
We ask this through our Lord Jesus
    Christ, your Son,
who lives and reigns with you
in the unity of the Holy Spirit,
one God, forever and ever.
Amen.

✠ *The heart of the just one is firm, trusting in the Lord.*

Optional memorial of St. Camillus de Lellis, priest

✜ *The Lord is my light and my salvation.*

PSALM 130   *page 418*

READING   *Matthew 12:46–50*

While Jesus was speaking to the crowds, his mother and his brothers appeared outside, wishing to speak with him. Someone told him, "Your mother and your brothers are standing outside, asking to speak with you." But he said in reply to the one who told him, "Who is my mother? Who are my brothers?" And stretching out his hand toward his disciples, he said, "Here are my mother and my brothers. For whoever does the will of my heavenly Father is my brother, and sister, and mother."

REFLECTION

When Jesus stretches out his hand, the power of God supersedes any human relationship. Just so, when Moses stretched out his hand over the Red Sea, God gave him dominion over nature. Over what part of our life or over what region of the world would we like to ask God to stretch out his hand? Imagine Jesus' hand, Moses' hand, even your own hand—reaching out over this problem and allowing the transformative power of God to work.

PRAYERS   *others may be added*

In times of trouble, we pray:

◆ Lord, stretch out your hand.

For the Christian faithful, we pray: ◆
For an end to division and confusion, we pray: ◆ *For an increase in unity, we pray:* ◆ *For an end to war, violence, and poverty throughout the world, we pray:* ◆ *For an end to grudges, hatred, and the inability to forgive, we pray:* ◆ *For healing in our own homes and neighborhoods, we pray:* ◆ *For pervasive peace, we pray:* ◆

Our Father . . .

All-powerful God,
you have dominion over the earth and
    all that lives on it.
When you stretch out your hand, you
    bring new beginnings, a new order.
Hold out your hand over our lives,
righting wrongs and healing ills.
Give us new life in you.
We ask this through Christ our Lord.
Amen.

✜ *The Lord is my light and my salvation.*

✦ *For ever I will sing the goodness of the Lord.*

PSALM 33   page 404

READING   *Exodus 16:9–12*

Then Moses said to Aaron, "Tell the whole congregation of the children of Israel: Present yourselves before the LORD, for he has heard your grumbling." When Aaron announced this to the whole assembly of the children of Israel, they turned toward the desert, and lo, the glory of the LORD, appeared in the cloud! The LORD spoke to Moses and said, "I have heard the grumbling of the children of Israel. Tell them: In the evening twilight you shall eat flesh, and in the morning you shall have your fill of bread, so that you may know that I, the LORD, am your God."

REFLECTION

If we were starving in the desert, we would not turn down what God offered us to eat. Yet, we are hungry for nourishment in this world and sometimes ignore the sustenance God offers us: the Word and Eucharist. We stumble about, lamenting our problems, and ignoring the solution in front of us. When we feel hungry or in need of God, let us go to the scriptures, to Mass, and to our community of faith.

PRAYERS   *others may be added*

Thanking God for sustaining us, we pray:

◆ Give us our daily bread.

That all Christians will draw upon the Word and sacraments for strength and life, we pray: ◆ *That those who have lost hope will see the message of God with new eyes, we pray:* ◆ *That we may not be oblivious to the nourishing food and drink Jesus offers us, we pray:* ◆ *That we may in turn offer the bread of life to others, we pray:* ◆

Our Father . . .

Benevolent God,
you sustained the Israelites in
   the desert,
and provide for all your children.
Help us to see the bread you offer us.
We ask this through our Lord Jesus
   Christ, your Son,
who lives and reigns with you
in the unity of the Holy Spirit,
one God, forever and ever.
Amen.

✦ *For ever I will sing the goodness of the Lord.*

✛ *The precepts of the Lord give joy to the heart.*

PSALM 16   *page 400*

READING   *Matthew 13:10–13*

The disciples approached Jesus and said, "Why do you speak to the crowd in parables?" He said to them in reply, "Because knowledge of the mysteries of the Kingdom of heaven has been granted to you, but to them it has not been granted. To anyone who has, more will be given and he will grow rich; from anyone who has not, even what he has will be taken away. This is why I speak to them in parables, because *they look but do not see and hear but do not listen or understand.*"

REFLECTION

It's amazing how we can be told something over and over and not hear. It is not only our children who are guilty of this. We, too, practice "selective hearing," whether by intention or by habit. Only after many times do we truly understand. It's shocking that we can see something but not realize it is there. Ask God to help you see what you are missing and hear what you have tuned out.

PRAYERS   *others may be added*

With open eyes, ears, and hearts, we pray:

◆ Reveal your truth to us.

For a deepening in understanding of the Christian tradition by the Church, we pray: ◆ *For solutions to problems in education, health care, and policy, we pray:* ◆ *For new understanding of children, parents, and friends with whom we have struggled, we pray:* ◆ *For commitment to prayer which brings deeper awareness of God's presence, we pray:* ◆

Our Father . . .

Omnipotent God,
you work in the natural world
    around us and in our daily
    interactions with others.
Signs and wonders surround us.
Open our eyes and ears to
    your presence,
giving us a heart of sensitivity to
    your grace.
Grant this through Christ our Lord.
Amen.

✛ *The precepts of the Lord give joy to the heart.*

✦ *Commit your life to the Lord, and he will help you.*

PSALM 40 *page 407*

READING *John 20:15–18*

Jesus said to [Mary Magdalene], "Woman, why are you weeping? Whom are you looking for?" She thought it was the gardener and said to him, "Sir, if you carried him away, tell me where you laid him, and I will take him." Jesus said to her, "Mary!" She turned and said to him in Hebrew, "Rabbouni," which means Teacher. Jesus said to her, "Stop holding on to me, for I have not yet ascended to the Father. But go to my brothers and tell them, 'I am going to my Father and your Father, to my God and your God.' " Mary Magdalene went and announced to the disciples, "I have seen the Lord," and then reported what he told her.

REFLECTION

In her devotion, Mary found herself at Jesus' tomb after his death. Jesus then chose her to be the first to reveal his Resurrection from the dead. When we draw close to Jesus, we will notice our lives change. The more time we spend with him, the more we will be affected by his ways. He calls us by name and sends us forth to love others. We will feel his presence and sense him urging us to help spread the Good News.

PRAYERS *others may be added*

Responding to the Teacher, we pray:

◆ Send us forth, O God.

For preachers and witnesses, sent by the Lord to share what they have seen and heard, we pray: ◆ *For journalists, international observers, and photographers, led to tell the stories of forgotten people to the world, we pray:* ◆ *For whistle blowers and witnesses to crime, who must speak truth boldly, we pray:* ◆ *For each of us, who spend a lifetime finding our own inner voice for Jesus, we pray:* ◆

Our Father . . .

Risen Lord,
you commissioned Mary Magdalene
to share the Good News with
the apostles.
You call forth men and women
to proclaim the kingdom in all times
and circumstances.
Make us bold in our dedication to and
telling of your truth.
You live and reign with God
the Father
in the unity of the Holy Spirit,
one God, forever and ever.
Amen.

✦ *Commit your life to the Lord, and he will help you.*

✝ *The Lord made us; we belong to him.*

PSALM 139 *page 420*

READING *Matthew 13:24–30*

Jesus proposed a parable to the crowds. "The Kingdom of heaven may be likened to a man who sowed good seed in his field. While everyone was asleep his enemy came and sowed weeds all through the wheat, and then went off. When the crop grew and bore fruit, the weeds appeared as well. The slaves of the householder came to him and said, 'Master, did you not sow good seed in your field? Where have the weeds come from?' He answered, 'An enemy has done this.' His slaves said to him, 'Do you want us to go and pull them up?' He replied, 'No, if you pull up the weeds you might uproot the wheat along with them. Let them grow together until harvest; then at harvest time I will say to the harvesters, " 'First collect the weeds and tie them in bundles for burning; but gather the wheat into my barn.' " "

REFLECTION

"The enemy" is indeed at work in our world alongside our God. Not everyone accepts the seed they are offered. We will continue our whole lives this way: aware of others around us making choices that distance themselves from God and eternal life. It may be difficult, but we must remain strong and growing in faith despite others' paths.

PRAYERS *others may be added*

Asking for God's guidance, we pray:

◆ Help us grow toward you, Lord Jesus.

That Christians may be strengthened in faith no matter what temptation or other influences cross their paths, we pray: ◆ *That voices for truth and justice are not intimidated or eliminated by evil forces, we pray:* ◆ *That those who are making bad choices may see the example of others struggling for good around them, we pray:* ◆ *That we find confidence in living our faith, so as not to be easily shaken, we pray:* ◆

Our Father . . .

Heavenly God,
you see the trajectory of time
and the path our choices take us.
You see the sincere of heart alongside
    those who are deceiving
    themselves.
Help us follow you steadfastly,
no matter what distractions may come
    our way.
We ask this through Christ our Lord.
Amen.

✝ *The Lord made us; we belong to him.*

✦ *For ever I will sing the goodness of the Lord.*

PSALM 100 page 414

READING Matthew 13:44–46

Jesus said to his disciples: "The kingdom of heaven is like a treasure buried in a field, which a person finds and hides again, and out of joy goes and sells all that he has and buys that field. Again, the kingdom of heaven is like a merchant searching for fine pearls. When he finds a pearl of great price, he goes and sells all that he has and buys it."

REFLECTION

What joy compares to this? What delights the human heart so entirely that one will give up everything else to retain it? We might consider forsaking our possessions for the sake of a true love. We would give up riches in order to save our precious child. We sacrifice time and sleep to complete our life's creative work. These beloved endeavors and people tell us something about the kingdom of heaven then, too. God's kingdom is akin to the greatest love we have known, the unique gift of a child, the culmination of years of effort.

PRAYERS *others may be added*

Rejoicing in the life God has promised us, we pray:

◆ Show us lasting treasure, Lord.

That the joy of everlasting life with God permeates the Church's identity, we pray: ◆ *That earthly experiences of deep happiness lead people to the ultimate happiness found in God, we pray:* ◆ *That we may hope in the transformation of the world, we pray:* ◆ *That we may be a joyful Christian people, celebrating all God has given us, we pray:* ◆

Our Father . . .

God our King,
you have riches and wealth beyond
    our wildest dreams awaiting us.
May we give thanks to you and take
    steps toward life with you
each time happiness touches
    our heart.
We ask this through our Lord Jesus
    Christ, your Son,
who lives and reigns with you
in the unity of the Holy Spirit,
one God, forever and ever.
Amen.

✦ *For ever I will sing the goodness of the Lord.*

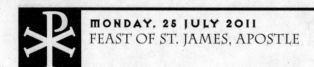

✦ *Commit your life to the Lord.*

PSALM 40 *page 407*

READING *Matthew 20:25–28*

But Jesus summoned them and said, "You know that the rulers of the Gentiles lord it over them, and the great ones make their authority over them felt. But it shall not be so among you. Rather, whoever wishes to be great among you shall be your servant; whoever wishes to be first among you shall be your slave. Just so, the Son of Man did not come to be served but to serve and to give his life as a ransom for many."

REFLECTION

Being called to follow Jesus implies a life of both joy and suffering. We may only want the joy. We sing, attend uplifting conferences, and spend our time with those who support our faith. Or, we may focus only on the suffering. We bear whatever we consider our "cross" silently, thinking no one could understand. To truly be a disciple requires holding in tension the delight in knowing the Lord and the pain of knowing the world's treatment of him.

PRAYERS *others may be added*

As your servants, Lord, we pray:

◆ Make us one with you in joy and sadness.

For all who follow Jesus, that they remain strong in suffering and rejoice in the promise of eternal life, we pray: ◆ *For converts to Christianity, that their initial zeal develops into steady faith, we pray:* ◆ *For those whose cup seems too much to bear, that they feel Jesus with them, we pray:* ◆ *For courage, honor, integrity, delight, and generosity in following Jesus, we pray:* ◆

Our Father . . .

Lord Jesus, Son of God,
even your apostles did not always
    understand
what it meant to follow you.
Your suffering and Crucifixion pained
    and confused them.
After your Resurrection, you came
    to them
and helped them understand.
St. James and others went on to give
    glory to you
by their commitment and sacrifice.
May we, too, drink the chalice with
    joy and strength.
You live and reign with God
    the Father
in the unity of the Holy Spirit,
one God, forever and ever.
Amen.

✦ *Commit your life to the Lord.*

✝ *Commit your life to the Lord, and he will help you.*

PSALM 40 page 407

READING *Matthew 13:16–17*

Jesus said to his disciples: "Blessed are your eyes, because they see, and your ears, because they hear. Amen, I say to you, many prophets and righteous people longed to see what you see but did not see it, and to hear what you hear but did not hear it."

REFLECTION

Faithful parenting is a mountainous task in our world. So many messages threaten to destroy parents' values, hopes, hard work, and love. Parents may lose faith, seeing their children go through phases that can only hurt them. St. Joachim and St. Anne were faithful parents who could not have imagined the way God would touch their daughter Mary. May all parents look to them for the inspiration to continue parenting with the love of Christ.

PRAYERS *others may be added*

With hearts of concern, we pray:

◆ Lord, hear our prayer.

That all parents will help their children prayerfully discern their vocation to serve Christ, we pray: ◆ *That all parents who fight for their children's well-being may have the help of the Church and the guidance of the Holy Spirit, we pray:* ◆ *That all grandparents will be rewarded by seeing the fruit of many years of love and teaching, we pray:* ◆ *That parents in our Church community will find each other supportive in raising Christian children, we pray:* ◆

Our Father . . .

God our Father,
St. Joachim and St. Anne model for
   us faithful parenting.
May we who are parents look to them
   for hope.
May we model the love of Christ in
   our parenting
and support of all families.
Grant this through Christ our Lord.
Amen.

✝ *Commit your life to the Lord, and he will help you.*

✝ *The Lord is my light and my salvation.*

PSALM 100   *page 414*

READING   *Exodus 34:29–30*

As Moses came down from Mount Sinai with the two tablets of the commandments in his hands, he did not know that the skin of his face had become radiant while he conversed with the LORD. When Aaron, then, and the other children of Israel saw Moses and noticed how radiant the skin of his face had become, they were afraid to come near him.

REFLECTION

A profound experience of God in prayer may leave a lasting impression of light, love, or joy. This reflection of God's nature is described as Moses' face becoming "radiant." Taking time to experience God in this most direct way will surely change us as well. Let us stay in prayer long enough to get glimpses into this mystical awareness of God.

PRAYERS   *others may be added*

Longing for God, we pray:

◆ Show us your face.

That the Pope, Bishops, and priests of the Church will have time for retreat and become radiant with joy, we pray: ◆ *That those who have experienced the divine goodness or light will search for truth in the story of Christianity, we pray:* ◆ *That busy workers, parents, and students will find time for prayer, recreation, and stillness that leads to God, we pray:* ◆ *That each of us will return again and again to God's love and light, we pray:* ◆

Our Father . . .

God of light and goodness,
Moses was privileged to stand before
     you in prayer,
and all who saw him afterward were
     awed by his appearance.
May we take time for prayer
and the opportunity to be blessed by
     your presence,
that we, too, may give you praise
     and glory.
We ask this through Christ our Lord.
Amen.

✝ *The Lord is my light and my salvation.*

✦ *The heart of the just one is firm, trusting in the Lord.*

PSALM 139 *page 420*

READING *Matthew 13:47–50*

Jesus said to the disciples: "The Kingdom of heaven is like a net thrown into the sea, which collects fish of every kind. When it is full they haul it ashore and sit down to put what is good into buckets. What is bad they throw away. Thus it will be at the end of the age. The angels will go out and separate the wicked from the righteous and throw them into the fiery furnace, where there will be wailing and grinding of teeth."

REFLECTION

Who is good, and who is bad? Who will or will not be saved? Pressing questions like these determine much of people's behavior regarding religion and ethics. But knowing what God asks of us and what will determine our "goodness" is more complicated than the rules regarding the Ark of the Covenant in Exodus. For Christians, it takes a lifelong journey to understand how to love God and neighbor.

PRAYERS *others may be added*

Desiring to be good in the eyes of God, we pray:

◆ Lead us to life in you.

That Christians eagerly await God's presence and guidance, we pray: ◆ *That God-fearing nations seek the kingdom of God, not a kingdom of power or wealth, we pray:* ◆ *That those who struggle financially may be led by God to stability, good choices, and gratitude, we pray:* ◆ *That we turn over to God our greed, and live anew in his sufficient love, we pray:* ◆

Our Father . . .

God, our final judge,
you remind us of the importance of
how we live our lives
to how we will spend our eternity.
And yet, you are full of mercy
and patience.
Show us how to live without
paralyzing fear,
and to live with motivating desire
for you.
We ask this through Christ our Lord.
Amen.

✦ *The heart of the just one is firm, trusting in the Lord.*

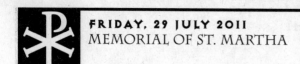
✦ *Commit your life to the Lord, and he will help you.*

PSALM 40   *page 407*

READING   *John 11:19–24*

Many of the Jews had come to Martha and Mary to comfort them about their brother [Lazarus, who had died]. When Martha heard that Jesus was coming, she went to meet him; but Mary sat at home. Martha said to Jesus, "Lord, if you had been here, my brother would not have died. But even now I know that whatever you ask of God, God will give you." Jesus said to her, "Your brother will rise." Martha said to him, "I know he will rise, in the resurrection on the last day."

REFLECTION

Martha and Mary provide us with two models of faithful women with different ways of living their faith. In today's Gospel, Mary retreats in mourning and prayer; Martha comes to Jesus with her questions and testifies to her faith that he can help Lazarus. It is good for us to know there are different ways of being in relationship with Jesus and living our faith.

PRAYERS   *others may be added*

Loving God in different ways, we pray:

◆ May we serve you with integrity.

For all holy men and women, past and present, who have been models of faith, we pray: ◆ *For those with inquisitive minds like Martha, who bring questions before God and the community, we pray:* ◆ *For contemplatives like Mary, who pray for the needs of the world, we pray:* ◆ *For friends who show us ways of praying, loving, and serving Jesus, we pray:* ◆ *For each of us, that we may be able to make heartfelt, honest statements of faith, we pray:* ◆

Our Father . . .

Lord Jesus,
you are the Way, the Truth, and
the Life.
May we trust in your goodness
and mercy,
as we dream of the day
when we will join you in your
Father's house of many rooms.
May we look forward to the day of
reuniting with loved ones
and all who have loved their God.
You live and reign with God the
Father
in the unity of the Holy Spirit,
one God, forever and ever.
Amen.

✦ *Commit your life to the Lord, and he will help you.*

✚ *The precepts of the Lord give joy to the heart.*

PSALM 33   *page 404*

READING   *Leviticus 25:10–17*

[The LORD said to Moses on Mount Sinai:] "This fiftieth year you shall make sacred by proclaiming liberty in the land for all its inhabitants. It shall be a jubilee for you, when every one of you shall return to his property, every one to his own family estate. In this fiftieth year, your year of jubilee, you shall not sow, nor shall you reap the aftergrowth or pick the grapes from the untrimmed vines. Since this is a jubilee, which shall be sacred for you, you may not eat of its produce, except as taken directly from the field.

"In this year of jubilee, then, every one of you shall return to his own property. Therefore, when you sell any land to your neighbor or buy any from him, do not deal unfairly. On the basis of the number of years since the last jubilee shall you purchase the land from your neighbor; and so also, on the basis of the number of years for crops, shall he sell it to you. When the years are many, the price shall be so much the more; when the years are few, the price shall be so much the less. For it is really the number of crops that he sells you. Do not deal unfairly, then; but stand in fear of your god. I, the LORD, am your God."

REFLECTION

The concept of jubilee years was meant to emphasize the Lord as true owner of the land and profits. A return to this understanding might help us in conservation of our earth, better care of our possessions, more reuse and less "disposable thinking" in our society. If we think of everything—land, goods, money, and objects—as rightfully belonging to God, we will treat them with loving care and a looser grip.

PRAYERS   *others may be added*

Aware of the sanctity of the earth, we pray:

◆ Lord, hear our prayer.

That the Church will continue to care for God's creation, we pray: ◆ *That nations will work toward sustainable energy sources, clean water and air, and protection of wildlife, we pray:* ◆ *That corporations will increasingly work toward fair trade that protects the earth and workers, we pray:* ◆ *That consumers will think carefully about purchases and patronage of businesses, we pray:* ◆

Our Father . . .

God of justice,
help us to be good stewards of the
    gifts you have given us,
in business and in personal spending.
We ask this through Christ our Lord.
Amen.

✚ *The precepts of the Lord give joy to the heart.*

Optional memorials of St. Peter Chrysologus, bishop, doctor of the Church; Blessed Virgin Mary

✠ *The Lord hears the cry of the poor.*

PSALM 42 *page 408*

READING *Matthew 14:15–20*

When it was evening, the disciples approached [Jesus] and said, "This is a deserted place and it is already late; dismiss the crowds so that they can go to the villages and buy food for themselves." Jesus said to them, "There is no need for them to go away; give them some food yourselves." But they said to him, "Five loaves and two fish are all we have here." Then he said, "Bring them here to me," and he ordered the crowds to sit down on the grass. Taking the five loaves and the two fish, and looking up to heaven, he said the blessing, broke the loaves, and gave them to the disciples, who in turn gave them to the crowds. They all ate and were satisfied.

REFLECTION

Jesus loved the people of God. He hated to see them in pain; he cured them; he fed them. This story about Jesus reveals the nature of our God. Our God is compassionate and is moved by our suffering to help us. It also tells us what our Christian nature should be. If we are not touched by others' hunger and pain, or if our inclination is to push people away rather than welcome them, we need to examine our faith.

PRAYERS *others may be added*

Awed by our God's love, we pray:

◆ Give us hearts of compassion.

For the shepherds of the Church, who respond to the needs of those who are hungry, thirsty, in pain, and are dying, we pray: ◆ *For Christians everywhere to work together to feed, clothe, and heal the world, we pray:* ◆ *For those who feel pushed away, that they feel the welcoming arms of God, we pray:* ◆ *For an examination of our faith and our feelings toward our brothers and sisters, we pray:* ◆

Our Father . . .

Compassionate God,
your Son could not turn away from
 those in need.
Give us hearts of mercy to do
 your will.
Make us healers, reconcilers, and
 advocates for those in need.
Make us compassionate in the name
 of Jesus the Christ,
through whom we ask this prayer.
Amen.

✠ *The Lord hears the cry of the poor.*

✚ *Commit your life to the Lord, and he will help you.*

PSALM 40   page 407

READING   Matthew 5:13–16

Jesus said to his disciples: "You are the salt of the earth. But if salt loses its taste, with what can it be seasoned? It is no longer good for anything but to be thrown out and trampled underfoot. You are the light of the world. A city set on a mountain cannot be hidden. Nor do they light a lamp and then put it under a bushel basket; it is set on a lampstand, where it gives light to all in the house. Just so, your light must shine before others, that they may see your good deeds and glorify your heavenly Father."

REFLECTION

The Redemptorist order, founded by St. Alphonsus, emphasizes the mission of the Church, making special efforts to catechize, evangelize, and uplift the faithful and unchurched. Do we take opportunities, individually or as a parish community, to bring the light of Christ to the world? What special speakers, events, and seasons do we employ as an opportunity for catechesis, formation, and service?

PRAYERS   others may be added

Seeking an increase in the light of Christ, we pray:

◆ Lord, hear our prayer.

For parish missions, diocesan conferences, spiritual speakers, Christian concerts, and all efforts to re-ignite Christian faith, we pray: ◆
For missionaries to go forth to the edges of society and developing parts of the world, that they reflect the light of Christ in their care for all people, we pray: ◆
For those living in darkness who need help coming into the light, we pray: ◆
For increased participation in local and regional opportunities for service projects, adult learning, and faith formation, we pray: ◆

Our Father . . .

Lord Jesus,
Light of the World,
you shine through our darkness,
reaching out to us by illuminating our
    path to you.
May we respond by reflecting your
    light to others,
with passion and truth,
You live and reign with God
    the Father
in the unity of the Holy Spirit,
one God, forever and ever.
Amen.

✚ *Commit your life to the Lord, and he will help you.*

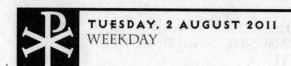
✦ *The heart of the just one is firm,*
   trusting in the Lord.

PSALM 139   page 420

READING   Matthew 14:22–27

Jesus made the disciples get into a boat
and precede him to the other side of the
sea, while he dismissed the crowds.
After doing so, he went up on the mountain by himself to pray. When it was
evening he was there alone. Meanwhile
the boat, already a few miles offshore,
was being tossed about by the waves,
for the wind was against it. During the
fourth watch of the night, he came
toward them, walking on the sea. When
the disciples saw him walking on the
sea they were terrified. "It is a ghost,"
they said, and they cried out in fear. At
once Jesus spoke to them, "Take courage, it is I; do not be afraid."

REFLECTION

Our faith can sometimes be weak, and
we can sin against our faith. Do we find
ourselves "terrified" like the disciples
just by the magnitude of God and his
power? Are we "frightened" like Peter
when we face a seemingly insurmount-
able obstacle? Do we cry out to be saved
at the first inclination that God is not
with us? This passage gives us a chance
to examine our doubts and how our
faith needs to grow.

PRAYERS   *others may be added*

With struggling faith, we pray:

◆ Calm our fears, O God.

That the Church does not intimidate
non-believers but gives them hope,
we pray: ◆ *That Christian faith is not*
easily overcome by the size of obstacles,
we pray: ◆ *That we hold fast to God and*
silence our doubts, we pray: ◆ *That we*
become people of great faith in God,
we pray: ◆

Our Father . . .

Awesome God,
let our awe of you be confident in
   your powers.
May we rely on you with trust.
You call us to cross the waters
   without fear.
Help us to walk, unafraid, with Jesus
   at our side.
We ask this through Christ our Lord.
Amen.

✦ *The heart of the just one is firm,*
   trusting in the Lord.

✦ *The heart of the just one is firm,*
trusting in the Lord.

PSALM 130   *page 418*

READING   *Matthew 15:21–28*

At that time Jesus withdrew to the region of Tyre and Sidon. And behold, a Canaanite woman of that district came and called out, "Have pity on me, Lord, Son of David! My daughter is tormented by a demon." But he did not say a word in answer to her. His disciples came and asked him, "Send her away, for she keeps calling out after us." He said in reply, "I was sent only to the lost sheep of the house of Israel." But the woman came and did him homage, saying, "Lord, help me." He said in reply, "It is not right to take the food of the children and throw it to the dogs." She said, "Please, Lord, for even the dogs eat the scraps that fall from the table of their masters." Then Jesus said to her in reply, "O woman, great is your faith! Let it be done for you as you wish." And her daughter was healed from that hour.

REFLECTION

Great faith gives one a powerful voice, persistent actions, and confidence in God. The Canaanite woman continued to plead with Jesus despite being ignored, despised, and told cultural, legal, and ethical reasons as to why she could not be helped. God's mercy and justice surpasses norms and laws.

PRAYERS   *others may be added*

With your law written on our hearts, we pray:

◆ Make us strong in you, O God.

For the Church to call forth actions rooted in justice and mercy, we pray: ◆ *For reconciliation and retribution for victims of genocide, war, slavery, and abuse, we pray:* ◆ *For an end to abortion and infanticide, we pray:* ◆ *For an end to the death penalty, we pray:* ◆

Our Father . . .

Merciful and just God,
those who love and serve you in faith
grow in wisdom and strength.
Like the Canaanite woman,
your servants work tirelessly for good.
Show us the way to speak
and act confidently.
Grant this through Christ our Lord.
Amen.

✦ *The heart of the just one is firm,*
trusting in the Lord.

✦ *The Lord is my shepherd, there is nothing I shall want.*

PSALM 40   *page 407*

READING   *Matthew 16:13b–19*

[Jesus asked], "Who do people say that the Son of Man is?" They replied, "Some say John the Baptist, others Elijah, still others Jeremiah or one of the prophets." He said to them, "But who do you say that I am?" Simon Peter said in reply, "You are the Christ, the Son of the living God." Jesus said to him in reply, "Blessed are you, Simon son of Jonah. For flesh and blood has not revealed this to you, but my heavenly Father. And so I say to you, you are Peter, and upon this rock I will build my Church, and the gates of the netherworld shall not prevail against it. I will give you the keys to the Kingdom of heaven. Whatever you bind on earth shall be bound in heaven; and whatever you loose on earth shall be loosed in heaven."

REFLECTION

A good pastor is known for his wisdom, guidance, and leadership. Today we remember and thank all pastors who have shepherded us well, and we praise and recognize those whose leadership skills are just beginning. Do we know how our Church is forming seminarians and new vocations? How can we support these efforts? Our seminaries and graduate schools of theology are places of intense prayer, faithful communities, and important theological study.

PRAYERS   *others may be added*

With gratitude for our pastors, we pray:

◆ Lord, hear our prayer.

For every parish priest, that he may grow ever more like Christ, our Good Shepherd, we pray: ◆ *For all who protect, serve, and lead others, we pray:* ◆ *For children, youths, and adults in need of mentors and spiritual directors, we pray:* ◆ *For our own pastor, that he may remain healthy and happy, we pray:* ◆ *For all pastors and pastoral leaders who have died, we pray:* ◆

Our Father . . .

Lord Jesus,
our Good Shepherd,
you care for each of us with
    unconditional love
and seek us when we are lost.
May the pastors of your Church lead
    with love
for every member of the flock
and deep faithfulness to God.
You live and reign with God
    the Father
in the unity of the Holy Spirit,
one God, forever and ever.
Amen.

✦ *The Lord is my shepherd, there is nothing I shall want.*

✤ *In you, O Lord, I have found my peace.*

PSALM 51   *page 409*

READING   *Matthew 16:24–27*

Jesus said to his disciples, "Whoever wishes to come after me must deny himself, take up his cross, and follow me. For whoever wishes to save his life will lose it, but whoever loses his life for my sake will find it. What profit would there be for one to gain the whole world and forfeit his life? Or what can one give in exchange for his life? For the Son of Man will come with his angels in his Father's glory, and then he will repay everyone according to his conduct."

REFLECTION

What are we trying to gain? Are we working hard in order to have a nicer house, a better car, more expensive clothes, an extravagant vacation? Do we desire recognition, power, or success? If we are able to "gain" these things, what do we achieve? Will happiness really come from these acquisitions?

PRAYERS   *others may be added*

Struggling with our disordered priorities, we pray:

◆ Show us the way to life in you.

For Christians who wrongly desire material wealth and success, that their deeper desires for life in Christ rise higher, we pray: ◆ For the very wealthy, that they recognize the limitations of their possessions and instead refocus on the state of their souls, we pray: ◆ For those who justifiably desire a living wage and adequate housing, that there may be a more equal distribution of wealth, we pray: ◆ For any of us in denial, that the question of our life's purpose stays before us, we pray: ◆

Our Father . . .

Lord Jesus,
you rule over every nation and
    earthly power.
The ultimate judgment day will wash
    away all human status and
    recognition;
all that will remain is our love for you
    and for others.
May we be worthy of life with you.
You live and reign with God
    the Father
in the unity of the Holy Spirit,
one God, forever and ever.
Amen.

✤ *In you, O Lord, I have found my peace.*

Optional memorial of the Dedication of the Basilica of St. Mary Major in Rome   **251**

✦ *For ever I will sing the goodness of the Lord.*

PSALM 100 *page 414*

READING Matthew 17:1–3

Jesus took Peter, James, and his brother, John, and led them up a high mountain by themselves. And he was transfigured before them; his face shone like the sun and his clothes became white as light. And behold, Moses and Elijah appeared to them, conversing with him.

REFLECTION *Anastasius of Sinai,
Bishop*

This is the saving revelation given us upon the mountain; this is the festival of Christ that has drawn us here. Let us listen, then, to the sacred voice of God so compellingly calling us from on high, from the summit of the mountain, so that with the Lord's chosen disciples we may penetrate the deep meaning of these holy mysteries, so far beyond our capacity to express. Jesus goes before us the way, both up the mountain and into heaven. . . . it is for us now to follow him with all speed, yearning for the heavenly vision that will give us a share in his radiance, renew our spiritual nature and transform us into his own likeness, making us for ever sharers in his Godhead and raising us to heights as yet undreamed of.

PRAYERS *others may be added*

Aware of Christ's pure light surrounding us, we pray:

◆ Show us your face, O Lord.

That the light of the Church may be a beacon of truth and hope, we pray: ◆
That the light of education may lead to greater harmony between nations, we pray: ◆ *That the light of justice may shine into the darkest corners where violence, crime, and cruelty have reigned, we pray:* ◆ *That the light of charity may pervade our community, making us generous with what we have, we pray:* ◆ *That the eternal light will lead all believers home, we pray:* ◆

Our Father . . .

Lord Jesus,
you faced the ordinariness of
    day-to-day life,
yet you transcended it with
    saving love.
Help us to believe in you,
and to bring the hope of transforma-
    tion to this world
through the Good News of your death
    and Resurrection.
You live and reign with God
    the Father
in the unity of the Holy Spirit,
one God, forever and ever.
Amen.

✦ *For ever I will sing the goodness of the Lord.*

✜ *I have found my peace.*

PSALM 42   page 408

READING   Matthew 14:26–31

When the disciples saw [Jesus] walking on the sea they were terrified. "It is a ghost," they said, and they cried out in fear. At once Jesus spoke to them, "Take courage, it is I; do not be afraid." Peter said to him in reply, "Lord, if it is you, command me to come to you on the water." He said, "Come." Peter got out of the boat and began to walk on the water toward Jesus. But when he saw how strong the wind was he became frightened; and, beginning to sink, he cried out, "Lord, save me!" Immediately Jesus stretched out his hand and caught him, and said to him, "O you of little faith, why did you doubt?"

REFLECTION   Pope John Paul II

Do not be afraid to go out on the streets and into public places, like the first Apostles who preached Christ and the Good News of salvation in the squares of cities, towns and villages. This is no time to be ashamed of the Gospel (cf. Rom 1:16). It is the time to preach it from the rooftops (cf. Mt 10:27). Do not be afraid to break out of comfortable and routine modes of living, in order to take up the challenge of making Christ known in the modern "metropolis." It is you who must "go out into the byroads" (Mt 22:9) and invite everyone you meet to the banquet which God has prepared for his people.

PRAYERS   *others may be added*

Searching for stillness, we pray:

◆ Be with us, Lord.

For all Christians, sought after by the world, that they find time to be alone in prayer, we pray: ◆ *For the beauty of the earth, which inspires us to turn to God, we pray:* ◆ *For students, teachers, coaches, and parents who feel the intensity of the school calendar approaching, that they are able to maintain times of silence to hear God's voice, we pray:* ◆ *For sacred spaces in our lives: church, nature, home, retreats, that we find them calling us to prayer, we pray:* ◆ *For an end to fear, to live freely in Christian love, we pray:* ◆

Our Father . . .

Prince of Peace,
calm our fears,
and open our hearts to your love.
As we remain in that serenity,
may we offer it to others.
You live and reign with God
    the Father
in the unity of the Holy Spirit,
one God, forever and ever.
Amen.

✜ *I have found my peace.*

✦ *Commit your life to the Lord, and he will help you.*

PSALM 40   page 407

READING   Luke 9:57–62

As Jesus and his disciples were proceeding on their journey someone said to him, "I will follow you wherever you go." Jesus answered him, "Foxes have dens and birds of the sky have nests, but the Son of Man has nowhere to rest his head." And to another he said, "Follow me." But he replied, "Lord, let me go first and bury my father." But he answered him, "Let the dead bury their dead. But you, go and proclaim the Kingdom of God." And another said, "I will follow you, Lord, but first let me say farewell to my family at home." He said, "No one who sets a hand to the plow and looks to what was left behind is fit for the Kingdom of God."

REFLECTION

St. Dominic inspired his followers to take the Word of God wherever they went. We may be challenged to proclaim the Gospel wherever we find ourselves. It is easiest to follow Christ when we are at Church or among like-minded Christians. Do we bring Christ to all our social circles, our workplace, shopping centers, recreational activities, and on vacations?

PRAYERS   *others may be added*

Following Christ wherever he calls us, we pray:

◆ Walk with us, Lord.

That Christians bring their faith into the world and daily life, we pray: ◆ *That all workers bring Christ into their words and actions, we pray:* ◆ *That all proclaim the Gospel at the margins of society, we pray:* ◆ *That traveling throughout life with the Word of God gives us confidence and joy, we pray:* ◆

Our Father . . .

Lord Jesus,
your disciples promised to follow you.
May we, like St. Dominic,
follow you in every aspect of
    our lives.
You make us strong and send us forth.
You live and reign with God
    the Father
in the unity of the Holy Spirit,
one God, forever and ever.
Amen.

✦ *Commit your life to the Lord, and he will help you.*

✛ *The Lord made us; we belong to him.*

PSALM 100   page 414

READING   Matthew 18:1–5

The disciples approached Jesus and said, "Who is the greatest in the Kingdom of heaven?" He called a child over, placed it in their midst, and said, "Amen, I say to you, unless you turn and become like children, you will not enter the Kingdom of heaven. Whoever becomes humble like this child is the greatest in the Kingdom of heaven. And whoever receives one child such as this in my name receives me."

REFLECTION

What is our attitude toward children? If our children are grown, or if we do not have children, we may not be exposed to them often. We might learn something about the kingdom of heaven by learning about children. We can pick up a book on children's development or reach out to a child in our life. How do we respond to children in need—in our neighborhood, our community, our world? Do we open our hearts, doors, and resources to all "little ones"?

PRAYERS   *others may be added*

*Challenged to open our hearts,
we pray:*

◆ May we see your face in every child.

For the children of the Church, that the Word and sacrament are made easily accessible to them, we pray: ◆
For children in need of adoptive and foster families, that they may be welcomed into homes, we pray: ◆
For children without enough food, shelter, or health care, that doors may open to them, we pray: ◆ *For children in our community, who bring Jesus into our midst, we pray:* ◆

Our Father . . .

Lord Jesus,
you were once a child
just like those children you loved.
Remind us to see your face
in the children we encounter.
May we embrace them with love
and generosity of spirit.
You live and reign with God
   the Father
in the unity of the Holy Spirit,
one God, forever and ever.
Amen.

✛ *The Lord made us; we belong to him.*

Optional memorial of St. Teresa Benedicta of the Cross, virgin, martyr

✦ *The Lord is my shepherd, there is nothing I shall want.*

PSALM 40   *page 407*

READING   *2 Corinthians 9:6–10*

Brothers and sisters: Whoever sows sparingly will also reap sparingly, and whoever sows bountifully will also reap bountifully. Each must do as already determined, without sadness or compulsion, for God loves a cheerful giver.

Moreover, God is able to make every grace abundant for you, so that in all things, always having all you need, you may have an abundance for every good work. As it is written:

He scatters abroad, he gives to the poor; / his righteousness endures forever.

The one who supplies seed to the sower and bread for food will supply and multiply your seed and increase the harvest of your righteousness.

REFLECTION

Most of us know a few cheerful givers. These people are inspiring. They give of their time or resources freely, neither resenting the sacrifice nor asking for recognition. As Christians, we also want to give gracefully, out of our gratitude to God and desire that all people share in God's love.

PRAYERS   *others may be added*

With joyful hearts, we pray:

◆ Inspire us to generosity.

For the Pope, Bishops, and priests of the Church who live their vocation with peace and happiness, we pray: ◆
For philanthropists who boldly fund initiatives to improve life for those in need, we pray: ◆ *For parents, volunteers, and neighbors who give endless amounts of time and money to support churches, schools, and community institutions, we pray:* ◆ *For each of us, when we can say "yes" to a request without grudge or self-righteousness, we pray:* ◆

Our Father . . .

Gracious God,
your heart knows no bounds to its
    generosity and mercy.
You have made us like you;
help us to find our own grounding
    in you,
that we may be genuinely joyful
    and generous.
We ask this through our Lord Jesus
    Christ, your Son,
who lives and reigns with you
in the unity of the Holy Spirit,
one God, forever and ever.
Amen.

✦ *The Lord is my shepherd, there is nothing I shall want.*

✙ *Commit your life to the Lord.*

PSALM 40 *page 407*

READING *Philippians 3:8–14*

I consider everything as a loss because of the supreme good of knowing Christ Jesus my Lord. For his sake I have accepted the loss of all things and I consider them so much rubbish, that I may gain Christ and be found in him, not having any righteousness of my own based on the law but that which comes through faith in Christ, the righteousness from God, depending on faith to know him and the power of his resurrection and the sharing of his sufferings by being conformed to his death, if somehow I may attain the resurrection from the dead.

It is not that I have already taken hold of it or have already attained perfect maturity, but I continue my pursuit in hope that I may possess it, since I have indeed been taken possession of by Christ Jesus.

REFLECTION *St. John of the Cross*

I wish I could persuade spiritual persons that the way of perfection does not consist in many devices, nor in much cogitation, but in denying themselves completely and yielding themselves to suffer everything for the love of Christ. And if there is failure in this exercise, all other methods of walking in the spiritual way are merely a beating about the bush, and profitless trifling, although a person should have very high contemplation and communication with God.

PRAYERS *others may be added*

With eyes on the prize of the kingdom, we pray:

◆ Lord, hear our prayer.

For all believers who are in pursuit of deeper life in Christ, we pray: ◆
For servants of the common good who renew their commitment to others daily, we pray: ◆ *For perfectionists, who will be freer by recognizing their humanity, we pray:* ◆ *For a parish community here that welcomes any sinner who wants to follow Christ today, we pray:* ◆ *For all who have died longing for eternal life, we pray:* ◆

Our Father . . .

Merciful God,
you know all too well our
    human failure,
and we know your never-ending
    goodness.
Lead us on the way to you again
    and again,
as we follow the saints who strive for
    life in the kingdom.
We ask this through our Lord Jesus
    Christ, your Son,
who lives and reigns with you
in the unity of the Holy Spirit,
one God, forever and ever.
Amen.

✙ *Commit your life to the Lord.*

✢ *The precepts of the Lord give joy to the heart.*

PSALM 139 — page 420

READING — *Matthew 19:3–6*

Some Pharisees approached Jesus, and tested him, saying, "Is it lawful for a man to divorce his wife for any cause whatever?" He said in reply, "Have you not read that from the beginning the Creator / *made them male and female* / and said, / *For this reason a man shall leave his father and mother and be joined to his wife, and the two shall become one flesh*? / So they are no longer two, but one flesh. Therefore, what God has joined together, man must not separate."

REFLECTION

A commitment to Marriage is a strong testament to God's love and the promise of the covenant. If we can be committed to each other with love and forgiveness, how much greater must be God's love and commitment! The world desperately needs models of this loving unity. Married couples commit themselves to witnessing to God's love by repeatedly forgiving one another, loving each other unconditionally, and sharing their love with children and the world.

PRAYERS — *others may be added*

Lifting up our love and commitment to God, we pray:

◆ Make us one in you.

For all Christian marriages that survive through faith, love, and God's grace, we pray: ◆ *For all civic marriages and marriages of other faiths that reflect the goodness and loyalty in human nature, we pray:* ◆ *For healing in marriages broken, battered, and painful, we pray:* ◆ *For this community to be a place of support and strength for all married couples, we pray:* ◆

Our Father . . .

O Holy Trinity,
you reveal yourself as a relationship
of three persons, but one God.
May we, too, be loving, forgiving,
and gracious in our love for
     each other.
May all married couples turn to you
     in trouble and in joy.
We ask this through Christ our Lord.
Amen.

✢ *The precepts of the Lord give joy to the heart.*

✚ *The Lord is my light and my salvation.*

PSALM 100   *page 414*

READING   *Joshua 24:14–15*

Joshua gathered together all the tribes of Israel at Shechem, and addressed them, saying: "Fear the LORD and serve him completely and sincerely. Cast out the gods your fathers served beyond the River and in Egypt, and serve the LORD. If it does not please you to serve the LORD, decide today whom you will serve, the gods your fathers served beyond the River or the gods of the Amorites in whose country you are dwelling. As for me and my household, we will serve the LORD."

REFLECTION

"As for me and my household, we will serve the LORD." Some homes have this verse cross-stitched or designed on a print hanging on the wall. Each of us—grandparent, parent, spouse, son, or daughter—has an impact on the faith of those with whom we live. Our "household" can grow closer to or further from God because of our words and actions.

PRAYERS   *others may be added*

With our own households in mind, we pray:

◆ Make us your servants, God.

For religious communities, that their "households" may bring each member prayerful support, companionship, and growth in faith, we pray: ◆
For households in which only one member is a Christian, that his or her life may be a powerful testimony of love and joy to others, we pray: ◆
For households made up entirely of Christians, that they may challenge one another to grow more deeply in relationship with Christ and serve one another, we pray: ◆ *For a welcoming of entire households into our faith community, we pray:* ◆

Our Father . . .

God, our master builder,
you have given us life in a unique set
   of circumstances.
May our households be filled with
   prayer, song, love, and mercy.
Grant this through Christ our Lord.
Amen.

✚ *The Lord is my light and my salvation.*

Optional memorials of St. Pontian, pope, martyr and St. Hippolytus, priest, martyr; Blessed Virgin Mary

✦ *The Lord hears the cry of the poor.*

PSALM 16   page 400

READING   *Matthew 15:22–28*

[A Canaanite woman called out] "Have pity on me, Lord, Son of David! My daughter is tormented by a demon." But Jesus did not say a word in answer to her. Jesus' disciples came and asked him, "Send her away, for she keeps calling out after us." He said in reply, "I was sent only to the lost sheep of the house of Israel." But the woman came and did Jesus homage, saying, "Lord, help me." He said in reply, "It is not right to take the food of the children and throw it to the dogs." She said, "Please, Lord, for even the dogs eat the scraps that fall from the table of their masters." Then Jesus said to her in reply, "O woman, great is your faith! Let it be done for you as you wish." And the woman's daughter was healed from that hour.

REFLECTION

This Canaanite woman does not fit the picture of who Jesus came to save. She bothers the disciples. Even Jesus ignores her, until she begs persistently for mercy. Who or what issue is outside the "box" of our faith, our Church, our usual perspective? Whose pleas are persistently calling to us?

PRAYERS   *others may be added*

Turning our eyes and ears beyond the edge of our viewpoint, we pray:

◆ Help us hear when we are called.

For those in exile from the Church, that we continue to reach out to them in compassion, we pray: ◆ *For members of non-Christian religions, that we maintain lines of communication and understanding, we pray:* ◆ *For the "untouchables" of society who make us uncomfortable, we pray:* ◆ *For the agitating voices within our own communities, that we come to greater understanding of one another, we pray:* ◆

Our Father . . .

Lord Jesus,
even you could change your mind
   and heart
when faced with persistent faith and
   deep need.
Help us to heed the voices
that keep calling out after us
and after you.
Show us how to grow in dialogue,
understanding, and mercy
when confronting difficult issues
and problematic people.
You live and reign with God
   the Father
in the unity of the Holy Spirit,
one God, forever and ever.
Amen.

✦ *The Lord hears the cry of the poor.*

✤ *Commit your life to the Lord.*

CANTICLE   page 422

READING   *Luke 1:27–28*

While Jesus was speaking, a woman from the crowd called out and said to him, "Blessed is the womb that carried you and the breasts at which you nursed." He replied, "Rather, blessed are those who hear the word of God and observe it."

REFLECTION

Mary's Song, the Magnificat, would be a good prayer to carry in our pocket, purse, or briefcase. It is a statement of faith for when we want to rejoice or need to rely on God. Pray it after a loved one is kept safe or a difficult obstacle has been overcome. It is a proclamation of trust when we need to call upon God. Pray it in a time of illness, betrayal, or anxiety. Whether we are strong or weak, we can stand with Mary in the footsteps of our ancestors of faith, relying on the Lord.

PRAYERS   *others may be added*

With Mary, our Mother, we pray:

◆ Saving God, hear us.

For the Church, the Body of Christ, that she always proclaims the greatness of the Lord, we pray: ◆ *For Christians to pray with Mary to the God who has done great things for us throughout all time, we pray:* ◆ *For all who are weary, hungry, alone, or frightened, that they will call upon Mary to lift them up to heaven, we pray:* ◆ *For us to remember Mary as our protectress and guide, we pray:* ◆ *For those who have died, that the arms of our mother Mary embrace them, we pray:* ◆

Our Father . . .

Son of Mary and Son of God,
you brought peace into the world at
    your birth,
a peace the world had never known.
Your mother accompanied and
    comforted you
throughout your earthly journey.
May she also guide and teach us
as we struggle to follow your path of
    justice and mercy,
that we might better walk in
    your ways.
You live and reign with God
    the Father
in the unity of the Holy Spirit,
one God, forever and ever.
Amen.

✤ *Commit your life to the Lord.*

Today's reading is from the vigil Mass, Lectionary #621.

✦ *The heart of the just one is firm, trusting in the Lord.*

PSALM 25   *page 403*

READING   *Matthew 19:27–30*

[Peter said to Jesus], "We have given up everything and followed you. What will there be for us?" Jesus said to them, "Amen, I say to you that you who have followed me, in the new age, when the Son of Man is seated on his throne of glory, will yourselves sit on twelve thrones, judging the twelve tribes of Israel. And everyone who has given up houses or brothers or sisters or father or mother or children or lands for the sake of my name will receive a hundred times more, and will inherit eternal life. But many who are first will be last, and the last will be first."

REFLECTION

Peter wants a sign from God that his faith has been worth it, is real, and will be rewarded. We, too, may flounder and seek some form of proof for God or confirmation of our faith. Jesus' response is that there will be a time of rejoicing, but it will not be in this lifetime. We may have to wait a very long time. This is the reality of our faith.

PRAYERS   *others may be added*

Feeling lost, we pray:

◆ Help us trust in you.

For believers experiencing a "dark night of the soul" beset by doubt, we pray: ◆ *For a world that can seem short on "signs" and long on the absence of God, we pray:* ◆ *For an end to our human need for proof, and a strengthening of our faith, we pray:* ◆ *For an ability to love without reward, believe without evidence, and hope without rationale, we pray:* ◆

Our Father . . .

God of mercy,
help us remember we believe in you
because of the gift of faith.
Help us let go of our need for signs.
Give us the strength to wait and trust.
We ask this through Christ our Lord.
Amen.

✦ *The heart of the just one is firm, trusting in the Lord.*

✦ *The precepts of the Lord give joy to the heart.*

PSALM 33   *page 404*

READING   *Matthew 20:8–16*

When it was evening the owner of the vineyard said to his foreman, 'Summon the laborers and give them their pay, beginning with the last and ending with the first.' When those who had started about five o'clock came, each received the usual daily wage. So when the first came, they thought that they would receive more, but each of them also got the usual wage. And on receiving it they grumbled against the landowner, saying, 'These last ones worked only one hour, and you have made them equal to us, who bore the day's burden and the heat.' He said to one of them in reply, 'My friend, I am not cheating you. Did you not agree with me for the usual daily wage? Take what is yours and go. What if I wish to give this last one the same as you? Or am I not free to do as I wish with my own money? Are you envious because I am generous?' Thus, the last will be first, and the first will be last."

REFLECTION

This passage may be a yardstick with which to measure our own jealousy and selfishness or generosity and openness. What is your reaction if you imagine yourself as one of the laborers who came at dawn? What is your response to the workers who came at five o'clock? We can be so focused on justice and equality, that we forget mercy and generosity. Our God never forgets these standards. He is just beyond our comprehension and merciful beyond our imagination.

PRAYERS   *others may be added*

Yearning for hearts like yours, Lord, we pray:

◆ Show us the way.

For generosity in the Church, to welcome and see all as equal in the eyes of God, we pray: ◆ *For generosity in our nation, to open our resources to those in need, we pray:* ◆ *For generosity in our friendships and families, to give others the benefit of the doubt, we pray:* ◆ *For hearts that rejoice when more are added to the flock of the faithful, without jealousy or selfish desires, we pray:* ◆

Our Father . . .

Generous God,
you surprise us with your ways of
    forgiveness and grace.
Open our hearts to those we think
    are less worthy
to be at the heavenly table.
Redefine our ideals of justice
    and mercy
and transform our world into
    your kingdom.
We ask this through Christ our Lord.
Amen.

✦ *The precepts of the Lord give joy to the heart.*

✛ *For ever I will sing the goodness of the Lord.*

PSALM 100   page 414

READING   Matthew 22:1b–9

[Jesus said:] "The Kingdom of heaven may be likened to a king who gave a wedding feast for his son. He dispatched his servants to summon the invited guests to the feast, but they refused to come. A second time he sent other servants, saying, 'Tell those invited: "Behold, I have prepared my banquet, my calves and fattened cattle are killed, and everything is ready; come to the feast." ' Some ignored the invitation and went away, one to his farm, another to his business. The rest laid hold of his servants, mistreated them, and killed them. The king was enraged and sent his troops, destroyed those murderers, and burned their city. Then the king said to his servants, 'The feast is ready, but those who were invited were not worthy to come. Go out, therefore, into the main roads and invite to the feast whomever you find.' "

REFLECTION

It seems odd that these guests would refuse to come to a feast, or would ignore an invitation. And yet, for many and diverse reasons we do the same. Not only do we turn down earthly banquets because of our personal grudges and divisions, but we may ignore God's invitation as well. We may think other things are more important, or we may not wish to associate with those we con-sider less desirable. We may decide for ourselves that we cannot possibly be worthy. We block God's grace at every turn.

PRAYERS   others may be added

Rejoicing at the invitation to the heavenly banquet, we pray:

◆ Open our hearts, Lord.

For Christians to be open to groups and gatherings where they might be surprised to find God calling them, we pray: ◆
For increased attention given to common ground and participation in international dialogue, we pray: ◆ *For openness at elite clubs to people of all backgrounds and circumstances, we pray:* ◆ *For all families, that bitterness and anger between members may be healed, we pray:* ◆ *For all those who have died, we pray:* ◆

Our Father . . .

Heavenly King,
you have promised a banquet for all
     who follow you
and have called us from every walk
     of life.
Open our hearts during this life,
that we may be ready and worthy
to share in that meal with our
     brothers and sisters in faith.
Grant this through Christ our Lord.
Amen.

✛ *For ever I will sing the goodness of the Lord.*

✦ *The Lord made us; we belong to him.*

PSALM 111   *page 417*

READING   *Ruth 1:3–6, 14b–16*

Elimelech, the husband of Naomi, died, and she was left with her two sons, who married Moabite women, one named Orpah, the other Ruth. When they had lived there about ten years, both Mahlon and Chilion died also, and the woman was left with neither her two sons nor her husband. She then made ready to go back from the plateau of Moab because word reached her there that the LORD had visited his people and given them food.

Orpah kissed her mother-in-law good-bye, but Ruth stayed with her. Naomi said, "See now! Your sister-in-law has gone back to her people and her god. Go back after your sister-in-law!" But Ruth said, "Do not ask me to abandon or forsake you! For wherever you go, I will go, wherever you lodge I will lodge, your people shall be my people, and your God my God."

REFLECTION

Loyalty that transcends family and culture is rare. Ruth demonstrates to Naomi a love, friendship, and kinship of great depth. Our primary loyalty must be to God. The people God has entrusted to us deserve our unending faithfulness. These may be family and friends, but above all, they should be our brothers and sisters in Christ.

PRAYERS   *others may be added*

With love for those God has given to us, we pray:

◆ We are your faithful people, O God.

For our brothers and sisters in Christ, who share our love for God and our desire for the coming of his kingdom, we pray: ◆ *For our spouses and most trusted friends, who walk with and support us in faith, we pray,* ◆ *For our children, to whom we give both stability and freedom, we pray:* ◆ *For our neighbors, whom we serve with Christ's love, we pray:* ◆ *For all who have died, those who wait to join them in heaven, and those who now go to be with their beloved, we pray:* ◆

Our Father . . .

God of faithfulness,
you modeled loyalty through your
    covenant with Israel,
and you sent your Son
to offer your unending love and life to
    all people.
May we be faithful servants and
    loyal friends.
We ask this through Christ our Lord.
Amen.

✦ *The Lord made us; we belong to him.*

Optional memorial of St. John Eudes, priest

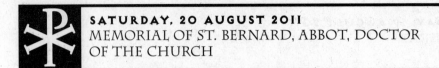
✦ *The Lord is my shepherd, there is nothing I shall want.*

PSALM 40 *page 407*

READING *Sirach 15:1–6*

He who fears the LORD will do this; / he who is practiced in the law will come to wisdom. / Motherlike she will meet him, / like a young bride she will embrace him, / Nourish him with the bread of understanding, / and give him the water of learning to drink. / He will lean upon her and not fall, / he will trust in her and not be put to shame. / She will exalt him above his fellows; / and in the midst of the assembly she will open his mouth / and fill him with the spirit of wisdom and understanding, / and clothe him with the robe of glory. / Joy and gladness he will find, / an everlasting name he will inherit.

REFLECTION

We can and should learn from many sources—education, our parents, reading, and experience. But the deepest wisdom we can ever know comes from God. Through prayer and spiritual guidance we gain inner clarity and understanding. These gifts surpass all our other knowledge. St. Bernard of Clairvaux and the monks who followed him were inspiring in their devotion to scripture, the Lord, and the heart of Christian faith in the trials of the Middle Ages. Wisdom can guide us, too, in trying times.

PRAYERS *others may be added*

Humbled by your wisdom, O God, we pray:

◆ Lord, hear our prayer.

For the Pope and Bishops of the Church, that wisdom nourishes them and quenches their thirst, especially in difficult times, we pray: ◆ *For leaders of nations, that wisdom offers them strength and guidance, to be faithful to their values despite outside pressures, we pray:* ◆ *For institutions of learning, that wisdom pervades their work, making them ethical and honest leaders at the service of society, we pray:* ◆ *For all of us who fear the Lord, that we call upon wisdom to lead us to eternal joy, we pray:* ◆

Our Father . . .

God of all power and might,
may wisdom come to us throughout
   our lives,
leading us ever closer to life in you.
May wisdom uphold us
when we are assaulted by lies, deceit,
   and the power of evil.
May St. Bernard of Clairvaux be a
   reminder to us
to be true to our faith in the face of
   cultural chaos.
We ask this through Christ our Lord.
Amen.

✦ *The Lord is my shepherd, there is nothing I shall want.*

✦ *The Lord made us; we belong to him.*

PSALM 16   *page 400*

READING   *Matthew 16:15–25*

[Jesus said to his disciples:] "But who do you say that I am?" Simon Peter said in reply, "You are the Christ, the Son of the living God." Jesus said to him in reply, "Blessed are you, Simon son of Jonah. For flesh and blood has not revealed this to you, but my heavenly Father. And so I say to you, you are Peter, and upon this rock I will build my church, and the gates of the netherworld shall not prevail against it.

REFLECTION   *St. Augustine*

Jesus chose his disciples before his passion and called them apostles; and among these almost everywhere Peter alone deserved to represent the entire Church. And because of that role which he alone had, he merited to hear the words: To you I shall give the keys of the kingdom of heaven. *For it was not one man who received the keys, but the entire Church considered as one. Now insofar as he represented the unity and universality of the Church, Peter's preeminence is clear from the words:* To you I give, *for what was given was given to all. For the fact that it was the Church that received the keys of the kingdom of God is clear from what the Lord says elsewhere to all the apostles:* Receive the Holy Spirit, *adding immediately,* whose sins you forgive, they are forgiven, and whose sins you retain, they are retained.

PRAYERS   *others may be added*

With respect and honor for our Church leadership, we pray:

✦ Strengthen the rock of your Church.

For the Pope, that he is attentive to his need for God and remains active in prayer, we pray: ✦ *For the Bishops, that they continue by the grace of God to lead in Christ's name, we pray:* ✦ *For repentance by and forgiveness for Church leaders, world leaders, and all who have fallen into sin, we pray:* ✦ *For all Christians, that we model ourselves after Peter, knowing and loving Christ, and remain in prayerful relationship with God, we pray:* ✦

Our Father . . .

Lord Jesus Christ,
inspire us to be firm in faith and
    humble in service.
May we be active members of the
    Body of Christ,
in our prayer, our learning, and our
    service to the Church,
each in our unique baptismal calling.
May our faith and that of our leaders
    come together
to strengthen and support all things
    done in your name.
You live and reign with God
    the Father
in the unity of the Holy Spirit,
one God, forever and ever.
Amen.

✦ *The Lord made us; we belong to him.*

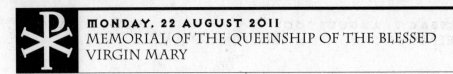

✦ *Blessed is the Virgin Mary, who kept the word of God and pondered it in her heart.*

CANTICLE   page 422

READING   Luke 2:15b–19

The shepherds said to one another, "Let us go, then, to Bethlehem to see this thing that has taken place, which the Lord has made known to us." So they went in haste and found Mary and Joseph and the infant lying in the manger. When they saw this, they made known the message that had been told them about this child. All who heard it were amazed by what had been told them by the shepherds. And Mary kept all these things, reflecting on them in her heart.

REFLECTION

Here Mary reflects her extraordinary role in the plan of salvation. She bore the Son of God, and throughout her life was witness to his saving life, death, and Resurrection. We can be like her, holding the mysteries of God's work in our hearts and reflecting on them. Today lift up your questions for God, hold concerns and confusion out to him, and ask him to reveal his peace to you. This type of prayer will lead us to gratitude, joy, and loving service.

PRAYERS   *others may be added*

With Mary, most blessed, we pray:

◆ Lord, hear our prayer.

That Christians may be guided by our queen and mother, Mary, who came from humble beginnings and great faith, we pray: ◆ *That Mary may be mother and queen to our troubled world, leading us to salvation, we pray:* ◆ *That all women and men who turn to Mary in prayer may gain insight into the presence of God in the world and his plan for the kingdom, we pray:* ◆ *That Mary may reside in our hearts, making us grateful and wise, we pray:* ◆

Our Father . . .

Mary, our Mother and Queen
   of Heaven,
we ask you to plead for us to
   the Father.
We pray with you, in the silence of
   our hearts,
for deep faith in the work of God.
Be with us as we struggle
to understand our world and our place
   in it.
We ask this through Christ our Lord.
Amen.

✦ *Blessed is the Virgin Mary, who kept the word of God and pondered it in her heart.*

✦ *I chose you from the world, to go and bear fruit that will last.*

PSALM 139   page 420

READING   Matthew 23:23–26

Jesus said: "Woe to you, scribes and Pharisees, you hypocrites. You pay tithes of mint and dill and cummin, and have neglected the weightier things of the law: judgment and mercy and fidelity. But these you should have done, without neglecting the others. Blind guides, who strain out the gnat and swallow the camel!

"Woe to you, scribes and Pharisees, you hypocrites. You cleanse the outside of cup and dish, but inside they are full of plunder and self-indulgence. Blind Pharisee, cleanse first the inside of the cup, so that the outside also may be clean."

REFLECTION

When we share the Gospel with others, we are also sharing how we ourselves live out the Good News. Take time to consider what your life tells others about God. How do you live? What words and attitudes come from your mouth? What actions do you take on your own behalf and on behalf of others? How do you love your brothers and sisters? If we claim to be faithful people, our lives should show it. This is often how people judge a religion: by those who profess and practice it.

PRAYERS   *others may be added*

Desiring to be pure for God's work in us, we pray:

◆ Make us worthy to serve you, O God.

That all Christians who bring the face of Christ to others may take time to renew their own hearts, we pray: ◆ *That Christians as an entire world religion may reflect God's kingdom of peace and justice to other world religions, we pray:* ◆ *That those with false faith and unclean hearts may repent and begin again, we pray:* ◆ *That we may hold one another accountable to a standard for Christ, we pray:* ◆

Our Father . . .

God of justice and mercy,
call us to confront the reality of our
    faith, inside and out.
Give us courage to cleanse
    from within.
Remind us of our responsibility
to bring the Gospel to others,
    undefiled.
Send us forth—humble, forgiven, and
    rooted in you.
We ask this through Christ our Lord.
Amen.

✦ *I chose you from the world, to go and bear fruit that will last.*

✦ *Commit your life to the Lord, and he will help you.*

PSALM 40   *page 407*

READING   *John 1:45–49*

Philip found Nathanael and told him, "We have found the one about whom Moses wrote in the law, and also the prophets, Jesus son of Joseph, from Nazareth." But Nathanael said to him, "Can anything good come from Nazareth?" Philip said to him, "Come and see." Jesus saw Nathanael coming toward him and said of him, "Here is a true child of Israel. There is no duplicity in him." Nathanael said to him, "How do you know me?" Jesus answered and said to him, "Before Philip called you, I saw you under the fig tree." Nathanael answered him, "Rabbi, you are the Son of God; you are the King of Israel."

REFLECTION

The heritage of our faith is the obedience and service of the apostles. They are our predecessors, the foundation of our Church. We can be inspired today by the honesty ascribed to Nathanael, who was perhaps also known as Bartholomew. Longing to be like the apostles, how can we be more honest in our life? We may be called to be more vulnerable in relationships and open our hearts. We may be asked to admit our faults more publicly. We may be encouraged to risk embarrassment, rejection, or ridicule because of our faith.

PRAYERS   *others may be added*

With hearts open to your Word, we pray:

◆ Cleanse us, O God.

For the successors to the apostles, our Bishops, that honesty may be a mark of their character, we pray: ◆ *For remarkable honesty among civil leaders, even when it is not popular, we pray:* ◆ *For the courage to be honest in relationships, the humility to be honest at work, and the wisdom to be honest when truth needs to be heard, we pray:* ◆ *For radical honesty among us, as brothers and sisters in Christ, we pray:* ◆

Our Father . . .

All-knowing God,
you see into our hearts and minds,
and recognize integrity
by raising up leaders who cling to it.
May we embrace honesty
in our personal, public,and
    ecclesial lives,
unafraid of the consequences,
and knowing that we are secure in
    your love.
Grant this through Christ our Lord.
Amen.

✦ *Commit your life to the Lord, and he will help you.*

✛ *The word of God is living and effective, able to discern reflections and thoughts of the heart.*

PSALM 111   page 417

READING   Matthew 24:42–44

Jesus said to his disciples: "Stay awake! For you do not know on which day your Lord will come. Be sure of this: if the master of the house had known the hour of night when the thief was coming, he would have stayed awake and not let his house be broken into. So too, you also must be prepared, for at an hour you do not expect, the Son of Man will come."

REFLECTION

It is our love for others that moves us to warn people of potential dangers such as fire, oncoming traffic, or weather alerts. Jesus' love for us is the reason he instructs his disciples to be vigilant. He knows of our human tendency to "slack off." We can grow lazy and apathetic about our faith. The Son of God knows the urgent need for us to reject sin and follow him. With this story, Jesus hopes to light a fire under us, reminding us of the important and immediate choice between good and evil.

PRAYERS   *others may be added*

With gratitude, we pray:

◆ Awaken our hearts.

For pastors, teachers, and spiritual directors who challenge and remind Christians of their commitment to God and the joy it brings, we pray: ◆ *For activists and prophets who warn secular societies when they have strayed far from moral values, we pray:* ◆ *For all who have grown indifferent to their faith, we pray:* ◆ *For our community, that we may joyfully prepare for the eternal life that awaits us, we pray:* ◆

Our Father . . .

God of our ancestors in faith,
you call all nations and peoples to
    your house;
help us to prepare for the time of
    judgment.
May your Word and sacrament
    fortify us
as we remain awake and ready,
anticipating the glorious return of
    your Son,
Jesus Christ, our Lord,
who lives and reigns with you
in the unity of the Holy Spirit,
one God, forever and ever.
Amen.

✛ *The word of God is living and effective, able to discern reflections and thoughts of the heart.*

✦ *The precepts of the Lord give joy to the heart.*

PSALM 130   *page 418*

READING   *1 Thessalonians 4:1–8*

Brothers and sisters, we earnestly ask and exhort you in the Lord Jesus that, as you received from us how you should conduct yourselves to please God—and as you are conducting yourselves—you do so even more. For you know what instructions we gave you through the Lord Jesus.

This is the will of God, your holiness: that you refrain from immorality, . . . For God did not call us to impurity but to holiness. Therefore, whoever disregards this, disregards not a human being but God, who also gives his Holy Spirit to you.

REFLECTION

What does it mean to be "holy"? It is not a way we hold our hands in church, how many times we say a prayer, or how loudly we sing a hymn. No, we please God when we treat our brothers and sisters with honor, respect, and equality. We reflect God's holiness when we treat another human being as sacred. Our actions show most clearly our morality and our innermost connection to the Lord. Our relationship with God is intricately related to our relationships with others. We cannot attend only to holy words and pious actions; we must love as Jesus did.

PRAYERS   *others may be added*

Loving God and loving neighbor, we pray:

◆ Sanctify us, O Lord.

That Christians may treat every person as a precious gift of God, we pray: ◆ *That Christian marriages and households may be models of love, chastity, and morality, we pray:* ◆ *That those who have given in to temptation may seek reconciliation with God and those they have hurt, we pray:* ◆ *That our holiness may not be self-righteous but rather an example of right relationship, we pray:* ◆

Our Father . . .

Gracious God,
you desire for us a life of holiness and
    happiness in you.
You know the choices that will lead
    us to joy.
Grant us your Spirit to guide our
    actions, thoughts, and lifestyle.
Help us to love you and one another
    as we should.
We ask this through Christ our Lord.
Amen.

✦ *The precepts of the Lord give joy to the heart.*

✚ *Commit your life to the Lord, and he will help you.*

PSALM 40 — page 407

READING — *Sirach 26:1–4, 13–16*

Blessed the husband of a good wife, / twice-lengthened are his days; / A worthy wife brings joy to her husband, / peaceful and full is his life. / A good wife is a generous gift / bestowed upon him who fears the LORD; / Be he rich or poor, his heart is content, and a smile is ever on his face.

A gracious wife delights her husband, / her thoughtfulness puts flesh on his bones; / A gift from the LORD is her governed speech, / and her firm virtue is of surpassing worth. / Choicest of blessings is a modest wife, / priceless her chaste soul. / A holy and decent woman adds grace upon grace; / indeed, no price is worthy of her temperate soul. / Like the sun rising in the LORD's heavens, / the beauty of a virtuous wife is the radiance of her home.

REFLECTION

We have the potential to bring great happiness and peace to our spouse and friends, and vice versa. When one or both of us are stressed or struggling, it may be hard to see this expectation as anything but a burden. How can we do more for yet one more person? We are exhausted from work, children, and other commitments. We must know our own selves and what we need to be nurtured. If we are committed, we can then be a support to each other's journey.

PRAYERS — *others may be added*

Keeping our spouse or married couples we know in mind, we pray:

◆ Lord, hear our prayer.

That married couples may be reminded in humility to turn to Christ and to one another in difficult times, we pray: ◆ *That all will foster the potential to bring joy to another person when we ourselves are healthy and centered, we pray:* ◆ *That joy may abound and carry newly married couples forward on their journey, we pray:* ◆ *That the wisdom married couples have gained by growing together can be shared with the world, we pray:* ◆ *That all who mourn a spouse who has died may be comforted, we pray:* ◆

Our Father . . .

Creator God,
be with all married and
    engaged couples,
and by your wisdom, love,
    and strength,
carry them through life's turmoils,
that they may come to the end of life,
having been blessed by one another.
We ask this through Christ our Lord.
Amen.

✚ *Commit your life to the Lord, and he will help you.*

SUNDAY, 28 AUGUST 2011
TWENTY-SECOND SUNDAY IN ORDINARY TIME

✦ *The Lord made us; we belong to him.*

PSALM 139   *page 420*

READING   *Matthew 16:21–25*

Jesus began to show his disciples that he must go to Jerusalem and suffer greatly from the elders, the chief priests, and the scribes, and be killed and on the third day be raised. Then Peter took Jesus aside and began to rebuke him, "God forbid, Lord! No such thing shall ever happen to you." He turned and said to Peter, "Get behind me, Satan! You are an obstacle to me. You are thinking not as God does, but as human beings do."

Then Jesus said to his disciples, "Whoever wishes to come after me must deny himself, take up his cross, and follow me. For whoever wishes to save his life will lose it, but whoever loses his life for my sake will find it."

REFLECTION

As Christians we are called to a life set apart. If we feel thoroughly comfortable in our secular culture, most likely we have succumbed to it. We are neither primarily citizens of our nation nor employees of our workplace. We should never feel fully "at home" with the values, trends, or mind-set of our culture. We are disciples of Christ. Our home, the place where we will feel at rest, is God's own home.

PRAYERS   *others may be added*

With the fire of the Holy Spirit burning in our hearts, we pray:

◆ Give us the mind of Christ.

For the Church, when she cries out in the name of justice and mercy, we pray: ◆
For government, that the mind and love of God permeates its offices, we pray: ◆
For those tempted to trade their souls for worldly desires, that they resist, we pray: ◆
For our community, that a spirit of service to others is our foundation, we pray: ◆

Our Father . . .

Holy, Holy, Holy Lord,
your awesome works attest to
    your greatness.
You continue to transform
and enliven the earth with your
    creative power.
May we place our trust in you,
hoping and dreaming of miracles.
Use us, your servants, to bring about
    your kingdom on earth.
You live and reign with God
    the Father
in the unity of the Holy Spirit,
one God, forever and ever.
Amen.

✦ *The Lord made us; we belong to him.*

✤ *Commit your life to the Lord, and he will help you.*

PSALM 40   *page 407*

READING   *Mark 6:17–20*

Herod was the one who had John the Baptist arrested and bound in prison on account of Herodias, the wife of his brother Philip, whom he had married. John had said to Herod, "It is not lawful for you to have your brother's wife." Herodias harbored a grudge against him and wanted to kill him but was unable to do so. Herod feared John, knowing him to be a righteous and holy man, and kept him in custody. When he heard him speak he was very much perplexed, yet he liked to listen to him.

REFLECTION

That which we fear, if we can, we keep "in custody." The truth is indeed powerful and life-changing. We may not be ready to face it. We push it aside; we compartmentalize it away from our focus. Consider what fears you have locked away—the gifts not shared, the responsibilities not fulfilled, the repentance or forgiveness being held back, or the truth that is difficult to confront. We are called, like John the Baptist, to proclaim truth, no matter what risks are involved.

PRAYERS   *others may be added*

Choosing to be like John the Baptist, we pray:

◆ Bring us face to face with truth.

For greater assent to Church teaching, through deep understanding of the word, tradition, and the love of God, we pray: ◆
For legislators, mayors, and all elected officials to make personal visits to crime scenes, drug houses, natural disaster areas, and isolated elderly, we pray: ◆
For service and mission trips to experience the life of the poor, and to help in any way that is possible, we pray: ◆
For the unspoken fears of our hearts, which have been held secret too long, we pray: ◆

Our Father . . .

Lord Jesus Christ,
the bold truth you proclaimed of the
    kingdom of God
inspired awe and fear in your
    listeners.
May we, like John the Baptist,
embrace your truth and continue to
    share it,
and reject the fearful vengeance
    of Herod.
You live and reign with God
    the Father
in the unity of the Holy Spirit,
one God, forever and ever.
Amen.

✤ *Commit your life to the Lord, and he will help you.*

✦ *In you, O Lord, I have found my peace.*

PSALM 130 — page 418

READING — *Luke 4:31–37*

Jesus went down to Capernaum, a town of Galilee. He taught them on the sabbath, and they were astonished at his teaching because he spoke with authority. In the synagogue there was a man with the spirit of an unclean demon, and he cried out in a loud voice, "What have you to do with us, Jesus of Nazareth? Have you come to destroy us? I know who you are—the Holy One of God!" Jesus rebuked him and said, "Be quiet! Come out of him!" Then the demon threw the man down in front of them and came out of him without doing him any harm. They were all amazed and said to one another, "What is there about his word? For with authority and power he commands the unclean spirits, and they come out." And news of him spread everywhere in the surrounding region.

REFLECTION

What are the things in your life or in the world that you feel powerless over? Racism, politics, war, terrorism, abuse? How would you react to seeing Jesus exert his power and authority over these evils, these "demons"? Imagine and ask for in prayer this very miracle: for Jesus to exorcise the demon of evil most feared in your heart.

PRAYERS — *others may be added*

In awe of the power of God's Word, we pray:

◆ Lord, hear our prayer.

That the Church may know and exercise her power to conquer evil in the world, we pray: ◆ That the demons of genocide, terror, and greed may be transformed by the power of God's Word, we pray: ◆ That those tormented by internal struggles may be set free by the touch of Jesus, we pray: ◆ That we may be harbingers of freedom, helping others and ourselves to break out of addiction, sin, and denial of the gifts Jesus offers, we pray: ◆

Our Father . . .

O Holy One of God,
your presence in our lives turns evil
    to good,
sin to grace, torment to joy.
As we experience you in our lives,
help us to share the gift of the Good
    News with others,
especially those most deeply in need
    of your freeing love.
You live and reign with God
    the Father
in the unity of the Holy Spirit,
one God, forever and ever.
Amen.

✦ *In you, O Lord, I have found my peace.*

✛　*I will sing the goodness of the Lord.*

PSALM 42　　　　　　*page 408*

READING　　　　　*Luke 4:38–39*

After Jesus left the synagogue, he entered the house of Simon. Simon's mother-in-law was afflicted with a severe fever, and they interceded with him about her. He stood over her, rebuked the fever, and it left her. She got up immediately and waited on them.

REFLECTION

Jesus did not turn away those in need of healing. We do not need to be afraid to turn to God and ask for relief from our suffering and that of others. Sometimes that is the first step in becoming whole again: allowing ourselves to admit the depth of our pain, and our need for God. What does it feel like to let down your guard and allow Jesus to see the pain you feel and the suffering you have endured?

PRAYERS　　　　*others may be added*

Aware of our dependence on God, we pray:

◆　God, heal us.

For those who offer the sacrament of Anointing of the Sick, that their touch, in God's name, may bring wholeness and healing, we pray: ◆ *For physicians, scientists, and philanthropists working creatively and untiringly to meet the needs of the world's poor for clean water, basic medicine, and nutritional building blocks, we pray:* ◆ *For those who are ill with stigmatized diseases such as AIDS, that medicinal and loving hands help bring them to greater health, we pray:* ◆ *For our own community's prayer hotlines, prayer chains, and prayer groups, that we see those in need around us and hold them in heartfelt prayer, we pray:* ◆

Our Father . . .

Merciful God,
you sent your own Son
to reach out to those in need
　　of healing.
The sick, the lepers, the outcast, and
　　the dying
were transformed by his touch.
May we ask for your healing embrace
　　when we are in need,
and be the first to offer the gentle,
　　transformative touch of your love.
Grant this through Christ our Lord.
Amen.

✛　*I will sing the goodness of the Lord.*

✠ For ever I will sing the goodness of the Lord.

PSALM 25 *page 403*

READING *Luke 5:4–10*

After [Jesus] had finished speaking, he said to Simon, "Put out into deep water and lower your nets for a catch." Simon said in reply, "Master, we have worked hard all night and have caught nothing, but at your command I will lower the nets." When they had done this, they caught a great number of fish and their nets were tearing. They signaled to their partners in the other boat to come to help them. They came and filled both boats so that the boats were in danger of sinking. When Simon Peter saw this, he fell at the knees of Jesus and said, "Depart from me, Lord, for I am a sinful man." For astonishment at the catch of fish they had made seized him and all those with him, and likewise James and John, the sons of Zebedee, who were partners of Simon. Jesus said to Simon, "Do not be afraid; from now on you will be catching men."

REFLECTION

What effort have you been making over and over with no result? Simon and the others had "worked hard all night and caught nothing." How will you respond to God when he asks you to keep trying? What do you learn from the realization that God can bring new results from your flawed, human attempts? You may work differently or have a changed attitude if you remember that God is active alongside you.

PRAYERS *others may be added*

Weary, we turn our prayers over to God:

◆ Fill us, O God.

For the Church, that her tireless efforts to spread the Gospel may continue faithfully and with renewed hope, we pray: ◆ *For flawed human governments, that good intentions dominate, and are transformed by God's grace into effective instruments of justice and peace, we pray:* ◆ *For all who are tired from efforts to be the face of love in a world of violence, that God gives them rest and new strength, we pray:* ◆ *For the cynics within us, that we are overcome by the hope only Jesus Christ can offer, we pray:* ◆

Our Father . . .

All-knowing God,
you have told us that your yoke is
    easy and your burden light.
Wake us from our weary, mindless,
    and repetitive efforts.
Blind us with the light of your grace,
which transforms our work into
    your work.
Give us the faith to try again in the
    face of defeat,
knowing that your power can bring
    miraculous results.
We ask this through Christ our Lord.
Amen.

✠ For ever I will sing the goodness of the Lord.

✦ *The heart of the just one is firm.*

PSALM 42 *page 408*

READING *Luke 5:33–39*

The scribes and Pharisees said to Jesus, "The disciples of John the Baptist fast often and offer prayers, and the disciples of the Pharisees do the same; but yours eat and drink." Jesus answered them, "Can you make the wedding guests fast while the bridegroom is with them? But the days will come, and when the bridegroom is taken away from them, then they will fast in those days." And he also told them a parable. "No one tears a piece from a new cloak to patch an old one. Otherwise, he will tear the new and the piece from it will not match the old cloak. Likewise, no one pours new wine into old wineskins. Otherwise, the new wine will burst the skins, and it will be spilled, and the skins will be ruined. Rather, new wine must be poured into fresh wineskins. And no one who has been drinking old wine desires new, for he says, 'The old is good.'"

REFLECTION

As Catholics, most of us treasure "the old": our rich, inspired tradition. But when does this reverence for ritual and consistency prevent us from tasting the new wine? Is there one area in your life where Jesus is calling you to embrace what is new and different? Think of ways in which others are inviting you to embrace your faith with new vigor—perhaps in the liturgy, a parish committee, speakers, or classes on faith.

PRAYERS *others may be added*

As we examine our faith, we pray:

◆ Renew us, Lord God.

That the wisdom of God, which is timeless, reaches every corner of the Church in old and new ways, we pray: ◆
That the Holy Spirit blows upon the nations of the earth with the winds of new life, we pray: ◆ *That those who are afraid of change are inspired by trust in God's providence, we pray:* ◆ *That our community values its wise ancestors as well as its young visionaries, we pray:* ◆

Our Father . . .

God of the beginning and the end,
you always have been, are, and always
will be with us.
Help us to embrace our tradition,
and the rich history of the people
of God,
and help us to see the Holy Spirit at
work today in the Church and in
the world.
Guide us to old and new ways to find
you in prayer, community,
and service.
We ask this through Christ our Lord.
Amen.

✦ *The heart of the just one is firm.*

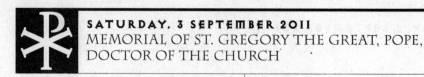

✦ *The Lord is my shepherd, there is
nothing I shall want.*

PSALM 40 page 407

READING Luke 22:24–30

An argument broke out among the
Apostles about which of them should
be regarded as the greatest. Jesus said
to them, "The kings of the Gentiles lord
it over them and those in authority over
them are addressed as 'Benefactors'; but
among you it shall not be so. Rather, let
the greatest among you be as the youngest, and the leader as the servant. For
who is greater: the one seated at table
or the one who serves? Is it not the one
seated at table? I am among you as the
one who serves. It is you who have stood
by me in my trials; and I confer a kingdom on you, just as my Father has con-
ferred one on me, that you may eat and
drink at my table in my Kingdom; and
you will sit on thrones judging the
twelve tribes of Israel."

REFLECTION

*Consider the opportunities we have to
serve others: holding open a door,
doing a favor, listening without inter-
rupting, anticipating needs, tending to
illness or injury, bringing a meal, reliev-
ing of duties. . . . These acts of kindness mean even more when they come
from one in a position of power. In what
way can we serve like Christ in our day
today? Can we surprise someone who
normally waits on us by reversing roles?
In doing so, let us show our love for
Christ and for our brothers and sisters.*

PRAYERS others may be added

*Following our servant leader,
we pray:*

◆ Make us graceful servants.

*For the Pope, Bishops, priests, and
deacons of the Church, that they may
follow in Christ's humble footsteps,
we pray:* ◆ *For coworkers, that small
efforts of consideration pervade the
workplace, we pray:* ◆ *For a recommitment
to loving acts for our family members
who we may take for granted, we pray:* ◆
*For a humble, service-oriented mind-set
in our parish ministries, we pray:* ◆

Our Father . . .

Lord Jesus,
you humbled yourself as a servant,
making yourself least among us.
May we, too, be servants of others,
models of thoughtfulness, gentleness,
    and kindness,
especially when we go against the
    standard norms of society.
You live and reign with God
    the Father
in the unity of the Holy Spirit,
one God, forever and ever.
Amen.

✦ *The Lord is my shepherd, there is
nothing I shall want.*

✚ *The heart of the just one is firm.*

PSALM 51 *page 409*

READING *Matthew 18:15–17*

Jesus said to his disciples: "If your brother sins against you, go and tell him his fault between you and him alone. If he listens to you, you have won over your brother. If he does not listen, take one or two others along with you, so that 'every fact may be established on the testimony of two or three witnesses.' If he refuses to listen to them, tell the church. If he refuses to listen even to the church, then treat him as you would a Gentile or a tax collector."

REFLECTION

Relationships matter. The sacrament of Reconciliation is one way the Church implores us to seek forgiveness from and offer forgiveness to one another. The way we live with those around us affects our relationship with God and our eternal happiness. We cannot make promises to God on Sunday and forget them on Monday at home or in the office. Our time on earth prepares us for life with Christ, and every day is a chance to practice our heavenly behavior.

PRAYERS *others may be added*

Connected to one another as part of the Body of Christ, we pray:

◆ Reconcile us to yourself and to one another.

For the Pope, the successor to St. Peter, that his deep relationship with Christ guides him as he leads the Church in showing justice and mercy to all, we pray: ◆ *For all priests, who in the sacrament of Reconciliation represent the whole Church and God's love, offering the liberating gift of absolution of sins, we pray:* ◆ *For all who make the sacrament of Reconciliation, that they make a genuine confession, make amends for their wrongdoing, and rejoice in being forgiven, we pray:* ◆ *For all who are chained to guilt, denial, and sin, that they may open their hearts to the freedom that comes with conversion, we pray:* ◆

Our Father . . .

Prince of Peace,
you came to conquer sin and death.
Help us to stop it and begin the
    process of reconciliation.
May our efforts inspire others to seek
    your forgiving love.
You live and reign with God
    the Father
in the unity of the Holy Spirit,
one God, forever and ever.
Amen.

✚ *The heart of the just one is firm.*

✦ *In you, O Lord, I have found my peace.*

PSALM 51   page 409

READING   Luke 6:6–11

On a certain sabbath Jesus went into the synagogue and taught, and there was a man there whose right hand was withered. The scribes and the Pharisees watched him closely to see if he would cure on the sabbath so that they might discover a reason to accuse him. But he realized their intentions and said to the man with the withered hand, "Come up and stand before us." Then Jesus said to them, "I ask you, is it lawful to do good on the sabbath rather than to do evil, to save life rather than to destroy it?" Looking around at them all, he then said to him, "Stretch out your hand." He did so and his hand was restored. But they became enraged and discussed what they might do to Jesus.

REFLECTION

How wrong it is to target and assassinate a person's reputation behind his or her back. We think of times when we have labeled an individual or group as sinful or evil. Perhaps we even waited for them to fall into our "trap" by erring again or proving our description of them true. We beg God to lead us away from the temptation to tear down another for our own gain.

PRAYERS   *others may be added*

Ashamed of our own competitiveness, we pray:

◆ Have mercy, O God.

For Christians, that we turn away from the temptation of personal gain, we pray: ◆ For dialogue, that stereotypes and assumptions may be broken down, we pray: ◆ For those who have been unjustly accused, that the truth may come to light, we pray: ◆ For us when we hear petty gossip, that we end it with proclamations of love and forgiveness, we pray: ◆

Our Father . . .

Lord Jesus, innocent victim,
you knew all too well what it meant
    to be targeted, humiliated, torn
    down, and accused.
You stand with all innocent victims of
    slander, injustice, and hatred.
Help us to accept the invitation to
    stand with you in solidarity
with those who are persecuted
    unfairly.
Give us the courage to do what
    is right.
You live and reign with God
    the Father
in the unity of the Holy Spirit,
one God, forever and ever.
Amen.

✦ *In you, O Lord, I have found my peace.*

✤ *Go out to all the world and tell the Good News.*

PSALM 33 — page 404

READING — Luke 6:12–19

Jesus departed to the mountain to pray, and he spent the night in prayer to God. When day came, he called his disciples to himself, and from them he chose Twelve, whom he also named Apostles: Simon, whom he named Peter, and his brother Andrew, James, John, Philip, Bartholomew, Matthew, Thomas, James the son of Alphaeus, Simon who was called a Zealot, and Judas the son of James, and Judas Iscariot, who became a traitor.

And he came down with them and stood on a stretch of level ground. A great crowd of his disciples and a large number of the people from all Judea and Jerusalem and the coastal region of Tyre and Sidon came to hear him and to be healed of their diseases; and even those who were tormented by unclean spirits were cured. Everyone in the crowd sought to touch him because power came forth from him and healed them all.

REFLECTION

How humbling it must have been to be called by name by a man who attracted crowds and healed those who were sick. Jesus, too, calls us by name. Hear him say your name today in prayer. Stand in awe of this leader, healer, miracle worker, and indeed, Savior of us all. Give thanks for his love and mercy.

PRAYERS — *others may be added*

Grateful that we are called by name, we pray:

◆ We praise you, Lord God.

For those called to be priests and to religious life, that they remain strong in their vocation, we pray: ◆ *For young leaders, that they answer the call to serve humankind, we pray:* ◆ *For those afflicted with cancer, heart problems, diabetes, and other destructive diseases, that they are touched by the healing Jesus, we pray:* ◆ *For us who are called in Baptism, that we remain humbled by the honor of being children of God, we pray:* ◆

Our Father . . .

Lord Jesus, our teacher,
you call us by name
just as you called your first disciples.
It is an awesome responsibility to be
   your brother or sister.
When we stray, call us by name again.
When we stand with you,
give us the courage to walk in
   your footsteps.
When we doubt, offer us your embrace.
You live and reign with God
   the Father
in the unity of the Holy Spirit,
one God, forever and ever.
Amen.

✤ *Go out to all the world, and tell the Good News.*

✦ *The Lord made us; we belong to him.*

PSALM 139   *page 420*

READING   *Luke 6:20–23*

Raising his eyes toward his disciples Jesus said: / "Blessed are you who are poor, / for the Kingdom of God is yours. / Blessed are you who are now hungry, / for you will be satisfied. / Blessed are you who are now weeping, / for you will laugh. / Blessed are you when people hate you, / and when they exclude and insult you, / and denounce your name as evil / on account of the Son of Man. /

"Rejoice and leap for joy on that day! Behold, your reward will be great in heaven."

REFLECTION

Jesus addresses his disciples directly with this challenging sermon. We cannot ignore it. Are we rich, satisfied, or held in high esteem? This could potentially cause us to look down upon others. How can we learn from those in our world who are poor, hungry, and hated on account of their faith? Consider missionaries, Catholic Worker communities, and peace and justice activists who risk their reputations and personal wealth. Read something they have written, visit their offices or homes, walk in their shoes for a day, and ask yourself: what is Jesus asking of you?

PRAYERS   *others may be added*

Longing for life with God, we pray:

◆ Lead me, Lord.

For Christians who have success, that they may learn from others to depend solely on God, we pray: ◆ *For power brokers and influential people, that they stop to hear the stories of those who are often forgotten, we pray:* ◆ *For those eager for entertainment, that they instead seek out those in need of true companionship, we pray:* ◆ *For a life in this world based on the values of the life beyond, we pray:* ◆

Our Father . . .

Lord Jesus, our brother,
you warned us of living too much in this world
without regard for the next.
Help us to prioritize our lives
so as to place our hopes and dreams in you.
Lead us to a life full of lasting meaning.
You live and reign with God the Father
in the unity of the Holy Spirit,
one God, forever and ever.
Amen.

✦ *The Lord made us; we belong to him.*

✛ *Blessed is the Virgin Mary who kept the word of God and pondered it in her heart.*

CANTICLE
page 422

READING
Matthew 1:18–21

Now this is how the birth of Jesus Christ came about. When his mother Mary was betrothed to Joseph, but before they lived together, she was found with child through the Holy Spirit. Joseph her husband, since he was a righteous man, yet unwilling to expose her to shame, decided to divorce her quietly. Such was his intention when, behold, the angel of the Lord appeared to him in a dream and said, "Joseph, son of David, do not be afraid to take Mary your wife into your home. For it is through the Holy Spirit that this child has been conceived in her. She will bear a son and you are to name him Jesus, because he will save his people from their sins."

REFLECTION

Mary was blessed to have the Holy Spirit uniquely at work through her. We, too, are blessed when the Spirit works in and through us. Call to mind a time when God offered you unique insight, creativity, or wisdom. Remember how God's message came to you. Was it subtle, attention-getting, gradual, or sudden? How did you respond? Be attentive to how the Spirit may be calling upon you now for a special gift only you can bring into the world.

PRAYERS
others may be added

Aware of God's blessings, we pray:

◆ Holy Spirit, fill us.

For Christians following Mary's example of faithfulness, that the Holy Spirit may guide them to do good in the world, we pray: ◆ For contemplative leaders, to whom the Spirit gives inspired ideas about the common good, we pray: ◆ For young and old who hear the voice of God in the hearts and respond, we pray: ◆ For each of us, pregnant with possibility in our life in Christ, we pray: ◆

Our Father . . .

Miraculous God,
you filled Mary with the life that
    would save the world.
May her faith and trust in you
inspire us as we allow your Spirit to
    lead us.
May we bring your love, mercy,
and justice into the world
and in our daily lives.
We ask this through our Lord Jesus
    Christ, your Son,
who lives and reigns with you
in the unity of the Holy Spirit,
one God, forever and ever.
Amen.

✛ *Blessed is the Virgin Mary who kept the word of God and pondered it in her heart.*

285

✦ *Commit your life to the Lord.*

PSALM 40 *page 407*

READING *Luke 6:39–42*

Jesus told his disciples a parable: "Can a blind person guide a blind person? Will not both fall into a pit? No disciple is superior to the teacher; but when fully trained, every disciple will be like his teacher. Why do you notice the splinter in your brother's eye, but do not perceive the wooden beam in your own? How can you say to your brother, 'Brother, let me remove that splinter in your eye,' when you do not even notice the wooden beam in your own eye? You hypocrite! Remove the wooden beam from your eye first; then you will see clearly to remove the splinter in your brother's eye."

REFLECTION

We have a responsibility to share Christ with others in our words and actions. We also must trust that God is at work in others' lives in ways we can neither see nor understand. This is especially important when we feel inclined to worry or try to control others. We rejoice, knowing that God reaches out to our family, friends, and strangers alongside our efforts. St. Peter Claver, in his work with African slaves in Latin America, could not have known his place in history, or how the cruelty he witnessed would ever end. Yet his faithful work in the name of Christ surely helped many and stands today as a testament to faith in the face of suffering.

PRAYERS *others may be added*

Grateful to God, we pray:

◆ We praise you, God of wonder.

For the presence of God at work in every heart, we pray: ◆ *For the power of God's love and mercy to inspire conversion, we pray:* ◆ *For the slowness and adequacy of God's time to counter life's rush, we pray:* ◆ *For the honor to cooperate with God's grace in the plan of salvation, we pray:* ◆ *For the unknown work of God in the lives of those who have died, we pray:* ◆

Our Father . . .

God of might,
you are a mystery of love and
    compassion.
We praise you for giving us a place in
    your plan of salvation.
May our service as disciples give
    you glory.
We ask this through our Lord Jesus
    Christ, your Son,
who lives and reigns with you
in the unity of the Holy Spirit,
one God, forever and ever.
Amen.

✦ *Commit your life to the Lord.*

✦ *The heart of the just one is firm, trusting in the Lord.*

PSALM 130   *page 418*

READING   *Luke 6:43–45*

Jesus said to his disciples: "A good tree does not bear rotten fruit, nor does a rotten tree bear good fruit. For every tree is known by its own fruit. For people do not pick figs from thornbushes, nor do they gather grapes from brambles. A good person out of the store of goodness in his heart produces good, but an evil person out of a store of evil produces evil; for from the fullness of the heart the mouth speaks."

REFLECTION

Take inventory of the ways your life bears fruit. What relationships have you tended this week? What support have you given? Who has been grateful for your small acts of kindness? When have you been faithful to keeping prayer time sacred? These actions strengthen the foundation of your life and your relationship with the Lord, so that you can stand firm against the storms of change. When we are feeling battered, we need to look to the roots of our own tree and provide nourishment.

PRAYERS   *others may be added*

Recognizing our need for you, O Lord, we pray:

◆ We give you thanks.

For the ministers and ministries of the Church that offer many ways to grow in relationship with God, we pray: ◆
For non-governmental organizations and international charities that resolutely protect those in need amid political and economical upheaval, we pray: ◆ *For opportunities given to us to serve those in need and respond to suffering, we pray:* ◆ *For friendships and small communities that support each of us in our Christian journey, we pray:* ◆

Our Father . . .

O God, our rock,
you offer us a foundation for
    eternal life.
When we take time for prayer,
    worship, and relationship with you,
we feel the strength you give us in our
    daily life.
When we are adrift,
we feel the loss that comes in being
    disconnected from you,
the source of all being.
Gather us in and re-root us in
    your love.
We ask this through Christ our Lord.
Amen.

✦ *The heart of the just one is firm, trusting in the Lord.*

✦ *The Lord hears the cry of the poor.*

PSALM 51 *page 409*

READING *Matthew 18:21–27*

Peter approached Jesus and asked him, "Lord, if my brother sins against me, how often must I forgive? As many as seven times?" Jesus answered, "I say to you, not seven times but seventy-seven times. That is why the kingdom of heaven may be likened to a king who decided to settle accounts with his servants. When he began the accounting, a debtor was brought before him who owed him a huge amount. Since he had no way of paying it back, his master ordered him to be sold, along with his wife, his children, and all his property, in payment of the debt. At that, the servant fell down, did him homage, and said, 'Be patient with me, and I will pay you back in full.' Moved with compassion the master of that servant let him go and forgave him the loan."

REFLECTION

Peter's question is the question of a person who has been hurt, repeatedly, by another. Jesus' answer challenges our sense of revenge or justice. Is there someone you have "given up on" or refused to give yet another chance? Perhaps Jesus' unending, forgiving love, when active in our hearts, will eventually break through to all sinners and convince them to change their ways.

PRAYERS *others may be added*

Aware of our sinfulness and our grudges, we pray:

◆ Show us your mercy, O God.

That the people of God may always forgive and welcome those who have lost hope, we pray: ◆ *That peace-making efforts which may seem pointless or off-track may be renewed with the Lord's guidance, we pray:* ◆ *That young people who have been forsaken by their families, schools, the criminal justice system, and law enforcement may find someone who believes in their potential, we pray:* ◆ *That we may always be grateful for God's unending forgiveness and express it in our loving kindness to others, we pray:* ◆

Our Father . . .

Merciful Father,
you have forgiven us every time we
    have strayed, fallen, or deserted you.
May we be mindful of our need
    for you,
and may you help us to forgive those
    who have sinned against us.
We ask this through our Lord Jesus
    Christ, your Son,
who lives and reigns with you
in the unity of the Holy Spirit,
one God, forever and ever.
Amen.

✦ *The Lord hears the cry of the poor.*

✠ *The heart of the just one is firm,*
trusting in the Lord.

PSALM 111   *page 417*

READING   *Luke 7:1–7*

When Jesus had finished all his words to the people, he entered Capernaum. A centurion there had a slave who was ill and about to die, and he was valuable to him. When he heard about Jesus, he sent elders of the Jews to him, asking him to come and save the life of his slave. They approached Jesus and strongly urged him to come, saying, "He deserves to have you do this for him, for he loves our nation and he built the synagogue for us." And Jesus went with them, but when he was only a short distance from the house, the centurion sent friends to tell him, "Lord, do not trouble yourself, for I am not worthy to have you enter under my roof. Therefore, I did not consider myself worthy to come to you; but say the word and let my servant be healed."

REFLECTION

The centurion's words here, "Lord, . . . I am not worthy to have you enter under my roof. . . . but say the word and let my servant be healed," are the source for one of our responses in the Communion Rite. Be the centurion in response to Jesus today as a statement of your faith. Like this faithful man, may we trust and hope in our Savior so much that we expect and rely on his healing power even when we cannot see or touch him.

PRAYERS   *others may be added*

Walking by faith alone, we pray:

◆ Help us trust in you.

For leaders of the Church, when they face doubts and fears, we pray: ◆
For our nation, when we are tempted to place patriotism, capitalism, and military might above God, we pray: ◆
For all who are suffering or struggling to survive and cannot see or feel God's presence, we pray: ◆ *For each of us in our moments of darkness, we pray:* ◆

Our Father . . .

Lord Jesus,
may our faith be so deep
that we trust wholly in you.
Make us humble and hopeful,
like the centurion,
that our light shines
for all the world to see
when darkness seems overwhelming.
You live and reign with God
   the Father
in the unity of the Holy Spirit,
one God, forever and ever.
Amen.

✠ *The heart of the just one is firm,*
trusting in the Lord.

Optional memorial of the Most Holy Name of the Blessed Virgin Mary

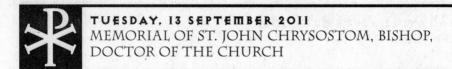
✦ *Commit your life to the Lord, and he will help you.*

PSALM 40 *page 407*

READING *Mark 4:1–2a*

Jesus began to teach by the sea. A very large crowd gathered around him so that he got into a boat on the sea and sat down. And the whole crowd was beside the sea on land. And he taught them at length in parables. . . .

REFLECTION

St. John Chrysostom, "the golden-mouthed preacher," inspired his hearers by his eloquence and passionate faith. Jesus himself taught his followers in creative, dynamic ways, especially by using parables. Naturally, we, too, seek out excellent preachers who bring the Gospel to life and offer inspiring applications for everyday Christians. We rightly recognize and commend teachers who seize our imaginations and bring us to new insights about our God.

PRAYERS *others may be added*

Yearning to hear the truth of Jesus, we pray:

◆ Teach us, Lord.

For preachers, retreat masters, spiritual directors, and teachers who bring alive the Gospel, we pray: ◆ For professors, scientists, musicians, and artists who explore the mysteries of life, we pray: ◆ For those who struggle with learning because of disabilities and illness, that creative therapies and methods reach them, we pray: ◆ For experiences of faith that bring each of us closer to God and to each other, we pray: ◆

Our Father . . .

Lord Jesus, our teacher,
you opened the mystery of God and
his kingdom
through stories and real-life
examples.
May your Gospel be brought to
every person
in creative, life-giving ways by
talented teachers and preachers.
You live and reign with God
the Father
in the unity of the Holy Spirit,
one God, forever and ever.
Amen.

✦ *Commit your life to the Lord, and he will help you.*

✦ *The Lord is my shepherd; there is nothing I shall want.*

PSALM 40   *page 407*

READING   *John 3:13–17*

Jesus said to Nicodemus: "No one has gone up to heaven except the one who has come down from heaven, the Son of Man. And just as Moses lifted up the serpent in the desert, so must the Son of Man be lifted up, so that everyone who believes in him may have eternal life."

For God so loved the world that he gave his only Son, so that everyone who believes in him might not perish but might have eternal life. For God did not send his Son into the world to condemn the world, but that the world might be saved through him.

REFLECTION

If you do not have a cross or crucifix in your home, bedroom, or other appropriate place, you might consider adding one. This sign powerfully summarizes our faith as the ultimate sign of God's love for all humanity. Since the sign of the cross is also used in popular culture, one might choose a unique cross so as to keep the sense of the image as sacred. It should call to mind the life, death, and Resurrection of our Savior, who calls us to follow him.

PRAYERS   *others may be added*

Meditating on the holy cross, we pray:

◆ Enliven our faith, Lord Jesus.

For churches and holy spaces, which reflect the heart of our Christian faith, we pray: ◆ *For governments with lingering ties to or influence from the Church, that, although separate, they may continue to be guided by the values of Christianity, we pray:* ◆ *For religious artists and their patrons, who expand and enrich understanding of the sign of the cross, we pray:* ◆ *For an exploration of faith through art and symbols in every Christian home, we pray:* ◆

Our Father . . .

Almighty God,
your love for us is conveyed in the
    mystery of the cross.
Call us to continually reflect on the
    life, death, and Resurrection of
    your Son
and the truth it reveals about
    ourselves and you, our Creator.
May the cross of Jesus be a holy,
    inspiring, and effective sign
    wherever it is found.
We ask this through our Lord Jesus
    Christ, your Son,
who lives and reigns with you
in the unity of the Holy Spirit,
one God, forever and ever.
Amen.

✦ *The Lord is my shepherd; there is nothing I shall want.*

✢ *Commit your life to the Lord.*

CANTICLE   page 422

READING   *John 19:25–27*

Standing by the cross of Jesus were his mother and his mother's sister, Mary the wife of Clopas, and Mary Magdalene. When Jesus saw his mother and the disciple there whom he loved he said to his mother, "Woman, behold, your son." Then he said to the disciple, "Behold, your mother." And from that hour the disciple took her into his home.

REFLECTION

In his mother's hour of greatest grief, Jesus entrusted her to the care of his beloved disciple. We are his disciples. All mothers are dependent on us for comfort, mercy, and protection. Today pray for your own mother, living or deceased. Notice mothers in public places, within your family, and in the news. What are their needs and how can you help meet them?

PRAYERS   *others may be added*

Calling to mind the sorrowful,
we pray:

◆ Be merciful, O God.

For mothers who raise their children with love for God, we pray: ◆ *For mothers who must watch their children suffer, go hungry, or be taken from them, we pray:* ◆ *For mothers whose children suffer because of bad choices, we pray:* ◆ *For mothers in our own community, and any sadness they hold in their hearts, unknown even to those around them, we pray:* ◆ *For mothers whose children have died, especially as infants or at a young age, we pray:* ◆

Our Father . . .

Compassionate God,
your daughter Mary held great sorrow
    in her heart
because of the suffering of her son.
May she accompany all who
    are tortured
by watching the pain of others.
May your infinite love
nurture and embrace those who face
    great evil and despair.
May we be your hands and feet as we
    behold all mothers.
We ask this through our Lord Jesus
    Christ, your Son,
who lives and reigns with you
in the unity of the Holy Spirit,
one God, forever and ever.
Amen.

✢ *Commit your life to the Lord.*

✛ *Commit your life to the Lord.*

PSALM 40 page 407

READING *2 Corinthians 4:7–11*

Brothers and sisters: We hold this treasure in earthen vessels, that the surpassing power may be of God and not from us. We are afflicted in every way, but not constrained; perplexed, but not driven to despair; persecuted, but not abandoned; struck down, but not destroyed; always carrying about in the body the dying of Jesus, so that the life of Jesus may also be manifested in our body. For we who live are constantly being given up to death for the sake of Jesus, so that the life of Jesus may be manifested in our mortal flesh.

REFLECTION

St. Cornelius and St. Cyprian faced Roman persecution and internal Christian schism in their struggle to remain faithful to Christ and preserve the Christian Church. The life of discipleship, the treasure of the Paschal Mystery, the core of our beliefs are always preserved and transmitted through human tools, means, and methods. The heritage of our faith comes to us through the efforts of countless faithful Christians over the ages. Our humanity is the only way through which we know God. It is imperfect, but incredibly resilient due to the grace of God.

PRAYERS *others may be added*

Acknowledging the fragile state of our faith, we pray:

◆ God, strengthen our faith.

For the Pope, clergy, theologians, and all who love the Catholic faith, that they find balance between wanting to know God and resting in his mystery, we pray: ◆
For all branches and services of government, that dedication to the law is balanced by love for people, we pray: ◆
For those who love their work and love their family, that each day and week brings appropriate prioritization of both, we pray: ◆ *For our emotional attachment to our faith, way of living, or communities, that we yet remain open to growth, we pray:* ◆

Our Father . . .

Merciful God,
you made us out of love.
You know our limitations
    and failures,
yet you continue to work in and
    through us.
Give us the faith, hope, and courage
to continue our journey
of discipleship as your servants.
We ask this through our Lord Jesus
    Christ, your Son,
who lives and reigns with you
in the unity of the Holy Spirit,
one God, forever and ever.
Amen.

✛ *Commit your life to the Lord.*

✛ *The Lord is my light and my salvation.*

PSALM 42 page 408

READING Luke 8:4–8a

When a large crowd gathered, with people from one town after another journeying to Jesus, he spoke in a parable. "A sower went out to sow his seed. And as he sowed, some seed fell on the path and was trampled, and the birds of the sky ate it up. Some seed fell on rocky ground, and when it grew, it withered for lack of moisture. Some seed fell among thorns, and the thorns grew with it and choked it. And some seed fell on good soil, and when it grew, it produced fruit a hundredfold."

REFLECTION

What conditions does the fruitful seed require? Consider how as parents, teachers, disciples, and friends we can nurture the soil for ourselves and others. Faithfulness to the sacraments of the Church, participation in the community, daily prayer, reading the Word of God, awareness of his presence in the world, and sharing of our time, talent, and treasure with others—in all these ways we till the soil of life in Christ.

PRAYERS others may be added

In order to support the seeds of faith around us, we pray:

◆ Lord, hear our prayer.

For liturgists and musicians, who form and enhance Christian worship, we pray: ◆ *For retreat houses and spiritual directors, who offer solitude and guidance to seeking Christians, we pray:* ◆ *For collaborating schools, parishes, and organizations that make service trips possible and greater understanding of global issues likely, we pray:* ◆ *For parents and teachers who answer questions about the Christian faith, we pray:* ◆

Our Father . . .

Creator God,
you sowed the seed and allowed us to develop it on our own.
We give thanks for the systems and institutions,
especially the Church,
that make it possible for us explore and shape our faith in community.
May we seek out chances to share and study faith with one another,
offering opportunities for faith development to young and old alike.
We ask this through Christ our Lord. Amen.

✛ *The Lord is my light and my salvation.*

Optional memorials of St. Robert Bellarmine, bishop, doctor of the Church; Blessed Virgin Mary

✚   *For ever I will sing the goodness of the Lord.*

PSALM 100   *page 414*

READING   *Matthew 20:8–15*

"When it was evening, the owner of the vineyard said to his foreman, 'Summon the laborers and give them their pay, beginning with the last and ending with the first.' When those who had started about five o'clock came, each received the usual daily wage. So when the first came, they thought that they would receive more, but each of them also got the usual wage. And on receiving it they grumbled against the landowner, saying, 'These last ones worked only one hour, and you have made them equal to us, who bore the day's burden and the heat.' He said to one of them in reply, 'My friend, I am not cheating you. Did you not agree with me for the usual daily wage? Take what is yours and go. Are you envious because I am generous?'"

REFLECTION

We may envy others' possessions, success, or looks. Do we also envy others who accept and enjoy God's saving love? If we have become self-righteous or self-critical to the point that we cannot understand God's love for all his creation, we need to examine our hearts. The cure for this envy is play, relaxation, and contentment in the gifts God has given us. We can be certain of his eternal grace. We can rejoice in it and share it with others.

PRAYERS   *others may be added*

Abandoning ourselves to God's care, we pray:

◆ Give us childlike delight in you.

That teachers of the Church may present the miraculous and stupendous love of God with great joy, we pray: ◆ *That business leaders who confuse generosity with competition may find the freedom to give and not count the cost, we pray:* ◆ *That those consumed with "keeping score" may rest in knowing God's providence is always enough, we pray:* ◆ *That Christian communities may inspire each other by their joy in being called disciples, we pray:* ◆

Our Father . . .

Beneficent God,
your abundant love overwhelms
    our sensibilities.
Show us how to rejoice in
    this mystery
rather than be caught up in concern
    over getting our share.
Give us generous and free hearts,
that we may love you and all
    your creation.
We ask this through our Lord Jesus
    Christ, your Son,
who lives and reigns with you
in the unity of the Holy Spirit,
one God, forever and ever.
Amen.

✚   *For ever I will sing the goodness of the Lord.*

✦ *Go out to all the world, and tell the Good News.*

PSALM 25   *page 403*

READING   *Luke 8:16–18*

Jesus said to the crowd: "No one who lights a lamp conceals it with a vessel or sets it under a bed; rather, he places it on a lampstand so that those who enter may see the light. For there is nothing hidden that will not become visible, and nothing secret that will not be known and come to light. Take care, then, how you hear. To anyone who has, more will be given, and from the one who has not, even what he seems to have will be taken away."

REFLECTION

The gifts given to us in Baptism and Confirmation necessarily lead us outward. If we only practice our faith in secret and private, we do not fulfill what is asked of us. Love should be given away and multiplied. The gifts of the Spirit pour out of us into the world. If this is difficult for us, we must ask why. What causes us to hide or deny the gifts God has given us? What do we fear will happen if we shine our light? The world may very well be waiting for our particular light to shine. When we do so there is a domino effect all around us.

PRAYERS   *others may be added*

Confident in our Baptism, we pray:

◆ Send us forth, O Lord.

That holy men and women everywhere shine the light of their faith out into the world, we pray: ◆ *That those whose practice of faith is forbidden are strengthened, we pray:* ◆ *That those who suffer from social phobias are emboldened by the Holy Spirit working through them to share faith, we pray:* ◆ *That our faith community looks for ways to carry our faith into the world, we pray:* ◆

Our Father . . .

Lord Jesus, Light of the World,
you are the source of our Baptism,
    our confidence,
and the Good News we carry.
Inspire us to overcome fear
    and hesitation
as we bring your love
and the promise of God's kingdom to
    those around us.
Make us your light in a sometimes
    dark world.
You live and reign with God
    the Father
in the unity of the Holy Spirit,
one God, forever and ever.
Amen.

✦ *Go out to all the world, and tell the Good News.*

✦ *Commit your life to the Lord.*

PSALM 40 page 407

READING Luke 9:23–26

Jesus said to all, "If anyone wishes to come after me, he must deny himself and take up his cross daily and follow me. For whoever wishes to save his life will lose it, but whoever loses his life for my sake will save it. What profit is there for one to gain the whole world yet lose or forfeit himself? Whoever is ashamed of me and of my words, the Son of Man will be ashamed of when he comes in his glory and in the glory of the Father and of the holy angels."

REFLECTION

We may be mostly unaware of the history of Christianity in Asia. It may surprise us to know that the Christian faith has survived there for hundreds of years, despite intense persecution and being the minority religion. What message might God have for the Church and the world in the perseverance of the Christian faith amid difficult opposition?

PRAYERS *others may be added*

Startled by the power and longevity of faith despite powerful obstacles, we pray:

◆ Holy Spirit, awaken us.

For the Church in the East, struggling against great odds, that we in the West may learn from its example, stories, and modern martyrs, we pray: ◆ *For a greater openness to religion in communist states, we pray:* ◆ *For increased exposure to and experience of cultures different from our own, we pray:* ◆ *For a prayerful kinship with our Christian brothers and sisters in all parts of the world, we pray:* ◆

Our Father . . .

Almighty God,
you gave great faith and strength to
     your disciples in Korea,
especially St. Andrew Kim Taegŏn
     and St. Paul Chong Hasang.
Your Spirit continues to lead the
     Christian Church in the East
     despite persecution.
May we be aware of ourselves as one
     global Christian family
and learn from our fellow disciples
     across the world.
We ask this through Christ our Lord.
Amen.

✦ *Commit your life to the Lord.*

✢ *The Lord is my shepherd, there is nothing I shall want.*

PSALM 40   *page 407*

READING   *Matthew 9:9–13*

As Jesus passed by, he saw a man named Matthew sitting at the customs post. He said to him, "Follow me." And he got up and followed him. While he was at table in his house, many tax collectors and sinners came and sat with Jesus and his disciples. The Pharisees saw this and said to his disciples, "Why does your teacher eat with tax collectors and sinners?" He heard this and said, "Those who are well do not need a physician, but the sick do. Go and learn the meaning of the words, *I desire mercy, not sacrifice.* I did not come to call the righteous but sinners."

REFLECTION

Jesus comes to us in the humdrum of our daily lives, wherever we work or spend our time, even "sitting at the customs post." Allow Jesus to spend time with you in your regular activities at work, at home, or at social outings. Be yourself with him; share with him your smallest tasks, your routine thoughts, and thereby, your true heart.

PRAYERS   *others may be added*

Welcoming Jesus into our day, we pray:

◆ Be with us, O Lord.

That all Christians, in every walk of life, at every age, in every place may pray: ◆
That all people, across nations, states, oceans, and deserts may learn to pray: ◆
That anyone who finds his or her life without meaning or purpose may pray: ◆
That each of us, when life seems overly complicated, may return to the simplest prayer: ◆

Our Father . . .

Lord Jesus,
you who became flesh and walked
    among us,
call us to be your brothers and sisters.
Remind us of this precious gift
and the great responsibility it brings.
May we turn to you in everything
    we do,
walking in the footsteps of St.
    Matthew, who followed you.
You live and reign with God the
    Father in the unity of the
    Holy Spirit,
one God, forever and ever.
Amen.

✢ *The Lord is my shepherd, there is nothing I shall want.*

✦ *Go out to all the world, and tell the Good News.*

PSALM 33 *page 404*

READING *Luke 9:7–9*

Herod the tetrarch heard about all that was happening and he was greatly perplexed because some were saying, "John has been raised from the dead"; others were saying, "Elijah has appeared"; still others, "One of the ancient prophets has arisen." But Herod said, "John I beheaded. Who then is this about whom I hear such things?" And he kept trying to see him.

REFLECTION

Today be reminded of the uniqueness and completeness of the revelation of God in Jesus Christ. His life and power forever changed the world and each of us. With all that competes for our attention, we strive to remain awed by and loyal to this perfect saving love.

PRAYERS *others may be added*

Giving glory to you, O God, we pray:

◆ Lord, hear our prayer.

For the Roman Catholic Church, may she continue to hold fast to the story of Jesus, lifting up the unique, saving truth within it, we pray: ◆ *For all the people of the world, may their lives give tribute to the majesty mystery of our triune God, we pray:* ◆ *For religious people who have become judgmental and hateful, may the love of Jesus be renewed within them, we pray:* ◆ *For our daily faith, may it retain a sense of awe and wonder when contemplating God's work, we pray:* ◆

Our Father . . .

Savior of us all,
you came that we might be reconciled
   to the Father in you.
Your life, death, and Resurrection
   changed the world forever.
May we return again and again to
   ponder the mystery of your love.
May your power and love shine
   through our adoring hearts.
You live and reign with God
   the Father
in the unity of the Holy Spirit,
one God, forever and ever.
Amen.

✦ *Go out to all the world, and tell the Good News.*

✦ *Commit your life to the Lord, and he will help you.*

PSALM 40   *page 407*

READING   *Luke 9:18–22*

Once when Jesus was praying in solitude, and the disciples were with him, he asked them, "Who do the crowds say that I am?" They said in reply, "John the Baptist; others, Elijah; still others, 'One of the ancient prophets has arisen.'" Then he said to them, "But who do you say that I am?" Peter said in reply, "The Christ of God." He rebuked them and directed them not to tell this to anyone. He said, "The Son of Man must suffer greatly and be rejected by the elders, the chief priests, and the scribes, and be killed and on the third day be raised."

REFLECTION

The world yearns for holy men and women like Padre Pio. We need to see that goodness and faithfulness to Christ is still possible. Whether we hope for someone to look up to, or have the chance to model virtue, use today's memorial to recognize and celebrate admirable ways of living and dying. We, too, can devote ourselves to Christ. We can intensely study his life, focus on living like him, and ask God to reveal the mystery of the cross to us. We, too, can look to those around us for extraordinary examples of living in Christ.

PRAYERS   *others may be added*

Longing for Christ, we pray:

◆ Lord, hear our prayer.

For the Pope, that he may continue to challenge young people to live in radical obedience to God and love for all people, we pray: ◆ *For the world, that contemporary men and women who live in devotion to the Lord may continue to be lifted up and recognized, so as to inspire us all to follow Christ, we pray:* ◆ *For all who desperately seek meaning and fulfillment, that they may revel in the rich depth of the mystery of faith, we pray:* ◆

Our Father . . .

Christ our Lord,
you suffered and died out of love
   for us.
Your servant, Padre Pio
devoted himself to you.
May we dedicate our lives to you,
even to the point of suffering or death.
May we take time to be moved,
   startled, excited, or amazed
by your great love and sacrifice
and the opportunity to cooperate
   with grace.
You live and reign with God
   the Father
in the unity of the Holy Spirit,
one God, forever and ever.
Amen.

✦ *Commit your life to the Lord, and he will help you.*

✠ *The heart of the just one is firm, trusting in the Lord.*

PSALM 16   *page 400*

READING   *Luke 9: 43b–45*

While they were all amazed at his every deed, Jesus said to his disciples, "Pay attention to what I am telling you. The Son of Man is to be handed over to men." But they did not understand this saying; its meaning was hidden from them so that they should not understand it, and they were afraid to ask him about this saying.

REFLECTION

As children, many of us were afraid to ask parents or teachers about things we did not understand. As adults, we may still harbor some fear regarding our ignorance, looking "stupid," or admitting a long-held mask of confidence. We cannot let this fear keep us from growth, from relationships, or from Jesus. If it is the sacrament of Reconciliation we fear after not having been reconciled for years, may we go today. If it is something we have never understood, let us seek out knowledge. If it is a person we need to forgive, let us seek that person out for dialogue, justice, and understanding.

PRAYERS   *others may be added*

Making today the day we take the first step away from fear, we come before God and pray:

◆ Give us courage.

For Christians who cling to childhood fears, that as adults they may seek truth and reject the prison of shame, we pray: ◆ *For nations whose pride and terrorization of others keeps them from honest dialogue, that they may strip away their own walls and weapons, we pray:* ◆ *For children paralyzed from learning or growth by fear of authority figures, that they find balance between respect for others and respect for self, we pray:* ◆ *For our community, that any barriers we have built may be torn down, we pray:* ◆

Our Father . . .

Lord Jesus,
you came to save us all,
by ending fear of death
and damnation by your eternal
    sacrifice.
May all in bondage be freed,
by trusting in you and your promise
    of salvation.
May all fear turn into liberation.
You live and reign with God
    the Father
in the unity of the Holy Spirit,
one God, forever and ever.
Amen.

✠ *The heart of the just one is firm, trusting in the Lord.*

✜ *The Lord made us; we belong to him.*

PSALM 51 *page 409*

READING *Matthew 21:28–31*

Jesus said to the chief priests and elders of the people: "What is your opinion? A man had two sons. He came to the first and said, 'Son, go out and work in the vineyard today.' He said in reply, 'I will not,' but afterwards changed his mind and went. The man came to the other son and gave the same order. He said in reply, 'Yes, sir,' but did not go. Which of the two did his father's will?" They answered, "The first." Jesus said to them, "Amen, I say to you, tax collectors and prostitutes are entering the kingdom of God before you."

REFLECTION

Most likely you think of heaven as a place of pleasure, happiness, and reunion with those we love. Would you still want to go if you knew you would be spending eternity with whomever you consider "undesirable"? Challenge yourself to consider who you assume is not going to heaven, and how your heart needs to change to spend eternal life with them. How will you live differently today with this understanding?

PRAYERS *others may be added*

Humbled by stubbornness and judgments, we pray:

◆ Open our hearts, Lord.

For unity among all Christians, we pray: ◆ *For a growing awareness of our interconnectedness to people of all parts of the world, we pray:* ◆ *For a new hospitality to those often treated as outcasts, we pray:* ◆ *For transformation of our hearts when we label or exclude others, we pray:* ◆ *For all saints and sinners who have died, that heaven's rewards may be even more enjoyable when shared together, we pray:* ◆

Our Father . . .

God of all,
you see all of your children as equals,
and offer mercy and love
to each person who seeks you.
May we see with your eyes
into the hearts of everyone around us,
dismissing judgments and stigmas.
We ask this through our Lord Jesus
    Christ, your Son,
who lives and reigns with you
in the unity of the Holy Spirit,
one God, forever and ever.
Amen.

✜ *The Lord made us; we belong to him.*

✦ *The Lord hears the cry of the poor.*

PSALM 111 *page 417*

READING *Luke 9:46–50*

An argument arose among the disciples about which of them was the greatest. Jesus realized the intention of their hearts and took a child and placed it by his side and said to them, "Whoever receives this child in my name receives me, and whoever receives me receives the one who sent me. For the one who is least among all of you is the one who is the greatest."

Then John said in reply, "Master, we saw someone casting out demons in your name and we tried to prevent him because he does not follow in our company." Jesus said to him, "Do not prevent him, for whoever is not against you is for you."

REFLECTION

Children bear the brunt of our society in many ways—from living through the everyday stresses of family life, unequal and unsatisfactory educational systems, to poverty, abuse, hunger, and wars around the world. If we find Jesus among the children, we will work to relieve their suffering and offer them hope. So many ways to do this exist locally and globally.

PRAYERS *others may be added*

Mindful of the littlest ones, we pray:

◆ Show us your face, Lord.

For the youngest members of the Church, that we welcome them in joy in Baptism and continue our support for them every year of their lives, we pray: ◆
For children of every nation, that we offer them opportunities to dialogue and learn together, so that they may achieve lasting peace, we pray: ◆ *For unborn children, that their development and birth is guided by the gentle hand of God, and they are then received into this world with love, we pray:* ◆ *For children who have died, that their short lives leave us a profound example, and that their rest in God brings them eternal joy, we pray:* ◆

Our Father . . .

Providential and protective God,
you designed our growth and
    development,
and the wonder of our minds
    and bodies.
Stay close to every child,
guarding each one from danger
    and evil.
Show us how to listen to and learn
    from their wisdom.
Make us more like them, pure in
    heart, and wise in soul.
Grant this through Christ our Lord.
Amen.

✦ *The Lord hears the cry of the poor.*

Optional memorial of St. Cosmas and St. Damian, martyrs

✦ *Commit your life to the Lord.*

PSALM 40   *page 407*

READING   *Matthew 25:31–46*

Jesus said to his disciples: "When the Son of Man comes in his glory, and all the angels with him, he will sit upon his glorious throne, and all the nations will be assembled before him. And he will separate them one from another, as a shepherd separates the sheep from the goats. He will place the sheep on his right and the goats on his left. Then the king will say to those on his right, 'Come, you who are blessed by my Father. Inherit the kingdom prepared for you from the foundation of the world. For I was hungry and you gave me food, I was thirsty and you gave me drink, a stranger and you welcomed me, naked and you clothed me, ill and you cared for me, in prison and you visited me.' Then the righteous will answer him and say, 'Lord, when did we see you hungry and feed you, or thirsty and give you drink? When did we see you a stranger and welcome you, or naked and clothe you? When did we see you ill or in prison, and visit you?' And the king will say to them in reply, 'Amen, I say to you, whatever you did for one of the least brothers of mine, you did for me.'"

REFLECTION

How do you feel when you are hungry, thirsty, unwelcome, unclothed, sick, or isolated? Does it dominate your thoughts, disrupt your composure, or distort your view of life? If you haven't felt the depth of these sufferings in a while, force yourself to face one of them today. Notice how your personality and very soul are deprived when your basic needs are not met. Those who truly are hungry, thirsty, unwelcome, and isolated have so much to overcome. Our help is needed to peel away the layers of difficulty and suffering to lead them to freedom in the Lord.

PRAYERS   *others may be added*

Moved with compassion, we pray:

◆ O God, hear us.

For the Church, we pray: ◆ *For the hungry, thirsty, unwelcome, unclothed, sick, and imprisoned, we pray:* ◆ *For awareness of our good fortune and voluntary sacrifices for those who have less, we pray:* ◆ *For all who see Christ in the face of the poor and respond, we pray:* ◆

Our Father . . .

God our father,
help us to grow in our understanding
    of suffering that we may give
    to others.
We ask this through Christ our Lord.
Amen.

✦ *Commit your life to the Lord.*

✝   *Commit your life to the Lord.*

PSALM 139   page 420

READING   *Luke 9:57–58*

As Jesus and his disciples were proceeding on their journey, someone said to him, "I will follow you wherever you go." Jesus answered him, "Foxes have dens and birds of the sky have nests, but the Son of Man has nowhere to rest his head."

REFLECTION

Those who have left behind family, friends, and old ways of life in order to follow Christ have much to teach us. Invite some of these "converts" to speak at church, at faith formation sessions, or to "one-on-one" outings. Inquire about their journey of faith. Have you, too, made this choice at some point in your life, in a big or small way?

PRAYERS   *others may be added*

Invested in our new life in Christ, we pray:

◆   Help us follow you.

For renewal movements and new members in the Church, that their questions and challenges help breathe new life into a lasting institution, we pray: ◆ *For new democracies, that leaders with integrity rise up and shape the future of their lands, we pray:* ◆ *For recovering addicts, that every day is a continued commitment to a life of sobriety, we pray:* ◆ *For those of us who have had to leave behind old habits, destructive friendships, and abusive family members, that our new start inspires change in others, we pray:* ◆ *For those who have left this life, that their new lives are in peace with God, we pray:* ◆

Our Father . . .

Sovereign God,
you invite us into your kingdom,
which is not of this world.
As we continue to say "yes" to you,
we sometimes have to let go of
    the old.
Give us courage and peace to not
    look back.
Remind us of the joy that begins now
and lasts forever in relationship
    with you.
We ask this through Christ our Lord.
Amen.

✝   *Commit your life to the Lord.*

Optional memorials of St. Wenceslaus, martyr; St. Lawrence Ruiz, martyr, and companions, martyrs

✦ *The Lord is my shepherd, there is nothing I shall want.*

PSALM 40 *page 407*

READING *John 1:47–51*

Jesus saw Nathanael coming toward him and said of him, "Here is a true child of Israel. There is no duplicity in him." Nathanael said to him, "How do you know me?" Jesus answered and said to him, "Before Philip called you, I saw you under the fig tree." Nathanael answered him, "Rabbi, you are the Son of God; you are the King of Israel." Jesus answered and said to him, "Do you believe because I told you that I saw you under the fig tree? You will see greater things than this." And he said to him, "Amen, amen, I say to you, you will see heaven opened and the angels of God ascending and descending on the Son of Man."

REFLECTION

Our cultural fascination with angels likely comes from a desire to know that God intervenes on earth. We long to see God's power at work, acting on behalf of his children. Since ancient times, people have shared in this hope. Scripture and tradition reassure us: we can rely upon God's protection and care. Whether angels are truly at our side caring for us, or whether we simply feel the love and guidance of God in an unknown way, we can count on not being alone.

PRAYERS *others may be added*

Needing the help of angels, we pray:

◆ Almighty God, hear us.

For all Christians, who long for heaven, that the angels may bring them to peace and eternal rest, we pray: ◆ *For the beauty of the earth and all that lives upon it, that the angels may protect it from evil, we pray:* ◆ *For desperate causes, that the messengers of God may hear the cries of those in pain, we pray:* ◆ *For each of us, when we call upon the Lord to show his power and might, we pray:* ◆

Our Father . . .

Eternal God,
you have power over all things
and archangels ready to do your will.
We pray that when the time and place
  is right,
you will bring about your kingdom,
with the glory of all that is good
  and holy,
and to the end of all that is evil.
We ask this through our Lord Jesus
  Christ, your Son,
who lives and reigns with you
in the unity of the Holy Spirit,
one God, forever and ever.
Amen.

✦ *The Lord is my shepherd, there is nothing I shall want.*

✤ *Commit your life to the Lord, and he will help you.*

PSALM 40 — page 407

READING — 2 Timothy 3:14–17

Beloved: Remain faithful to what you have learned and believed, because you know from whom you learned it, and that from infancy you have known the sacred Scriptures, which are capable of giving you wisdom for salvation through faith in Christ Jesus. All Scripture is inspired by God and is useful for teaching, for refutation, for correction, and for training in righteousness, so that one who belongs to God may be competent, equipped for every good work.

REFLECTION

St. Jerome, doctor of the Church, labored tirelessly to translate and explain the scriptures. We, too, should spend significant time reading, reflecting on, and praying with the Bible. Regular reading of the Word of God, especially with periodic discussion and the addition of scholarly commentary, can exponentially deepen our faith.

PRAYERS — *others may be added*

Hoping to grow in wisdom and faith, we pray:

◆ Word of God, teach us.

For Biblical scholars, archaeologists, anthropologists, and historians, whose ongoing work enriches our understanding of Jesus, God's Word, and the early Church, we pray: ◆ *For the early Bishops, theologians, and scholars whose devotion to exploration of the faith assisted in the creation of the Spirit-filled Church we know, we pray:* ◆ *For ongoing transliteration and transmission of the Bible to every language and culture in the world, we pray:* ◆ *For a renewed dedication to Bible study in our parish and our homes, we pray:* ◆

Our Father . . .

Word of God,
your story and mysteries are revealed
   in scripture and tradition.
May we recommit ourselves studying
   our faith
and learning of your ways.
You live and reign with God
   the Father
in the unity of the Holy Spirit,
one God, forever and ever.
Amen.

✤ *Commit your life to the Lord, and he will help you.*

✦ *The Lord is my shepherd, there is nothing I shall want.*

PSALM 40   *page 407*

READING   *Matthew 18:1–4*

The disciples approached Jesus and said, "Who is the greatest in the Kingdom of heaven?" He called a child over, placed it in their midst, and said, "Amen, I say to you, unless you turn and become like children, you will not enter the Kingdom of heaven. Whoever humbles himself like this child is the greatest in the Kingdom of heaven."

REFLECTION

This passage humbles our complicated, arrogant ways. Each small child is a model for us of how to renew our faith. Let us learn from their joy, simplicity, and love. Spend time this day observing and learning from children or just one little child. How do they show joy? How do they express sadness? What do they do when they're afraid? What do they know and share of love?

PRAYERS   *others may be added*

In search of the wisdom of children, we pray:

◆ God, show us your ways.

For Christian children, that they be brought fully into the life of the Church for the good of the whole community, we pray: ◆ *For all children, that their innocence may be protected and their hope lifted up, we pray:* ◆ *For those who are like children in their way of living, that their simple ways may be appreciated, we pray:* ◆ *For a strong religious education program for our children, in our schools, parish programs, and homes, we pray:* ◆ *For children who have died, we pray:* ◆

Our Father . . .

Lord Jesus,
you called the children to yourself.
Your disciple St. Thérèse
modeled the "little way" we can all
    follow to you.
Help us to simplify, enjoy, and trust
    this life we have been given.
Help us to protect all those children
    who show us your face.
You live and reign with God
    the Father
in the unity of the Holy Spirit,
one God, forever and ever.
Amen.

✦ *The Lord is my shepherd, there is nothing I shall want.*

✛ *For ever I will sing the goodness of the Lord.*

PSALM 111 *page 417*

READING *Matthew 21:33 – 35, 38–41*

Jesus said to the chief priests and elders of the people: "Hear another parable. There was a landowner who planted a vineyard, put a hedge around it, dug a wine press in it, and built a tower. Then he leased it to tenants and went on a journey. When vintage time drew near, he sent his servants to the tenants to obtain his produce. But the tenants seized the servants and one they beat, another they killed, and a third they stoned. Finally, he sent his son to them, thinking, 'They will respect my son.' . . . They seized him, threw him out of the vineyard, and killed him. What will the owner of the vineyard do to those tenants when he comes?" They answered him, "He will put those wretched men to a wretched death and lease his vineyard to other tenants who will give him the produce at the proper times."

REFLECTION

God challenges our expectations and assumptions. He chooses disciples from among the lowly; God prefers those who are forgotten; God welcomes the outcasts to his table. God's blessings flow; they are not tied to convention or external regulations. We can trust God and allow our presuppositions to be questioned and our biases to be overturned.

PRAYERS *others may be added*

Opening our eyes to seeing as God sees, we pray:

◆ Bring life out of death, O Lord.

That the Church may welcome and lift up all who have been "rejected" by society, we pray: ◆ *That downtrodden and forgotten peoples may be transformed into sources of knowledge, wisdom, and truth, we pray:* ◆ *That those excluded from clubs, groups, and friendships may rise up as loving servants of Christ, we pray:* ◆ *That parts of our community seeming to lack life may spring forth anew in faith, we pray:* ◆ *That those discarded in this life may dance and sing in the heavenly kingdom, we pray:* ◆

Our Father . . .

God of wisdom,
you see the strength and potential in
    every person and group.
What the world rejects, you can
    use, nurture,
and transform into goodness
    and light.
May we be blessed to be witness to
    and a part of that process.
We ask this through our Lord Jesus
    Christ, your Son,
who lives and reigns with you
in the unity of the Holy Spirit,
one God, forever and ever.
Amen.

✛ *For ever I will sing the goodness of the Lord.*

✚ *The Lord hears the cry of the poor.*

PSALM 130 — page 418

READING — Luke 10:30, 33–35

Jesus replied, "A man fell victim to robbers as he went down from Jerusalem to Jericho. They stripped and beat him and went off leaving him half-dead. But a Samaritan traveler who came upon him was moved with compassion at the sight. He approached the victim, poured oil and wine over his wounds and bandaged them. Then he lifted him up on his own animal, took him to an inn, and cared for him. The next day he took out two silver coins and gave them to the innkeeper with the instruction, 'Take care of him. If you spend more than what I have given you, I shall repay you on my way back.'"

REFLECTION

What does cleansing and binding wounds, carrying a wounded person and waiting on them, imply? The ability to look at someone else's pain and brokenness, to share in his or her disfigurement, to "get messy," to become weighted down by his or her sorrow, and to disrupt one's own life for the other's needs—these sacrifices may be hard to make. Try to be with one who is truly suffering, instead of walking away. Spend more time rather than less with a friend or stranger who makes you sad or uncomfortable. Rather than avoid what is difficult, may Jesus be with us as we face the heartbreak of life.

PRAYERS — others may be added

Without avoiding what is painful, we pray:

◆ Be with us, Lord.

For truth, healing, and change to come forth from the sin and scandals in the Church, we pray: ◆ *For increased awareness of how the lives of wealthy nations depend on the suffering of impoverished peoples, we pray:* ◆ *For exposure of policies and decisions that have treated human persons as waste, expendable, or worthless, we pray:* ◆ *For honesty about our own sin, ability to hurt, evil desires and participation in wrongdoing, we pray:* ◆ *For those who have died in a state of sin, that God's mercy be upon them, we pray:* ◆

Our Father . . .

Healing God,
our capacity for sin has been
    demonstrated
in the history of time and in this
    very moment,
yet you still love us.
Be with us as we face our own evils
and contribute to the brokenness in
    our world.
We beg for forgiveness,
and we ask that you show us a new
    way to live.
We ask this through Christ our Lord.
Amen.

✚ *The Lord hears the cry of the poor.*

✦ *Commit your life to the Lord, and he will help you.*

PSALM 40   page 407

READING   Galatians 6:14–18

Brothers and sisters: May I never boast except in the cross of our Lord Jesus Christ, through which the world has been crucified to me, and I to the world. For neither does circumcision mean anything, nor does uncircumcision, but only a new creation. Peace and mercy be to all who follow this rule and to the Israel of God.

From now on, let no one make troubles for me; for I bear the marks of Jesus on my body.

The grace of our Lord Jesus Christ be with your spirit, brothers and sisters. Amen.

REFLECTION

The idea that our salvation is tied up with the salvation of the world permeates Catholic theology. We do not believe in a personal Savior alone. God's plan of redemption is for all. We are forever linked to our brothers and sisters throughout the earth, and our practice should reflect this belief. St. Francis devoted himself to all people and all of creation, especially those who were suffering, poor, and forgotten.

PRAYERS   *others may be added*

With love and peace toward all, we pray:

◆ Save us, O Lord.

For the mission of the Church to the world, made manifest in our leaders, ministries, and communities, we pray: ◆
For the entirety of creation, for every life threatened, and for an end to the destruction of its goodness, we pray: ◆
For a unity between believers that models for others the Body of Christ, we pray: ◆ *For ourselves, that we are never content with our personal salvation alone, we pray:* ◆ *For those who have died, we pray:* ◆

Our Father . . .

Saving Lord,
on the cross you bore the sins and
    suffering of all the world.
Your servant St. Francis carried your
    grace and peace to everyone
    he met.
May we do the same,
honoring your sacrifice by our
    own solidarity
with our brothers and sisters in
    every nation.
You live and reign with God
    the Father
in the unity of the Holy Spirit,
one God, forever and ever.
Amen.

✦ *Commit your life to the Lord, and he will help you.*

✦ *In you, O Lord, I have found my peace.*

PSALM 130   *page 418*

READING   *Luke 11:1–4*

Jesus was praying in a certain place, and when he had finished, one of his disciples said to him, "Lord, teach us to pray just as John taught his disciples."

He said to them, "When you pray, say:

Father, hallowed be your name, / your Kingdom come. / Give us each day our daily bread / and forgive us our sins, / for we ourselves forgive everyone in debt to us, / and do not subject us to the final test."

REFLECTION

What a gift it is to have Jesus himself give us the words to offer prayer to God. The Lord's Prayer can help us when we are feeling lost, are in despair, or when we need focus. It gives comfort when life seems chaotic. Use it often today, trusting in God's grace and providence. Give thanks for knowing we do not have to find the perfect words for God to hear us. He knows our hearts.

PRAYERS   *others may be added*

Asking Jesus to help us, we pray:

◆ Lord, hear our prayer.

That honor and glory is given to the name of God by the Church through her actions, we pray: ◆ *That the kingdom of God prevails over the death and destruction ravaging the earth, we pray:* ◆ *That those who hunger for their most basic needs find nourishment, we pray:* ◆ *That we sinners repent and freely give forgiveness to those around us, we pray:* ◆ *That those who have died in faith have been enveloped in God's love, we pray:* ◆

Our Father . . .

Heavenly Father,
your Son Jesus gave us words we use
to grasp at knowing and loving you.
Thank you for the mercy you show us
   and the guidance you give us.
Remind us to listen to your Word,
in which the way to you is revealed.
Help us to trust in your providence
over all that is and all that will come.
Grant this through Christ our Lord.
Amen.

✦ *In you, O Lord, I have found my peace.*

✦ *Forever I will sing the goodness of the Lord.*

PSALM 100 *page 414*

READING *Luke 11:9–13*

[Jesus said:] "And I tell you, ask and you will receive; seek and you will find; knock and the door will be opened to you. For everyone who asks, receives; and the one who seeks, finds; and to the one who knocks, the door will be opened. What father among you would hand his son a snake when he asks for a fish? Or hand him a scorpion when he asks for an egg? If you then, who are wicked, know how to give good gifts to your children, how much more will the Father in heaven give the Holy Spirit to those who ask him?"

REFLECTION

Sometimes we see our lives as static. We do not know how much change is possible. The opening of a door to something new may be a radical, life-giving new path. In prayer we may ask God to open the door when we knock. It may be time for a shift in a relationship, a career change, a new outlook on our community or world. May we allow God to work in ways we never dreamed possible.

PRAYERS *others may be added*

Asking for what we truly need and desire, we pray:

◆ Surprise and delight us.

That the gift of the Holy Spirit continues to renew and strengthen the Church, we pray: ◆ *That visions of peace for the world may come in new and practical ways to world leaders, we pray:* ◆ *That the unemployed and underemployed may find life-giving work, we pray:* ◆ *That our desires for deeper relationship may be met in those around us in new ways, we pray:* ◆

Our Father . . .

Father in heaven,
we seek you,
we ask much of you,
and we knock at the door of
   eternal life.
You know our heart's desires
even before we speak.
Help us to comprehend the
   magnanimity of your love,
and to accept the possibility of
   transformational change.
We ask this through Christ our Lord.
Amen.

✦ *Forever I will sing the goodness of the Lord.*

✦ *Commit your life to the Lord.*

CANTICLE   *page 422*

READING   *Luke 1:28–30a, 35b–38b*

[The angel Gabriel said to Mary,] "Hail, full of grace! The Lord is with you." But she was greatly troubled at what was said and pondered what sort of greeting this might be. Then the angel said to her, "Do not be afraid, Mary . . . the Holy Spirit will come upon you, and the power of the Most High will over-shadow you. Therefore the child to be born will be called holy, the Son of God. And behold, Elizabeth, your relative, has also conceived a son in her old age, and this is the sixth month for her who was called barren; for nothing will be impossible for God." Mary said, "Behold, I am the handmaid of the Lord. May it be done to me according to your word."

REFLECTION

God chose Mary for a unique role in salvation. He blessed her with grace sufficient for this responsibility. When we pray the Rosary, we ask God to grant us the grace we need to live out our roles and responsibilities with love. We ask that God's love and grace may be enough. May our prayers, with Mary's, help us live as Christians who know and reflect God's goodness and mercy.

PRAYERS   *others may be added*

With Mary, we pray:

◆ Lord, fill us with your grace.

For all Christians, uniquely chosen for their vocations to serve God, we pray: ◆ *For civil leaders facing challenges that seem too great, we pray:* ◆ *For parents, struggling to guide, discipline, and nurture, we pray:* ◆ *For our parish, striving to be the Body of Christ in our community, we pray:* ◆ *For all to walk with our mother Mary in following God's will, we pray:* ◆ *For leaders to engage tirelessly in peaceful efforts, we pray:* ◆ *For all pregnant women to choose life, we pray:* ◆ *For new babies to be welcomed in love and bring delight, we pray:* ◆ *For those facing death, that they know of God's mercy, we pray:* ◆

Our Father . . .

Loving God,
you chose Mary and filled her with
   your grace.
May her example remind us of your
   presence with us.
May we know that you are enough
   for us,
no matter how we are called to serve.
We ask this through Christ our Lord.
Amen.

✦ *Commit your life to the Lord.*

✛ *Forever I will sing the goodness of the Lord.*

PSALM 33   *page 404*

READING   *Luke 11:27–28*

While Jesus was speaking, a woman from the crowd called out and said to him, "Blessed is the womb that carried you and the breasts at which you nursed." He replied, "Rather, blessed are those who hear the word of God and observe it."

REFLECTION

We give thanks for the many blessings we have received. These include the Creator, who gave us life and faith; parents or others who taught us the faith; the Word, accessible to us in the Bible and in our daily individual and communal life; the Spirit, who continually guides us; saints and holy men and women who have inspired us; the community that lifts us up; and the sacraments that fortify us. All of these are reasons to live by and share the Good News!

PRAYERS   *others may be added*

With joy and gratitude, we give thanks:

◆ *Glory and praise to you, O God.*

For the community of believers that supports us in good times and in bad, we pray: ◆ *For the stability of our country where we are able to live freely and express faith, we pray:* ◆ *For family members, mentors, teachers, and friends who have accompanied us on our life's journey, we pray:* ◆ *For the availability of the sacraments and ministries in our area, which enrich our being and keep us in relationship with God, we pray:* ◆

Our Father . . .

Creator God,
all the world and the cosmos is
   your gift.
From our conception until our life
   with you,
you have sent the Word, sacraments,
   and the Holy Spirit to sustain us.
We give thanks for your foresight
in knowing what we needed along
   the way.
We joyfully look forward to
   the celebration
that will be when we see you face
   to face.
We ask this through Christ our Lord.
Amen.

✛ *Forever I will sing the goodness of the Lord.*

✜ *The Lord made us; we belong to him.*

PSALM 100 *page 414*

READING *Matthew 22:8–10*

"Then he said to his servants, 'The feast is ready, but those who were invited were not worthy to come. Go out, therefore, into the main roads and invite to the feast whomever you find.' The servants went out into the streets and gathered all they found, bad and good alike, and the hall was filled with guests."

REFLECTION

Wearing certain attire for an event shows one's preparedness for and awareness of its significance. In what ways are we unprepared, or "undressed," for life with God? Are we unclean or unforgiven? Do we slight God's role in our lives? Or, are we overdressed, thus emphasizing ourselves rather than God? Stand before God in prayer, considering your own spiritual attire.

PRAYERS *others may be added*

Considering in what garments we come before God, we pray:

◆ Form us for life in Christ, O God.

For the Church, in the ways she prepares believers, that her being rooted in Christ's leadership brings emphasis on what really matters, we pray: ◆ For a growing understanding between cultures and religions of different ways to pray, customs for relating to one another, and ethical standards, we pray: ◆ For those seeking religious education, spiritual direction, and companionship as they journey toward God, we pray: ◆ For those who have died, that they have been welcomed to the heavenly banquet, regardless of their attire, we pray: ◆

Our Father . . .

God of heaven and earth,
you give us this life to know and
    serve you.
Do not let us come to death
    unprepared,
but offer us many opportunities
    to choose
a deepening of our relationship
    with you.
We ask this through our Lord Jesus
    Christ, your Son,
who lives and reigns with you
in the unity of the Holy Spirit,
one God, forever and ever.
Amen.

✜ *The Lord made us; we belong to him.*

✦ *In you, O Lord, I have found*
my peace.

PSALM 42   *page 408*

READING   *Luke 11:29–32*

While still more people gathered in the crowd, Jesus said to them, "This generation is an evil generation; it seeks a sign, but no sign will be given it, except the sign of Jonah. Just as Jonah became a sign to the Ninevites, so will the Son of Man be to this generation. At the judgment the queen of the south will rise with the men of this generation and she will condemn them, because she came from the ends of the earth to hear the wisdom of Solomon, and there is something greater than Solomon here. At the judgment the men of Nineveh will arise with this generation and condemn it, because at the preaching of Jonah they repented, and there is something greater than Jonah here."

REFLECTION

The deep wisdom and truth of Christianity keeps us coming back, even when we are excited by or interested in other viewpoints. We may read about Eastern religions, explore New Age spiritual practices, and learn something from them. Ultimately, however, they inform and enrich our Christian faith. Our heart, soul, and mind return to the lasting testament of Jesus, his teaching, his death and Resurrection, and what is uniquely revealed about God.

PRAYERS   *others may be added*

Awed by wisdom, we pray:

◆ Lord, hear our prayer.

For the Church, as she holds fast to ancient truth, amid the mix of other religious beliefs and practices, we pray: ◆
For attorneys, judges, and legal systems, that civil law points them toward the eternal law of lasting truth, justice, and mercy, we pray: ◆ *For consumers of media, that the lure of wealth, beauty, and fame may quickly diminish, we pray:* ◆
For ourselves, that as we grow in understanding of other religions, we give at least equal time to the story of our own faith, we pray: ◆

Our Father . . .

All-knowing God,
throughout time, your infinite truth
    has remained.
As we explore the cultures and
    religions known to us,
lead us to deeper understanding of the
    unique story of Christianity.
May we see the "something greater"
    that awaits us beyond all
    speculation.
Grant this through Christ our Lord.
Amen.

✦ *In you, O Lord, I have found*
my peace.

✦ *The Lord made us; we belong to him.*

PSALM 139 *page 420*

READING *Luke 11:37–41*

After Jesus had spoken, a Pharisee invited him to dine at his home. He entered and reclined at table to eat. The Pharisee was amazed to see that he did not observe the prescribed washing before the meal. The Lord said to him, "Oh you Pharisees! Although you cleanse the outside of the cup and the dish, inside you are filled with plunder and evil. You fools! Did not the maker of the outside also make the inside? But as to what is within, give alms, and behold, everything will be clean for you."

REFLECTION

We ask ourselves: How does our outer appearance compare with what lies within our hearts? Do we present ourselves as attractive, pleasant, and welcoming, but secretly harbor jealousy, hatred, or harsh judgments? Or do we hide our inner generosity and gifts by avoiding interaction, sticking to exclusive friendships, and refusing to participate in the community? Our maker, the God of all creation, made both our outside appearances and our inner personalities. Let us give him praise and thanks by being people of integrity who are comfortable sharing who we are with others.

PRAYERS *others may be added*

Bringing our prayers to God, we pray:

◆ May we be united in love.

That the beauty of our Christian Churches is always matched by the generosity and openness of our members, we pray: ◆ *That the wealth and glamor of America is balanced by abundant aid to international need and just trade policies, we pray:* ◆ *That obsession with exercise, beautiful bodies, and makeovers is countered by emphasis on learning compassion and practicing peaceful conflict resolution, we pray:* ◆ *That expression of talent and sharing of treasure spreads from our homes and churches outward into the wider community, we pray:* ◆

Our Father . . .

Maker of us all,
you challenged the Pharisees to
    cleanse their hearts,
rather than solely follow the law.
May we observe the new law you
    gave to us: love of God
    and neighbor.
As we bare our inner selves
    before you,
show us how we can join our inward
    and outward selves
as we live in imitation of your Son.
Make us whole as we accept the
    creation you made in us.
We ask this through Christ our Lord.
Amen.

✦ *The Lord made us; we belong to him.*

✛ *The precepts of the Lord give joy to the heart.*

PSALM 51   *page 409*

READING   *Luke 11:42–46*

The Lord said: "Woe to you Pharisees! You pay tithes of mint and of rue and of every garden herb, but you pay no attention to judgment and to love for God. These you should have done, without overlooking the others. Woe to you Pharisees! You love the seat of honor in synagogues and greetings in marketplaces. Woe to you! You are like unseen graves over which people unknowingly walk."

Then one of the scholars of the law said to him in reply, "Teacher, by saying this you are insulting us too." And he said, "Woe also to you scholars of the law! You impose on people burdens hard to carry, but you yourselves do not lift one finger to touch them."

REFLECTION

Today is a hard time to be a leader or intellectual—or so it seems. Jesus challenges all of us to value love over money, service over prestige, and mercy over judgment. Our culture honors these misconstrued values, and we as Christians should be first to subvert them and live as examples of Jesus' servant leadership.

PRAYERS   *others may be added*

With humble hearts, we pray:

◆ Make us servant leaders, Lord.

For the Pope, Bishops, priests, and all ministers of the Church, that love for God eliminates all desire for power and honor, we pray: ◆ *For attorneys, legislators, judges, and professors, that upholding truth and justice is a humble service rather than a judgmental condemnation of others, we pray:* ◆ *For those burdened by unjust punishments and excessive sentences, that freedom may come soon, we pray:* ◆ *For each of us in our interactions with others, that we hold a Christian perspective regarding money, justice, and mercy, we pray:* ◆

Our Father . . .

Lord Jesus,
you challenged the status quo
and upset cultural and religious leaders,
not for spite but to remind them of
    God's justice.
Help us find the balance between
    power and service, mercy and
    judgment, prestige and humility.
Help us to carry out our civil duties
    with a heart like yours.
You live with God the Father in the
    unity of the Holy Spirit,
one God, forever and ever.
Amen.

✛ *The precepts of the Lord give joy to the heart.*

✦ *In you, O Lord, I have found
my peace.*

PSALM 42   *page 408*

READING   *Luke 11:47–52*

The Lord said: "Woe to you who build the memorials of the prophets whom your fathers killed. Consequently, you bear witness and give consent to the deeds of your ancestors, for they killed them and you do the building. Therefore, the wisdom of God said, 'I will send to them prophets and Apostles; some of them they will kill and persecute' in order that this generation might be charged with the blood of all the prophets shed since the foundation of the world, from the blood of Abel to the blood of Zechariah who died between the altar and the temple building. Yes, I tell you, this generation will be charged with their blood! Woe to you, scholars of the law! You have taken away the key of knowledge. You yourselves did not enter and you stopped those trying to enter."

REFLECTION

"Woe to you!" This type of phrasing leads many people to believe the Church, and even Christ, intends to punish or cause to suffer those with whom they disagree. But the "woe" sayings are not so much a condemnation as a warning of concern. The teachings of Christ and the wisdom of the Church share, in love, knowledge of what brings true happiness and what brings despair.

PRAYERS   *others may be added*

Trusting in God's care for us, we pray:

✦ Lead us to life in you, O Christ.

That the Magisterium holds dear the tradition of the Church, and expresses it with true compassion for all Christians, we pray: ✦ *That wisdom figures in all parts of the world lead people away from false and unlasting happiness, we pray:* ✦ *That addicts and workaholics realize the despair gripping them and trade it for the true happiness that comes in God, we pray:* ✦ *That we who share faith help each other to see the path Christ leads us on toward real contentment and genuine peace, we pray:* ✦

Our Father . . .

God of wisdom,
in love you have sent us prophets,
    teachers, saints,
and above all, your Son,
to show us the way to you.
May we use the tools and resources
at our disposal to choose the way
    of life,
the source of goodness, the truth that
    surpasses understanding,
the Good News of your love.
Grant this through Christ our Lord.
Amen.

✦ *In you, O Lord, I have found
my peace.*

✦ *The heart of the just one is firm, trusting in the Lord.*

PSALM 111 *page 417*

READING *Luke 12:2–7*

[Jesus said to his disciples:] "There is nothing concealed that will not be revealed, nor secret that will not be known. Therefore whatever you have said in the darkness will be heard in the light, and what you have whispered behind closed doors will be proclaimed on the housetops."

REFLECTION

Do not fear, but rather, trust. As blessed, beloved children of God, we know that our future is in his hands. We can trust wholeheartedly in the goodness of God and his plan for our lives. We can open ourselves to be ever more trusting, thereby allowing him to work ever more beautifully in the world. This attitude alone, through the grace of God, has the potential to change our entire world.

PRAYERS *others may be added*

Bringing our prayers to God, we pray:

◆ Remember your people, O Lord.

For the Pope, Bishops, and ministers of the Church, that the challenges the world presents never outweigh the hope offered in Christ, we pray: ◆ *For modern-day prophets facing injustice and violence, that they are filled with the joy and courage of the Holy Spirit, we pray:* ◆ *For those in the media and politics who manipulate others, that they live anew in trust, we pray:* ◆ *For parents and teachers who are tempted with fears for their children, that they conquer violence and hatred with Christ's love, we pray:* ◆ *For those martyred because of their radical hope in Christ, that they celebrate today in heaven, we pray:* ◆

Our Father . . .

Merciful Father,
you have sheltered your people
    through natural disasters
and human wars.
You have walked with survivors
    and martyrs.
You conquered even death with
    your love.
Help us stand with all holy men
    and women
who have resisted fear and chosen
    trust in you.
We ask this through Christ our Lord.
Amen.

✦ *The heart of the just one is firm, trusting in the Lord.*

Optional memorial of St. Callistus I, pope, martyr

✦ *Commit your life to the Lord, and he will help you.*

PSALM 40 *page 407*

READING *John 15:1–8*

Jesus said to his disciples: "I am the true vine, and my Father is the vine grower. He takes away every branch in me that does not bear fruit, and everyone that does he prunes so that it bears more fruit. You are already pruned because of the word that I spoke to you. Remain in me, as I remain in you. Just as a branch cannot bear fruit on its own unless it remains on the vine, so neither can you unless you remain in me. I am the vine, you are the branches. Whoever remains in me and I in him will bear much fruit, because without me you can do nothing."

REFLECTION

Do not underestimate how fruitful God may make your life. If we are committed to prayer, joyful in relationship with God, and humble in our service of others, he may use us in ways we could not have dreamed. St. Teresa, a woman of the sixteenth century, developed a mystical spirituality that influenced many. She is one of only three women recognized as a doctor of the Church. God may amaze us with the plans he has for our lives.

PRAYERS *others may be added*

Clinging to God, we pray:

◆ Bring forth the fruit of your kingdom.

For the men and women of the Church in whom God is making a new creation, we pray: ◆ For activists and agents for positive change in government, education, and health care, we pray: ◆ For young people beginning careers and retirees entering transition, we pray: ◆ For an openness to the surprises God has in store for us, we pray: ◆

Our Father . . .

Creator God,
you imagined and gave life to
　the world.
Your Spirit is at work in all who live
　by faith.
May your call to us continually
　surprise and amaze us
with the fruit you bring forth.
We ask this through our Lord Jesus
　Christ, your Son,
who lives and reigns with you
in the unity of the Holy Spirit,
one God, forever and ever.
Amen.

✦ *Commit your life to the Lord, and he will help you.*

✝ *The Lord made us; we belong to him.*

PSALM 100 *page 414*

READING *Matthew 22:15, 17–21*

The Pharisees . . . plotted how they might entrap Jesus in speech, . . . saying, "Tell us, then, what is your opinion: Is it lawful to pay the census tax to Caesar or not?" Knowing their malice, Jesus said, "Why are you testing me, you hypocrites? Show me the coin that pays the census tax." Then they handed him the Roman coin. He said to them, "Whose image is this and whose inscription?" They replied, "Caesar's." At that he said to them, "Then repay to Caesar what belongs to Caesar and to God what belongs to God."

REFLECTION

Jesus avoids the trap of discussing taxes and legalities, but he raises a question for us: what belongs to God? What areas of our life do we see as God's domain? If we think only of Sunday mornings, we need to grow. How much time do we give to God? What resources belong to him? Who has ownership of our gifts?

PRAYERS *others may be added*

Reflecting on our lives, we pray:

◆ Lord, hear our prayer.

That teachers of the Church may present the miraculous and stupendous love of God with great joy, we pray: ◆ *That business leaders who confuse generosity with competition may find the freedom to give and not count the cost, we pray:* ◆ *That those consumed with "keeping score" may rest in knowing God's providence is always enough, we pray:* ◆ *That Christian communities may inspire each other by their joy in being called disciples, we pray:* ◆

Our Father . . .

Generous God,
you have blessed us with life itself
    and every gift within it.
May we never forget that you are
    our Creator
and giver of all good things.
Help us to see our lives as belonging
    to you,
and return to you our gratitude, our
    service, and our love.
We ask this through our Lord Jesus
    Christ, your Son,
who lives and reigns with you
in the unity of the Holy Spirit,
one God, forever and ever.
Amen.

✝ *The Lord made us; we belong to him.*

✛ *Commit your life to the Lord, and he will help you.*

PSALM 40   *page 407*

READING   *Philippians 3:17–21*

Join with others in being imitators of me, brothers and sisters, and observe those who thus conduct themselves according to the model you have in us. For many, as I have often told you and now tell you even in tears conduct themselves as enemies of the cross of Christ. Their end is destruction. Their God is their stomach; their glory is in their "shame." Their minds are occupied with earthly things. But our citizenship is in heaven, and from it we also await a savior, the Lord Jesus Christ. He will change our lowly body to conform with his glorified Body by the power that enables him also to bring all things into subjection to himself.

REFLECTION

An "athlete" and "soldier" for Christ, St. Ignatius (of the early Church) gives us a passionate model of discipleship. At times we may grow slack in living our Christian faith. Think of athletes— their hours of practice, regimented eating and sleeping—and do the same for Christ. Think of soldiers—rigorous self-discipline, devotion to the cause—and do the same for Christ. St. Paul's words call us to serve Christ by our conduct and our citizenship. Promise Christ today to follow him with zeal.

PRAYERS   *others may be added*

Confident in God, we pray:

◆ Make us strong in you.

For our Pope, Bishops, clergy, deacons, and all servants of Christ, we pray: ◆
For militaries protecting justice, human rights, and peace, we pray: ◆
For students, athletes, workers, and volunteers who dedicate their efforts to Christ, we pray: ◆ *For our faith, our prayer life, our commitment to the Church, we pray:* ◆ *For those who have crossed the finish line of faith, that the race leads them to the arms of God, we pray:* ◆

Our Father . . .

God of power and might,
you rule with justice and mercy.
You call us, your disciples,
to serve you with steadfast hearts.
May St. Ignatius, an early believer,
inspire us by his dedication
   and passion.
May we, too, be soldiers for Christ.
May we, too, run the race for Christ.
We ask this through Christ our Lord.
Amen.

✛ *Commit your life to the Lord, and he will help you.*

✦ *Commit your life to the Lord, and he will help you.*

PSALM 40 page 407

READING Luke 10:1–3, 8–9

The Lord Jesus appointed seventy-two disciples whom he sent ahead of him in pairs to every town and place he intended to visit. He said to them, "The harvest is abundant but the laborers are few; so ask the master of the harvest to send out laborers for his harvest. Go on your way; behold, I am sending you like lambs among wolves. Whatever town you enter and they welcome you, eat what they set before you, cure the sick in it and say to them, 'The Kingdom of God is at hand for you.'"

REFLECTION

The word evangelism *might intimidate us or carry negative connotations. Yet, some of us have a special gift for evangelizing. It is a gift of love for every person one meets, so much so as to want to share the miracle of God's love and mercy with every human heart. If this is your call, respond quickly. Many are in need of the message of healing, forgiveness, and eternal life. If you are unsure of how to evangelize, see each person you meet as a child of God in need of his love.*

PRAYERS *others may be added*

Aware of the hunger for God, we pray:

◆ Send us forth with the Good News.

For missionaries, preachers, and teachers, who share the Gospel with fervor, we pray: ◆ *For creative media, technology, and communication, which can facilitate sharing God's love with the young, the isolated, and the far away, we pray:* ◆ *For new models of evangelization, which are inspired by love for others, not judgment, we pray:* ◆ *For each of us, called to share the Gospel in our own way, we pray:* ◆

Our Father . . .

Lord Jesus, our teacher,
you told your disciples to peacefully
   and earnestly
spread the news of the coming of
   God's reign.
We, too, are called to share the Good
   News with love.
Make us evangelists, like St. Luke, in
   the way we can best serve.
You live and reign with God
   the Father
in the unity of the Holy Spirit,
one God, forever and ever.
Amen.

✦ *Commit your life to the Lord, and he will help you.*

✛ *The Lord is my shepherd, there is nothing I shall want.*

PSALM 40   *page 407*

READING   *Matthew 10:28–33*

Jesus said to his Apostles: "Do not be afraid of those who kill the body but cannot kill the soul; rather, be afraid of the one who can destroy both soul and body in Gehenna. Are not two sparrows sold for a small coin? Yet not one of them falls to the ground without your Father's knowledge. Even all the hairs of your head are counted. So do not be afraid; you are worth more than many sparrows. Everyone who acknowledges me before others I will acknowledge before my heavenly Father. But whoever denies me before others, I will deny before my heavenly Father."

REFLECTION

The children's rhyme "sticks and stones . . ." gave us an early distinction between physical and verbal attacks. In fact, both types of violence can hurt us. Most of us have learned to persevere through pain, ignore cruel comments, or cling to our faith when faced with cruelty. God wants to be with us, holding us up and reassuring us of safety, when we encounter danger. He tells us: Do not be afraid of those who kill the body but cannot kill the soul.

PRAYERS   *others may be added*

Strong in body and soul, we pray:

◆ Lord, be with us.

For all Christians faced with persecution for their beliefs, we pray: ◆ *For soldiers tortured for protecting justice and peace, we pray:* ◆ *For police officers, emergency medical personnel, and fire fighters who risk their lives to protect others, we pray:* ◆ *For growth in confidence and strength through God, no matter what obstacles lie in our path, we pray:* ◆

Our Father . . .

God of mercy,
you were with your sons in North
    America,
who died for their beliefs.
You are always with us when we
    face difficulty.
Your Holy Spirit pervades our soul,
    giving us strength, courage,
    and calm.
We ask this through our Lord Jesus
    Christ, your Son,
who lives and reigns with you
in the unity of the Holy Spirit,
one God, forever and ever.
Amen.

✛ *The Lord is my shepherd, there is nothing I shall want.*

✝ *Go out to all the world, and tell the Good News.*

PSALM 33 page 404

READING Luke 12:49–53

Jesus said to his disciples: "I have come to set the earth on fire, and how I wish it were already blazing! There is a baptism with which I must be baptized, and how great is my anguish until it is accomplished! Do you think that I have come to establish peace on the earth? No, I tell you, but rather division. From now on a household of five will be divided, three against two and two against three; a father will be divided against his son and a son against his father, a mother against her daughter and a daughter against her mother, a mother-in-law against her daughter-in-law and a daughter-in-law against her mother-in-law."

REFLECTION

The divisions between believers and non-believers in our country do seem to set issues on fire and cause turmoil within families. The divisions among Christians themselves seem to do the same. We cannot pretend that our differences are not real. Our only hope is greater understanding by each of us of our own position, an awareness of the history that led us to today, and then open and honest dialogue with a goal of peace. The Prince of Peace knows the difficulty of the road ahead, and he will guide us.

PRAYERS *others may be added*

Burdened by divisions, we pray:

◆ Reconcile us in you, Prince of Peace.

For dialogue leading to greater unity within the Church, we pray: ◆ *For successful negotiations between warring parties all over the world, we pray:* ◆ *For a politics of hope and reconciliation in the United States of America and in all nations, we pray:* ◆ *For continued improving ecumenical and interreligious relations, we pray:* ◆ *For each of us to gain the ability to understand another's perspective, we pray:* ◆

Our Father . . .

God of the lion and the lamb,
true peace will only come in
   your kingdom.
Until then, help us take steps
   individually and communally
toward greater understanding,
   dialogue, and common goals.
May we challenge our assumptions
   and fears
for the sake of a lasting peace.
Grant this through Christ our Lord.
Amen.

✝ *Go out to all the world, and tell the Good News.*

Optional memorial of St. Paul of the Cross, priest

✛ *The Lord is my light and my salvation.*

PSALM 139   page 420

READING   Luke 12:54–59

Jesus said to the crowds, "When you see a cloud rising in the west you say immediately that it is going to rain—and so it does; and when you notice that the wind is blowing from the south you say that it is going to be hot—and so it is. You hypocrites! You know how to interpret the appearance of the earth and the sky; why do you not know how to interpret the present time?

"Why do you not judge for yourselves what is right? If you are to go with your opponent before a magistrate, make an effort to settle the matter on the way; otherwise your opponent will turn you over to the judge, and the judge hand you over to the constable, and the constable throw you into prison. I say to you, you will not be released until you have paid the last penny."

REFLECTION

We often make things more difficult than they need to be. Here is some practical advice from Jesus: settle what we can on our own by being direct with one another. Just as we are practical with money, weather, and business matters, how can we be straightforward in our faith? If we need to be more up front with friends, let's do it. If we need to be firm with our children, let's do it. If we need to be honest before God, let's do it.

PRAYERS   *others may be added*

With uncluttered thoughts, we pray:

◆ Give us wisdom.

For the good of the Church, the community of the faithful, as she acts on earth, we pray: ◆ *For the good of the people of the world, as their communities struggle to find meaning, happiness, and health, we pray:* ◆ *For those who are suffering and in need, that they are reached by others and touched with the compassion of Jesus, we pray:* ◆ *For all of us in the Body of Christ, that we live out of joy, in service to God and others, we pray:* ◆

Our Father . . .

God our Father,
you created all.
You sustain all.
You redeem all.
As we are overwhelmed with the gift
    of your love,
may we always live out of that joy,
    offering forgiveness
and love to all whom we meet.
May we have open hearts and clean
    consciences.
Grant this through Christ our Lord.
Amen.

✛ *The Lord is my light and my salvation.*

✤ *In you, O Lord, I have found my peace.*

PSALM 51   *page 409*

READING   *Luke 13:6–9*

[Jesus told them] this parable: "There once was a person who had a fig tree planted in his orchard, and when he came in search of fruit on it but found none, he said to the gardener, 'For three years now I have come in search of fruit on this fig tree but have found none. So cut it down. Why should it exhaust the soil?' He said to him in reply, 'Sir, leave it for this year also, and I shall cultivate the ground around it and fertilize it; it may bear fruit in the future. If not you can cut it down.' "

REFLECTION

It is easy to find fault with others. We could surely make a long list of those around us or in the news who have sinned. Jesus asks us to repent of our own sins. Humble yourself today and ask forgiveness specifically for all the ways you have failed to be a follower of Christ. Like the fig tree, you have been given yet another chance.

PRAYERS   *others may be added*

With contrite hearts, we pray:

◆ Show us your compassion.

For gratitude for God's mercy among all the faithful, we pray: ◆ For humility among authorities in every arena of life, we pray: ◆ For a second chance for those who repent and hope to start anew, we pray: ◆ For forgiveness for those times when we have grown arrogant, we pray: ◆

Our Father . . .

Lord Jesus,
you took our sins upon you,
bearing them upon the cross.
By your death and Resurrection,
you have redeemed humanity.
May we glorify you in how we live,
that we may rejoice with you
where you live and reign with God
   the Father
in the unity of the Holy Spirit,
one God, forever and ever.
Amen.

✤ *In you, O Lord, I have found my peace.*

Optional memorial of the Blessed Virgin Mary

✛ *The heart of the just one is firm,*
trusting in the Lord.

PSALM 42   *page 408*

READING   *Matthew 22:36–40*

[The Sadducees asked Jesus:] "Teacher, which commandment in the law is the greatest?" He said to him, "You shall love the Lord, your God, with all your heart, with all your soul, and with all your mind. This is the greatest and the first commandment. The second is like it: You shall love your neighbor as yourself. The whole law and the prophets depend on these two commandments."

REFLECTION

Even today we resist Jesus' answer to the question, Which commandment in the law is the greatest? We want to believe that the most important thing we can do is follow a rule, such as attending Mass on Sunday, or be obedient to the tenets of the faith. But the greatest commandment involves loving God and loving our neighbor. Love is hard. Loving neighbors, strangers, widows, and orphans as much as we love ourselves and our own family is difficult. No wonder this commandment is the greatest of all. It defines everything else.

PRAYERS   *others may be added*

Rising to the challenge to love,
we pray:

◆ Show us our neighbors.

For Christians, who love God and want to follow his law, we pray: ◆ *For citizens of our nation, our state, and our local communities, when we forget our connectedness to others, we pray:* ◆ *For those whom we love, and those whom we cannot stand, that we open our eyes to who they really are, we pray:* ◆ *For all relationships in our lives, that we treat each other with gentleness, civility, and loving concern, we pray:* ◆

Our Father . . .

Lord Jesus, our teacher,
you revealed to us the hardest lesson
    of all:
love in its truest, self-sacrificing form.
May we live in this love,
surpassing your commandments and
    treating others with deep love.
You live and reign with God
    the Father
in the unity of the Holy Spirit,
one God, forever and ever.
Amen.

✛ *The heart of the just one is firm,*
trusting in the Lord.

✢ *The Lord hears the cry of the poor.*

PSALM 100   *page 414*

READING   *Luke 13:10–13*

Jesus was teaching in a synagogue on the sabbath. And a woman was there who for eighteen years had been crippled by a spirit; she was bent over, completely incapable of standing erect. When Jesus saw her, he called to her and said, "Woman, you are set free of your infirmity." He laid his hands on her, and she at once stood up straight and glorified God.

REFLECTION

In what ways might we be bent over? Are we in bondage to some force that has shaped our lives for many years? Perhaps addiction, depression, perfectionism, unhealed wounds from a trauma, a bad habit, or a learned yet sinful way of relating to others? Christ wants us to be freed from these crippling afflictions. We need our faith, and often we need to take steps ourselves, with the help of others such as professionals, in order to finally stand erect and give glory to God.

PRAYERS   *others may be added*

In need of God's healing touch, we pray:

◆ Make straight our paths.

For all who serve the Church, that the transformative power of God's grace reaches to their innermost depths anywhere it is needed, we pray: ◆ *For all who serve their countries, that the freedom that comes from Christ's presence in their life takes hold, we pray:* ◆ *For all who serve in caregiving professions, that burnout and stress may be alleviated through fair labor practices and God's guidance, we pray:* ◆ *For all who dream of standing tall, free of their inner demons, that Christ's love may be the miracle they seek, we pray:* ◆

Our Father . . .

Lord Jesus, our healer,
your touch on earth changed lives.
Your touch from heaven does
   the same.
We bring our maladies and tormented
   souls to you,
desperate for your powerful touch.
Help us to accept your grace.
You live and reign with God
   the Father
in the unity of the Holy Spirit,
one God, forever and ever.
Amen.

✢ *The Lord hears the cry of the poor.*

Optional memorial of St. Anthony Mary Claret, bishop

✦ *Forever I will sing the goodness of the Lord.*

PSALM 100 page 414

READING Luke 13:18–21

Jesus said, "What is the Kingdom of God like? To what can I compare it? It is like a mustard seed that a man took and planted in the garden. When it was fully grown, it became a large bush and *the birds of the sky dwelt in its branches.*"

Again he said, "To what shall I compare the Kingdom of God? It is like yeast that a woman took and mixed in with three measures of wheat flour until the whole batch of dough was leavened."

REFLECTION

The yeast and the mustard seed demonstrate the mystery of transformation. Look around you today and notice the signs of God's transformation—the beauty of fall, the kindness of neighbors, forgiveness between children, hope for the world despite violence and war. Receive Eucharist today or this week and ask for the mystery of the transformation you witness at Mass to take place again in your heart and in your actions.

PRAYERS others may be added

Awed by God, we pray:

◆ May your kingdom come.

For the miraculous endurance of the Church, even in times of great resistance, we pray: ◆ *For the efforts of national leaders for good, even when immoral agendas compete for priority, we pray:* ◆ *For random acts of kindness and justice, no matter how small, because they give rise to ripples of results, we pray:* ◆ *For the gift of Eucharist in which we find Christ, his unique and mysterious presence in the bread and wine, we pray:* ◆

Our Father . . .

Creator God,
you reveal yourself to us in the
  wonder of the tiny seed
and in the awesomeness of the
  infinite universe.
All around us, you work in and
  through your children.
Attune our ears and train our eyes to
  notice your presence.
Show us how to meditate on the
  mystery of your kingdom.
We ask this through Christ our Lord.
Amen.

✦ *Forever I will sing the goodness of the Lord.*

✦ *The Lord made us; we belong to him.*

PSALM 111 *page 417*

READING *Luke 13:23–25, 29*

Someone asked [Jesus], "Lord, will only a few people be saved?" He answered them, "Strive to enter through the narrow gate, for many, I tell you, will attempt to enter but will not be strong enough. After the master of the house has arisen and locked the door, then will you stand outside knocking and saying, 'Lord, open the door for us.' He will say to you in reply, 'I do not know where you are from.' And people will come from the east and the west and from the north and the south and will recline at table in the Kingdom of God."

REFLECTION

God's justice turns our sensibilities on their heads. Who do you consider least likely to be saved? Who do you consider most likely? What if you found out that the exact opposite was true? What does this tell you about your own biases, fears, and judgments? How can we live out of an openness and humility that assumes we do not know the heart of every person? Let us truly treat each and every person as a son or daughter of God.

PRAYERS *others may be added*

With hope in the Lord, we pray:

◆ Lord, hear our prayer.

For the Roman Catholic Church, that her leaders may always be servants of others, we pray: ◆ *For international trade, that a spirit of God's justice may surpass the sense of competition and domination, we pray:* ◆ *For those convinced they would be last to be welcome in God's house, that their eyes may be opened to his surprising love, we pray:* ◆ *For the followers of Christ, that we may honestly consider our own biases and judgments of others, we pray:* ◆

Our Father . . .

God of heaven and earth,
you gave us the servant-leader for all
    time, our brother Jesus.
You give us now the opportunity to
    serve in his name.
May we choose to be last;
may we choose to be open;
may we choose to be welcoming to
    each man, woman,
and child who seeks God.
Grant this through Christ our Lord.
Amen.

✦ *The Lord made us; we belong to him.*

✠ *The Lord is my light and my salvation.*

PSALM 130   *page 418*

READING   *Luke 13:31–35*

Some Pharisees came to Jesus and said, "Go away, leave this area because Herod wants to kill you." He replied, "Go and tell that fox, 'Behold, I cast out demons and I perform healings today and tomorrow, and on the third day I accomplish my purpose. Yet I must continue on my way today, tomorrow, and the following day, for it is impossible that a prophet should die outside of Jerusalem.'

"Jerusalem, Jerusalem, you who kill the prophets and stone those sent to you, how many times I yearned to gather your children together as a hen gathers her brood under her wings, but you were unwilling! Behold, your house will be abandoned. But I tell you, you will not see me until the time comes when you say, / Blessed is he who comes in the name of the Lord."

REFLECTION

We often do not recognize Christ in our midst, just as the people of Jerusalem did not. We do not slow down enough to hear his voice and spend time in prayer with him. We do not notice the lowly ones who have much to teach us about our Lord. We look only in certain circles for companions in faith. We set such parameters on our lives that we refuse to accept the possibility that God is working in a way we did not expect.

PRAYERS   *others may be added*

Looking for Christ among us, we pray:

◆ Open our eyes and ears.

That Christian retreat houses offer solitude and peace in a rushed world, we pray: ◆ *That quiet beaches, undeveloped rain forests, and barren deserts remain unspoiled and serve as an oasis in a crowded world, we pray:* ◆ *That muted voices of the forgotten can still be heard over the din of everyday life, we pray:* ◆ *That our community holds dear its empty spaces, quiet hearts, and moments of peace, we pray:* ◆

Our Father . . .

Lord Jesus Christ,
you are blessed;
you are God's own Son;
you are with us, yet we often fail
    to notice.
Open our eyes to see your face in
    unexpected places.
Help us to choose rest and restoration,
that we might spend more time
    with you,
and in so doing, bring more peace to
    our entire world.
You live and reign with God
    the Father
in the unity of the Holy Spirit,
one God, forever and ever.
Amen.

✠ *The Lord is my light and my salvation.*

✦ *Commit your life to the Lord, and he will help you.*

PSALM 40 *page 407*

READING *Luke 6:12–16*

Jesus went up to the mountain to pray, and he spent the night in prayer to God. When day came, he called his disciples to himself, and from them he chose Twelve, whom he also named Apostles: Simon, whom he named Peter, and his brother Andrew, James, John, Philip, Bartholomew, Matthew, Thomas, James the son of Alphaeus, Simon who was called a Zealot, and Judas the son of James, and Judas Iscariot, who became a traitor.

REFLECTION

Jesus sounds a bit like the CEO of a corporation, or the head of a leadership training program. How is his calling and his choosing different from appointments with which we are familiar? Business leaders choose standout achievers. Jesus is one with God in discernment. He sees the inner heart of his followers. Star salespeople and those receiving bonuses for their work have the bottom line of the company as their goal. Jesus gives to us and our Church leaders a much richer mission: the saving of souls.

PRAYERS *others may be added*

Hearing the divine call, we pray:

◆ May we be worthy.

For the Pope, Bishops, priests, deacons, religious, and all baptized Christians called to serve, we pray: ◆ For our leaders asked to serve our country, we pray: ◆ For spouses called to lifelong commitment and love, we pray: ◆ For neighbors asked to love each other as themselves, we pray: ◆ For those who have been called home for eternity, we pray: ◆

Our Father . . .

Lord Jesus, our Light,
you have called us and have chosen us
    to be God's children.
You have missioned each of us for a
    particular role in the kingdom.
May we respond with
    generous hearts,
and give glory to you in our service.
May we recognize this unique and
    holy call.
You live and reign with God
    the Father
in the unity of the Holy Spirit,
one God, forever and ever.
Amen.

✦ *Commit your life to the Lord, and he will help you.*

✠ *In you, O Lord, I have found my peace.*

PSALM 139   page 420

READING   Luke 14:7–11

[Jesus] told a parable to those who had been invited [to the Sabbath], noticing how they were choosing the places of honor at the table. "When you are invited by someone to a wedding banquet, do not recline at table in the place of honor. A more distinguished guest than you may have been invited by him, and the host who invited both of you may approach you and say, 'Give your place to this man,' and then you would proceed with embarrassment to take the lowest place. Rather, when you are invited, go and take the lowest place so that when the host comes to you he may say, 'My friend, move up to a higher position.' Then you will enjoy the esteem of your companions at the table. For everyone who exalts himself will be humbled, but the one who humbles himself will be exalted."

REFLECTION

Have you ever tried to look "better" than you are? Bought a nicer house, car, jewelry, clothing, or possessions than you could afford? What drives us to try to position ourselves as wealthy, successful, or well-off? What if you tried to humble yourself? What steps would you have to take to stand among the poor and humble? What pressures would be relieved by taking this path, and what priorities would stand out?

PRAYERS   *others may be added*

Standing before God just as we are, we pray:

◆ Humble our hearts, O Lord.

For all Christian clergy, that vestments and collars give glory to God, not to the wearer, we pray: ◆ *For a celebration of the gifts of native cultures and simple living around the globe, we pray:* ◆ *For an end to the obsession with glamor, perfect bodies, and wealth in American media, we pray:* ◆ *For each of us to stand in solidarity with the least among us, rather than jockey for position with the elite, we pray:* ◆

Our Father . . .

Lord Jesus,
you spoke truth to the Pharisees,
who had lost sense of their priorities.
You speak boldly to us as well.
Everywhere we go,
help us to seek the place of the lowly,
to avoid the clamor for appreciation
    and recognition.
May we stand firmly in line with you
and all who seek you with
    humble hearts.
You live and reign with God
    the Father
in the unity of the Holy Spirit,
one God, forever and ever.
Amen.

✠ *In you, O Lord, I have found my peace.*

✦ *The heart of the just one is firm.*

PSALM 25 *page 403*

READING *Matthew 23:1–12*

Jesus spoke to the crowds and to his disciples, saying, "The scribes and the Pharisees have taken their seat on the chair of Moses. Therefore, do and observe all things whatsoever they tell you, but do not follow their example. For they preach but they do not practice. They tie up heavy burdens hard to carry and lay them on people's shoulders, but they will not lift a finger to move them. All their works are performed to be seen. They widen their phylacteries and lengthen their tassels. They love places of honor at banquets, seats of honor in synagogues, greetings in marketplaces, and the salutation 'Rabbi.' "As for you, do not be called 'Rabbi.' You have but one teacher, and you are all brothers. Call no one on earth your father; you have but one Father in heaven. Do not be called 'Master'; you have but one master, the Christ. The greatest among you must be your servant. Whoever exalts himself will be humbled; but whoever humbles himself will be exalted."

REFLECTION

Have you been led astray by a false mentor, friend, or role model? Examine carefully those whose lives you admire. Are they doing the hard work of life themselves? Are they only too happy to be rewarded or praised? Distance yourself from anyone who leads you away from the one, true God of love and humility.

PRAYERS *others may be added*

Seeking truth, we pray:

◆ Show us the right way, Master.

For Christians who have put too much emphasis on any human person and have strayed from worship of God alone, we pray: ◆ *For nations to be led by selfless acts, we pray:* ◆ *For young people, especially those vulnerable to manipulation, we pray:* ◆ *For a review of the examples we follow, and direction for our choices, we pray:* ◆

Our Father . . .

Jesus Christ, true Lord,
false prophets and Pharisees have
   always tried to recruit
   your followers.
Lead us to the one light, the one path,
   the one truth, found in you.
You live and reign with God
   the Father
in the unity of the Holy Spirit,
one God, forever and ever.
Amen.

✦ *The heart of the just one is firm.*

✦ *The Lord hears the cry of the poor.*

PSALM 100 — page 414

READING — Luke 14:12–14

On a sabbath Jesus went to dine at the home of one of the leading Pharisees. He said to the host who invited him, "When you hold a lunch or dinner, do not invite your friends or your brothers or sisters or your relatives or your wealthy neighbors, in case they may invite you back and you have repayment. Rather, when you hold a banquet, invite the poor, the crippled, the lame, the blind; blessed indeed will you be because of their inability to repay you. For you will be repaid at the resurrection of the righteous."

REFLECTION

Imagine who you would invite to the banquet if Jesus said these words to you today. Picture your dining room table filled with those in need. Recall their names if you know them, call to mind their faces, remember their stories from the news on TV or in the newspaper. If you cannot actually invite them to your home, what could you do for them today in the name of Jesus?

PRAYERS — others may be added

Startled by your generous love, O God, we pray:

✦ May the spirit of goodness fill the earth.

That the Eucharistic table of the Church is a place of welcome, we pray: ◆
That humanitarian efforts continue to bring the world's poor to a banquet of bounty, we pray: ◆ *That the disabled, ill, and outcast are welcomed into community celebrations, we pray:* ◆
That our holiday feasts this year welcome new faces to our homes, we pray: ◆

Our Father . . .

Loving Father,
you offer the invitation to life in you
   to every person.
As we respond in gratitude,
may we model your generosity
as we welcome others into our hearts
   and homes.
We ask this through Christ our Lord.
Amen.

✦ *The Lord hears the cry of the poor.*

✠ *Commit your life to the Lord, and he will help you.*

PSALM 40   page 407

READING   *Matthew 5:1–12a*

When Jesus saw the crowds, he went up the mountain, and after he had sat down, his disciples came to him. He began to teach them, saying: / "Blessed are the poor in spirit, / for theirs is the Kingdom of heaven. / Blessed are they who mourn, / for they will be comforted. / Blessed are the meek, / for they will inherit the land. / Blessed are they who hunger and thirst for righteousness, / for they will be satisfied. / Blessed are the merciful, / for they will be shown mercy. / Blessed are the clean of heart, / for they will see God. / Blessed are the peacemakers, / for they will be called children of God. / Blessed are they who are persecuted for the sake of righteousness, / for theirs is the Kingdom of heaven. / Blessed are you when they insult you and persecute you and utter every kind of evil against you falsely because of me. Rejoice and be glad, for your reward will be great in heaven."

REFLECTION

As we remember today all the saints, we call to mind those who have especially influenced us. Our personal patrons, patrons of our Church, those whose names we took at Confirmation are all important saints in our lives. Which recognized and unrecognized saints have showed you what it means to live according to the Beatitudes?

PRAYERS   *others may be added*

With all holy men and women, we pray:

◆ Bless us, O Lord.

For the communion of saints that has guided the Church throughout history, we pray: ◆ *For all saints who have reached across culture and language to spread the Gospel, we pray:* ◆ *For saints past and present who have touched the lepers of their time, we pray:* ◆ *For saints among us, who inspire us to live our faith deeply, we pray:* ◆ *For saints who have gone before us to prepare our heavenly home, we pray:* ◆

Our Father . . .

God of heaven and earth,
we thank you for the way you have uniquely
touched the lives of the saints.
They inspire us in our love for you.
Show us how we, too, are called to be saints.
Give us clean and joyful hearts.
We ask this through our Lord Jesus Christ, your Son,
who lives and reigns with you
in the unity of the Holy Spirit,
one God, forever and ever.
Amen.

✠ *Commit your life to the Lord, and he will help you.*

✚ *The Lord is my shepherd, there is nothing I shall want.*

PSALM 23
page 402

READING
John 14:1–6

Jesus said to his disciples: "Do not let your hearts be troubled. You have faith in God; have faith also in me. In my Father's house there are many dwelling places. If there were not, would I have told you that I am going to prepare a place for you? And if I go and prepare a place for you, I will come back again and take you to myself, so that where I am you also may be. Where I am going you know the way." Thomas said to him, "Master, we do not know where you are going; how can we know the way?" Jesus said to him, "I am the way and the truth and the life. No one comes to the Father except through me."

REFLECTION

Does death frighten you? What comfort do you find in today's Gospel? Concentrate on the word or phrase that brings you the most peace or trust about death for you and for those you have loved. Use it today to center your mind and heart when worry and doubt creep in. Offer it as a prayer for those you have loved who are even now struggling to trust in the embrace of God in the next life.

PRAYERS
others may be added

With vulnerable hearts, we pray:

◆ Heal us, O God.

That the compassion of Jesus permeates the Church's ministry to the dying and to those who mourn, we pray: ◆
That countries that have experienced mass deaths find healing, we pray: ◆
That those who die alone receive the Holy Spirit to accompany them, we pray: ◆ *That all who fear death turn to God for guidance, insight, and growth, we pray:* ◆ *That all those who have died find eternal peace, we pray:* ◆

Our Father . . .

O God, Alpha and Omega,
you created us in love
and desire to see our return to you
    in love.
May our uncertainty and fears
    about death
lead us on a journey to knowing you
and finding solace in your community
    on earth.
We ask this through our Lord Jesus
    Christ, your Son,
who lives and reigns with you
in the unity of the Holy Spirit,
one God, forever and ever.
Amen.

✚ *The Lord is my shepherd, there is nothing I shall want.*

✢ *The Lord made us, we belong to him.*

PSALM 111 *page 417*

READING *Luke 15:8–10*

[So Jesus addressed this parable to the disciples.] "What woman having ten coins and losing one would not light a lamp and sweep the house, searching carefully until she finds it? And when she does find it, she calls together her friends and neighbors and says to them, 'Rejoice with me because I have found the coin that I lost.' In just the same way, I tell you, there will be rejoicing among the angels of God over one sinner who repents."

REFLECTION

Have you ever almost lost a child in a store or on a field trip, or have you waited up late at night worrying about someone who had not yet come home? What a sense of relief and renewed gratitude we feel when that child or loved one finally shows up. We want to embrace him or her and never let go. God sees each of us this way. We are all precious to him, no matter how late or lost or disobedient we have been.

PRAYERS *others may be added*

In gratitude, we pray:

◆ Lord, hear our prayer.

For the Holy Spirit to continue to guide and inspire leaders and servants of the Church, we pray: ◆ *For rescue workers who continue searching in disaster areas for lost and wounded victims, we pray:* ◆ *For shelter workers and supporters who reach out to runaway teens and neglected children, we pray:* ◆ *For friends and neighbors who watch out for one another, we pray:* ◆ *For lost souls who find their way home to God in heaven, we pray:* ◆

Our Father . . .

Lord Jesus,
our Good Shepherd,
you know us each by name
and love us despite our sin.
Lead us back to the Father's arms
 when we are lost,
that we might give thanks for his
 loving embrace.
You live and reign with God
 the Father
in the unity of the Holy Spirit,
one God, forever and ever.
Amen.

✢ *The Lord made us; we belong to him.*

✛ *Commit your life to the Lord and he will help you.*

PSALM 40   *page 407*

READING   *John 10:11–16*

Jesus said: "I am the good shepherd. A good shepherd lays down his life for the sheep. A hired man, who is not a shepherd and whose sheep are not his own, sees a wolf coming and leaves the sheep and runs away, and the wolf catches and scatters them. This is because he works for pay and has no concern for the sheep. I am the good shepherd, and I know mine and mine know me, just as the Father knows me and I know the Father; and I will lay down my life for the sheep. I have other sheep that do not belong to this fold. These also I must lead, and they will hear my voice, and there will be one flock, one shepherd."

REFLECTION

Consider your relationship with your local Bishop(s). Do you see him as a shepherd? Have you read anything he has written in your (arch)diocesan newspaper or for a wider audience? We are blessed with many good leaders; let's take advantage of their prayerful wisdom to help us grow in faith and knowledge.

PRAYERS   *others may be added*

Yearning for guidance, we pray:

◆ Send us a good shepherd.

For all priests who follow Christ and will soon serve as Bishops, we pray: ◆ *For heirs to thrones and political nominees, we pray:* ◆ *For hiring committees for our schools, agencies, and hospitals, we pray:* ◆ *For our parish community, which needs volunteers for various roles, we pray:* ◆

Our Father . . .

Lord Jesus,
our Good Shepherd,
you know your people and we
    know you.
You know our need for protection
    and guidance.
Send us bishops, priests, deacons,
    religious, and active laity
to enliven and lead your Church.
You live and reign with God
    the Father
in the unity of the Holy Spirit,
one God, forever and ever.
Amen.

✛ *Commit your life to the Lord and he will help you.*

✚ *The heart of the just one is firm,*
trusting in the Lord.

PSALM 42   page 408

READING   Luke 16:9–13

Jesus said to his disciples: "I tell you, make friends for yourselves with dishonest wealth, so that when it fails, you will be welcomed into eternal dwellings. The person who is trustworthy in very small matters is also trustworthy in great ones; and the person who is dishonest in very small matters is also dishonest in great ones. If, therefore, you are not trustworthy with dishonest wealth, who will trust you with true wealth? If you are not trustworthy with what belongs to another, who will give you what is yours? No servant can serve two masters. He will either hate one and love the other, or be devoted to one and despise the other. You cannot serve God and mammon."

REFLECTION

What is your attitude about small transgressions concerning money? Have you cheated on your taxes? Have you short-changed a tip? Overlooked a financial error that favored your account? Taken something small that wasn't yours? Today we are reminded that these small actions reflect our character and our trustworthiness. Let us vow to be honest in all ways, big and small, and to make amends where necessary for the past.

PRAYERS   *others may be added*

Searching our consciences, we pray:

◆ Make us pure of heart.

That audits and overseers in the Church serve well to maintain a house of integrity and order, we pray: ◆
That checks and balances in our own government succeed in defeating corruption and raising up honesty, we pray: ◆ *That all who struggle with money concerns find wise counsel and strength to make good decisions, we pray:* ◆ *That our own community may be a generous and smart steward of resources, we pray:* ◆

Our Father . . .

God of justice and mercy,
may we always follow the path that
leads to you.
When we stray, bring us back,
that our hearts may be renewed
and our lives may honor you.
Grant this through Christ our Lord.
Amen.

✚ *The heart of the just one is firm,*
trusting in the Lord.

✢ *In you, O Lord, I have found my peace.*

PSALM 139 *page 420*

READING *Matthew 25:1–13*

Jesus told his disciples this parable: "The kingdom of heaven will be like ten virgins who took their lamps and went out to meet the bridegroom. Five of them were foolish and five were wise. The foolish ones, when taking their lamps, brought no oil with them, but the wise brought flasks of oil with their lamps. Since the bridegroom was long delayed, they all became drowsy and fell asleep. At midnight, there was a cry, 'Behold, the bridegroom! Come out to meet him!' Then all those virgins got up and trimmed their lamps. The foolish ones said to the wise, 'Give us some of your oil, for our lamps are going out.' But the wise ones replied, 'No, for there may not be enough for us and you. Go instead to the merchants and buy some for yourselves.' While they went off to buy it, the bridegroom came and those who were ready went into the wedding feast with him. Then the door was locked. Afterwards the other virgins came and said, 'Lord, Lord, open the door for us!' But he said in reply, 'Amen, I say to you, I do not know you.' Therefore, stay awake, for you know neither the day nor the hour.'"

PRAYERS *others may be added*

Preparing our hearts for God, we pray:

◆ Lord, hear our prayer.

For all Christians who have grown slack in their faith, that they may turn again to God with earnestness, we pray: ◆ *For all busy Americans caught up in so many of life's opportunities, who have put faith on the back burner, we pray:* ◆ *For friends and family ignoring the call to repentance and forgiveness, that they may attend to the most important relationships in life, we pray:* ◆ *For our community, when it moves away from service to others and generous stewardship, that it be renewed, we pray:* ◆

Our Father . . .

Lord Jesus Christ,
we await your Second Coming,
and the chance to eat with you at the
    heavenly banquet.
May we not be like the foolish
    bridesmaids, forgetting to prepare
    ourselves for you.
May we attend to your presence in
    our life,
praying and serving you at all times.
You live and reign with God
    the Father
in the unity of the Holy Spirit,
one God, forever and ever.
Amen.

✢ *In you, O Lord, I have found my peace.*

✦ *The precepts of the Lord give joy to the heart.*

PSALM 51   page 409

READING   Luke 17:1–6

Jesus said to his disciples, "Things that cause sin will inevitably occur, but woe to the one through whom they occur. It would be better for him if a millstone were put around his neck and he be thrown into the sea than for him to cause one of these little ones to sin. Be on your guard! If your brother sins, rebuke him; and if he repents, forgive him. And if he wrongs you seven times in one day and returns to you seven times saying, 'I am sorry,' you should forgive him."

And the Apostles said to the Lord, "Increase our faith." The Lord replied, "If you have faith the size of a mustard seed, you would say to this mulberry tree, 'Be uprooted and planted in the sea,' and it would obey you."

REFLECTION

It takes great faith to forgive. It can be easy for us to hold a grudge or insist that the other person is unforgivable. We can be a sign of hope for the world when we see goodness in another, even one who has wronged us. Think of those who have forgiven even murderers of family members and how the media takes notice. Ask God for the desire and strength to initiate reconciliation with someone who has hurt you. Call for justice and offer forgiveness. Pray for the ability to move past this pain.

PRAYERS   *others may be added*

Yearning for wisdom and courage, we pray:

◆ Soften our hearts, O Lord.

For the judicial ministries of the Church, that Christ's justice and mercy be their guide, we pray: ◆ *For the judicial courts and incarceration systems in our country, that the opportunity for forgiveness and reconciliation remains an option, we pray:* ◆ *For those in conflict, that God grants them the wisdom to know when to seek justice and when to seek forgiveness, we pray:* ◆ *For an ability to let go of resentment in all of us, we pray:* ◆

Our Father . . .

Merciful God,
great faith demands great sacrifice and great vulnerability.
Help us to trust you when we must face those who wronged us.
Help us not to be dominated by anger and revenge, but mercy.
May we be instruments in bringing peace to the world.
We ask this through Christ our Lord.
Amen.

✦ *The precepts of the Lord give joy to the heart.*

✝ *In you, O Lord, I have found
my peace.*

PSALM 139   page 420

READING   Luke 17:7–10

Jesus said to the Apostles: "Who among you would say to your servant who has just come in from plowing or tending sheep in the field, 'Come here immediately and take your place at table'? Would he not rather say to him, 'Prepare something for me to eat. Put on your apron and wait on me while I eat and drink. You may eat and drink when I am finished'? Is he grateful to that servant because he did what was commanded? So should it be with you. When you have done all you have been commanded, say, 'We are unprofitable servants; we have done what we were obliged to do.'"

REFLECTION

Today we take a lesson from service workers everywhere. Watch the wait staff next time you are in a restaurant—or better yet, the cooks and busboys. What humility it takes to serve without reward or appreciation! What about housekeeping staff in the last hotel you stayed in? Did you notice them? What must their days be like, cleaning up after others for little pay? We, as servants of God, should serve with as much humility. Let us go about obeying, loving, assisting, witnessing, and sharing what we have, all without asking for any recognition. We rest in God's love and faithfulness and need nothing more.

PRAYERS   *others may be added*

*In humility, we bring our prayers
to God:*

◆ May life in Christ be our reward.

For all the faithful, that we receive each day of opportunities to love and serve as a gift, we pray: ◆ *For the lowly around the world, that they be richly blessed for the example they are to the powerful of how to live as Christ did, we pray:* ◆ *For religious women, who have served God in hospitals, schools, parishes, and charity work, we pray:* ◆ *For those who perform the most demeaning and low-paid jobs, we pray:* ◆ *For those who search through garbage heaps to survive, we pray:* ◆ *For those who suffer humiliation, that God may lift them out of their pain, we pray:* ◆

Our Father . . .

Merciful and just God,
you have made us your own
and sent us into the world to serve.
Give us humble hearts, eager to do
    your will.
Help us learn from your little ones,
who serve tirelessly in their work,
their families, and their communities.
Open our eyes to see them
    everywhere,
and lead us in your way of service.
We ask this through Christ our Lord.
Amen.

✝ *In you, O Lord, I have found
my peace.*

✦ *The Lord is my shepherd, there is nothing I shall want.*

PSALM 40   *page 407*

READING   *John 2:13–17*

Since the Passover of the Jews was near, Jesus went up to Jerusalem. He found in the temple area those who sold oxen, sheep, and doves, as well as the money-changers seated there. He made a whip out of cords and drove them all out of the temple area, with the sheep and oxen, and spilled the coins of the money-changers and overturned their tables, and to those who sold doves he said, "Take these out of here, and stop making my Father's house a market-place." His disciples recalled the words of Scripture, *Zeal for your house will consume me.*

REFLECTION

Remember the beautiful and varied churches you have worshipped in throughout your life. How has their structure, their soaring ceilings, their detailed art inspired your faith? These important "temples" give us sacred space, where we may more easily be in touch with the holy presence of God, and be mindful of our own baptismal call to holiness. Thus inspired, we go out to address the needs of the world.

PRAYERS   *others may be added*

Aware of God's presence in our lives, we pray:

◆ May we honor what is sacred.

For the beautiful diversity of Church architecture, which glorifies God and offers a holy setting for worship, we pray: ◆ *For churches that are the last sanctuaries of peace in violent neighborhoods and war zones, we pray:* ◆ *For all who try to carve out sacred time and space in a secular culture, we pray:* ◆ *For those who clean, maintain, and fund the needs of our church buildings, we pray:* ◆

Our Father . . .

Almighty God,
we are your children,
made for you,
and we need glimpses of the
    transcendent.
May our places of worship
give you glory and lead souls to you.
Grant this through Christ our Lord.
Amen.

✦ *The Lord is my shepherd, there is nothing I shall want.*

✦ *Commit your life to the Lord, and he will help you.*

PSALM 40   page 407

READING   Matthew 16:15–19

[Jesus] said to [the disciples], "But who do you say that I am?" Simon Peter said in reply, "You are the Christ, the Son of the living God." Jesus said to him in reply, "Blessed are you, Simon son of Jonah. For flesh and blood has not revealed this to you, but my heavenly Father. And so I say to you, you are Peter, and upon this rock I will build my Church, and the gates of the netherworld shall not prevail against it. I will give you the keys to the Kingdom of heaven. Whatever you bind on earth shall be bound in heaven; and whatever you loose on earth shall be loosed in heaven."

REFLECTION

As Catholics, we firmly believe that the Holy Spirit has worked and continues to work in and through our Church and our apostolic leaders. This thought can sustain us when we are unsure of the direction of our world, or even struggling with a question of the Church. As we read, question, dialogue, and discuss the issues of our time, we know that the Holy Spirit is working within it all. No matter how dismal things may seem, God has permanently reached into and allowed grace to flourish in our world.

PRAYERS   others may be added

Standing on the rock, we pray:

◆ Holy Spirit, lead us to victory.

For the Roman Catholic Church, which has withstood the tests of time, that she may follow the Spirit's lead through any struggle today or in the future, we pray: ◆ *For peace and justice to win in the battle against all evil, we pray:* ◆ *For places that seem destroyed, abandoned, and without hope, that God may bring forth new life, we pray:* ◆ *For any of us, when we falter, that we may find absolute goodness in the foundation of our faith, Jesus Christ, we pray:* ◆

Our Father . . .

God, our rock,
when all the world swirls with chaos
   and confusion,
you are there.
Give us confidence and courage
in the face of struggles,
knowing your Church is filled with
   your Spirit.
We ask this through our Lord Jesus
   Christ, your Son,
who lives and reigns with you
in the unity of the Holy Spirit,
one God, forever and ever.
Amen.

✦ *Commit your life to the Lord, and he will help you.*

✦ *Commit your life to the Lord, and he will help you.*

PSALM 40   *page 407*

READING   *Matthew 25:35–40*

Jesus said to his disciples: For I was hungry and you gave me food, I was thirsty and you gave me drink, a stranger and you welcomed me, naked and you clothed me, ill and you cared for me, in prison and you visited me.' Then the righteous will answer him and say, 'Lord, when did we see you hungry and feed you, or thirsty and give you drink? When did we see you a stranger and welcome you, or naked and clothe you? When did we see you ill or in prison, and visit you?' And the king will say to them in reply, 'Amen, I say to you, whatever you did for one of the least brothers of mine, you did for me.'"

REFLECTION

Who is hungry? The children of the developing world, for starters. Who is a stranger to you? One you cannot understand? Perhaps a teenager, expressing him or herself in dark clothes and bizarre music. Who is naked? The victims of child pornography, certainly. Who is ill? The homeless addict, most likely suffering also from mental illness and without medical care. Who is in prison? A greatly disproportionate number of young black men. What have we done for each of these brothers and sisters of Christ?

PRAYERS   *others may be added*

Seeing Christ in the faces of those in need, we pray:

◆ Lord, hear our prayer.

For the Church, that she reaches out to all those whom the world ignores, we pray: ◆ *For bold servants to the poor, like St. Martin, we pray:* ◆ *For all those who are in need, especially those we do not remember, we pray:* ◆ *For saint-like love for the poor among all of us, we pray:* ◆ *For those who have died of hunger, thirst, and sickness, we pray:* ◆

Our Father . . .

Merciful God,
you know the hungers and suffering
   of all the world.
Your Son Jesus walks with all who
   are in need.
May we follow in the footsteps
of St. Martin of Tours
and respond to the cries of the poor.
Grant this through Christ our Lord.
Amen.

✦ *Commit your life to the Lord, and he will help you.*

✦ *The Lord is my shepherd, there is nothing I shall want.*

PSALM 40 — page 407

READING — John 17:20–22, 24a

Jesus raised his eyes to heaven and said: "Holy Father, I pray not only for these, but also for those who will believe in me through their word, so that they may all be one, as you, Father, are in me and I in you, that they also may be in us, that the world may believe that you sent me. And I have given them the glory you gave me, so that they may be one, as we are one, I in them and you in me, that they may be brought to perfection as one, that the world may know that you sent me, and that you loved them even as you loved me. Father, they are your gift to me."

REFLECTION

Christ's loving desire that all of us be unified through him comes through strongly in this reading. Today we can focus on what we hold in common with our brothers and sisters. When divisions arise, lovingly bring to the forefront what is most important and unifies us. As we do this in our homes, schools, parishes, and communities, we cooperate in Christ's desire that we may be one. We can be unifiers, organizers, peacemakers, and foundation builders.

PRAYERS — *others may be added*

Desiring unity, we pray:

◆ Make us one in you, O Lord.

For all followers of Christ, we pray: ◆ *For all peoples of the earth, surpassing national boundaries, languages, and cultures, we pray:* ◆ *For schools, neighborhoods, and communities, that our common goals may supersede our differences, we pray:* ◆ *For our community of faith, that we may grow in our relationship with God and one another, we pray:* ◆

Our Father . . .

Lord Jesus, our brother,
you called upon the Father
to bring about unity for
    your followers.
You knew the importance of being of
    one mind and heart.
May we today work toward that ideal,
overcoming divisions and focusing on
    life in you.
You live and reign with God the
    Father
in the unity of the Holy Spirit,
one God, forever and ever.
Amen.

✦ *The Lord is my shepherd, there is nothing I shall want.*

    Today's reading is from the memorial, Lectionary #674.

✦ *Forever I will sing the goodness of the Lord.*

PSALM 100 *page 414*

READING *Matthew 25:14–15, 19–21*

Jesus told his disciples this parable: "A man going on a journey called in his servants and entrusted his possessions to them. To one he gave five talents; to another, two; to a third, one—to each according to his ability. Then he went away.

"After a long time the master of those servants came back and settled accounts with them. The one who had received five talents came forward bringing the additional five. He said, 'Master, you gave me five talents. See, I have made five more.' His master said to him, 'Well done, my good and faithful servant. Since you were faithful in small matters, I will give you great responsibilities. Come, share your master's joy.'"

REFLECTION

Are we tempted to say "It's not fair!" or "Others have it easy"? We may feel the weight of our responsibilities at times, but God's use of us is a reward for the way we have served in the past. If we can see the opportunities we have to welcome others, help where needed, use our gifts, and be leaders for Christ as God's blessings, we can then "share [the] master's joy."

PRAYERS *others may be added*

As faithful servants, we pray:

◆ Let us share in your joy.

For the Pope, Bishops, and all leaders of the Church, that large workloads and great influence are seen as privileged ways to serve God, we pray: ◆ *For all Christians who use and develop their talents to their greatest degree, we pray:* ◆ *For those who mistakenly think other lives look easy, that they will refocus on the best ways they can love and serve the Lord, we pray:* ◆ *For our attentiveness to every task and opportunity God sets before us, big or small, we pray:* ◆

Our Father . . .

Wise God,
grower of the vineyard,
you see the big picture:
each person's choices and life journey.
May we silence our inner doubts
    and jealousies
and rejoice in doing your will.
May we aspire to be your good and
    faithful servants.
We ask this through our Lord Jesus
    Christ, your Son,
who lives and reigns with you in the
    unity of the Holy Spirit,
one God, forever and ever.
Amen.

✦ *Forever I will sing the goodness of the Lord.*

✛ *Go out to all the world, and tell the Good News.*

PSALM 25   *page 403*

READING   *Luke 18:35–43*

As Jesus approached Jericho a blind man was sitting by the roadside begging, and hearing a crowd going by, he inquired what was happening. They told him, "Jesus of Nazareth is passing by." He shouted, "Jesus, Son of David, have pity on me!" The people walking in front rebuked him, telling him to be silent, but he kept calling out all the more, "Son of David, have pity on me!" Then Jesus stopped and ordered that he be brought to him; and when he came near, Jesus asked him, "What do you want me to do for you?" He replied, "Lord, please let me see." Jesus told him, "Have sight; your faith has saved you." He immediately received his sight and followed him, giving glory to God. When they saw this, all the people gave praise to God.

REFLECTION

When the other people saw the change in the blind man, they, too, gave praise to God. When we are faithful to him, others notice. If we do something wrong, and ask forgiveness, we stand out. If we consider ourselves equal to others, and no better, people see that. When we make changes in our lives, we can inspire those around us. If we accept God's gifts to us and the Holy Spirit working in us, we help build the kingdom of God.

PRAYERS   *others may be added*

Conscious of others looking to us for an example, we pray:

◆ Change us, Lord, and change the world.

For Church leaders, that extraordinary use of their own gifts inspires others to give time, talent, and treasure on behalf of Christ, we pray: ◆ *For faithful Christians committed to daily prayer, service to others, joy, and purity, that they carry a revolution wherever they go, we pray:* ◆ *For anyone waiting for a reason to change, that their own salvation and the salvation of others is reason enough, we pray:* ◆ *For attention to our brothers and sisters in Christ, that we give praise to God when one among us is healed, forgiven, reborn, or found, we pray:* ◆

Our Father . . .

Lord Jesus, our healer,
your love and forgiveness changes us
    again and again.
May our faithful response be a model
    to others.
May they feel welcomed and turn to
    you in their needs.
You live and reign with God
    the Father
in the unity of the Holy Spirit,
one God, forever and ever.
Amen.

✛ *Go out to all the world, and tell the Good News.*

✝ *The Lord made us; we belong to him.*

PSALM 130 *page 418*

READING *Luke 19:2–10*

Now a man there named Zacchaeus, who was a chief tax collector and also a wealthy man, was seeking to see who Jesus was; but he could not see him because of the crowd, for he was short in stature. So he ran ahead and climbed a sycamore tree in order to see Jesus, who was about to pass that way. When he reached the place, Jesus looked up and said, "Zacchaeus, come down quickly, for today I must stay at your house." And he came down quickly and received him with joy.

REFLECTION

Ask Christ to be a guest in your home for dinner tonight. Can you be so bold as to ask others at the table to also consider Christ present? What habits have you formed that need to be purged, such as disparaging others' reputations, hateful comments, sarcasm that hurts one another, silence meant to cut off relationship, or greed in consumption when others have so little? Find a symbol or object to place on your table as a reminder that Christ is present every evening.

PRAYERS *others may be added*

Opening ourselves, we pray:

◆ Lord, hear our prayer.

For an awareness of Christ's presence in the offices, rectories, sanctuaries, and meeting places of the Church, we pray: ◆ *For a sense of Christ's spirit in community forums, business deals, and public debates, we pray:* ◆ *For a sharing of the love of Christ in families and neighborhoods, we pray:* ◆ *For openness to Christ in every conversation we have, we pray:* ◆

Our Father . . .

Lord Jesus Christ,
you sat down with Zacchaeus,
and you sit down with each of us
each time we gather for a meal.
May our meals and our lives be
    worthy of your company.
Though we are sinners,
help us to welcome you in faith.
You live and reign with God
    the Father
in the unity of the Holy Spirit,
one God, forever and ever.
Amen.

✝ *The Lord made us; we belong to him.*

✦ *The Lord is my light and my salvation.*

PSALM 33 — page 404

READING — *2 Maccabees 7:1, 27–29*

It happened that seven brothers with their mother were arrested and tortured with whips and scourges by the king, to force them to eat pork in violation of God's law.

In derision of the cruel tyrant, [the mother] leaned over close to her [youngest] son and said in their native language: "Son, have pity on me, who carried you in my womb for nine months, nursed you for three years, brought you up, educated and supported you to your present age. I beg you, child, to look at the heavens and the earth and see all that is in them; then you will know that God did not make them out of existing things; and in the same way the human race came into existence. Do not be afraid of this executioner, but be worthy of your brothers and accept death, so that in the time of mercy I may receive you again with them."

REFLECTION

What would you say to your child in your last hour? This mother wanted to convince her son of the lasting truth of God's existence and creative power. She wanted, more than anything, for her son to remain faithful to God and to share with her in eternal life. Consider writing this down for your loved ones even now.

PRAYERS — *others may be added*

Thinking of our own children and dear ones, we pray:

◆ Lord, hear our prayer.

For pastors, full of love for their flocks, that they may convert hearts to knowing Jesus, we pray: ◆ *For wise old ones, whose knowledge of the human and divine story is vast, that they may pass on their insights, we pray:* ◆ *For those who are dying alone, that they may find someone with whom to share their final words, we pray:* ◆ *For the courage to speak our heart's deepest convictions to our children, parents, and loved ones, we pray:* ◆

Our Father . . . .

Magnificent God,
our belief in you is inspired
by your revelation in the world and in
    your Son Jesus.
May we not hold this truth inside,
but share it with those whom we love
    and those who will listen.
Bring all to their knees in wonder
    at you.
We ask this through Christ our Lord.
Amen.

✦ *The Lord is my light and my salvation.*

✦ *Commit your life to the Lord, and he will help you.*

PSALM 40 · *page 407*

READING *Luke 6:27–31, 35*

Jesus said to his disciples: "To you who hear I say, love your enemies, do good to those who hate you, bless those who curse you, pray for those who mistreat you. To the person who strikes you on one cheek, offer the other one as well, and from the person who takes your cloak, do not withhold even your tunic. Give to everyone who asks of you, and from the one who takes what is yours do not demand it back. Do to others as you would have them do to you . . . . love your enemies and do good to them, and lend expecting nothing back; then your reward will be great and you will be children of the Most High, for he himself is kind to the ungrateful and the wicked."

REFLECTION

With whom is it hard for you to spend time? Spend more time with them. With whom is it hard for you to do business? Do more business with them. With whom is it hard for you to work on a project? Choose him or her for a partner. Who has asked you to share more than is fair? Ask what more you can do for them. This counter intuitive instruction shows us what it really means to love our enemies. We must spend time with them, get to know them, welcome them into our lives.

PRAYERS *others may be added*

With obedience to God, we pray:

◆ Teach us to love our enemies.

For clergy and laity, traditional and progressive, old and young within the Church, we pray: ◆ *For ethnic rivals, tribal groups, and religious avengers, we pray:* ◆ *For Republicans and Democrats, conservatives and liberals, libertarians, greens, and independents, we pray:* ◆ *For employers and employees, sparring neighbors, opposing gangs, and angry citizens, we pray:* ◆ *For our social acquaintances, close friends, and dearest family members, we pray:* ◆

Our Father . . .

Lord Jesus,
you taught that the greatest love is for
    one's enemies,
as well as one's friends.
Show us our enemies,
those we avoid and about whom
    we gossip.
Show us how to love them and see
    them as your children.
Challenge us to face our discomfort,
    dislike, and lack of love.
You live and reign with God
    the Father
in the unity of the Holy Spirit,
one God, forever and ever.
Amen.

✦ *Commit your life to the Lord, and he will help you.*

✦ *The Lord made us, we belong to him.*

PSALM 130 *page 418*

READING *Luke 19:45–48*

Jesus entered the temple area and proceeded to drive out those who were selling things, saying to them, "It is written, *My house shall be a house of prayer, but you have made it a den of thieves.*" And every day he was teaching in the temple area. The chief priests, the scribes, and the leaders of the people, meanwhile, were seeking to put him to death, but they could find no way to accomplish their purpose because all the people were hanging on his words.

REFLECTION

What is the atmosphere in our churches? Is our mission to spread the Good News intact? Are we engaged with the person of Jesus, and taking his love out into the world? Is prayer at the heart of our worship? We do not want to fall into other malicious or even benign agendas. We do not want to become obsessed with our "bottom line." Let us be conscious of our role and responsibilities as a people of God building his kingdom.

PRAYERS *others may be added*

Aware of our need for God, we pray:

◆ Wash clean our houses of worship.

For the one, holy, catholic and apostolic church, that it is firmly rooted in Jesus Christ, we pray: ◆ *For the local church of every diocese, that it is guided in times of transition and restructuring, we pray:* ◆ *For Church leaders from Rome to parish councils, that they spend significant time listening to God's voice, we pray:* ◆ *For the welcoming ministries of our Church, that we reach out to all our members, we pray:* ◆

Our Father . . .

Gracious God,
you enliven our communities,
our worship, and our service
   to others.
Guide our Church at all times,
that we may be a sign to the world
of your goodness.
Eliminate any other agendas
   or purposes,
save that of doing your will.
We ask this through Christ our Lord.
Amen.

✦ *The Lord made us, we belong to him.*

Optional memorials of the Dedication of the Basilicas of St. Peter and St. Paul in Rome, apostles; St. Rose Philippine Duchesne, virgin

✦ *In you, O Lord, I have found*
my peace.

PSALM 100 *page 414*

READING *Luke 20:27–36*

Some Sadducees, those who deny that there is a resurrection, came forward and put this question to Jesus, saying, "Teacher, Moses wrote for us, *If someone's brother dies leaving a wife but no child, his brother must take the wife and raise up descendants for his brother.* Now there were seven brothers; the first married a woman but died childless. Then the second and the third married her, and likewise all the seven died childless. Finally the woman also died. Now at the resurrection whose wife will that woman be? For all seven had been married to her." Jesus said to them, "The children of this age marry and remarry; but those who are deemed worthy to attain to the coming age and to the resurrection of the dead neither marry nor are given in marriage. They can no longer die, for they are like angels; and they are the children of God because they are the ones who will rise."

REFLECTION

The mystery of life after death is hard to explain to an adult, let alone a child. How do you describe the reality of a God of the living? What lesson is there for us in life in our images and understanding of heaven? Many great writers have explored ideas of what heaven might be like. These depictions tell us something of the writers' ideas about God and humanity. *Explore your own ideas about eternal life, and consider exploring other creative images in order to develop your images of God, self, and others. Above all, live today as if you are already in the embrace of God (for you are!).*

PRAYERS *others may be added*

Awed by our God, we pray:

◆ Bring us to life with you.

That the house of the Lord on earth may reflect the house of the Lord in heaven, we pray: ◆ That humanity's search for meaning and understanding of life after death leads to relationship with the God of creation, we pray: ◆ That human attempts to understand eternal life through art and literature glorify God, we pray: ◆ That each of us lives in such joy that we witness to the promise of life in God, we pray: ◆

Our Father . . .

Eternal God,
your ways are unknown to us.
Your view of time and space is
    beyond us.
We know only your love and the gift
    of your Son.
May our curiosity and longing for you
lead us ever deeper into the mystery
    of life with you.
We ask this through Christ our Lord.
Amen.

✦ *In you, O Lord, I have found*
my peace.

✠ *Go out to all the world, and tell the Good News.*

PSALM 23 *page 402*

READING *Matthew 25:31–34*

Jesus said to his disciples: "When the Son of Man comes in his glory, and all the angels with him, he will sit upon his glorious throne, and all the nations will be assembled before him. And he will separate them one from another, as a shepherd separates the sheep from the goats. He will place the sheep on his right and the goats on his left. Then the king will say to those on his right, 'Come, you who are blessed by my Father. Inherit the kingdom prepared for you from the foundation of the world.'"

REFLECTION

In the end, we all are and will be equal before God. Our nationality, race, gender, age, career, and possessions mean nothing. When God judges us on our readiness for eternal life with him, it will be our love, faith, and service to others on which our status will rest. We may have fulfilled this mission in culturally specific ways, but behind all of our actions lies a deeper motivation.

PRAYERS *others may be added*

Assembled before you as one, O God, we pray:

◆ Judge us by our love.

For all members of the Church from every continent and in every nation, we pray: ◆ *For all kings, presidents, heads of state, as well as those who cook for, clean up after, and serve others, we pray:* ◆ *For divided classes, groups, cliques, and families, we pray:* ◆ *For our community, that we may be one in Christ despite our differences, we pray:* ◆

Our Father . . .

Lord Jesus Christ our King,
you rule over every nation and earthly
    power.
The ultimate judgment day will
    wash away
all human status and recognition.
All that will remain
is our love for you and for others.
May we be worthy of life with you.
You live and reign with God
    the Father
in the unity of the Holy Spirit,
one God, forever and ever.
Amen.

✠ *Go out to all the world, and tell the Good News.*

✠ *Blessed is the Virgin Mary who kept the word of God and pondered it in her heart.*

CANTICLE   page 422

READING   Matthew 12:46–50

While Jesus was speaking to the crowds, his mother and his brothers appeared outside, wishing to speak with him. Someone told him, "Your mother and your brothers are standing outside, asking to speak with you." But he said in reply to the one who told him, "Who is my mother? Who are my brothers?" And stretching out his hand toward his disciples, he said, "Here are my mother and my brothers. For whoever does the will of my heavenly Father is my brother, and sister, and mother."

REFLECTION

What is the youngest age you can remember being aware of God? Loving God? The children in our lives or at church around us may be sensing God's presence and searching for answers. We may learn more about him from reflecting on our first memories of divine love or guidance, or from reaching out to children we know and asking them to tell us what they sense of God.

PRAYERS   *others may be added*

In the presence of our loving God, we pray:

◆ Lord, hear our prayer.

For all clergy and lay ministers of the Church, that they call upon their earliest days of faith for inspiration, we pray: ◆ *For all children, that their eager, curious minds lead them to the story of Jesus, we pray:* ◆ *For all who doubt or struggle with faith, that they may be comforted, we pray:* ◆ *For our church, that it be a place of uplifting prayer and the presence of God, we pray:* ◆

Our Father . . .

Lord Jesus, Lamb of God,
your mother Mary stood out for
her faithfulness.
May we call to mind how our hearts
stirred at the presence of God.
May we be renewed to a
child-like faith.
You live and reign with God
the Father
in the unity of the Holy Spirit,
one God, forever and ever.
Amen.

✠ *Blessed is the Virgin Mary who kept the word of God and pondered it in her heart.*

✢ *The Lord is my shepherd, there is nothing I shall want.*

PSALM 40   page 407

READING   *Hosea 2:16b, 17cd, 21–22*

Thus says the LORD: / I will lead her into the desert / and speak to her heart. / She shall respond there as in the days of her youth, / when she came up from the land of Egypt. /

I will espouse you to me forever: / I will espouse you in right and in justice, / in love and in mercy; / I will espouse you in fidelity, / and you shall know the Lord.

REFLECTION

Physical and symbolic deserts abound, but we usually avoid them. Think of empty waiting rooms, long stretches of highway, "boring" Sunday afternoons, and our own churches apart from Mass times. God may want to lead you to a desert such as this, in order to speak. Linger a little longer in the "deserts" of your life, and listen.

PRAYERS   *others may be added*

Allowing ourselves to be led, we pray:

◆ Bring me to the desert.

For Christians busy with the routines of life, that stillness and slowness may be seen with new eyes, we pray: ◆
For urban dwellers, surrounded by concrete and industry, that open spaces may be found, we pray: ◆ *For members of the military, overseas travelers, and those forced to be away from family for long periods of time, that grace may enter their loneliness, we pray:* ◆ *For a welcoming stance toward God when we are lonely, bored, lost, or trapped by a desert, we pray:* ◆

Our Father . . .

Faithful God,
you called your daughter Cecilia and
    she heard your voice.
May we follow your lead, even into
    the desert,
and know your presence in our hearts.
May we see silence and solitude as
    your gifts to us.
We ask this through our Lord Jesus
    Christ, your Son,
who lives and reigns with you
in the unity of the Holy Spirit,
one God, forever and ever.
Amen.

✢ *The Lord is my shepherd, there is nothing I shall want.*

✦ *Go out to all the world, and tell the Good News.*

PSALM 139   *page 420*

READING   *Luke 21:12–19*

Jesus said to the crowd: "They will seize and persecute you, they will hand you over to the synagogues and to prisons, and they will have you led before kings and governors because of my name. It will lead to your giving testimony. Remember, you are not to prepare your defense beforehand, for I myself shall give you a wisdom in speaking that all your adversaries will be powerless to resist or refute. You will even be handed over by parents, brothers, relatives, and friends, and they will put some of you to death. You will be hated by all because of my name, but not a hair on your head will be destroyed. By your perseverance you will secure your lives."

REFLECTION

What public speaker has moved you through charisma and content? Often raw honesty, vulnerability, and personal stories have the greatest impact on others. Do you believe that you, too, with the help of the Holy Spirit, have the ability to influence others' lives for good? Prayerfully reflect on your own story and what in it God is asking you to share with someone else who needs to hear it. If you need motivation to do it now, consider if this were not just the end of the liturgical year, but the end of all time.

PRAYERS   *others may be added*

Inspired by God working in us, we pray:

◆ Let your voice be heard, O Lord.

That representatives of the Church inspire others by their integrity, humility, and faithfulness to God, we pray: ◆ *That cross-cultural exchange through technology may be a conduit for witness to God's love, we pray:* ◆ *That Catholic media inspires its audiences to live like Christ, we pray:* ◆ *That each of us has the courage to tell the truth of what God has done in our lives to those with whom we are closest, we pray:* ◆

Our Father . . .

Almighty God,
may the Spirit of wisdom fill us
as we share the Good News as we
    have experienced it.
May the fire of your love burn
    brightly within us.
We ask this through Christ our Lord.
Amen.

✦ *Go out to all the world, and tell the Good News.*

Optional memorials of St. Clement I, pope, martyr; St. Columban, abbot; Bl. Miguel Agustín Pro, priest, martyr

✦ *The Lord is my shepherd, there is nothing I shall want.*

PSALM 40 page 407

READING John 12:24–26

Jesus said to his disciples: "Amen, amen, I say to you, unless a grain of wheat falls to the ground and dies, it remains just a grain of wheat; but if it dies, it produces much fruit. Whoever loves his life loses it, and whoever hates his life in this world will preserve it for eternal life. Whoever serves me must follow me, and where I am, there also will my servant be. The Father will honor whoever serves me."

REFLECTION

Even as Christians it is hard to see good in death. We think first of loss and what is missing. But if we can think of sacrifice and death in terms of nature, we are reminded that from death comes life. May the courageous, loving martyrs of Vietnam, who knew life would come out of their deaths, lead us forward. May we value what comes from death as much as we value the precious gift of life.

PRAYERS *others may be added*

Opening ourselves to the closeness of death, we pray:

◆ Give us peace in life and death.

That the Church teaches the preciousness of life and the power of death, which leads to life eternal, we pray: ◆ *That Christians may be inspired by those who walk alongside death—the poor, the elderly, hospice workers, and potential martyrs, we pray:* ◆ *That those who face death alone and in fear may feel the martyrs lifting them up, we pray:* ◆ *That all facing death in our community may receive the Anointing of the Sick and the love of their families, we pray:* ◆ *That those who have died experience new life in eternity, we pray:* ◆

Our Father . . .

Crucified Lord,
you knew the hearts of St. Andrew
    Dung-Lac
and his companions.
They gave up life for love of you
and the future of the faith in Vietnam.
May we be open to sacrifice
and the possibility of new life coming
    out of our death.
You live and reign with God
    the Father
in the unity of the Holy Spirit,
one God, forever and ever.
Amen.

✦ *The Lord is my shepherd, there is nothing I shall want.*

✛ *Forever I will sing the goodness of the Lord.*

PSALM 42 — page 408

READING — *Luke 21:29–33*

Jesus told his disciples a parable. "Consider the fig tree and all the other trees. When their buds burst open, you see for yourselves and know that summer is now near; in the same way, when you see these things happening, know that the Kingdom of God is near. Amen, I say to you, this generation will not pass away until all these things have taken place. Heaven and earth will pass away, but my words will not pass away."

REFLECTION

Do you long for the next season? Do you eagerly wait for an approaching holiday? On a deeper level, what do your heart and soul most desire? Jesus tells us, "The Kingdom of God is near." All those holy desires of our hearts, the goodness we ache for—love, justice, peace, harmony, unity, eternal life for all—are near at hand. May we become aware of how deeply we long for and need our God.

PRAYERS — *others may be added*

With deep longing, we pray:

◆ Be with us, Lord.

That the people of God reflect the knowledge that he is with us and also yearn for full unity with him in heaven, we pray: ◆ *That people all over the earth who yearn for world peace will continue to pray and work in hopes of its fulfillment at the end of time, we pray:* ◆ *That all who long for Marriage may find the right person with whom to share life, we pray:* ◆ *That the longing of children and for good things may remind us of our heart's deepest desires, we pray:* ◆ *That all who have died rejoice in the fulfillment of their deepest longings for God, we pray:* ◆

Our Father . . .

Lord of heaven and earth,
you made us in love,
and you wait to welcome us into your
   kingdom.
May our time on earth be spent
   glorifying you
and working to build your kingdom
   on earth.
Call to us;
invite us ever closer to the joy
that will come in seeing you face
   to face.
Grant this through Christ our Lord.
Amen.

✛ *Forever I will sing the goodness of the Lord.*

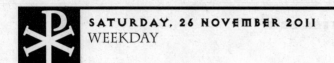

✦ *The Lord is my light and my salvation.*

PSALM 25
page 403

READING
Luke 21:34–36

Jesus said to his disciples: "Beware that your hearts do not become drowsy from carousing and drunkenness and the anxieties of daily life, and that day catch you by surprise like a trap. For that day will assault everyone who lives on the face of the earth. Be vigilant at all times and pray that you have the strength to escape the tribulations that are imminent and to stand before the Son of Man."

REFLECTION

Tiredness—such a familiar feeling. Do we bring it on ourselves at times? Where have we "wasted" energy lately? Watching TV, fulfilling commitments we felt pressured into, passing gossip, being angry or worried? Let us conserve our energy and time for what really matters. Avoiding negative drains on our minds and hearts can help. Taking time for stillness, rest, and reflection can refocus our energy into living as a disciple.

PRAYERS
others may be added

Weary with life's distractions, we pray:

◆ Lord, hear our prayer.

That Christians living in solitude, simplicity, and vowed religious life challenge us all to remain focused on life in Christ, we pray: ◆ *That those in developing countries who live with so little inspire us to give up our excess, we pray:* ◆ *That anyone addicted to food, television, shopping, and other gluttonies may break free of this prison and embrace a life of service, we pray:* ◆ *That we support one another in choosing ways to spend our time that reflects our life as disciples, we pray:* ◆

Our Father . . .

Loving God,
you know the many ways we are
    distracted and lose our focus.
Thank you for your Son,
who warned us and offered us new
    life in you.
Pull us away from temptation
and open our hearts to true happiness.
Renew our spirits, that we might walk
    once again with you.
We ask this through Christ our Lord.
Amen.

✦ *The Lord is my light and my salvation.*

✦ *Show us Lord, your love; and grant us your salvation.*

PSALM 67 *page 411*

READING *Mark 13:33–37*

Jesus said to his disciples: "Be watchful! Be alert! You do not know when the time will come. It is like a man traveling abroad. He leaves home and places his servants in charge, each with his own work, and orders the gatekeeper to be on the watch. Watch, therefore; you do not know when the Lord of the house is coming, whether in the evening, or at midnight, or at cockcrow, or in the morning. May he not come suddenly and find you sleeping. What I say to you, I say to all: 'Watch!'"

REFLECTION

As we begin Advent, we long for the return of our God. We re-awaken, roused to renew our faith. Perhaps we have wandered away from God. Perhaps we have become mired in doubt. Or, it may be that we have simply grown apathetic or slack in our faith. Now we become alert. We watch. We wait. We ask God to show his face in the birth of Jesus, once again.

PRAYERS *others may be added*

As we enter the dark stillness of Advent, we pray:

◆ Awaken our hearts, O Lord.

That all Christians will renew their faithful waiting for the Lord this Advent, we pray: ◆ *That leaders who have grown indifferent to suffering and economic disparity in their nations and in the world renew their commitment to serve all people, we pray:* ◆ *That those who have been traveling through life alone open their eyes to the presence of God in the people around them, we pray:* ◆ *That this community practices watchfulness over the forgotten unborn, elderly, and needy of our world, we pray:* ◆

Our Father . . .

Watchful God,
we grow weary and afraid
when we are apart from you.
This Advent, show us your face
in the Church and in the world.
Wrap us in your love,
and show us how to be vigilant
in our love for others and for you,
as we prepare for your Son's coming.
We ask this through Christ our Lord.
Amen.

✦ *Show us Lord, your love; and grant us your salvation.*

✛ *Let us go rejoicing to the house of the Lord.*

PSALM 67   page 411

READING   *Isaiah 2:2–3abc, 5*

In days to come, / the mountain of the LORD's house / shall be established as the highest mountain / and raised above the hills. / All nations shall stream toward it; / many peoples shall come and say: / "Come, let us climb the LORD's mountain, / to the house of the God of Jacob, / That he may instruct us in his ways, / and we may walk in his paths."

O house of Jacob, come, / let us walk in the light of the LORD!

REFLECTION

As we grow more aware of the nations of the world, and our brothers and sisters in faith around the globe, Advent calls us to imagine our heavenly home occupied by "all nations." Just as this was hard to imagine for the Hebrew people who lived very differently from their neighbors, it may be a challenge for us. When we see a woman or man on the news from India, do we imagine our salvation linked with theirs? When we hear of someone suffering in Somalia, do we hope to one day rejoice with them in eternal life? When we meet an immigrant from China, do we realize how much we hold in common because of our Creator? One day we may "climb the LORD's mountain" together and be instructed in his ways. Start today embracing members of all nations.

PRAYERS   *others may be added*

Envisioning the house of the Lord, we pray:

◆ King of Kings, hear our prayer.

For the Pope and all Bishops, that they continue to teach Christians of the global needs of the Church, we pray: ◆
For communication between members of different nations, that increased dialogue leads to greater understanding, we pray: ◆
For an end to poverty and war in every corner of the world, we pray: ◆
For opportunities to welcome and learn from missionaries, exchange students, immigrants, and visitors from foreign countries, we pray: ◆

Our Father . . .

Lord God,
as we await your Son's
    Second Coming,
we imagine the unity of all nations
    under you.
We dream of the reign that you desire:
    peace, justice, and harmony.
May this Advent bring us closer to
    that reality
as we take steps to learn from and
    love all people.
We ask this through Christ our Lord.
Amen.

✛ *Let us go rejoicing to the house of the Lord.*

✚ *Justice shall flourish in his time, and fullness of peace for ever.*

PSALM 67 *page 411*

READING *Isaiah 11:1 – 5, 10*

On that day, / A shoot shall sprout from the stump of Jesse, / and from his roots a bud shall blossom. / The Spirit of the LORD shall rest upon him: / a Spirit of wisdom and of understanding, / a Spirit of counsel and of strength, / a Spirit of knowledge and of fear of the LORD, / and his delight shall be the fear of the LORD. / Not by appearance shall he judge, / nor by hearsay shall he decide, / But he shall judge the poor with justice, / and decide aright for the land's afflicted. / He shall strike the ruthless with the rod of his mouth, / and with the breath of his lips he shall slay the wicked. / Justice shall be the band around his waist, / and faithfulness a belt upon his hips . . .

On that day, / The root of Jesse, / set up as a signal for the nations, / The Gentiles shall seek out, / for his dwelling shall be glorious.

REFLECTION

Watching wild animals on television or even one's own dog chasing a squirrel teaches us something about "animal instinct." There is a natural order of predator and prey, and the struggle for survival can make the consequences severe. How hard, then, it is to imagine the wolf and the lamb side by side, the cow and the bear at peace together, or a little child alone with a lion or cobra.

If God's transformation of the world is powerful enough to tame wild beasts, surely there is hope for us. If we have given up on a bitter grudge, a decimated relationship, or a hard heart, let us renew our hope this Advent. For the Lord says, "There shall be no harm or ruin on all my holy mountain" (Isaiah 11:9).

PRAYERS *others may be added*

Before God, we pray:

◆ Heal us, Prince of Peace.

For a spirit of counsel and strength, a spirit of knowledge and of fear of the Lord among all believers, we pray: ◆
For childlike openness to negotiations for peace among world leaders, we pray: ◆
For relationships broken by hard words, jealousy, or betrayal, we pray: ◆ *For the courage to face our enemies with love, we pray:* ◆

Our Father . . .

Merciful God, you sent your
　　Son Jesus
to bring peace to the earth.
May our Advent preparation be a time
　　of peace making in our families,
　　our communities, and our world.
May your presence among us bring
　　patience, healing, and
　　understanding.
We ask this through Christ our Lord.
Amen.

✚ *Justice shall flourish in his time, and fullness of peace for ever.*

367

✦ *Blessed are all who wait for the Lord.*

PSALM 40   page 407

READING   *Matthew 4:18–22*

As Jesus was walking by the Sea of Galilee, he saw two brothers, Simon who is called Peter, and his brother Andrew, casting a net into the sea; they were fishermen. He said to them, "Come after me, and I will make you fishers of men." At once they left their nets and followed him. He walked along from there and saw two other brothers, James, the son of Zebedee, and his brother John. They were in a boat, with their father Zebedee, mending their nets. He called them, and immediately they left their boat and their father and followed him.

REFLECTION

For fear of being overly pushy with our faith, we may shirk our responsibility for others' souls. To be "fishers of men," we must care deeply about the current and future happiness of those around us. When we see injustice being done, we cannot simply stand aside. When we know someone is being self-destructive, we must reach out. When we sense despair in another, we are obligated to bring hope. This is not a judgmental evangelism; this is the abiding, unconditional love of our God who asks us to follow him by seeking all who are lost.

PRAYERS   *others may be added*

Following Jesus, we pray:

◆ Make us compassionate disciples, O God.

For the pastors of the Church, who are entrusted with the care of souls, that they may tend their flocks with love and mercy, we pray: ◆ For leaders of government at every level, that their stewardship of resources, human potential, and financial investments may be wise and just, we pray: ◆ For those who search the streets of our cities for the homeless, addicts, and lost souls, we pray: ◆ For all Christians, that they know the call to reach out to hurting souls with the love of Christ, we pray: ◆

Our Father . . .

Lord Jesus, our teacher,
as you showed Peter and Andrew the
    way to follow you,
so you show us how to be
    your disciples.
May we listen well,
respond with humility,
and serve you by loving others.
You live and reign with God
    the Father
in the unity of the Holy Spirit,
one God, forever and ever.
Amen.

✦ *Blessed are all who wait for the Lord.*

✦ *Let us go rejoicing to the house of the Lord.*

PSALM 67 page 411

READING *Matthew 7:24–27*

[Jesus said to his disciples:] "Everyone who listens to these words of mine and acts on them will be like a wise man who built his house on rock. The rain fell, the floods came, and the winds blew and buffeted the house. But it did not collapse; it had been set solidly on rock. And everyone who listens to these words of mine but does not act on them will be like a fool who built his house on sand. The rains fell, the floods came, and the winds blew and buffeted the house. And it collapsed and was completely ruined."

REFLECTION

What does rain and wind feel like when it buffets our home? How does it feel when life's trials try to knock us down spiritually? We may have a clue as to the quality of our foundation in Christ, depending on how well we withstand the storms of daily life. If we are resilient, bouncing back from obstacles and challenges with hope and renewed faith, we are probably well-rooted in God. If we find that any new temptation or difficulty threatens to wipe out our faith entirely, we may want to look carefully at our core. Do we harbor doubt, fear, or guilt? These damaging emotions eat away at our trust in God.

PRAYERS *others may be added*

Aware of our strengths and our weaknesses, we pray:

◆ Make us people of great faith.

For the domestic Church, that we build trust and hope in God, we pray: ◆
For those facing intense pressures in the military, government, and law enforcement, that they remain strong amid storms of difficulty, we pray: ◆
For those who are without shelter, adequate food, and basic health care, that their needs may be met, we pray: ◆
For attentiveness to prayer, by which we grow closer to God, we pray: ◆

Our Father . . .

Provident God,
the surest, strongest foundation we
    can find is in you.
May we prioritize our lives according
    to our faith,
trusting in you no matter what storms
    come our way.
You are the rock of our lives,
and our hope is in you.
We ask this through Christ our Lord.
Amen.

✦ *Let us go rejoicing to the house of the Lord.*

✦ *Show us Lord, your love; and grant us your salvation.*

PSALM 67   page 411

READING   *Matthew 9:27–31*

As Jesus passed by, two blind men followed him, crying out, "Son of David, have pity on us!" When he entered the house, the blind men approached him and Jesus said to them, "Do you believe that I can do this?" "Yes, Lord," they said to him. Then he touched their eyes and said, "Let it be done for you according to your faith." And their eyes were opened. Jesus warned them sternly, "See that no one knows about this." But they went out and spread word of him through all that land.

REFLECTION

Are you involved in healing ministries? The skilled work of doctors, nurses, and other health care professionals brings immeasurable relief to patients. But each of us can help heal another as a person of faith. Christ's healing touch cured physical illness, alleviated mental suffering, renewed or sparked faith, returned alienated members of the community, and revealed truth that had been ignored or denied. When we work toward peace, offer comfort, pray for others, listen, and witness to God's work in our lives, we help bring about healing.

PRAYERS   *others may be added*

Offering our gifts for the healing of others, we pray:

◆ Lord, hear our prayer.

For those who administer the sacrament of the Anointing of the Sick, that they may touch those who need physical, mental, or spiritual healing and mediate God's grace, we pray: ◆ *For the American Red Cross, World Health Organization, and all agencies that serve to curtail disease, lessen suffering, and improve health, we pray:* ◆ *For those who are ill, dying, or cut off from relationships because of poor health, that they may be comforted, we pray:* ◆ *For each of us to know how we can help in the healing ministry of Christ, we pray:* ◆

Our Father . . .

Compassionate God,
you know how we long for wholeness
    with you.
You sent your Son Jesus to give sight
    to the blind
and to make the mute speak.
You sent him to cure diseases
and bring all to eternal life.
May we participate in your loving
    plan of salvation
each time we assist another in
    becoming whole.
We ask this through Christ our Lord.
Amen.

✦ *Show us Lord, your love; and grant us your salvation.*

✦ *Blessed are all who wait for the Lord.*

PSALM 40   page 407

READING   Mark 16:15–20

Jesus appeared to the Eleven and said to them: "Go into the whole world and proclaim the Gospel to every creature. Whoever believes and is baptized will be saved; whoever does not believe will be condemned. These signs will accompany those who believe: in my name they will drive out demons, they will speak new languages. They will pick up serpents with their hands, and if they drink any deadly thing, it will not harm them. They will lay hands on the sick, and they will recover." So the Lord Jesus, after he spoke to them, was taken up into heaven and took his seat at the right hand of God. But they went forth and preached everywhere, while the Lord worked with them and confirmed the word through accompanying signs.

REFLECTION

What a privilege it is to be an instrument of God's grace! The apostles "went forth and preached everywhere," and "the Lord worked with them and confirmed the word through accompanying signs." God worked through them, and they cooperated with grace. This Advent, God is waiting to do something great through you. Will you open yourself to the Holy Spirit and work with God? What wondrous results may come!

PRAYERS   *others may be added*

Humbled by God's abundant grace, we pray:

◆ Lord, hear our prayer.

That the grace bestowed on the Church, and all who have cooperated with it, continue to spread God's loving mercy throughout the world, we pray: ◆
That the Spirit of God calls forth men and women to cooperate in bringing about justice, mercy, and peace, we pray: ◆ *That those who feel powerless recognize God's power and submit to his service, we pray:* ◆ *That we believers follow in the footsteps of the apostles, proclaiming the Gospel to all, we pray:* ◆

Our Father . . .

Lord Jesus,
you commissioned your apostles to go
    out into the world,
carrying on your work.
Your servant St. Francis Xavier
    courageously followed this call.
May we, too, humbly take on
    your mission,
healing, preaching, and bringing the
    lost to you,
through the grace of God the Father,
who lives and reigns with you
in the unity of the Holy Spirit,
one God, forever and ever.
Amen.

✦ *Blessed are all who wait for the Lord.*

✦ *Let us go rejoicing to the house of the Lord.*

PSALM 67 *page 411*

READING *Mark 1:1–5, 7–8*

The beginning of the gospel of Jesus Christ the Son of God.

As it is written in Isaiah the prophet: / *Behold, I am sending my messenger ahead of you; / he will prepare your way. / A voice of one crying out in the desert: / "Prepare the way of the Lord, / make straight his paths." /* John the Baptist appeared in the desert proclaiming a baptism of repentance for the forgiveness of sins. People of the whole Judean countryside and all the inhabitants of Jerusalem were going out to him and were being baptized by him in the Jordan River as they acknowledged their sins. . . . And this is what he proclaimed: "One mightier than I is coming after me. I am not worthy to stoop and loosen the thongs of his sandals. I have baptized you with water; he will baptize you with the Holy Spirit."

REFLECTION

How are you preparing for the birth of Christ this Advent? You might picture John the Baptist, with even the detail of how he is dressed, what he is eating, and of course what he is doing — baptizing and proclaiming the coming of the Lord. How does one prepare for the birth of the Christ child, not according to secular norms, but according to a heart of faith? You might dress simply or joyfully. You might eat mindfully, remembering Christ at each meal. You might spend special time in prayer, or share forgiveness with family and friends. You might serve others out of gratitude for the gift we are about to receive.

PRAYERS *others may be added*

Awaiting Christ with joy, we pray:

◆ May our lives give glory to God.

For all Christians, that we help bring the gifts of joy, forgiveness, and rebirth to the world this Advent, we pray: ◆ *For a straightening of the paths of justice before the coming of the Christ child, we pray:* ◆ *For the coming of all sinners to the waters of Baptism, we pray:* ◆ *For physical and spiritual signs of preparation among the members of our parish this Advent, we pray:* ◆

Our Father . . .

Lord Jesus Christ,
John the Baptist calls us to prepare
  for your coming.
May we repent, live intentionally, and
  rejoice in your nearness to us.
May our lives show our deep faith
  in you.
You live and reign with God
  the Father
in the unity of the Holy Spirit,
one God, forever and ever.
Amen.

✦ *Let us go rejoicing to the house of the Lord.*

✛ *Show us Lord, your love; and grant us your salvation.*

PSALM 67   page 411

READING   *Luke 5:21–26*

Then the scribes and Pharisees began to ask themselves, "Who is this who speaks blasphemies? Who but God alone can forgive sins?" Jesus knew their thoughts and said to them in reply, "What are you thinking in your hearts? Which is easier, to say, 'Your sins are forgiven,' or to say, 'Rise and walk'? But that you may know that the Son of Man has authority on earth to forgive sins"—he said to the one who was paralyzed, "I say to you, rise, pick up your stretcher, and go home."

He stood up immediately before them, picked up what he had been lying on, and went home, glorifying God. Then astonishment seized them all and they glorified God, and, struck with awe, they said, "We have seen incredible things today."

REFLECTION

Picture yourself as one of the people bringing a stretcher to Jesus with someone on it who needs healing. This person faces daily suffering; his or her life is permanently affected by some kind of paralysis or illness. Who is this person, that you would find a way through the rooftop to get him or her to Jesus? Opening your eyes to this kind of suffering, and helping bring healing to others are acts of faith. Pray for and reach out to someone suffering today.

PRAYERS   *others may be added*

Aware of our need for Jesus' healing touch, we pray:

◆ Raise us up, and bring us home, Lord.

For Catholic hospitals, their ministry of healing, and all those who come to them in pain, we pray: ◆ *For caregivers of homebound patients, who continue to walk with the suffering toward healing and new life, we pray:* ◆ *For individuals and families facing addiction, illness, depression, and unemployment, that they may overcome these paralyzing obstacles, we pray:* ◆ *For all friends, that we take care of one another, we pray:* ◆

Our Father . . .

Merciful God,
you have deep compassion
for those who are lost and suffering,
and are moved by the faith
of those who bring loved ones to you.
May we continually reach out to all
who are in need of your salvation.
May we be true friends, loving
    companions, and devoted disciples.
We ask this through Christ our Lord.
Amen.

✛ *Show us Lord, your love; and grant us your salvation.*

✛ *Show us Lord, your love; and grant us your salvation.*

PSALM 67   *page 411*

READING   *Isaiah 40:1–2, 9–11*

Comfort, give comfort to my people, / says your God. / Speak tenderly to Jerusalem, and proclaim to her / that her service is at an end, / her guilt is expiated; / Indeed, she has received from the hand of the LORD / double for all her sins.

Go up onto a high mountain, / Zion, herald of glad tidings; / Cry out at the top of your voice, / Jerusalem, herald of good news! / Fear not to cry out / and say to the cities of Judah: / Here is your God! / Here comes with power / the Lord GOD, / who rules by his strong arm; / Here is his reward with him, / his recompense before him, / Like a shepherd he feeds his flock; / in his arms he gathers the lambs, / Carrying them in his bosom, / and leading the ewes with care.

REFLECTION

All of us need comforting. This reading tells us about the gentle love of God, who is like a shepherd to his sheep. Who gave or gives you the greatest comfort? Can you remember being held as a child? Do you have a spouse or friend who speaks to you tenderly, who cares deeply about you? God is like this person. God wants to hold us gently and carefully guide us. Open up to God and allow him to respond with love. Then, in turn, let us be gentle with others and ourselves.

PRAYERS   *others may be added*

Yearning for a gentle touch, we pray:

◆ Comfort us, O God.

For leaders of the Church, who face daily pressures, that they may feel the gentle hand of God upon them, we pray: ◆
For heads of state and military commanders, that they govern with justice and mercy, we pray: ◆
For parents and grandparents, who offer loving care to children from their first days, we pray: ◆ *For those who are unhappy, stressed, and anxious, that they will find peace, we pray:* ◆

Our Father . . .

Loving God,
you are our shepherd,
tending to your flock with great care.
Help us to learn gentleness from you,
and practice it with all those around us.
Forgive us when we go astray,
and make harsh demands of ourselves
    and others.
We ask this through Christ our Lord.
Amen.

✛ *Show us Lord, your love; and grant us your salvation.*

✝ *Blessed are all who wait for
the Lord.*

PSALM 40   *page 407*

READING   *John 10:11–16*

Jesus said: "I am the good shepherd. A
good shepherd lays down his life for the
sheep. A hired man, who is not a shepherd and whose sheep are not his own,
sees a wolf coming and leaves the sheep
and runs away, and the wolf catches and
scatters them. This is because he works
for pay and has no concern for the
sheep. I am the good shepherd, and I
know mine and mine know me, just as
the Father knows me and I know the
Father; and I will lay down my life for
the sheep. I have other sheep that do not
belong to this fold. These also I must
lead, and they will hear my voice, and
there will be one flock, one shepherd."

REFLECTION

*A visit to the Web site of the United
States Conference of Catholic Bishops
reveals the complicated work of shepherding. Not only do our Bishops attend
to the needs of their respective dioceses,
but they work to guide the conscience
of the nation. Their voices address health
care, education, poverty, justice, and
theology. We can learn from their writ-
ings, support the causes they promote,
educate others, and pray for our Bishops and their staff.*

PRAYERS   *others may be added*

*Keeping in mind our earthly
shepherds, we pray:*

◆ Shepherd us, O God.

*For all Bishops, that the source of their
work and their constant companion is
Jesus, we pray: ◆ For the members of
Congress, that the voice of the USCCB
is recognized as a defender of human
dignity, we pray: ◆ For the USCCB staff,
that their eyes and ears are attentive to
the most neglected causes of our world,
we pray: ◆ For greater awareness on our
part about the priorities of our nation's
Bishops, and for action on their behalf,
we pray: ◆*

Our Father . . .

God of wisdom,
we pray for our shepherds,
   the Bishops.
As they lead our communities, cities,
   and countries,
they help shape the world's response
   to you.
May their ministry be strong,
   effective, compassionate,
   and focused.
May we, their flock, be responsive,
   supportive, and faithful,
that, together, may we help bring
   about justice and peace.
We ask this through Christ our Lord.
Amen.

✝ *Blessed are all who wait for
the Lord.*

✦ *Commit your life to the Lord.*

CANTICLE   *page 422*

READING   *Luke 1:38b*

Mary said, "Behold, I am the handmaid of the Lord. May it be done to me according to your word."

REFLECTION

Acceptance does not come easily for many of us. We are more likely to doubt, question, argue, or deny. In some ways, we can only practice acceptance, not "achieve" it. Listen to Mary's words: "Behold, I am the handmaid of the Lord. May it be done to me according to your word." They perfectly capture the attitude of acceptance. Repeating this phrase and asking Mary to show us how to embrace it can lead to deeper acceptance. When we face a difficult situation, a disappointment, or change from expectations, we can choose to stand in Mary's place. We can turn away from knee-jerk reactions and choose to be servants of the Lord. Trusting in God, even if things are very difficult, will ultimately bring us deep peace.

PRAYERS   *others may be added*

Learning from Mary, we pray:

◆ May it be done to us according to your word, O God.

For the people of God, the Church, that this Advent opens our hearts wide to God's plans, we pray: ◆ *For policy makers and strategic planners, that the will of God—for the good of all— permeates our agendas, we pray:* ◆ *For those who are bitter, frustrated, and demanding, that Mary's peace envelops our souls, we pray:* ◆ *For our parish, that the spirit of renewal comes to us in this time of preparation, in whatever form it is needed, we pray:* ◆

Our Father . . .

Holy Son of God,
your mother Mary exemplified
  perfect faith.
May we carefully examine our hearts
  and minds,
that we may adopt the attitude
  of Mary,
trusting you completely
and opening ourselves to the life you
  have planned for us.
You live and reign with God
  the Father
in the unity of the Holy Spirit,
one God, forever and ever.
Amen.

✦ *Commit your life to the Lord.*

✦ *Justice shall flourish in his time, and fullness of peace for ever.*

PSALM 67   page 411

READING   *Matthew 11:16–19*

Jesus said to the crowds: "To what shall I compare this generation? It is like children who sit in marketplaces and call to one another, 'We played the flute for you, but you did not dance, we sang a dirge but you did not mourn.' For John came neither eating nor drinking, and they said, 'He is possessed by a demon.' The Son of Man came eating and drinking and they said, 'Look, he is a glutton and a drunkard, a friend of tax collectors and sinners.' But wisdom is vindicated by her works."

REFLECTION

We quickly judge and easily condemn. In so doing, do we miss something? Could we even miss Jesus himself? Think of times when you have dismissed someone you disliked or disagreed with: She's a snob. He's worthless. That family is a mess. I can't get a thing out of him. I don't know what her problem is. We blame the other, but what would happen if we looked with new eyes? When we humble ourselves and give people the benefit of the doubt, God reveals new things to us. He is present in those we don't understand, from whom we feel different, and of whom we are afraid. All people are children of God, and we learn more about who he is when we open ourselves to the stories and experiences of others.

PRAYERS   *others may be added*

Looking for the face of God, we pray:

◆ Lord, hear our prayer.

That Christians may be known by their attentiveness to all people, no matter how small, frail, or marginalized, we pray: ◆ *That people of different cultures, tribes, and religions will see each other with new eyes, we pray:* ◆ *That first impressions may give way to radical openness to the truth of another, we pray:* ◆ *That our community may be a place of welcome for all people, we pray:* ◆

Our Father . . .

Emmanuel,
you are with us and all around us in
    the hearts of others.
Make us slow to judge and quick
    to welcome.
Help us to see you in every age, race,
    gender, and religion.
Make us the generation that believes
    in you
and brings that faith to others.
You live and reign with God
    the Father
in the unity of the Holy Spirit,
one God, forever and ever.
Amen.

✦ *Justice shall flourish in his time, and fullness of peace for ever.*

Optional memorial of St. Juan Diego Cuauhtlatoatzin

✦ *Show us Lord, your love; and grant us your salvation.*

PSALM 67 *page 411*

READING *Sirach 48:1–4, 9–11*

In those days, / like a fire there appeared the prophet Elijah / whose words were as a flaming furnace. / Their staff of bread he shattered, / in his zeal he reduced them to straits; / By the Lord's word he shut up the heavens / and three times brought down fire. / How awesome are you, Elijah, in your wondrous deeds! / Whose glory is equal to yours? / You were taken aloft in a whirlwind of fire, / in a chariot with fiery horses. / You were destined, it is written, in time to come / to put an end to wrath before the day of the LORD, / To turn back the hearts of fathers toward their sons, / and to re-establish the tribes of Jacob. / Blessed is he who shall have seen you / and who falls asleep in your friendship.

REFLECTION

At times we need God to turn our hearts back to him with ferocity. Human nature grows apathetic now and then. We fall into sin. We need a "flaming furnace" or a "whirlwind of fire" to "turn back" our hearts. When this happens, we usually complain. Our lives turn upside down, our priorities are shaken, and we face our worst fears. Yet, this tumult may be God himself speaking. Smaller signs have gone unnoticed. It took chaos and disaster to get our attention. If we recognize God in the whisper or the whirlwind, we are blessed.

PRAYERS *others may be added*

Awed by God's love for us, we pray:

◆ Turn our hearts to you, Lord.

That Christians know God's presence in life's ups and downs, as well as the day-to-day plateaus in between, we pray: ◆ *That natural disasters spare human life but remind us of our powerlessness, we pray:* ◆ *That life's fires can be put out quickly and lessons learned smoothly, we pray:* ◆ *That those in need of dramatic conversion experience the majestic power of God, we pray:* ◆

Our Father . . .

God of wind and flame,
you revealed yourself to prophets
    and kings, sinners and saints.
Each of us comes to know you in a
    unique way.
When we are lost or cannot find you,
turn our hearts back to you.
May we be blessed to know you
and live with you forever.
We ask this through Christ our Lord.
Amen.

✦ *Show us Lord, your love; and grant us your salvation.*

✚ *Let us go rejoicing to the house of the Lord.*

PSALM 67   *page 411*

READING   *John 1:6 – 8, 23–28*

A man named John was sent from God. He came for testimony, to testify to the light, so that all might believe through him. He was not the light, but came to testify to the light.

[John] said: "I am *the voice of one crying in the desert, / make straight the way of the Lord,* as Isaiah the prophet said." Some Pharisees were also sent. They asked him, "Why, then, do you baptize if you are not the Christ or Elijah or the Prophet?" John answered them, "I baptize with water; but there is one among you whom you do not recognize, the one who is coming after me, whose sandal strap I am not worthy to untie." This happened in Bethany across the Jordan where John was baptizing.

REFLECTION

Today is Gaudete *Sunday, and we rejoice at the nearness of the coming of Christ. Even as we prepare for Christmas, we know that Christ is already with us. John the Baptist says that "there is one among you whom you do not recognize." Look carefully. Listen quietly. Where is Christ in our midst? What has brought gladness to your heart of late? Give thanks for his presence in that moment. The kingdom is at hand; we need only notice.*

PRAYERS   *others may be added*

Opening our eyes to the presence of Christ in our midst, we pray:

◆ Let us rejoice and be glad in the Lord.

For all Christians, that our faith may make us people of hope and love, which we extend to our families, friends, and all we meet, we pray: ◆ *For those who serve their countries and the common good of all the world's people, that they celebrate and share the stories of peace, healing, and unity, we pray:* ◆ *For all who experience joy, but know not its source, that they may come to realize the love God has for them, we pray:* ◆ *For all who have died, that they live in eternal peace, we pray:* ◆

Our Father . . .

Lord Jesus Christ,
you are hidden in the faces and
    experiences of life around us.
Reveal yourself to us this Advent,
reminding us of the great joy we feel
    when we are close to you.
May we bring the joy of life in you to
    all the world,
leading to the day when we will
    rejoice together in heaven,
where you live and reign with God
    the Father,
in the unity of the Holy Spirit,
one God, forever and ever.
Amen.

✚ *Let us go rejoicing to the house of the Lord.*

✦ *Commit your life to the Lord.*

CANTICLE
page 422

READING
Luke 1:39–45

Mary set out and traveled to the hill country in haste to a town of Judah, where she entered the house of Zechariah and greeted Elizabeth. When Elizabeth heard Mary's greeting, the infant leaped in her womb, and Elizabeth, filled with the Holy Spirit, cried out in a loud voice and said, "Most blessed are you among women, and blessed is the fruit of your womb. And how does this happen to me, that the mother of my Lord should come to me? For at the moment the sound of your greeting reached my ears, the infant in my womb leaped for joy. Blessed are you who believed that what was spoken to you by the Lord would be fulfilled."

REFLECTION

Mary appeared on a hillside in rural Mexico to Juan Diego, an ordinary man. Mary and Elizabeth were also ordinary people visiting with one another in a small town. Like Juan Diego, they were stunned by what God could do in their lives. We, too, are ordinary people. We may think this means we can do nothing exceptional. We may diminish our role or responsibility in the world. How blessed we are if we can believe that God will fulfill his Word. If we believe, God can come to us, too, in whatever way that will most move us to be "ordinary" faithful servants.

PRAYERS
others may be added

In gratitude for an extraordinary God who works through ordinary people, we pray:

◆ Lord, hear our prayer.

For vocations to the priesthood, religious life, and lay ministry that ordinary men and women respond to God's call, we pray: ◆ *For a joining of voices of faith from around the globe, "to do the right and to love goodness, and to walk humbly with [our] God" (Micah 6:8), we pray:* ◆ *For service workers in the lowest ranks of society, that they walk with confidence, knowing they are beloved and equal in the eyes of God, we pray:* ◆ *For this community, that we hold each other accountable to being ordinary people of faith who live courageously, we pray:* ◆

Our Father . . .

God of fulfilled promises,
all things are possible with you.
Make us women and men of
      great faith,
who await your miraculous work in
      the ordinary acts of life.
May we rejoice in the blessing of our
      simple lives.
We ask this through Christ our Lord.
Amen.

✦ *Commit your life to the Lord.*

✚ *Come, Lord Jesus.*

PSALM 40 — page 407

READING — Matthew 25:1–7, 13

Jesus told his disciples this parable: "The Kingdom of heaven will be like ten virgins who took their lamps and went out to meet the bridegroom. Five of them were foolish and five were wise. The foolish ones, when taking their lamps, brought no oil with them, but the wise brought flasks of oil with their lamps. Since the bridegroom was long delayed, they all became drowsy and fell asleep. At midnight, there was a cry, 'Behold, the bridegroom! Come out to meet him!' Then all those virgins got up and trimmed their lamps. Therefore, stay awake, for you know neither the day nor the hour."

REFLECTION

If someone urges us to go out into the dark and we have no light to guide us, what will happen? We may be afraid to go forward, head off in the wrong direction, or fall on our way. If we do not prepare for life with God, we may resist it when it arrives out of fear, misunderstanding, or lack of familiarity. Most people do not like the unknown. Therefore, to prepare for heavenly life, we can learn about and experience God in his fullness, opening ourselves to new ways of knowing him. We can spend time in silence and prayer, allowing God's grace to work in us.

PRAYERS — *others may be added*

Before God, we pray:

◆ Fill us with your presence.

For retreat centers, spiritual directors, and schools of spirituality who explore the mystery of God and offer us experiences of the divine, we pray: ◆ *For travelers and adventurers, who seek out new lands and ways of life, thereby growing in knowledge of God's creation, we pray:* ◆ *For an end to prejudice, which prevents us from experiencing the fullness of God, we pray:* ◆ *For deep respect amid our community when one shares the ways they have come to know God more deeply, we pray:* ◆

Our Father . . .

Light of the World,
by your coming, you revealed the
   mystery of God.
May we continue to explore
   that mystery
by meditating on your life, death,
   and Resurrection
in old and new ways.
Send us pastors and teachers
who will expand our hearts'
   understanding of you
so that we may live in the peace of
   God forever,
where you live and reign forever
   and ever.
Amen.

✚ *Come, Lord Jesus.*

✝ *Blessed are all who wait for the Lord.*

PSALM 40 page 407

READING Luke 14:25–27

Great crowds were traveling with Jesus, and he turned and addressed them, "If anyone comes to me without hating his father and mother, wife and children, brothers and sisters, and even his own life, he cannot be my disciple. Whoever does not carry his own cross and come after me cannot be my disciple.

REFLECTION

St. John of the Cross, a mystic of the Church, guides us when we carry our heaviest crosses. He endured physical and spiritual trials to the point of breaking, but that led him deep into the heart of God. Think of your burdens, what brings you to tears, even that which threatens to destroy you. In these struggles, God is at work. By these fires, we become more dependent on God, more attuned to his ways, and stronger in our life of faith. Can we embrace this process of sanctification?

PRAYERS *others may be added*

Carrying our crosses, we pray:

◆ Make us your disciples.

For holy men and women who face deathly trials and embrace them in the name of God, we pray: ◆ *For political figures tempted by power and wealth, that they choose instead the cross of honest public service, we pray:* ◆ *For those who suffer in prisons, that the demons of despair and loneliness are overcome by faith, we pray:* ◆ *For a sensitivity to the crosses carried by our brothers and sisters in faith, that we offer to help carry the load, we pray:* ◆

Our Father . . .

Lord Jesus,
you endured every human hardship
    for our salvation.
You walk with us through
    every difficulty.
May the fortitude and faith of St. John
    of the Cross
inspire us to pick up our crosses and
    follow you daily.
You live and reign with God
    the Father
in the unity of the Holy Spirit,
one God, forever and ever.
Amen.

✝ *Blessed are all who wait for the Lord.*

✦ *Show us Lord, your love; and grant us your salvation.*

PSALM 67   *page 411*

READING   *Isaiah 54:6–10*

The LORD calls you back, / like a wife forsaken and grieved in spirit, / A wife married in youth and then cast off, says your God. / For a brief moment I abandoned you, / but with great tenderness I will take you back. / In an outburst of wrath, for a moment / I hid my face from you; / but with enduring love I take pity on you, / says the LORD, your redeemer. /

This is for me like the days of Noah, / when I swore that the waters of Noah / should never again deluge the earth; / So I have sworn not to be angry with you, / or to rebuke you. Though the mountains leave their place / and the hills be shaken, / My love shall never leave you / nor my covenant of peace be shaken, / says the LORD, who has mercy on you.

REFLECTION

The prophet Isaiah describes what many of us have felt: surely God is so angry with me that I can never be forgiven. These are human experiences: abandonment, broken covenants, and severed familial ties. But our God is different. He is full of mercy and will never stop loving us. He is a spouse that never leaves. He is a parent that never gives up. He is a friend that never betrays. He is a leader that never disappoints. Let us put our trust in him.

PRAYERS   *others may be added*

Knowing we are sinners, we repent and give praise to our God:

◆ Show us your mercy.

For all Christians who have broken covenants with God, loved ones, and the community, we pray: ◆ For all leaders who have lost the public's trust due to unethical and illegal acts, we pray: ◆ For families broken by divorce, betrayal, abuse, and lack of forgiveness, we pray: ◆ For relationships where we need to make amends or grant forgiveness, we pray: ◆

Our Father . . .

Gracious God,
you are merciful and just,
and give us the gift of salvation.
May we recognize that you alone are
   perfectly loving and perfectly loyal.
May we seek forgiveness for straying
   from you
and seek to forgive those who have
   hurt us.
We ask this through Christ our Lord.
Amen.

✦ *Show us Lord, your love; and grant us your salvation.*

✦ *Justice shall flourish in his time, and fullness of peace for ever.*

PSALM 67 *page 411*

READING *Isaiah 56:1–3a, 6–7*

Thus says the LORD: / Observe what is right, do what is just; / for my salvation is about to come, / my justice, about to be revealed. / Blessed is the man who does this, / the son of man who holds to it; / Who keeps the sabbath free from profanation, / and his hand from any evildoing. / Let not the foreigner say, / when he would join himself to the LORD, / "The LORD will surely exclude me from his people."

The foreigners who join themselves to the LORD, / ministering to him, / Loving the name of the LORD, /and becoming his servants—/ All who keep the sabbath free from profanation / and hold to my covenant, / Them I will bring to my holy mountain / and make joyful in my house of prayer; / Their burnt offerings and sacrifices / will be acceptable on my altar, / For my house shall be called / a house of prayer for all peoples.

REFLECTION

We hear the call of the prophet in our hearts this Advent. We should do what is right and just. As children, we knew well that feeling of doing something wrong. We were afraid of being caught or of what our parents would say. Have we kept that internal sensor, that knowledge of God's law, on alert? When we stray from his covenant, do we immediately realize it? We may have grown accustomed to ignoring that little voice, at least in certain areas. We hear Isaiah's voice resonate in our hearts. We pledge to hold to God's covenant.

PRAYERS *others may be added*

Knowing ourselves as God's people, we pray:

◆ May we walk in your ways.

For all who call themselves servants of the Lord, that we listen to the voice of God in our hearts, we pray: ◆ *For all peoples, that an end comes to territorial and exclusionary practices, we pray:* ◆ *For those who have gone astray, acting unethically or unlawfully, that Advent is a time of repentance and renewal, we pray:* ◆ *For this house of worship, that it holds a community which welcomes all to the mountain of the Lord, we pray:* ◆

Our Father . . .

God of the old and new covenants,
you sent priests, prophets, and kings
to proclaim a time of repentance and
a new reign of justice.
You call all your sons and daughters
to follow you in word and deed.
May we be worthy of this calling,
aligning our hearts with your law
and praising your holy name.
We ask this through Christ our Lord.
Amen.

✦ *Justice shall flourish in his time, and fullness of peace for ever.*

✦ *Justice shall flourish in his time, and fullness of peace for ever.*

PSALM 67 *page 411*

READING *Genesis 49:2, 8, 9b, 10*

Jacob called his sons and said to them: "Assemble and listen, sons of Jacob, / listen to Israel, your father.

"You, Judah, shall your brothers praise / —your hand on the neck of your enemies; / the sons of your father shall bow down to you. He crouches like a lion recumbent, / the king of beasts— who would dare rouse him? / The scepter shall never depart from Judah, / or the mace from between his legs, / While tribute is brought to him, / and he receives the people's homage."

REFLECTION

Judah was a leader among his brothers and his people because of his strength, his wisdom, and the blessing of the Lord. His leadership was part of a lineage that culminated in Jesus. Leaders today can learn from these faithful figures. What does it take to gain the praise and respect of one's own family, community, or church? A start includes deep connectedness, listening skills, the wisdom that comes from experience, and being centered in God. We each play a part in identifying Christian leaders, supporting our priests and ministers, and ensuring that the line of leadership remains faithful to Jesus.

PRAYERS *others may be added*

Longing for the justice and leadership of God, we pray:

◆ Lord, hear our prayer.

For the Pope, Bishops, clergy, and all ministers and servants of the Church, in gratitude for their service and in petition for their well-being, we pray: ◆ *For civil leaders who truly represent their constituencies, and listen with compassionate hearts to the needs of their regions, we pray:* ◆ *For young people learning from their leaders, that they find fine examples of humility, wisdom, and collaboration, we pray:* ◆ *For the leaders of various ministries in our parish, that they perform their duties with dedication and care, and take time to train others, we pray:* ◆

Our Father . . .

Provident God,
you raised up leaders in every period
    to proclaim your Word.
When we feel a crisis in leadership,
    help us to trust in you;
when we are grateful for inspiring
    leaders, help us to praise you;
open our eyes and hearts to those
    who are called to share their
    unique gifts
for the service of the common good.
We ask this through Christ our Lord.
Amen.

✦ *Justice shall flourish in his time, and fullness of peace for ever.*

✦ *Come, Lord Jesus.*

PSALM 67 *page 411*

READING *Luke 1:26–35a*

The angel Gabriel was sent from God to a town of Galilee called Nazareth, to a virgin betrothed to a man named Joseph, of the house of David, and the virgin's name was Mary. And coming to her, he said, "Hail, full of grace! The Lord is with you." But she was greatly troubled at what was said and pondered what sort of greeting this might be. Then the angel said to her, "Do not be afraid, Mary, for you have found favor with God.

"Behold, you will conceive in your womb and bear a son, and you shall name him Jesus. He will be great and will be called Son of the Most High, and the Lord God will give him the throne of David his father, and he will rule over the house of Jacob forever, and of his kingdom there will be no end." But Mary said to the angel, "How can this be, since I have no relations with a man?" And the angel said to her in reply, "The Holy Spirit will come upon you, and the power of the Most High will overshadow you."

REFLECTION

Our joy is building with the nearness of Jesus' birth. The words of the angel confirm our greatest hopes. Jesus' rule will surpass all worldly rulers. His kingship will never end. We may be knocked down from time to time. Doubt may creep in. But underneath every fear and worry, we rest on a foundation of certitude that the kingdom of God lies ahead.

PRAYERS *others may be added*

As people of hope, we pray:

◆ Come, Lord Jesus!

That all Christians spread joy to others in Jesus, we pray: ◆ *That all who long for world peace continue to pray for and work toward bringing it to fulfillment, we pray:* ◆ *That those who are standing on the edge of despair refuse to give in and lean instead on faith, we pray:* ◆ *That our joy bursts forth in song, service, prayer, and fellowship, we pray:* ◆

Our Father . . .

Saving Lord,
come to us quickly, now, and renew
    our hearts and our world.
You live and reign with God
    the Father
in the unity of the Holy Spirit,
one God, forever and ever.
Amen.

✦ *Come, Lord Jesus.*

✦ *Come, Lord Jesus.*

PSALM 67   page 411

READING   Luke 1:13–17

But the angel said to him, "Do not be afraid, Zechariah, because your prayer has been heard. Your wife Elizabeth will bear you a son, and you shall name him John. And you will have joy and gladness, and many will rejoice at his birth, for he will be great in the sight of the Lord. He will drink neither wine nor strong drink. He will be filled with the Holy Spirit even from his mother's womb, and he will turn many of the children of Israel to the Lord their God. He will go before him in the spirit and power of Elijah to turn the hearts of fathers toward children and the disobedient to the understanding of the righteous, to prepare a people fit for the Lord."

REFLECTION

John the Baptist, and others, help us prepare to be "a people fit for the Lord." How has your heart become more ready to receive Christ this Advent? How do you prepare to receive Christ at each Eucharist? The angel says that John the Baptist will "turn" hearts. Ask God in prayer to turn your heart—from addiction to freedom, from despair to hope, from negativity to optimism, from judgment to forgiveness, from selfishness to generosity, from pride to humility, or from control to openness. You may be amazed at how it feels to be "fit for the Lord!"

PRAYERS   *others may be added*

As people of God, we pray:

◆ Turn our hearts, Lord.

For all those gathered at the Eucharistic banquet this day and every day, we pray: ◆ *For a new vision of the earth as God's creation, we pray:* ◆ *For those who abuse others physically or verbally, we pray:* ◆ *For our community as we approach the birth of Christ, we pray:* ◆ *For the human hands and hearts of the Church, when we doubt or falter, we pray:* ◆ *For leaders of nations, that their efforts may be grounded in love of God, we pray:* ◆ *For the conversion of hearts, minds, and actions, we pray:* ◆ *For those who have died, we pray:* ◆

Our Father . . .

Gracious God,
you sent John the Baptist
to prepare your people for the coming
    of your Son.
You continue to reveal your love and
    salvation to us
as we prepare for the celebration of
    the Incarnation.
May we continually turn our hearts
    to you,
leaving behind all that keeps us from
    life in you.
We ask this through Christ our Lord.
Amen.

✦ *Come, Lord Jesus.*

✦ *Show us Lord, your love.*

PSALM 67 *page 411*

READING *Luke 1:26–35a*

In the sixth month, the angel Gabriel was sent from God to a town of Galilee called Nazareth, to a virgin betrothed to a man named Joseph, of the house of David, and the virgin's name was Mary. And coming to her, he said, "Hail, full of grace! The Lord is with you." But she was greatly troubled at what was said and pondered what sort of greeting this might be. Then the angel said to her, "Do not be afraid, Mary, for you have found favor with God. Behold, you will conceive in your womb and bear a son, and you shall name him Jesus. He will be great and will be called Son of the Most High, and the Lord God will give him the throne of David his father, and he will rule over the house of Jacob forever, and of his Kingdom there will be no end."

But Mary said to the angel, "How can this be, since I have no relations with a man?" And the angel said to her in reply, "The Holy Spirit will come upon you, and the power of the Most High will overshadow you."

REFLECTION

"Hail, full of grace! The Lord is with you." The Holy Spirit will come so close it will be palpable. The power of God will be felt within and around you. We hear these words with Mary, and we know that in Christ's birth God is with us. It is good to be overcome with awe in the presence of God. It is good to stand in silence before the holy infant. The Incarnation takes our breath away.

PRAYERS *others may be added*

Longing for God, we pray:

◆ Come, Emmanuel.

For those Christians who wait for you in silent prayer or with loud pleas, we pray: ◆ *For lands stricken by disease, war, or poverty, we pray:* ◆ *For all mothers, especially those who are expecting new life, we pray:* ◆ *For the renewal of our faith and our community life, we pray:* ◆

Our Father . . .

Father, Son, and Holy Spirit,
awe us with your wondrous works.
You have always been with us.
You are with us.
You are all that is to come.
May we stand in your shadow
    and rejoice.
We ask this through Christ our Lord.
Amen.

✦ *Show us Lord, your love.*

✦ *Justice shall flourish in his time, and fullness of peace for ever.*

PSALM 67   *page 411*

READING   *Song of Songs 2:10–14*

My lover speaks; he says to me, / "Arise, my beloved, my dove, my beautiful one, / and come! / "For see, the winter is past, / the rains are over and gone. / The flowers appear on the earth, / the time of pruning the vines has come, / and the song of the dove is heard in our land. / The fig tree puts forth its figs, / and the vines, in bloom, give forth fragrance. / Arise, my beloved, my beautiful one, / and come!

    "O my dove in the clefts of the rock, / in the secret recesses of the cliff, / Let me see you, / let me hear your voice, / For your voice is sweet, / and you are lovely."

REFLECTION

We know the rejoicing that comes with spring, especially after the darkness of winter. We know the bliss that comes with love, especially when it is rediscovered. Our loving, devoted God calls to us: "Arise . . . and come!" We are his beloved. We have reason to rejoice. Whatever pain or sorrow we have experienced, we are invited into the heart of God this Advent. We are healed, comforted, and loved. We can hope once again.

PRAYERS   *others may be added*

Rejoicing, we pray:

◆ May we know your bountiful love, O God.

For the Pope, Bishops, clergy, and all the people of God, when they are down or afraid, we pray: ◆ *For countries being developed, restructured, or reborn from darkness, we pray:* ◆ *For those in love, that they may recognize the source of their great happiness in God, we pray:* ◆ *For any who doubt their beauty in the eyes of the Creator, we pray:* ◆

Our Father . . .

God of love,
you created us, delight in us, and
    love us.
May we recognize ourselves as
    beloved and arise,
coming to you with open hearts.
May we rejoice in the gift of
    your love.
We ask this through our Lord Jesus
    Christ, your Son,
who lives and reigns with you
in the unity of the Holy Spirit,
one God, forever and ever.
Amen.

✦ *Justice shall flourish in his time, and fullness of peace for ever.*

Optional memorial of St. Peter Canisius, priest, doctor of the Church

✛ *Justice shall flourish in his time, and fullness of peace for ever.*

PSALM 67   *page 411*

READING   *Luke 1:46–55*

Mary said: / "My soul proclaims the greatness of the Lord; / my spirit rejoices in God my savior. / for he has looked upon his lowly servant. / From this day all generations will call me blessed: / the Almighty has done great things for me, / and holy is his Name. / He has mercy on those who fear him / in every generation. / He has shown the strength of his arm, / and has scattered the proud in their conceit. / He has cast down the mighty from their thrones / and has lifted up the lowly. / He has filled the hungry with good things, / and the rich he has sent away empty. / He has come to the help of his servant Israel / for he remembered his promise of mercy, / the promise he made to our fathers, / to Abraham and his children for ever."

REFLECTION

God fulfills promises. But which kind? He remembers "his promise of mercy." We are wasting our time if we are asking God for riches and worldly success. But, if we are hoping with all our hearts for loving families, an end to hunger and injustice, a lasting peace, care for neighbor, a healthy planet, and eternal life for all who believe, our expectations are not too high. God is merciful and mighty. He has promised to save all who count on him.

PRAYERS   *others may be added*

With Advent hope, we pray:

◆ Be merciful, O Lord.

For all Christians who hold onto hope in the promise of God's mercy, we pray: ◆ *For the powerful who ignore the reign of God, we pray:* ◆ *For the poor of this world, who have long suffered, we pray:* ◆ *For communities that work to bring about God's dreams for his children, we pray:* ◆ *For all who have died with faith in God's promises, we pray:* ◆

Our Father . . .

God of Abraham, of Isaac, and of
    your people Israel,
Mary proclaimed the hope of
    generations in your promise
    of mercy.
We, too, proclaim our hope in you.
May your merciful rule come to pass
    over the earth.
May the birth of your Son Jesus
    renew our hope,
and bring us to your eternal kingdom,
where you live and reign, with your
    Son Jesus,
in the unity of the Holy Spirit,
one God, forever and ever.
Amen.

✛ *Justice shall flourish in his time, and fullness of peace for ever.*

✚ *Show us Lord, your love; and grant us your salvation.*

PSALM 67   page 411

READING   *Luke 1:57, 62–66*

When the time arrived for Elizabeth to have her child she gave birth to a son. So they made signs, asking his father what he wished him to be called. He asked for a tablet and wrote, "John is his name," and all were amazed. Immediately his mouth was opened, his tongue freed, and he spoke blessing God. Then fear came upon all their neighbors, and all these matters were discussed throughout the hill country of Judea. All who heard these things took them to heart, saying, "What, then, will this child be? For surely the hand of the Lord was with him."

REFLECTION

"What, then, will this child be?" What will the birth of Christ mean for you this year? Will it resonate with the birth of something in you? Does it represent a gift from God? Is it a moment of renewal or new beginnings? Is it a letting go of other priorities, and refocusing on the presence of Christ in your life? Take this question "to heart." "What, then, will this child be"—for you?

PRAYERS   *others may be added*

Preparing for the birth of Christ, we pray:

◆ Come, Lord Jesus.

For the people of God, that all are open to the new life we are offered daily, we pray: ◆ *For the educational system in our country, that a vision of our children's fullest potential drives policy, we pray:* ◆ *For all considering ending a pregnancy, that they are filled with awareness of the life growing within them, we pray:* ◆ *For leaders in parishes, that Christmas renews their faith and inspires rebirth, we pray:* ◆ *For all who are dying, that they are filled with peace, imagining who they will be in the embrace of God, we pray:* ◆

Our Father . . .

Omnipotent God,
you revealed your plan of salvation
    with many signs and wonders,
preparing your people for your
    greatest revelation.
Open our eyes and hearts
to how you are preparing us for the
    Christ child.
May we respond with awe and
    gratitude in your marvelous works.
We ask this through Christ our Lord.
Amen.

✚ *Show us Lord, your love; and grant us your salvation.*

✦ *Let us go rejoicing to the house of the Lord.*

PSALM 67 *page 411*

READING *Luke 1:67, 76–79*

Zechariah his father, filled with the Holy Spirit, prophesied, saying: "You, my child, shall be called the prophet of the Most High, / for you will go before the Lord to prepare his way, / to give his people knowledge of salvation / by the forgiveness of their sins. / In the tender compassion of our God / the dawn from on high shall break upon us, / to shine on those who dwell in darkness and the shadow of death, / and to guide our feet into the way of peace."

REFLECTION

As the dawn of a new day breaks upon us, the fullness of God's salvation is revealed further. We are all on a life-long journey, with God guiding us "into the way of peace." Every step of our lives, a little more of Zechariah's prophecy is complete. We, too, are children of God. We prepare the way of the Lord. Do we believe this? Do we acknowledge our destiny and the purpose of our lives? Can we read this passage and consider how our choices and our lives reflect this prophecy? Greet the dawn of Christmas with "yes."

PRAYERS *others may be added*

Answering God's call, we pray:

◆ Guide us in the way of peace.

For the mission of the Church in the world, giving people knowledge of salvation by the forgiveness of their sins, we pray: ◆ For an end to darkness and death brought by rulers who do not believe in the sanctity of all human life, we pray: ◆ For all who need the tender compassion of God, especially victims of sex trafficking, child pornography, and physical and emotional abuse, we pray: ◆ For the courage to respond to God's call, we pray: ◆

Our Father . . .

Loving God,
on the eve of Christmas,
we hear the call to prepare the way
    of the Lord
by giving witness to you and your
    divine call.
May we respond with a
    resounding "yes,"
helping bring the light of Christ
to every part of the world.
We ask this through Christ our Lord.
Amen.

✦ *Let us go rejoicing to the house of the Lord.*

✛ *Let the heavens be glad and the earth rejoice!*

PSALM 98   *page 413*

READING   *John 1:1–5, 9–11*

In the beginning was the Word, / and the Word was with God, / and the Word was God. / He was in the beginning with God. / All things came to be through him, / and without him nothing came to be. / What came to be through him was life, / and this life was the light of the human race; / the light shines in the darkness, / and the darkness has not overcome it. /
The true light, which enlightens everyone, was coming into the world. / He was in the world, / and the world came to be through him, / but the world did not know him. / He came to what was his own, / but his own people did not accept him.

REFLECTION

This is a day to revel in the "grace in place of grace" (John 1:16) that blesses us. Not only do we have a provident God who has guided his people throughout history, but he is compassionate. God came to us in human form to fully reveal himself as merciful love redeeming our brokenness and our chaotic world by his salvific sacrifice. We are blessed, loved, called, chosen, enlightened— through no act of our own, but only because of the great love God has for us.

PRAYERS   *others may be added*

With the joy of children, we pray:

◆ *Rejoice in the Lord!*

For the people of God, that Christmas morning brings a renewed joy to their hearts, we pray: ◆ *For the people of the world, that the fullness of revelation made known again today reaches every heart with love, we pray:* ◆ *For all children, that their natural curiosity and awe remains with them throughout their lives, we pray:* ◆ *For our families and friends, that the birth of Christ brings them every blessing, we pray:* ◆

Our Father . . .

Lord Jesus,
Son of God and Son of Man,
you are born this day to save us.
By coming into the world, you
    reconcile all to the Father.
We are endlessly blessed by the gift
    of this day.
We praise you and thank you, and
    give glory to God the Father,
who lives and reigns with you in the
    unity of the Holy Spirit,
one God, forever and ever.
Amen.

✛ *Let the heavens be glad and the earth rejoice!*

✦ *The Lord takes delight in his people.*

PSALM 149   page 421

READING   *Acts of the Apostles 6:8,*
9b, 10; 7:54–58a, 59

Stephen, filled with grace and power, was working great wonders and signs among the people. Certain . . . people from Cilicia and Asia, came forward and debated with Stephen, but they could not withstand the wisdom and the spirit with which he spoke.

When they heard this, they were infuriated, and they ground their teeth at him. But he, filled with the Holy Spirit, looked up intently to heaven and saw the glory of God and Jesus standing at the right hand of God, and he said, "Behold, I see the heavens opened and the Son of Man standing at the right hand of God." But they cried out in a loud voice, covered their ears, and rushed upon him together. They threw him out of the city, and began to stone him. As they were stoning Stephen, he called out "Lord Jesus, receive my spirit."

REFLECTION

We switch quickly from the joy of Christmas to this tragic story of Christianity's first martyr. However, the Gospel tells us not to worry, but rather to trust in God. This is exactly what St. Stephen did, of course. He was filled with the Holy Spirit, and his mind was on Jesus until his last breath. Surely, if he can remain centered in faith under these conditions, no amount of distraction during the holidays can tear us from our love for God. Let us continue *to rejoice, to pray, to evangelize, to prophesy, drawing upon St. Stephen for strength and inspiration.*

PRAYERS   *others may be added*

Living our faith in a busy and even hostile world, we pray:

◆ Be with us, Lord Jesus.

For Christians who face distraction, temptation, and persecution that leads them away from faith, we pray: ◆
For missionaries and human rights activists in countries intolerant of religion, we pray: ◆ *For young people walking by faith amid a secularized culture, we pray:* ◆ *For a community of support here for all who are committed to carrying forth Christmas joy, we pray:* ◆

Our Father . . .

Provident God,
no matter what trials or obstacles
    we face,
you remain with us,
and send the saints to lift us up.
As we carry the Christmas message
    out into the world,
may we stay strong in faith,
persistent in prayer, and joyful
    in hope.
We ask this through Christ the Lord.
Amen.

✦ *The Lord takes delight in his people.*

✙ *The Lord takes delight in his people.*

PSALM 149   *page 421*

READING   *1 John 1:1–4*

Beloved: / What was from the beginning, / what we have heard, / what we have seen with our eyes, / what we looked upon / and touched with our hands, / concerns the Word of life— / for the life was made visible; / we have seen it and testify to it / and proclaim to you the eternal life / that was with the Father and was made visible to us—/ what we have seen and heard / we proclaim now to you, / so that you too may have fellowship with us; / for our fellowship is with the Father / and with his Son, Jesus Christ. / We are writing this so that our joy may be complete.

REFLECTION

Using this reading, take some time to recount your story of faith. At each line, note how God was present: something you heard, saw, and touched. Then consider how you gave witness to God's work. Finally, write an account of this faith and pass it on to someone: a child, a friend, or even a stranger. Take notice of the joy that fills you.

PRAYERS   *others may be added*

Learning to be evangelists, we pray:

◆ Help us share our joy, O Lord.

For an increase in witnessing to God's work by all Christians, we pray: ◆ *For journalists, novelists, poets, songwriters, and all writers, who have the opportunity to reach hearts and minds with stories of the grace of God present in everyday experiences, we pray:* ◆ *For greater unity between Christians who take different approaches to evangelization, that we may learn from one another, we pray:* ◆ *For the humility and courage to share our story of God's love with others, we pray:* ◆

Our Father . . .

God of mystery,
it brings us joy to know you
and grow in relationship with you.
Help us to make our joy "more
    complete" by sharing you
    with others.
Show us the moments and
    experiences of our lives that
    changed our hearts.
Make us vulnerable and
    articulate enough
to bring others to you by way of
    these stories.
Grant this through Christ our Lord.
Amen.

✙ *The Lord takes delight in his people.*

✝ *The Lord takes delight in his people.*

PSALM 149 *page 421*

READING *1 John 1:8–10*

[Beloved:] If we say, "We are without sin," / we deceive ourselves, and the truth is not in us. / If we acknowledge our sins, he is faithful and just / and will forgive our sins and cleanse us from every wrongdoing. / If we say, "We have not sinned," we make him a liar, / and his word is not in us.

REFLECTION

Great danger lies in seeing the sin of others but not ourselves. Yet, human nature leads us that way often. We read the paper and think, "tsk, tsk," or worse. We listen to a friend and later gossip about her shocking admissions. But we are deceiving ourselves, as John says in today's reading, if we see ourselves as so different from others. Rather than condemn, let us ask ourselves how our personality flaws make us susceptible to the same wrongdoing we read about in the paper or hear on TV. Let us imagine ourselves standing next to the criminals and neighbors we have judged, begging for forgiveness from our God.

PRAYERS *others may be added*

Keeping in mind the Holy Innocents and our own sinfulness, we pray:

◆ Save us, O Lord.

For leaders of the Church, that they maintain a sense of their own created status before the Creator and those who look up to them, we pray: ◆
For upstanding citizens and public servants, that their good works never surpass their sense of humility and service to others, we pray: ◆ *For parents, that in providing good role models to their children, that they do not become haughty, condescending, or judgmental, we pray:* ◆ *For humility and gratitude for the grace of God in hearing of others' bad decisions, we pray:* ◆

Our Father . . .

Merciful God,
We pray for all who are
  truly innocent:
the unborn, babies, the disabled,
  and the powerless.
Give us insight into our
  own sinfulness,
so we can see how it leads to ever
  greater evil.
Make us repentant and dependent
  on you.
May we then act humbly and justly to
  bring the joy of forgiveness to all.
We ask this through your Son, our
  Lord Jesus Christ.
Amen.

✝ *The Lord takes delight in his people.*

✦ *A light will shine on us this day.*

PSALM 98   *page 413*

READING   *1 John 2:8–11*

[Beloved:] And yet I do write a new commandment to you, which holds true in him and among you, for the darkness is passing away, and the true light is already shining. Whoever says he is in the light, yet hates his brother, is still in the darkness. Whoever loves his brother remains in the light, and there is nothing in him to cause a fall. Whoever hates his brother is in darkness; he walks in darkness and does not know where he is going because the darkness has blinded his eyes.

REFLECTION

In the afterglow of Christmas we are filled with love and joy. We are surrounded by family and friends, we have time off from work, and we attend parties. All of this is good, but on one condition— are we truly "in the light?" Who is missing from our celebrations? Who have we shunned or ignored? If we are at odds with a friend or family member, or holding prejudice against members of our community, we are actually in the dark. The true light of Christ shines into every corner of our life, and calls us to love each and every person. This is the true Christmas celebration.

PRAYERS   *others may be added*

Walking in the light of Christ, we pray:

◆ Give us love for one another.

For all Christians from every denomination and perspective, that we find common ground in the Gospel, we pray: ◆ *For peace talks, negotiations, and development planning, that representatives are present from every nation and class of people, we pray:* ◆ *For men and women, that we see how our lives are fuller when we live in harmony, we pray:* ◆ *For honesty within our community about whom we exclude or find it hard to love, that we may be a place of welcome, we pray:* ◆

Our Father . . .

Lord Jesus,
Light of the World,
you shine radiantly in this
    Christmas season.
May the joy we feel in our hearts
spread to enlighten every interaction
    we have,
every relationship we nurture,
and every enemy with whom we need
    to reconcile.
Lead us from darkness into your
    marvelous, transformative light.
You live and reign with God
    the Father
in the unity of the Holy Spirit,
one God, forever and ever.
Amen.

✦ *A light will shine on us this day.*

✦ *The Lord takes delight in his people.*

PSALM 149 *page 421*

READING *Luke 2:36–40*

There was a prophetess, Anna, the daughter of Phanuel, of the tribe of Asher. She was advanced in years, having lived seven years with her husband after her marriage, and then as a widow until she was eighty-four. She never left the temple, but worshipped night and day with fasting and prayer. And coming forward at that very time, she gave thanks to God and spoke about the child to all who were awaiting the redemption of Israel.

When they had fulfilled all the prescriptions of the law of the Lord, they returned to Galilee, to their own town of Nazareth. The child great and became strong, filled with wisdom; and the favor of God was upon him.

REFLECTION

Parents wish their child maturity, wisdom, and trust in God. Mary and Joseph sought this for Jesus by bringing him to the temple and asking for the blessing of their religious tradition. Parents today do this by preparing their children for the sacraments. When parents understand these graced moments and discuss them with their children, the children become aware of God's presence in their lives.

PRAYERS *others may be added*

Honoring our children, we pray:

◆ Fill us with wisdom, O God.

For priests, catechists, liturgists, and parents preparing children and families for the sacraments, we pray: ◆
For worldwide relief and educational efforts on behalf of children, we pray: ◆
For all children, who are close to God in unique ways, that they grow and become strong in mind, spirit, and body, we pray: ◆ *For the religious education of children in our parish, that adult involvement is strong and child participation is joyful, we pray:* ◆

Our Father . . .

Lord Jesus,
your Holy Family followed the Jewish
    faith with devotion.
They lived as examples of obedience
    to God.
May our families follow in
    their footsteps,
giving priority to our children's
    formation in faith.
May we recognize the precious gift of
    each child
and how closely God is present
    to them.
You live and reign with God
    the Father
in the unity of the Holy Spirit,
one God, forever and ever.
Amen.

✦ *The Lord takes delight in his people.*

✛ *A light will shine on us this day: the Lord is born for us.*

PSALM 98 · page 413

READING 1 John 2:18–21

Children, it is the last hour; and just as you heard that the antichrist was coming, so now many antichrists have appeared. Thus we know this is the last hour. They went out from us, but they were not really of our number; if they had been, they would have remained with us. Their desertion shows that none of them was of our number. But you have the anointing that comes from the Holy One, and you all have knowledge. I write to you not because you do not know the truth/but because you do, and because every lie is alien to the truth.

REFLECTION

Lest we doubt our ability to follow our loving Savior, we hear John's words: "you have the anointing that comes from the Holy One, and you all have knowledge." As children of God, we possess within ourselves knowledge, truth, and power. We have everything we need to live faithfully, serve joyfully, and love completely. It will certainly be difficult at times, but there can be no excuses. We are blessed! God's marvelous light shines on us every day, in every moment, no matter where we are. We go forward in confidence and hope.

PRAYERS *others may be added*

Humbled by our calling, we pray:

◆ Send us forth.

For the Pope, Bishops, clergy, and the people of God, that each one lives out his or her baptismal call to follow in the footsteps of Jesus, we pray: ◆ *For all who feel a call to make the world a better place, that they seize opportunities for education, reconciliation, community building, and peace, we pray:* ◆ *For all the anointed who are waiting for a sign, a different day, or courage, that they may be filled with the Holy Spirit, we pray:* ◆ *For all who doubt the power of God to use his children to heal the world and one another, we pray:* ◆

Our Father . . .

O Holy God,
you created us in love
and call us forth by the life, death,
    and Resurrection of your Son.
May we honor you as your sons
    and daughters
by living bold lives that embody and
    share the Good News with all.
We ask this through our Lord Jesus
    Christ, your Son,
who lives and reigns with you
in the unity of the Holy Spirit,
one God, forever and ever.
Amen.

✛ *A light will shine on us this day: the Lord is born for us.*

Optional memorial of St. Sylvester I, pope

PSALTER

PSALM 16:5, 8, 9–10, 11

O Lord, my allotted portion and my cup,
  you it is who hold fast my lot.
I set the Lord ever before me;
  with him at my right hand I shall not be disturbed.
Therefore my heart is glad and my soul rejoices,
  my body, too, abides in confidence;
Because you will not abandon my soul to the nether world,
  nor will you suffer your faithful one to undergo corruption.

You will show me the path to life,
  fullness of joys in your presence,
  the delights at your right hand forever.

PSALM 22:8-9, 17-18A, 19-20, 23-24

All who see me scoff at me;
    they mock me with parted lips, they wag their heads:
"He relied on the LORD ; let him deliver him,
    let him rescue him, if he loves him."

Indeed, many dogs surround me,
    a pack of evildoers closes in upon me;
They have pierced my hands and my feet;
    I can count all my bones.

They divide my garments among them,
    and for my vesture they cast lots.
But you, O LORD, be not far from me;
    O my help, hasten to aid me.

I will proclaim your name to my brethren;
    in the midst of the assembly I will praise you:
"You who fear the LORD, praise him;
    all you descendants of Jacob, give glory to him."

PSALM 23:1–3, 3–4, 5, 6

The LORD is my shepherd; I shall not want.
  In verdant pastures he gives me repose;
Beside restful waters he leads me;
  he refreshes my soul.

He guides me in right paths
  for his name's sake.
Even though I walk in the dark valley
  I fear no evil; for you are at my side
With your rod and your staff
  that give me courage.

You spread the table before me
  in the sight of my foes;
You anoint my head with oil;
  my cup overflows.

Only goodness and kindness follow me
  all the days of my life;
And I shall dwell in the house of the LORD
  for years to come.

PSALM 25:4–5, 6–7, 8–9

Your ways, O LORD , make known to me;
    teach me your paths,
Guide me in your truth and teach me,
    for you are God my savior.

Remember that your compassion, O LORD,
    and your kindness are from of old.
In your kindness remember me,
    because of your goodness, O LORD.

Good and upright is the LORD;
    thus he shows sinners the way.
He guides the humble to justice,
    he teaches the humble his way.

PSALM 33:4–5, 18–19, 20, 22

Upright is the word of the LORD,
   and all his works are trustworthy.
He loves justice and right;
   of the kindness of the LORD the earth is full.

See, the eyes of the LORD are upon those who
      fear him,
   upon those who hope for his kindness,
To deliver them from death
   and preserve them in spite of famine.

Our soul waits for the LORD,
   who is our help and our shield.
May your kindness, O LORD, be upon us
   who have put our hope in you.

PSALM 34:2-3, 4-5, 6-7

I will bless the LORD at all times;
   his praise shall be ever in my mouth.
Let my soul glory in the LORD;
   the lowly will hear me and be glad.

Glorify the LORD with me,
   let us together extol his name.
I sought the LORD, and he answered me
   and delivered me from all my fears.

Look to him that you may be radiant with joy,
   and your faces may not blush with shame.
When the afflicted man called out, the LORD heard,
   and from all his distress he saved him.

PSALM 37:3–4, 5–6, 23–24, 39–40

Trust in the LORD and do good,
  that you may dwell in the land and enjoy
    security.
Take delight in the LORD,
  and he will grant you your heart's requests.

Commit to the LORD your way;
  trust in him, and he will act.
He will make justice dawn for you like the light;
  bright as the noonday shall be your vindication.

By the LORD are the steps of a man made firm,
  and he approves his way.
Though he fall, he does not lie prostrate,
  for the hand of the LORD sustains him.

The salvation of the just is from the LORD;
  he is their refuge in time of distress.
And the LORD helps them and delivers them;
  he delivers them from the wicked and saves them,
    because they take refuge in him.

PSALM 40:2, 4, 7–8, 8–9, 10

I have waited, waited for the LORD,
    and he stooped toward me and heard my cry.
And he put a new song into my mouth,
    a hymn to our God.

Sacrifice or oblation you wished not,
    but ears open to obedience you gave me.
Holocausts or sin-offerings you sought not;
    then said I, "Behold I come."

"In the written scroll it is prescribed for me,
To do your will, O my God, is my delight,
    and your law is within my heart!"

I announced your justice in the vast assembly;
    I did not restrain my lips, as you, O LORD, know.

PSALM 42:2-3; 43, 3-4

As the hind longs for the running waters,
  so my soul longs for you, O God.
A thirst is my soul for God, the living God.
  When shall I go and behold the face of God?

Send forth your light and your fidelity;
  they shall lead me on
And bring me to your holy mountain,
  to your dwelling-place.

Then will I go in to the altar of God,
  the God of my gladness and joy;
Then will I give you thanks upon the harp,
  O God, my God!

PSALM 51:3–4, 5–6, 12–13, 14, 17

Have mercy on me. O God, in your goodness;
   in the greatness of your compassion wipe
      out my offense.
Thoroughly wash me from my guilt
   and of my sin cleanse me.

For I acknowledge my offense,
   and my sin is before me always:
"Against you only have I sinned,
   and done what is evil in your sight."

A clean heart create for me, O God,
   and a steadfast spirit renew within me.
Cast me not out from your presence,
   and your holy spirit take not from me.

Give me back the joy of your salvation,
   and a willing spirit sustain in me.
O Lord, open my lips,
   and my mouth shall proclaim your praise.

PSALM 66:1–3, 4–5, 6–7, 16, 20

Shout joyfully to God, all you on earth,
    sing praise to the glory of his name;
    proclaim his glorious praise.
Say to God, "How tremendous are your deeds!

Let all on earth worship and sing praise to you,
    sing praise to your name!"
Come and see the works of God,
    his tremendous deeds among men.

He has changed the sea into dry land;
    through the river they passed on foot;
    therefore let us rejoice in him.
He rules by his might forever.

Hear now, all you who fear God, while I declare
    what he has done for me.
Blessed be God who refused me not
    my prayer or his kindness!

PSALM 67:2 –3, 5, 6, 8

May God have pity on us and bless us;
    may he let his face shine upon us.
So may your way be known upon earth;
    among all nations, your salvation.

May the nations be glad and exult
    because you rule the peoples in equity;
    the nations on the earth you guide.

May the peoples praise you, O God;
    may all the peoples praise you!
May God bless us,
    and may all the ends of the earth fear him!

PSALM 85:9, 10, 11–12, 13–14

I will hear what God proclaims;
    the LORD—for he proclaims peace to his people.
Near indeed is his salvation to those who fear him,
    glory dwelling in our land.

Kindness and truth shall meet;
    justice and peace shall kiss.
Truth shall spring out of the earth,
    and justice shall look down from heaven.

The LORD himself will give his benefits;
    our land shall yield its increase.
Justice shall walk before him,
    and salvation, along the way of his steps.

PSALM 98:1, 2–3, 3–4, 5–6

Sing to the LORD a new song,
    for he has done wondrous deeds;
His right hand has won victory for him,
    his holy arm.

The LORD has made his salvation known:
    in the sight of the nations he has revealed
        his justice.
He has remembered his kindness and his
        faithfulness
    toward the house of Israel

All the ends of the earth have seen
    the salvation by our God.
Sing joyfully to the LORD, all you lands:
    break into song; sing praise.

Sing praise to the LORD with the harp,
    with the harp and melodious song.
With trumpets and the sound of the horn
    sing joyfully before the King, the LORD.

Psalm 100:1–2, 3, 5

Sing joyfully to the LORD, all you lands;
    serve the LORD with gladness;
    come before him with joyful song.

Know that the LORD is God;
    he made us, his we are;
    his people, the flock he tends.

[The LORD] is good:
    his kindness endures forever,
    and his faithfulness, to all generations.

PSALM 103:1–2, 3 – 4, 6–7, 8, 11

Bless the LORD, O my soul;
    and all my being, bless his holy name.
Bless the LORD, O my soul,
    and forget not all his benefits.

He pardons all your iniquities,
    he heals all your ills.
He redeems your life from destruction,
    he crowns you with kindness and compassion.

The LORD secures justice
    and the rights of all the oppressed.
He has made known his ways to Moses,
    and his deeds to the children of Israel.

Merciful and gracious is the LORD,
    slow to anger and abounding in kindness.
For as the heavens are high above the earth,
    so surpassing is his kindness toward those who fear him.

PSALM 104:1-2, 5-6, 10, 12, 13-14, 24, 35B

Bless the LORD, O my soul!
 O LORD, my God, you are great indeed!
You are clothed with majesty and glory,
 robed in light as with a cloak.

You fixed the earth upon its foundation,
 not to be moved forever;
With the ocean, as with a garment, you covered it;
 above the mountains the waters stood.

You send forth springs into the watercourses
 that wind among the mountains.
Beside them the birds of heaven dwell;
 from among the branches they send forth their song.

You water the mountains from your palace;
 the earth is replete with the fruit of your works.
You raise grass for the cattle,
 and vegetation for men's use,
Producing bread from the earth.

How manifold are your works, O LORD!
 In wisdom you have wrought them all—
 the earth is full of your creatures.
Bless the LORD, O my soul! Alleluia.

PSALM 111:1-2, 4-5, 9-10

I will give thanks to the LORD with all my heart
    in the company and assembly of the just.
Great are the works of the LORD,
    exquisite in all their delights.

He has won renown for his wondrous deeds;
    gracious and merciful is the LORD.
He has given food to those who fear him;
    he will forever be mindful of his covenant.

He has sent deliverance to his people;
    he has ratified his covenant forever;
    holy and awesome is his name.
    His praise endures forever.

PSALM 130:1–2, 3–4, 5–6, 7–8

Out of the depths I cry to you, O LORD;
    LORD, hear my voice!
Let your ears be attentive
    to my voice in supplication.

If you, O LORD, mark iniquities,
    LORD, who can stand?
But with you is forgiveness,
    that you may be revered.

I trust in the LORD;
    my soul trusts in his word.
More than sentinels wait for the dawn,
    let Israel wait for the LORD.

For with the LORD is kindness
    and with him is plenteous redemption;
And he will redeem Israel
    from all their iniquities.

PSALM 138:1-2, 2-3, 4-5, 7-8

I will give thanks to you, O LORD, with all my heart,
    [for you have heard the words of my mouth;]
      in the presence of the angels I will sing your praise,
I will worship at your holy temple
    and give thanks to your name.

Because of your kindness and your truth;
    for you have made great above all things
    your name and your promise.
When I called you answered me;
    you built up strength within me.

All the kings of the earth shall give thanks to you, O LORD,
    when they hear the words of your mouth;
And they shall sing of the ways of the LORD:
    "Great is the glory of the LORD."

    Your right hand saves me.
The LORD will complete what he has done for me;
    your kindness, O LORD, endures forever;
    forsake not the work of your hands.

PSALM 139:7–8, 9–10, 11–12

Where can I go from your spirit?
    from your presence where can I flee?
If I go up to the heavens, you are there;
    if I sink to the nether world, you are present there.

If I take the wings of the dawn,
    if I settle at the farthest limits of the sea,
Even there your hand shall guide me,
    and right hand hold me fast.

If I say, "Surely the darkness shall hide me,
    and night shall be my light"—
For you darkness itself is not dark,
    and night shines as the day.

PSALM 149:1-2, 3-4, 5-6, 9

Sing to the LORD a new song
   of praise in the assembly of the faithful.
Let Israel be glad in their maker,
   let the children of Zion rejoice in their king.

Let them praise his name in the festive dance,
   let them sing praise to him with timbrel and harp.
For the LORD loves his people,
   and he adorns the lowly with victory.

Let the faithful exult in glory;
   let them sing for joy upon their couches;
let the high praises of God be in their throats.
   This is the glory of all his faithful.

THE CANTICLE OF MARY

My soul proclaims the greatness of the Lord,
my spirit rejoices in God my savior
for he has looked with favor on his lowly servant.

From this day all generations will call me blessed:
the Almighty has done great things for me,
and holy is his Name.

He has mercy on those who fear him
in every generation.

He has shown the strength of his arm,
he has scattered the proud in their conceit.

He has cast down the mighty from their thrones,
and has lifted up the lowly.

He has filled the hungry with good things,
and the rich he has sent away empty.

He has come to the help of his servant Israel
for he has remembered his promise of mercy,
the promise he made to our fathers,
to Abraham and his children for ever.

Acknowledgments continued from page ii.

Excerpts from the *New American Bible* with Revised New Testament Copyright © 1986, 1970 Confraternity of Christian Doctrine, Inc., Washington, DC. Used with permission. All rights reserved. No portion of the *New American Bible* may be reprinted without permission in writing from the copyright owner.

Excerpts from *The Lectionary for Mass for Use in Dioceses of the United States of America* Copyright © 1998, 1997, 1970, Confraternity of Christian Doctrine, Inc., Washington, DC. Used with permission. All rights reserved. No portion of this text may be reproduced by any means without permission in writing from the copyright owner.

Reflections on pages 31, 33, 42, 43, 201, 204, 252, 257, and 267 are excerpts from *The Liturgy of the Hours*, © 1973, 1974, 1975, International Commission on English in the Liturgy (ICEL). All rights reserved.

The English translation of some Psalm responses, Alleluia and Gospel Verses from *Lectionary for Mass* © 1969, 1981, 1997, International Committee on English in the Liturgy, Inc. (ICEL); excerpts from the English translation of *The Liturgy of the Hours* © 1974, ICEL. All rights reserved. The closing prayer on page 54 was adapted from the English translation of *The Liturgy of the Hours* © 1974.